T proto-
in ustries
w Often
th vanced
te heories
ha ormed
de utions,
ar zation.
E cisms,
ar hapters
w des an
es nomic
ar

This collection of essays provides an up-to-date introduction to 'proto-industrialization': the growth of export-oriented domestic industries which took place all over Europe between about 1500 and 1800. Often these industries expanded alongside agriculture, without advanced technology or centralized factories. Since the 1970s, numerous theories have been proposed, arguing that proto-industrialization transformed demographic behaviour, social structure and traditional institutions, and was a major cause of capitalism and factory industrialization. *European proto-industrialization* summarizes the theories and criticisms and includes a reconsideration of the original theories, and chapters written by experts on different European countries. It provides an essential guide to an important, yet often confusing, field of economic and social history.

European proto-industrialization

European proto-industrialization

Edited by
Sheilagh C. Ogilvie
University of Cambridge
and
Markus Cerman
University of Vienna

CAMBRIDGE
UNIVERSITY PRESS

Published by the Press Syndicate of the University of Cambridge
The Pitt Building, Trumpington Street, Cambridge CB2 1RP
40 West 20th Street, New York, NY 10011–4211, USA
10 Stamford Road, Oakleigh, Melbourne 3166, Australia

First published in German (in a shorter version) as Markus Cerman and Sheilagh C. Ogilvie (eds.), *Protoindustrialisierung in Europa: Industrielle Produktion vor dem Fabrikszeitalter*, Volume 5 of Beiträge zur Historischen Sozialkunde 1994 and © Verlag für Gesellschaftskritik in Vienna 1994.

First published 1996

Printed in Great Britain at the University Press, Cambridge

A catalogue record for this book is available from the British Library

Library of Congress cataloguing in publication data

European proto-industrialization / edited by Sheilagh C. Ogilvie and
Markus Cerman.
p. cm.
Includes bibliographical references.
ISBN 0 521 49738 8. – ISBN 0 521 49760 4 (pbk.)
1. Industrialization – Europe. 2. Industries – Europe – History.
I. Ogilvie, Sheilagh C. II. Cerman, Markus.
HD2329.E95 1996
338.094–dc20 95–13491 CIP

ISBN 0 521 49738 8 hardback
ISBN 0 521 49760 4 paperback

CE

Contents

Illustrations

Figures

Maps

Tables

Contributors

Carlo Marco Belfanti, Department of Social Studies, University of Brescia, Italy
Markus Cerman, Department of Economic and Social History, University of Vienna, Austria
L. A. Clarkson, Department of Economic and Social History, The Queen's University of Belfast, Northern Ireland
Pierre Deyon, Department of History, University of Lille, France
Pat Hudson, Department of Economic and Social History, University of Liverpool, England
Lars Magnusson, Department of Economic History, University of Uppsala, Sweden
Milan Myška, Department of History, University of Ostrava, Czech Republic
Sheilagh C. Ogilvie, Faculty of Economics and Politics, and Trinity College, University of Cambridge, England
Ulrich Pfister, Department of Economic History, University of Geneva, Switzerland
Jürgen Schlumbohm, Max-Planck-Institut für Geschichte, Göttingen, Germany
J. K. J. Thomson, School of European Studies, University of Sussex, England
Christiaan Vandenbroeke, Faculty of Arts, University of Ghent, Belgium

1 The theories of proto-industrialization

Sheilagh C. Ogilvie and Markus Cerman

'Proto-industrialization' is the name given to the expansion of domestic industries producing goods for non-local markets which took place in many parts of Europe between the sixteenth and the nineteenth centuries. Often, although not always, such industries arose in the countryside where they were practised alongside agriculture; usually, they expanded without adopting advanced technology or centralizing production into factories.

This widespread industrial growth in early modern Europe has long been a subject of specialized study. But in the 1970s it began to attract much wider interest, when a series of stimulating articles and books christened it 'proto-industrialization', and argued that it was a major cause of the transition to capitalism and factory industrialization.

Proto-industrialization as the first step in industrialization

The term 'proto-industrialization' was invented by Franklin Mendels, and first used in his 1969 doctoral dissertation on the Flemish linen industry (Mendels 1969/1981). It became widely known after the publication in 1972 of a now-famous article based on this research (Mendels 1972). For Mendels, proto-industrialization was the first phase of industrialization: 'pre-industrial industry', he argued, 'preceded and prepared modern industrialization proper' (Mendels 1972: 241). During this proto-industrial phase, a rural labour force became involved in domestic industries producing for supra-regional markets. The population was liberated from the agrarian resource base, and labour which had previously been unused because of the seasonal nature of agrarian production found employment. Subsequently, in order for production to expand further, specialization into regions of rural industry and commercial agriculture became necessary.

Mendels took for granted that all of early modern Europe (not just Flanders) saw the decline of traditional urban and guild regulation of industry, as manufacturing moved into the unregulated countryside. There, according to Mendels, proto-industrialization also broke down the traditional regulation mechanisms of agrarian society – inheritance systems and other institutional controls – which had adjusted population growth to available economic resources. For the regions of Flanders which he studied, Mendels sought to show that periods of economic upturn in proto-industry led to an increase in the number of marriages, and that this increase was irreversible – that is, even in periods of economic downturn, the marriage rate did not decline again. This, he argued, generated higher fertility and rapid population growth, which in turn led to further expansion in rural domestic industries. It was this self-sustaining proto-industrial spiral, Mendels argued, which ultimately generated the labour, capital, entrepreneurship, commercial agriculture and supra-regional consumer markets required for factory industrialization. Mendels explored and extended these theses over the years that followed (see Mendels 1975; and especially Mendels 1980).

Proto-industrialization and proletarianization

During the 1970s and 1980s, Mendels' arguments were eagerly taken up by other historians, giving rise to separate schools of proto-industrial theory. One emanated from David Levine, who, in his doctoral dissertation on two villages in nineteenth-century Leicestershire, also viewed proto-industry as having revolutionized demographic behaviour (later published as Levine 1977). But for Levine, proto-industry and the associated population explosion were important mainly because they 'proletarianized' the workforce. By this he meant that they broke down the social structure and landownership pattern of traditional rural society, creating a large group of people who had no land to live from, and therefore had to work for wages. Levine viewed proto-industrialization as only one aspect of this larger process of proletarianization, which for him was the crucial precondition for capitalism and industrialization.

Proto-industrialization and surplus labour

Another view of proto-industrialization, much less widely known than others but indirectly quite influential, was put forward by Joel Mokyr. Mokyr rejected almost all the arguments advanced by Mendels (Mokyr 1976: 377–9). However, he was convinced that proto-industrialization provided cheap 'surplus' labour, which fuelled European industrialization by means of the mechanisms described by W. A. Lewis in his dualistic growth model for modern developing economies (Lewis 1954).

While Lewis' model had been (and still is) enormously influential, it was becoming clear that there was little empirical evidence for the existence of much 'surplus' labour in the agricultural sectors of present-day less developed economies (Kao, Anschel and Eicher 1964: 141; Little 1982: 90). But Mokyr argued that in the pre-industrial European economy, surplus labour was provided not by agriculture but by proto-industry. Although for the most part this version of the theory has not been pursued, it is important because of its direct links with the economics of development, and because it is close to the view of proto-industrialization adopted by Jan de Vries in his influential theories concerning early modern European urbanization (de Vries 1984).

Proto-industrialization and the transition from feudalism to capitalism

The proto-industrialization debate was intensified, first in German (in 1977) and then in English (in 1981), by the publication of a book by Peter Kriedte, Hans Medick and Jürgen Schlumbohm. Combining Mendels' and Levine's findings with earlier literature on domestic industry, particularly that of the German Historical School of National Economy, they turned the theory of proto-industrialization into a general model of European social and economic change in the period between the Middle Ages and the nineteenth century. In their own words,

> Proto-industrialization ... as 'industrialization before industrialization' ... can be defined as the development of rural regions in which a large part of the population lived entirely or to a considerable extent from industrial mass production for inter-regional and international markets ... Viewed from the long-range perspective, it belongs to the great process of transformation which seized the feudal European agrarian societies and led them toward industrial capitalism. (Kriedte, Medick and Schlumbohm 1981: 6)

For them, proto-industrialization represented the 'second phase' of this transformation process, for it 'could establish itself only where the ties of the feudal system had either loosened or were in the process of full disintegration' (Kriedte, Medick and Schlumbohm 1981: 6). The cause of this loosening of feudalism in the 'first phase' of the transition to capitalism was, they argued, an increased differentiation in agrarian class structure and a bifurcation of agrarian production into commercial and subsistence types. This in turn had been caused by the commutation of feudal dues paid in kind into money rents, which had occurred in European feudal societies, particularly in western and north-western areas of the continent. The polarization of the rural population into two different groups – 'peasants' (who owned enough land to live solely from agricultural production), and a landless or land-poor 'rural sub-stratum' (who could not live from agriculture alone) – provided the basis, it was argued, for the subsequent integration of the rural sub-stratum into domestic industry. This integration was triggered by the expansion of supra-regional and international markets, and a resulting need to increase production. Industrial production could only be expanded if it was shifted to the countryside, because in the towns guilds restricted growth.

Once proto-industries had arisen in the countryside, according to this account, they led to a transformation in the organization of industrial production, through a succession of different stages of development (although it was emphasized that these stages should not be viewed as rigid or deterministic). The first stage was the 'Kaufsystem' (artisanal or workshop system), in which rural producers retained autonomy over production and selling. An increasing penetration of merchant capital into production led to a greater dependency of producers on merchants and putters-out, bringing about a general transition to the 'Verlagssystem' (putting-out system). The most important element in this dependency was that the rural producers no longer had independent access to the market, either for buying raw materials or for selling their product. In the putting-out system, the merchants bought up the raw material inputs, 'put them out' to the rural producers who processed them in return for a wage, whereupon the merchants collected the output for transfer either to the finishing stages of production or to the final consumer market. Ultimately, according to this view, industrial production made the transition to a third organizational stage, the concentration of production into centralized manufactories and then into mechanized factories. Kriedte, Medick and Schlumbohm – like Mendels – explicitly mentioned (although without explaining) the possibility that this line of development might fail, resulting in de-industrialization and re-agrarianization.

As in the theory of Mendels, so too in that of Kriedte, Medick and Schlumbohm, the demographic consequences of proto-industrialization occupied a central position. The so-called 'demo-economic system' of proto-industrialization, developed by Hans Medick (and discussed in greater detail in Jürgen Schlumbohm's contribution to the present volume), drew a systematic set of theoretical connections between demographic development and the family economy of the proto-industrial household. Medick's concept thus sought to go beyond the direct relationships between proto-industry and marriage behaviour as they had been interpreted by Mendels.

Something often not acknowledged by either critics or proponents of the concepts advanced by Kriedte, Medick and Schlumbohm is that their theory actually advances two distinct assessments of proto-industrialization. Peter Kriedte and Hans Medick, in what they call their 'system concept', regard the proto-industrialization phase as a separate economic system: that is, it was a separate mode of production which prevailed during the transition from feudalism to capitalism, and which united elements of both feudal and capitalist modes. Jürgen Schlumbohm, by contrast, holds that although the proto-industrialization phase did have features of both feudal and capitalistic modes of production, it did not constitute a system of its own: it was a process, and remained part of the feudal mode of production.

Extensions to the theories of proto-industrialization

At latest by 1977, therefore, the concept of proto-industrialization had proliferated into a family of different theories, which adopted rather different definitions of proto-industry and which disagreed quite fundamentally about the causes of economic development. Almost all that they had in common was that they located these causes in a certain sector of the economy – export-oriented domestic industries – and viewed this sector as having broken down the demographic equilibrium of traditional European society. Over the following years and decades, these various branches of proto-industrialization theory stimulated a huge outpouring of research into regions of domestic industry throughout Europe – and, indeed, beyond it (on the application of proto-industrialization theories to the non-European world, see the literature cited in Ogilvie 1993a: 178 n. 6).

By 1982, so influential and yet so variegated had the field of proto-industrialization become that Franklin Mendels and Pierre Deyon were invited to convene one of the three main sessions of the Eighth International Economic History Congress in Budapest, with proto-industrialization as their theme. Deyon and Mendels pre-circulated a draft definition and a set of hypotheses, forty-eight researchers contributed empirical papers (Deyon and Mendels 1982), and Mendels summarized the findings of the session in a 'General report', containing a revised definition and a set of hypotheses which have provided a basis for subsequent debate (Mendels 1982; revised version published in French as Mendels 1984).

The 1982 definition of proto-industrialization stressed certain key characteristics. Proto-industrialization was held to take place (and thus be most properly studied) not nationally or internationally, but *regionally*:

'within a small radius around a regional capital'. Within regions, proto-industries were held to combine three characteristics. First, they were distinguished from old-fashioned crafts in that they produced not for local or regional consumption, but for sale to export markets located outside the region. Second, 'the most significant aspect of proto-industrialization' was that it 'provided employment in the countryside above all': it was practised part time by peasants who also laboured in agriculture, and only in its 'extreme or ultimate form' did it involve full-time employment. Third, proto-industrialization involved the 'symbiosis of rural industry with the regional development of a commercial agriculture'. A supplementary characteristic was 'the dynamic element': proto-industrialization was defined as a *growth* over time in the industrial employment of rural workers (Mendels 1982: 77–9).

Deyon and Mendels also put forward four hypotheses concerning the *effects* of proto-industrialization. First, it was supposed to have led to population growth and land fragmentation, by breaking down traditional regulation of demographic behaviour by peasants, landlords or inheritance systems. Second, it created profits which formed the capital for factory industrialization. Third, it provided merchants with the skills and experience they would need for factory industrialization. And fourth, it caused the commercialization of agriculture, which enabled subsequent urbanization and factory industrialization. The authors argued that it was through these four mechanisms that proto-industrialization led to factory industrialization, although they admitted that sometimes it led to de-industrialization instead (Mendels 1982: 80).

In his 'General report' of 1982, Mendels also proposed a list of revisions to some of the original proto-industrialization hypotheses of the 1970s. First, he admitted that the chronology of proto-industrialization varied, and had to be investigated in the context of the economic history of the particular region in question. Second, he acknowledged that proto-industrialization did not invariably lead to impoverishment; he suggested that producers' incomes depended on the production function of the specific wares they produced. Third, although he still held that proto-industry invariably disturbed the demographic system, he admitted that its impact might be felt not just on nuptiality, but also on fertility and migration; and that it depended on household organization, the prevalence of a Hajnal-type 'European' family system (Hajnal 1965, 1983), the social position of women and adolescents, the degree of population pressure and the nature of domestic relations in the particular society in question. Fourth, he admitted that proto-industry could lead to either industrialization or de-industrialization, depending on a variety of factors, among which he highlighted transportation costs.

Fifth, he acknowledged that the effect of proto-industrialization depended on the larger world economy, which might make it risky to extrapolate to the modern developing world. Finally, he argued that the study of proto-industrialization should warn modern development economists of the dangers of simple linear views of development, involving straightforward transitions from static feudal societies to dynamic capitalist ones (Mendels 1982: 93–8).

Criticisms of the theories of proto-industrialization

Somewhat more slowly than they attracted support, the theories of proto-industrialization also began to draw criticisms. Several components of the *definition* of proto-industry evoked lively controversy (Kriedte, Medick and Schlumbohm 1992: 70ff). For one thing, the precise size and structure of unit that qualified as a 'region' was unclear. Proto-industries could and often did extend beyond the radius around a single market town, or alternatively were sometimes found in only one or two communities in such a radius. Thus it was undesirably constraining to adopt this narrow geographers' definition of a region. On the other hand, defining the region as simply the area within which a certain proto-industry was practised seemed, although pragmatic, to leach the concept of the 'region' of much of its analytic content. Moreover, there was no agreement about how large a proportion of the regional labour force must have been employed in proto-industry, nor how fast or sustained the growth of this labour force must have been, in order to qualify as 'proto-industrialization'. Many researchers emphasized the importance of specific characteristics of the particular region, including the economic trends it experienced historically, and its situation within the wider national or international framework, in affecting the course of proto-industrialization.

There was also confusion about the precise theoretical importance of *export markets* for proto-industries; this is especially important given the criticisms from a number of historians of crafts and industry about the neglect of locally oriented rural and urban crafts. Even now, it remains unclear what proportion of production had to be exported in order for any given industry to qualify as a proto-industry instead of a craft. Finally, it is not clear how distant the final markets must have been, in order for trade in industrial products to count as 'supra-regional' rather than 'local' – especially given the ambiguity in defining the 'region' which has already been discussed. In sum, the precise demarcation between locally oriented crafts and export-oriented proto-industries remains indistinct.

Many commentators, especially historians of crafts and industry, criticized the *neglect of other forms of industry*. The theories of proto-industrialization concentrated solely on one sort of pre-industrial industry – namely domestic industry. These critics advanced strong arguments against such an over-emphasis on the role played by this single sort of industry in the transition to industrialization proper. They urged that historians also take into account the quantitative and qualitative importance of locally oriented rural and urban crafts, export-oriented urban industries, and centralized manufactories – all of which had been consciously neglected by the theories of proto-industrialization (Kaufhold 1986; Stromer 1986; Schremmer 1980: 422–3, 425–7, 442).

A related issue was the apparent *neglect of industrial technology and physical geography*. Although Mendels made passing references to the role of the production functions of particular industries in affecting rural impoverishment, and the key role of transportation costs in determining industrialization or de-industrialization of proto-industrial regions, these references remained for many years largely unexplored. Only recently have they been developed into a more systematic consideration of the role in proto-industries of technical requirements of different branches of industry and the effect on production costs of geographical and physical characteristics of the region (Mager 1993).

A fundamental substantive criticism levelled at all the theorists, but particularly Kriedte, Medick and Schlumbohm, was that they adopted a mistaken view of the structure and functioning of the *traditional societies* out of which proto-industrialization is supposed to have developed. This criticism was directed both at their view of the preconditions for the dissolution of feudalism during the 'first phase' of the transition to capitalism, and at their picture of agrarian society, especially that part of it which they termed the 'subsistence type' (Coleman 1983: 440ff; Eley 1984: 525ff; Houston and Snell 1984: 491; Linde 1980: 106ff; Schremmer 1980: 434ff; cf. on this Kriedte, Medick and Schlumbohm 1983: 92ff and the contribution by Schlumbohm in the present volume). This raised the question whether the model of the peasant family economy which they – like Mendels – had taken over from Alexander Chayanov, who had developed it for early-twentieth-century Russian peasants (Chayanov 1966), was really applicable to early modern European societies. Further criticisms were levelled at the contrasts drawn between subsistence-oriented proto-industrial producers and profit-oriented (i.e. capitalistically motivated) putters-out and entrepreneurs (Mosser 1981: 404ff). The exclusive subsistence orientation assumed for rural domestic workers was not found in empirical studies, and was inconsistent with the observed fact that proto-industrial producers sometimes became traders, factors, putters-out and even manufactory operators; nor was it altogether consistent with the observed practice whereby proto-industrial workers saved up proto-industrial earnings to invest in land and agriculture.

Closely related to this issue was the argument that the theories were *inapplicable to certain European societies*. Some commentators argued that the preconditions for proto-industrialization assumed in the theory actually prevailed only in north-west Europe, so that the model could not claim to be generally applicable (Houston and Snell 1984: 476). However, others contended that England – an important part of north-west Europe – had to be excluded from the model, because commercialization and capitalistic structures were already far advanced in England before the establishment of proto-industries, and thus proto-industrialization cannot have brought them into being. It was also argued that the demographic postulates of the theory and the view it advanced concerning factory industrialization were not appropriate in the English context (Coleman 1983: 439ff; Houston and Snell 1984: 476). Ironically, German historians also claimed that the theories of proto-industrialization were inapplicable to Germany, which is often seen as having followed a 'special path' toward industrialization and modernization (Kuczynski 1981; Schultz 1983; Linde 1980).

Most commentaries also criticized the *demographic* component to the theories: both Mendels' view of the relationship between proto-industry and demographic growth, and Medick's 'demo-economic system'. Because the demographic regime was subject to so many different influences in the various regions of early modern Europe, it seemed unlikely that all local and regional studies would support the postulates of the theory in all respects. As a consequence, the explanatory power and the validity of Mendels' and Medick's demographic postulates were questioned by a wide variety of critics, from both theoretical and empirical perspectives. Empirical case-studies of proto-industrial regions all over Europe were adduced to show that not all proto-industrial regions had greater population density, faster demographic growth, lower ages of marriage, higher fertility rates, larger households or a breakdown in the family and gender division of labour – all of which had been postulated in the original theories. Furthermore, case-studies of agrarian regions were used to demonstrate that many – even all – of these demographic characteristics could also be found in regions and time-periods when agricultural production was intensified and expanded (Coleman 1983: 442f; Linde 1980: 113ff; Houston and Snell 1984: 479ff; Schremmer 1980: 429ff; Kriedte, Medick and Schlumbohm 1993: 219–26).

The relationship between proto-industry and *agriculture* also remained unclear. It was pointed out that proto-industries were practised in the same region as many different kinds of agriculture, including both subsistence and commercial farming. Moreover, proto-industries derived their food and raw material supplies both from their own farming and from that of neighbouring or more distant regions of surplus. By-employment in proto-industry and agriculture was not the norm, but rather was sometimes present and sometimes absent. Finally, it was pointed out that in a number of proto-industrial regions, traditional agrarian institutions survived unaltered and rural social structure remained stable (Houston and Snell 1984; Linde 1980).

The theories were also accused of neglecting the economic role of *urban centres*. Although Deyon and Mendels acknowledged that 'the entire handicraft sector was organized or coordinated from the town', they appear to have regarded proto-industry as exclusively the *rural* component of this handicraft sector (Mendels 1982: 78). This is one aspect of the theories of proto-industrialization which has been most strongly criticized. An important current of thought argues that large *urban* export industries, or those involving centralized production units, should also be included under the rubric of proto-industrialization (Cerman 1993; Hohenberg 1991; Poni 1985).

A final major criticism focussed on *factory industrialization and de-industrialization*, and questioned the role of proto-industrialization in preparing the way for industrialization. It was widely acknowledged by both proponents and critics of the theories of proto-industrialization that de-industrialization and a return to agriculture were a not infrequent outcome in proto-industrial regions. According to the critics, this fact removed a great deal of the empirical content from any theory about proto-industrialization, especially since the factors which decided whether a proto-industrial region would industrialize or de-industrialize remained largely unclear (Clarkson 1985: 34ff; Houston and Snell 1984: 488ff; cf. on this the contribution by Clarkson in the present volume).

Each of the *mechanisms* by which proto-industrialization is supposed to have led to industrialization was shown to have weak empirical and theoretical bases. Research showed that the demographic effects of proto-industrialization were extremely various, as was its impact on the fragmentation of landholdings (as is acknowledged in Kriedte, Medick and Schlumbohm 1993: 219ff, 226ff). Proto-industrialization appears to have been only one of many sources of capital for industrialization, and in some cases proto-industrial profits flowed into agriculture, land-holding, or socio-political investments. Proto-industrialization was also only one of many sources of entrepreneurial skills for industrialization, and sometimes took place in such a constraining framework that it did not involve the development of the appropriate entrepreneurial skills at all. Furthermore, there is no evidence that it was proto-industrialization which led to the development of commercial agriculture, rather than agricultural surpluses which led to the growth of both proto-industries and – crucially – towns and cities. Commercial agriculture developed in many cases earlier than proto-industry, and not always in neighbouring regions. In many proto-industrial regions these mechanisms themselves cannot have operated, since they did not industrialize, but rather stayed proto-industrial or moved back to agriculture, and there is no agreement about what factors decided whether a proto-industry would generate the appropriate 'industrializing' mechanisms or not; thus the predictive power of the theory is greatly reduced (Clarkson 1985; Houston and Snell 1984; Hudson 1990; Mokyr 1976).

The theories of proto-industrialization thus touch upon almost every aspect of pre-industrial society: people's thoughts and motivations, their sexual and family behaviour, their use of time in work and play, their ownership of land and equipment, their standard of living and nutrition, their inequalities and conflicts, the social institutions which they used (but were also constrained by) in the attempt to survive and the mechanisms by which their society and economy gradually changed between *c.* 1500 and *c.* 1800. Around each of these fields of pre-industrial Europeans' lives, the theories of proto-industrialization have put forward daring hypotheses, which have aroused lively and often acrimonious debate. In different ways, all of these debates are discussed in the chapters of this book. However, most chapters place special emphasis on those issues which are crucial for understanding a particular European society. This is only appropriate, given that, in the early modern period just as today, Europe was a continent with a rich range of regional differences, as well as an equally rich array of shared concerns. Among these shared concerns are social inequality, demographic change and economic well being. How these evolved in Europe between the medieval period and the nineteenth century continues to be illuminated by the debate about proto-industrialization.

2 'Proto-industrialization' as a research strategy and a historical period – a balance-sheet*

Jürgen Schlumbohm

Ever since they were established by Franklin Mendels (Mendels 1969/1981, 1972), the theories of proto-industrialization have had a twofold direction of impact. On the one hand, they aimed to introduce into economic and social history a new approach which would overcome the divorce between previously separate fields of research. On the other, they advanced hypotheses with empirical content, which proposed for discussion a number of specific postulates about the period of transition from a 'pre-industrial' to an 'industrial' – or from a 'feudal' to a 'capitalist' – economy and society. These two aspects of the theory had quite separate pre-histories. The significance of (rural) domestic industry for the emergence of capitalism and factory industrialization had been discussed in various ways since the nineteenth century (Kriedte, Medick and Schlumbohm 1981: 1ff); the concept of an integrated research strategy, by contrast, was an original project of the 1970s. The two aspects must also be distinguished as far as the effects, achievements and limits of the theories of proto-industrialization are concerned.

The theory of proto-industrialization as a research strategy

The research strategy implied in the concept of proto-industrialization sought above all to overcome the barriers which had arisen between various sub-fields of economic and social history. It was a question of bringing together industrial and agrarian history, adding to them historical demography and the history of the household and the family, and also including the history of everyday culture and the development of institutions. The theories of proto-industrialization focussed on the inter-penetration between these fields, which in previous research had for the most part been separate; the central hypotheses of proto-industrialization concerned inter-dependencies between various aspects of social reality. This integrative approach was largely followed by the regional and local case-studies which were carried out in subsequent

* This chapter is translated from the German by Sheilagh C. Ogilvie.

years. In this sense, the theoretical anticipation showed itself to be enormously fruitful.

As far as the relationship between industrial and agrarian development was concerned, Franklin Mendels, on the basis of the findings of English agricultural historians and his own research on Flanders, placed at centre-stage the 'bifurcation' of the regional economy. According to this view, in the course of proto-industrialization there arose a contrasting and complementary specialization of neighbouring economic areas. While one area shifted into domestic industrial mass production for supra-regional and international markets, a neighbouring zone turned to the commercial production of foodstuffs (Mendels 1972: 247f; for a modified version, Mendels 1984: 990). This insight into the close reciprocal relationship between the industrial and the agrarian economy, precisely in the process of the emergence of capitalism, showed itself to be basic to further research: admittedly, such research soon revealed this 'bifurcation' of regions to be merely a special case of a much more complex connection. On the basis of a careful comparison of the literature on western, central and eastern European regions, Peter Kriedte already came to a more differentiated view (Kriedte, Medick and Schlumbohm 1981: 25ff). Since then, further research has enriched the picture (for example, Gullickson 1983; Dewerpe 1985; Kriedte, Medick and Schlumbohm 1993: 226ff; Pfister 1992a: 393ff).

The most important methodological impulse emanating from Franklin Mendels' theorem was that he put forward a sharply defined thesis about the relationship between rural industrial and demographic development as a central component of the concept of proto-industrialization. On the basis of aggregative data from the linen region he studied in Belgian Flanders, he arrived at a model of the mechanism through which demographic behaviour and economic changes were transmitted. Linen producers responded to economic upturns with increased frequency of marriage, while there was no corresponding demographic reaction to economic downturns. Mendels saw this asymmetry as the basis for the widespread population growth in proto-industrial regions; he sought the causes of this 'short-sighted' behaviour in the 'conditions of general backwardness and illiteracy' (Mendels 1971: 270, 1972: 249ff).

It was here that the ideas of Hans Medick intervened (Kriedte, Medick and Schlumbohm 1981: 74–93). Medick sketched out a model of the strategies of proto-industrial families, in order to show that there was an internal logic and rationality to their demographic behaviour. In so doing, he formulated, in a much more stringent way, a 'demo-economic system' of proto-industrialization, admittedly in a provisional form, in the sense of a 'hypothetical model'. As point of departure and comparison, he referred to the 'demo-economic system which regulated the feudal agrarian societies of Europe', as this had been sketched out by historical demographers following Malthus or Mackenroth. Whereas in the agrarian system, population growth was basically limited by marriage being linked to a 'niche' (a peasant farm, a craftsman's workshop) which was as a rule obtainable only through inheritance, proto-industrialization broke the iron 'chain between reproduction and inheritance' (in the formulation of Tilly and Tilly 1971: 189). Three reasons were suggested for this. First, early marriage was made *possible* for proto-industrial producers by the fact that they relied for subsistence not on inherited property but on their own labour: thus they were not subject to the seigneurial or communal control mechanisms of agrarian society. Secondly, because of their typical lifetime earnings curve, it was *useful* for proto-industrial workers (both female and male) to marry and have children early. Finally, the form of the domestic industrial work process actually made marriage and family formation a *necessary* precondition for independent production: the unit of production was the family, with the husband, wife and children working in co-operation.

These hypotheses thus immediately brought the research on the history of the household and the family, which had developed into a new field of historical studies in the 1970s, into the ambit of the theory of proto-industrialization. Above all, they stressed the importance of a methodological connection between the macro-level and the micro-level. It was a question of explaining the great developments encompassing the economy and population of whole regions and countries in terms of the life-cycles and family strategies of individual persons and families.

Admittedly, the many empirical studies stimulated by the hypotheses about the demographic behaviour of proto-industrial populations have led to highly differentiated findings; the same is true for studies of family structures and life-cycle patterns (Kriedte, Medick and Schlumbohm 1993: 219–26). In this process it has emerged that the proto-industrial family was by no means always a unit of production involving co-operation and a division of labour, but rather that – especially in the putting-out system – it was not infrequent that several persons would carry out individual wage labour side by side in the same household. Co-operation in work, involving a division of labour, thus did not necessarily have to take place within a household, but could also take place between households. For this reason alone, the link between the work process on the one hand and the family as the unit of demographic reproduction on the other is a complex one. Furthermore, the demographically relevant acts of marriage and begetting children were not the only ways in which households adapted to the requirements of work and survival. The social acts of the leaving home of unmarried offspring, or the taking in of persons who did not belong to the nuclear family, could also serve this purpose. Given this, although the relationship between work process, household structure and demographic behaviour remains central, the requirements of the proto-industrial working economy could no longer be viewed one-sidedly as the determining factor, generating a necessity for early marriage and a high number of children. The economic stimulus to early marriage, too, was less strongly felt where young people could already earn their own wages without marrying and establishing a household, whether as inmates in the houses of others or in a loosened dependency within the parental family. And if young people left the parental household early in life, the hope that adult children would contribute significantly to the family income when the parents' own ability to work declined because of ageing was an uncertain one. Finally, with respect to the effectiveness of seigneurial and communal mechanisms of control over marriage and household formation, on the one hand it has been found that not only proto-industrial workers were freed from this sort of restriction, but also other more or less 'proletarianized' labour forces, such as rural labourers in the course of the transition to agrarian capitalism, and possibly also workers in centralized industrial concerns and early factories. On the other hand, the proto-industrial population not infrequently remained linked into peasant-dominated society to such an extent that their demographic behaviour was thereby subjected to considerable restrictions.

Thus, the multitude of empirical findings which have in the meantime become available have revealed that no single behavioural pattern can be traced for all proto-industrial populations, but rather that an array of differentiating perspectives must be taken into account. In this, the proto-industrial demographic model shares the fate of its counterpart, the concept of a pre-industrial/agrarian demographic pattern. Whereas in the 1970s this was understood very much in the sense of a homogeneous system characterized by the 'European marriage pattern' (Hajnal 1965), in the meantime not only have fundamental criticisms been directed at the premises of this model (Ehmer 1991: 36ff, 62ff), but also empirical research has demonstrated the extraordinary variability of actual behaviour. The demography of early modern Europe therefore appears to be more complex than could be conceptualized by the antithesis between two models, one agrarian and one proto-industrial. Two fundamental methodological impulses, which emanate not least from the theories of proto-industrialization, appear however to remain influential: on the one hand, the attempt to integrate economy, demographic behaviour and household and family structure; on the other, the effort to explain the macro-structures of pre-industrial and proto-industrial societies in terms of the logic of micro-entities, namely life-cycles and family strategies. Both in the formulation of theoretical models (e.g. Pfister 1992b) and in empirical research, these two impulses are still operating vigorously (e.g. Kriedte 1991; Medick 1992/forthcoming; Schlumbohm 1994).

The pioneering study by Rudolf Braun on the Zürich highlands (Braun 1990) represented a decisive step in the linking of the social history of domestic industry with questions of everyday culture, which had traditionally been analysed by anthropology. In the framework of the theorem of proto-industrialization, it was sought to develop a more systematic connection between the concepts of the 'family economy' and 'plebeian culture' (Kriedte, Medick and Schlumbohm 1981: 64–73). Particularly in the course of the reciprocal rapprochement between history and cultural anthropology, this perspective, too, provided fundamental stimuli for succeeding debates and empirical studies.

The proto-industrialization theories of the 1970s already encompassed the approach of studying political, social and legal institutions in their reciprocal relationship with economic structures and strategies (Kriedte, Medick and Schlumbohm 1981: 126–34, cf. 23ff, 94ff, 136ff). These questions were initially not widely pursued in the general discussion, but they did play a large role in the special field of research on eastern central Europe and eastern Europe. Here, it was especially a question of the significance of the system of *Gutsherrschaft* (an agrarian system with very strong institutional powers for the landlords) for industrial development in the countryside (Myška 1979; Komlos 1980; Fenster 1983; Rudolph 1985; Melton 1987; Klíma 1991; Kulczykowski 1989, 1991). In recent years, the general debate and the western European discussion have turned more intensively to these problems. In so doing, it has been stressed – in accordance with the original hypotheses – that proto-industrialization not only could contribute to legal and institutional change, but in turn was also itself deeply imprinted, in both its course and its nature, by the political and social framework (Hudson 1981; Ogilvie 1993a; Pfister 1992a: 139–256).

Proto-industrialization as an element in an epoch of transition?

When Franklin Mendels introduced the term 'proto-industrialization' into scholarly discussion, he characterized the significance of the phenomenon decisively from an *ex post* perspective: for him, proto-industrialization was the 'first phase of the industrialization process'; it created essential conditions for the latter, in that it enabled a substantial accumulation of capital, prepared entrepreneurs and a usable labour force and developed the domestic market (Mendels 1972: esp. 244f).

Although the word *proto*-industrialization refers strongly to a precursor phase to 'actual' industrialization, the theory of an 'industrialization before industrialization' sought to free the concept from this relatively narrow definition. On the one hand, it stressed much more strongly that regions and branches of industry by no means regularly passed from proto-industrialization to factory industrialization, but rather that in numerous cases rural domestic industries ended in de-industrialization and re-agrarianization (Kriedte, Medick and Schlumbohm 1981: 145). On the other hand, it was a question of determining the historical significance of proto-industrialization not only from the perspective of the period which followed it, but also from that of the period which preceded it. Only in an all-encompassing perspective such as this could the weight of this phenomenon in the long epoch of the transition from the primarily agrarian feudal society of old Europe to industrial capitalism be more closely determined (Kriedte, Medick and Schlumbohm 1981: 6ff, 12ff; Kriedte, Medick and Schlumbohm 1986: 263ff).

Considering the misunderstandings which arose not only among the critics but also among some adherents to this conceptualization, it must be recalled that it was not claimed that the theorem of proto-industrialization explained this transition in its totality. It was merely one section of the transition, although admittedly an important one. In chronological terms, proto-industrialization was assigned to a 'second phase' in the process of transformation which encompassed feudal society in Europe: this 'second' phase assumed the existence of a 'first' phase, which had since the high Middle Ages led to the appearance of a dense network of towns, a division of labour between town and country mediated by the market, and – in agrarian production – the predominance of small peasant farms relative to the demesne estates of landlords. But within the 'second phase', as well, the rural export industries which stood in the centre of the theory of proto-industrialization were not the only relevant factor. Although agrarian change was included in the theory in a number of ways, on the other hand it must be regarded as an element with its own dynamic; and even the industrial sector was consciously not dealt with by the proto-industrialization concept in its full breadth: crafts working for local needs remained out of consideration, and early centralized concerns such as mines, iron works and manufactories were considered only as a borderline case.

Nevertheless, from the point of view of the concept it is unfortunate that the centre of gravity of most of the empirical studies on proto-industrialization still lies in the eighteenth or even in the nineteenth century. Of course, the documentary sources for this late period are much more favourable, and therefore investigating the relationship between various aspects of the historical process is easier. However, from a systematic point of view, studies of the origins of proto-industrialization in the late Middle Ages or in the sixteenth century are just as important as those of its end in industrialization or de-industrialization; given the state of research, they are perhaps even the greater desideratum. The studies which have appeared in the last fifteen years on the important case of Upper Swabia, especially on its industrial production of fustians (mixed fabrics made of linen and cotton), show that significant progress on this early period is quite possible (Stromer 1978, 1986; Clasen 1981; Paas 1981; Kießling 1989, 1991; Zorn 1988).

Precisely – although not exclusively – for this early period, the relationship between proto-industrialization and the urban economy and society must be re-thought. Originally, the towns were either largely excluded from the concept, or the relationship between rural export industries and towns was mainly, and rather one-sidedly, assessed in negative terms: considering the low elasticity of supply of the urban economy, guild restrictions and high living costs, the centre of gravity of export industry shifted from the towns to the countryside in the early modern period. However, this was not always an out-migration of a hitherto urban branch of industry into the surrounding countryside (thus woollen cloth production, for example, settled increasingly in the countryside around Aachen, while the importance of the town declined); it could also consist of new products whose production emerged directly in the countryside (such as, for the most part, the production of 'New Draperies', light woollen cloths, in the southern Netherlands); or it consisted of articles which the peasants had hitherto produced for their own needs, but were now being brought into trade by merchants or putters-out (as was often the case with linen).

Admittedly, studies of urbanization argue that proto-industrialization was an important factor slowing down the growth of towns in the course of the early modern period (de Vries 1984: esp. 220f, 238ff). But a closer analysis shows that the relationship between the urban economy and the rural industrial economy was a complex one (Kriedte 1982a). The problems begin already with the definition of the line of demarcation between 'town' and 'countryside', which is not everywhere unambiguous, whether economically, socially or as far as size and density of population are concerned. Furthermore, although not a few urban export crafts fell into crisis because of competition from cheaper rural labour forces, the towns mostly remained the centres of trade, finance and organization. Often only particularly labour-intensive stages of production took place in the countryside (thus, in the textile industry, regularly the spinning and often the weaving stage), while other stages, such as the important end processing, remained in the town. Where an especially skilled labour force was used, a great deal of capital was at risk or precise monitoring was required (as in silk weaving), the towns retained their advantage. In addition, in the course of the industrial development of the countryside in various parts of Europe, there arose new agglomerations which concentrated themselves into towns or quasi-towns. Overall, therefore, in the framework of proto-industrialization there were not only competitive relations, but also co-operation and mutual supplementation, between town and country.

The inter-penetration between town and countryside, and the structural similarity between urban and rural export industries, appear to support the notion of abandoning the original demarcations and fully integrating urban production centres into the concept of proto-industrialization. In this sense, some have spoken of 'proto-industrial cities' (Poni 1982a, 1990; Hohenberg and Lees 1985: 125ff; Kriedte 1991: esp. 19ff; Cerman 1993). Such arguments coming from the history of industry, however, confront no less important doubts. The social context of production was quite different in the countryside and the city, not only because of the relationship between industry and agriculture, but also because of the institutional framework.

The arguments for and against fully incorporating the industrial concerns which were already centralized before factory industrialization into the concept of proto-industrialization show a certain structural similarity to the debate sketched out above. The theory of 'industrialization before industrialization' directed attention, in conscious contrast to a dogmatically narrow view of the 'period of manufactures', above all to the breadth of rural domestic industry, without conclusively clarifying its relationship with the early 'large concerns' (Kriedte, Medick and Schlumbohm 1981: 7f, 10, 34, 52, 91, 107ff, 112, 142). Since then, authors arguing in the tradition of industrial history in particular have extended the concept in this direction (Cerman 1993; Mager 1993: 199ff).

Since the 1980s, new light has also fallen on the core area of Mendels' theory, the relationship between proto-industrialization and 'actual' industrialization. Here, several of the new tendencies in the literature on the industrial revolution are of considerable relevance. Particularly deserving of consideration in this perspective is the debate about the case of England, since in this 'pioneer' country the relationship between early factories and proto-industries can be investigated without the additional refractions which arise with 'catching-up industrialization'.

Three tendencies in recent research should be mentioned. On the one hand, historians and economists working quantitatively on the macro-level in the 1980s came to a wide-ranging consensus that during the 'industrial revolution' British economic growth was much slower and change was much more gradual than had been generally assumed in the 1950s and 1960s (Harley 1982; Williamson 1984; Crafts 1985). There is considerable disagreement about the causes for this; but it is widely accepted that the level of development before the beginning of the industrial revolution – whether in 1760 or as early as 1700 – was clearly higher than earlier assumed. The proportion of the labour force working in processing industries was greater, that in agriculture was smaller; and the per capita income of the population was higher. Admittedly, this 'revisionist' view of British industrialization has in the mean time been criticized in its turn (Hoppit 1990; Berg and Hudson 1992; Jackson 1992); and even its proponents insist that their macro-economic series are only 'best guesses' and 'controlled conjectures' (Crafts and Harley 1992: 703f). Nevertheless there is agreement that growth and change – at least insofar as they can be grasped quantitatively – were not compressed into the decades of the 'industrial revolution' to anything like the extent previously assumed, but rather extended over much longer periods. This yields the conclusion that Mendels' attention to the changes which took place before factory industrialization was altogether justified.

In addition to – and partially in opposition to – the current of research oriented around macro-economic aggregates, another strand of the recent literature stresses that industrialization was not a national, but a 'regional phenomenon': 'the process of industrialization . . . is essentially one of regions, operating in a European context' (Pollard 1981: vii, 14, 1980; Hudson 1989). This approach essentially corresponds to that of the theory and study of proto-industrialization: here, too, it is a question of a level below that of national aggregates, and likewise a question of exchange and competition between regions in Europe and the world, beyond the borders of the individual state.

Finally, there has recently been a re-awakening of interest in qualitative studies, and in a 'new microeconomics of the Industrial Revolution' (Berg 1985: 17). This current of research has found that there was not a sudden breakthrough at the end of the eighteenth century, but rather that a large number of small improvements and changes in so-called traditional industries and forms of organization had already taken place much earlier (cf. Leboutte 1988: 95ff, 125ff, 478ff) – an insight which is well suited to underlining the importance of proto-industrialization.

Admittedly, these findings make drawing a demarcation between the 'first' phase (proto-industrialization) and the 'second' phase (factory industrialization) more problematic than it seemed in a more emphatic view of the industrial revolution. But even the revisionist current of argument does not dispute that several branches of industry (such as cotton production) were indeed revolutionary; it is only that it assesses them as making up a smaller proportion of the economy as a whole. Nevertheless, they do not deny the fundamental change in the structure of the economy. Others have recently again stressed qualitative breaks and social discontinuities, thereby 'rehabilitating' the industrial *revolution* (Berg and Hudson 1992; Hudson 1992).

Even though on this side the approach of proto-industrialization can find some support from recent research tendencies, it must not be ignored that fundamental doubts are emanating from another side. The growing scepticism in the last two decades about traditional thinking on progress – whether technocratic and growth-oriented, or Marxian – has not been without its consequences for our views of historical processes. In this, increasing weight has been given to the accusation that all the theories of proto-industrialization are more or less massively teleological in nature, and explicitly or implicitly contain the idea of a succession of stages in economic and social development (Coleman 1983: 439f; Perlin 1983: 36ff, 1985: 389ff). Certainly, this criticism does not strike all versions of the theory with equal severity. When the transition from proto-industrialization to factory industrialization is not assumed to be regular and normal, but rather the outcome is conceived as being one which is in principal open – even to the extent of re-agrarianization – a great deal has been done to take such doubts into account. Such a more open concept can even take into account that in some regions industrial development broke off not only under competition from factories, but rather already during the epoch of proto-industrialization (Kriedte, Medick and Schlumbohm 1981: 145f; Thomson 1982, 1983).

However, the question arises whether one must not go substantially further: is there, in the history of industry, really a great line of development which in the last few centuries led from dispersed small craft production to ever more centralized and mechanized structures? Or is it more appropriate to speak of a series of cyclical fluctuations between centralized and de-centralized – and between smaller-scale and larger-scale – production? It is not disputed that the beginning of factory industrialization did not by any means start a unilinear decline in domestic industry: in addition to domestic industries displaced by mechanization, there were also those which endured for a long time, others which even expanded greatly and still others which were newly established, and experienced an enormous upswing – not least in cities (Kriedte, Medick and Schlumbohm 1993: 232–8). In the present day in advanced industrial countries, domestic work is once again expanding, not least in the service sector, extending to 'electronic domestic work'; particularly, however, in the less-developed world this form of production is used to a very considerable extent. Already in the nineteenth century, and certainly in our own time, 'alternatives to mass production' may have existed, and do exist, for instance in the form of 'flexible specialization' of smaller concerns (Piore and Sabel 1985; Sabel and Zeitlin 1985). Finally, there are certain analogies between the decentralized organization of a proto-industrial putting-out system, in which separate stages of work took place in different sub-regions, and the 'new international division of labour' of our own day, in which substages of production are distributed across various countries in the centre, semi-periphery and periphery according to cost advantages (Fröbel, Heinrichs and Kreye 1980). However, it is important not to ignore the fact that such new tendencies toward de-centralization are taking place on a quite different spatial scale and technological level than in the epoch before factory industrialization. To this extent – despite all justified criticisms of linear views of development – the picture of a cyclical movement which in some ways returns to the point of departure does not in fact seem justified.

Given the wide-ranging criticisms of the specific content of the proto-industrialization hypotheses, must one conclude that this theory was a 'mistake' – even if possibly a 'talented' one which led to interesting debates and studies and thus may have been more fruitful than many tedious truths (Kuczynski 1984: 152)? Certainly, the heuristic usefulness of the concept as a research strategy finds broader recognition than the concrete content of proto-industrialization as a chronological category. And without question, nowadays proto-industrialization appears to be less a homogeneous system than a many-sided and differentiated phenomenon; and demarcating it is not without its problems. However, now as ever, there is a range of good reasons for concluding that this concept enables the conceptualization of a number of features of social and economic processes and structures which were essential for Europe between the late Middle Ages and factory industrialization.

3 Social institutions and proto-industrialization

Sheilagh C. Ogilvie

Introduction: proto-industry and the social framework

Theories about proto-industrialization have, over the last twenty years, encouraged a flowering of research on early modern European industrial regions. This research has revealed both important common characteristics in early modern economies, and important differences and divergences among them. Perhaps the most important common feature is regional specialization. By the end of the sixteenth century, few parts of Europe remained autarkic 'less developed economies' engaging in subsistence production. Instead, Europe was turning into a differentiated patchwork of inter-dependent regions, specializing in a variety of different branches of agriculture and industry, and trading among themselves through a network of towns and cities (de Vries 1976). Proto-industries and regions of commercial agriculture were arising almost everywhere in early modern Europe.

But important differences and divergences within Europe have also emerged from studying proto-industrialization. Although proto-industries arose everywhere, different proto-industrial regions developed in radically different ways. A few underwent demographic, social and economic changes close to those postulated by the original theories, but many others did not. These differences can be very enlightening – not just about proto-industrialization, but also about the wellsprings of social, demographic and economic change in general. It is now the task of the 'second generation' of proto-industrialization studies to explain the *divergences*, as well as the similarities, among different European proto-industrial regions. In this chapter, I will try to show that a great deal of this divergence – although not all – was caused by profound and enduring differences in *social institutions* among European societies.

By 'social institutions' I refer to the sets of established rules and practices through which people organized their economic, social, demographic, political and cultural activities. For economic development, the most important *existing* institutions in early modern Europe were landholding systems, communities (villages, towns, cities) and corporate groups (guilds and merchant companies). There were also two *new* institutions which expanded rapidly during the early modern period: the state and the market.

All of these institutions varied a great deal among different societies – sometimes even among different regions of the same country. All of these institutions also changed over time, as they interacted with one another and were influenced by demographic, economic and political changes. In the brief space at my disposal here it is naturally impossible to provide a complete survey of the numerous social and institutional frameworks which existed in European proto-industrial regions. Here, I will simply point out some important general features of the social and institutional framework, its wide variability across the continent of Europe, and its development over time, which were not recognized in the early literature on proto-industrialization, and suggest ways in which they may constitute an important focus for future research.

Social institutions constrained most forms of economic, social, demographic and cultural activity in early modern European societies, yet they have been surprisingly neglected by both the theories of proto-industrialization and the criticisms of them. A central component of the original theories proposed in the 1970s was that proto-industrialization cleared away the obstacles to industrial capitalism in Europe by *breaking down* traditional social institutions (seigneurial systems, village communities, privileged towns, guilds, merchant companies), and replacing them with unregulated markets. Yet this was theoretically assumed, rather than empirically demonstrated, and subsequent research on proto-industrialization has not confirmed it.

In some parts of Europe, village communities and the institutions regulating access to land and settlement rights were already weak, without proto-industrialization. This was the case, for example, in most areas of England, Flanders and the Netherlands, and in parts of highland Switzerland (e.g. Kanton Zürich, Appenzell-Ausserrhoden) and of the Rhineland (e.g. Krefeld and the Wuppertal) (Braun 1978; de Vries 1974; Kisch 1981b; Kriedte 1982b; Macfarlane 1978; Tanner 1982; Wrightson 1982). The causes of this weakness of community and seigneurial institutions are a matter for lively debate by historians; however, proto-industrialization is clearly not the cause, since communities were weak in these societies in agrarian areas as well as proto-industrial ones. There were also many parts of Europe, as we will see on pp. 27–30 of this chapter, in which community and seigneurial institutions remained strong despite the existence of proto-industry, and played a major role in the development of the economy and society during proto-industrialization.

Likewise, in some parts of Europe, craft guilds and merchant companies could easily be evaded by moving industry outside the towns. This was the case in England, where the state was too weak to provide support or enforcement for the institutional privileges of towns over the countryside (Clark and Slack 1976). It was also the case in Flanders and the Netherlands, where the large number and density of cities created too much inter-urban competition for effective control of the countryside, or effective capture by a single city of state enforcement for its privileges against all the other cities (de Vries 1974). But, as we will see on pp. 30–3 below, in most other parts of Europe cities and corporate groups exercised considerable influence over rural industry, throughout proto-industrialization. Seldom, outside England and the Low Countries, were putting-out and proto-industrial exporting the domain of individual 'capitalist' entrepreneurs; instead, they were monopolized by guild-like companies of finishers and merchants with state privileges. In some parts of Europe, proto-industrial workers were unregulated and unorganized; in others they set up guilds, even in the countryside, to defend themselves against the merchant companies, and to exploit their own employees and suppliers (especially females and young people, who were often legally prohibited from engaging in the more lucrative stages of production).

Social institutions thus varied widely across European regions, both before and during proto-industrialization. It cannot be said that in general strong non-market institutions prevented proto-industries from arising. Indeed, as we will see, there are many cases in which it was precisely the strength of specific non-market institutions which artificially created favourable conditions for proto-industry, for instance by lowering the cost of labour. Nor can it be claimed that in general proto-industrialization broke down non-market institutions and replaced them with markets. Indeed, in most regions, social institutions other than markets profoundly and enduringly influenced how proto-industries developed.

Social institutions and costs

Why and in what ways did social institutions have such strong effects on proto-industry? A useful way to think about this question is in terms of *costs*. Like any form of production, proto-industries faced costs for their inputs – raw materials, labour, capital and sometimes land. They also faced what are called 'transactions costs' – costs of transportation, negotiation, information, contract enforcement, protection from coercion and so on. Transactions costs affected many aspects of production itself (such as embezzlement of raw materials, quality maintenance and responsiveness to changes in demand). They also affected almost every aspect of marketing and selling proto-industrial output. A proto-industry was more likely to arise in a region where the particular mix of inputs required by its technology could be obtained, and where export markets could be reached, at lowest cost. Once in existence, an industry would tend to organize production so as to take advantage of the characteristics of the region, in order to continue to minimize costs. Any industry which failed to exploit cost advantages would find itself undercut in all but very monopolistic export markets, since input costs were a major, although not the only, influence on output prices.

Especially in a pre-industrial economy, cost should be understood in the usual economic sense of *opportunity cost* – not just in money, but in terms of foregone alternatives. For example, in a region with fertile soils and easy access to land people had good potential earnings in agriculture, and the opportunity cost of working in proto-industry was high; infertile soil or institutional restrictions on access to land lowered the opportunity cost of proto-industrial labour. In pre-industrial Europe, just as in modern developing economies, many inputs were not formally traded in markets, and thus did not have money prices, but they did have opportunity costs for the economic agents concerned, and it is this cost which is analytically important.

What determined these costs? One important determinant was physical geography: climate, soil, natural resources, energy supplies, topographical barriers to transportation, location near trade routes and so on (Mager 1988). But proto-industries arose in regions with no special physical characteristics to favour their development. Even industries with the same technical requirements could arise in a variety of environments, and could develop very differently as a consequence. Moreover, many regions with infertile soils, good energy supplies, or cheap sources of raw materials failed to develop proto-industries. Physical factors alone, therefore, were neither necessary nor sufficient to cause proto-industries to arise or to develop in specific ways.

This is not surprising: input costs and output prices can be affected by other things than characteristics of the physical environment. In particular, they are affected by the *social institutions* governing the transactions through which inputs are obtained, production is organized and output is sold. In European proto-industries, this means we must examine the ways in which markets in land, labour, capital, raw materials, and industrial output were regulated by village communities, landholding systems, urban centres, occupational corporations such as guilds and merchant companies, and – not least – the emerging early modern state. What mattered was not so much the strength or weakness of these institutions, but the precise way in which they inflated or reduced costs.

Community institutions

Community institutions often regulated whether people could settle, work, hold land, use common resources or marry. This was especially the case in societies in which landlords were relatively weak, but village communities could also be strong in areas of the 'second serfdom', even though in these areas seigneurial institutions were stronger and had the final word. Because of the regulatory powers they enjoyed, communities often controlled the availability, and thus the cost, of labour, land and natural resources. The original hypotheses argued that proto-industrialization required, and furthered, the breakdown of community institutions (Mendels 1982: 80; Kriedte, Medick and Schlumbohm 1981: 8, 16–17, 40). But research does not confirm this.

Where weak community institutions lowered industrial costs, proto-industry might, holding other factors constant, seek out communities whose institutions were already weak; this appears to have happened in Switzerland (Braun 1960) and in England (Levine 1977). But other factors also affected costs, and we therefore find proto-industry in areas of strong community institutions where other factors favoured it. An example is Scotland, where proto-industries arose in arable regions with strong communities because the 'cottar system' in such regions lowered the costs of proto-industrial labour compared to pastoral regions where communities were weaker but other factors were unfavourable (Whyte 1989: 231, 237–8, 243–5).

Certain strong community institutions actually encouraged proto-industry by lowering its costs. Thus in Twente, in the Netherlands, the strong community institution of the *marken* system gave hereditary rights of access to common land to a group of established peasant families, excluding the rest of the population, which therefore turned to proto-industrial work; that is, community institutions in Twente reduced the opportunity costs of labour in proto-industry by preventing a part of the population from engaging in agriculture (Hendrickx 1993: 330–1).

In Cento, in northern Italy, access to all land was regulated by a community institution called the *partecipanza*, which distributed a share of land to each family according to its size, but only as long as family members remained resident in the village. However, each share was not sufficient for a family's subsistence, so instead of emigrating (which would have lost their family its right to a land share), a large part of the population stayed in the community but turned to proto-industry to supplement their earnings from farming their insufficient land share. That is, community institutions in Cento provided strong incentives to the population to remain in the countryside but engage in industry, thereby reducing the opportunity cost of proto-industrial labour (Belfanti 1993: 265–6).

In most European regions, including proto-industrial ones, communities laid down a dense network of rules about how land could be held, sold and inherited, how labour could settle, reproduce and be employed, how capital could be lent and borrowed, how natural resources could be used, and how agricultural products could be bought and sold. In the dense worsted proto-industry in the south German duchy of Württemberg, for instance, throughout the seventeenth and eighteenth centuries strong communities regulated marriage, settlement, labour mobility, output markets and women's work, and helped enforce market regulation by rural proto-industrial guilds (Ogilvie 1986, 1995). Similarly, in the rural cotton proto-industry in the Waldviertel of Lower Austria, until the 1780s village communities strictly enforced the one-heir inheritance system, stringently controlled new settlement and restricted access to and use of common lands, thereby affecting labour costs, demographic behaviour and social structure (Berkner 1973; Komlosy 1988).

Community rules, which varied enormously across Europe, affected the costs and prices of most factor inputs and most products. Counter to the original arguments of the theories of proto-industrialization, communities were not broken down, weakened, or even uniformly affected, by proto-industry. The influence of proto-industry on communities was extremely various: in some parts of Europe they were already weak, even where the regional economy remained agrarian; in others, communities remained strong, even where the regional economy shifted over to proto-industry. In such regions, community institutions themselves shaped proto-industry, helping to decide whether a rural population would turn to proto-industrial work, which groups would do so, which tasks they would engage in and whether their demographic behaviour would change.

Landholding institutions

Proto-industry is supposed to have required, and furthered, the breakdown of traditional institutions governing landholding and agriculture, and is portrayed as a major force in the transition from feudalism to capitalism (Kriedte, Medick and Schlumbohm 1981: 8, 16–17, 40; Mendels 1982: 80). But this theoretical proposition has not been borne out empirically. For one thing, proto-industries arose throughout eastern central and eastern Europe, where feudal institutions continued to survive for centuries. It was originally argued that these 'feudal proto-industries' arose only in areas where feudalism had begun to weaken. But Rudolph has shown that they arose throughout Russia in areas of classic feudal production on large estates, and were not associated with even such a partial 'breakdown' of the serf system as the commutation of labour dues to money payments (Rudolph 1980: 111, 1985: 48, 54, 57–61, 63). Strong feudal institutions could positively *encourage* proto-industries by decreasing their costs. Thus in Bohemia after 1650, the so-called 'second serfdom' strengthened lords' powers to benefit from their peasants' industrial activities (through feudal dues and contract payments from foreign merchants), to urge (and even occasionally compel) their peasants into proto-industrial work, and to keep proto-industrial costs low through 'forced wage labour', exploitation of labour services for proto-industrial auxiliary tasks, and restricting peasants' alternative options (Klíma 1959: 35, 38, 1974: 51, 53; Myška 1979: 59–63). In addition, strong feudal institutions encouraged proto-industry in both eastern Europe and northern Italy by weakening the industrial monopolies of urban guilds (Belfanti 1993; Klíma 1991). In the Swedish iron proto-industry, seigneurial institutions remained strong enough to prevent the rise of a land-poor proto-industrial labour force on the English pattern, but had weakened too much to provide an adequate supply of forced labour for transport and charcoal burning as in Russia (Florén *et al.* 1993). Thus what mattered for proto-industry was not so much the 'strengthening' or 'weakening' of feudalism, but rather the specific effect of feudal institutions on industrial costs.

Non-feudal landholding institutions also affected industrial costs. In eastern Rumelia in Bulgaria, for instance, landholding institutions supported by the Ottomans enabled large landowners and graziers to hinder settlement of wastes and restrict access to land until 1878, artificially creating cost conditions favouring proto-industry (Palairet 1982). In Tuscany, sharecropping tenancies adjusted farm size to family membership and contractually obliged tenants to labour for the landlord, thereby precluding proto-industrial employments (Belfanti 1993). In Ravensberg in Westphalia, the 'Heuerling' ('cottager') system interlinked landholding with labour relationships: peasants permitted *Heuerlinge* to settle on their farms and to make *de facto* (although not legal) use of the common lands, in exchange for having a right to demand their labour when it was needed on the farm. The combination of agricultural day-labouring for the peasants and use of commons was not enough for *Heuerlinge* to survive, so they also engaged in proto-industry in the interstices left by the labour demands of the peasants. Empirical research has shown that this agrarian institution affected the labour available for proto-industry, the seasonality of production, the demographic and familial behaviour of proto-industrial producers and the resulting social structure (Kriedte, Medick and Schlumbohm 1992: 85, 240–2; Schlumbohm 1992).

As research such as this shows, landholding institutions also affected social structure and demographic behaviour in proto-industrial regions. In the Waldviertel in Lower Austria, for instance, strong seigneurial and communal controls over landholding and settlement permitted the existence of a rural cotton proto-industry, but prevented proletarianization and population explosion (Mitterauer 1986). In proto-industrial areas of Switzerland, France, Württemberg and Upper Lusatia, smallholding systems remained strong, and proto-industrialization failed to transform the rural social structure or abolish agricultural by-employments (Kriedte, Medick and Schlumbohm 1992). Even where proto-industrial groups were landless, institutions such as the *Heuerling* system continued to influence the organization of proto-industrial labour within the family. By affecting the opportunity costs of labour and other resources, landholding institutions had far-reaching effects on the options of proto-industrial workers.

Guilds and companies

Proto-industrial costs were also affected by corporate groups such as guilds and merchant companies. According to the original theory, proto-industries arose in the countryside precisely to avoid corporate regulations; by doing so, they are supposed to have hastened the breakdown of guilds and companies (Kriedte, Medick and Schlumbohm 1981: 7, 13, 22, 106, 115, 128; Mendels 1981: 16, 26). But this idea is based on an unjustified generalization of the experiences of England and the Low Countries, where urban and guild powers over the countryside appear to have been breaking down in the sixteenth century independently of proto-industrialization (de Vries 1974; Kellett 1958). It is important to recognize that this was quite exceptional. Almost everywhere else in Europe, proto-industries were regulated by corporate groups of 'capitalists', and often also of 'workers', well into the eighteenth century.

In this context, the corporate groups of 'capitalists' – the merchant companies which enjoyed monopolies and other state privileges over most European proto-industries outside England, Flanders and the Netherlands – should not be confused with modern capitalist corporations. Merchant companies were much closer in nature to guilds: indeed, they often originated as 'merchant guilds' or guilds of finishing crafts (such as dyers), and were issued with state charters which strongly resembled those of guilds. Merchant companies and guilds shared many characteristics. As a general rule, a merchant company was not a voluntary association any more than a guild was: it was a corporate organization which one was compelled to join if one desired to operate as a merchant in a particular community, or if one wished to trade in a particular commodity. Many proto-industrial merchant companies either altogether refused to admit any new member who was not the son or relative of an existing member, or charged prohibitively high fees for the admission of outsiders, much higher than the admission fees charged by ordinary craft guilds (Kisch 1972; Thomson 1982; Troeltsch 1897). Above all, both guilds and merchant companies enjoyed legal monopolies and other state privileges over production and trade in particular sectors of the economy, which they used to prevent competition by non-members of the corporate group, and to increase their own profits by charging higher than competitive prices to customers and paying lower than competitive prices to their suppliers and employees.

The privileges of guilds and merchant companies were often, but not always, associated with the institutional powers of urban centres. One frequent criticism directed at the original theories of proto-industrialization is that they ignored the many stages of proto-industry carried out in towns and cities (Cerman 1993; Poni 1985). In few European towns outside England and the Low Countries did guilds and merchant companies lose power before the late eighteenth century, whatever happened in the countryside. France was a transitional case, in which towns gradually began to lose their powers during the first half of the eighteenth century, although they retained a number of privileges until at least 1760 (Gayot 1981; Guignet 1979; Lewis 1993; Poni 1985). Since a corporate monopoly sought to reduce prices paid to suppliers and increase prices charged to customers, an effective guild or company in an *urban* stage of proto-industry was very likely to affect the costs faced by rural workers, irrespective of whether these also possessed a corporate organization. Urban guilds in one industry could also increase costs of other industries, as shown by the successful lobbying of woollen- and silk-weaving guilds to impose restrictions on the cotton industry (Mager 1993; Thomson 1991).

Rural proto-industrial workers also formed their own guilds. In the small iron goods industry of Berg (in western Germany) and the trimmings industry of the Erzgebirg-Vogtland (in eastern Germany), rural workers 'formed corporate groups in the same way as urban craftsmen, to secure the "livelihood", regulate training, enforce quality standards, and implement their interests vis-à-vis the entrepreneurs and putters-out' (Mager 1993: 188). Rural or 'regional' guilds formed under similar pressures, and sought similar forms of control over input and output markets, in a wide variety of other industries, particularly in central Europe and northern Italy: in the Wuppertal linen proto-industry (Kisch 1972); the Württemberg linen and worsted proto-industries (Medick 1983a, 1983b; Ogilvie 1986, 1990); the east Swabian textile region around Ulm and Augsburg (Kießling 1991: 44–5); the Austrian linen-weaving (Hoffmann 1952: 103ff), cotton-production (Berkner 1973: 123ff; Komlosy 1988, 1991; Matis 1991), scythe-making (Fischer 1966: 19ff) and small-iron-goods proto-industries (Hassinger 1986: 950); the linen and woollen proto-industries of northern and north-eastern Bohemia (Klíma 1991); and the Trompia valley gun-making industry of northern Italy (Belfanti 1993). Other rural proto-industries, such as the Prato woollen industry in northern Italy (Belfanti 1993) simply retained their medieval guilds.

What was the economic impact of these proto-industrial guilds and companies? It is sometimes claimed that the negative impact of guilds has been exaggerated. In the sense that guilds did not prevent proto-industrialization altogether, this is certainly true. But whether they benefited any given social group or proto-industry, let alone the wider economy, can only be established by detailed study. Corporate groups sought to reduce input costs and increase output prices for their own members. To achieve this they implemented a variety of measures – entry barriers, output quotas, quality regulations, technical restrictions, wage ceilings, price floors – which were enforced with varying effectiveness. How any given corporate group affected costs and prices in any given proto-industry therefore requires detailed investigation, of a sort which has, in most cases, not yet been carried out. However, some general results can be identified.

Although guilds and companies were not invariably opposed to productivity-enhancing changes in technology or the organization of production *in themselves*, they did oppose such changes where these threatened their corporate ability to prevent competition, charge monopoly prices and restrict the pay of their employees and suppliers (such as the female spinners, undoubtedly the most numerous and surely the most exploited proto-industrial workforce in Europe). Violent political struggles broke out when attempts were made to reduce guild and company privileges in proto-industries as far afield as

Austria (Cerman 1993), Bohemia (Klíma 1991), Württemberg (Medick 1983a; Ogilvie 1986), the Wuppertal (Kisch 1972), France (Thomson 1982), Italy (Belfanti 1993; Poni 1982a), and Spain (Thomson 1991; Torras 1991). Many of these struggles did not reach their climax until the late eighteenth century. The abolition of corporate privileges was often followed by an industrial boom, as with the abolition in 1770 of the Prato rural weavers' guild in northern Italy, or that of the Schwechat company in Austria in 1762. This, combined with the fact that people do not expend resources to defend valueless privileges, strongly suggests that these corporate groups were able to exercise significant influence over costs and prices, and that they constrained growth in many proto-industries until the late eighteenth or early nineteenth centuries.

Guilds and companies were particularly important for proto-industries in regions where the dominant political institution was the city-state, such as in central and northern Italy (Belfanti 1993). German and Austrian guilds and companies also owed their power to their symbiotic relationship with the state (Ogilvie 1992). Few if any proto-industrial guilds or merchant companies survived without state support, as is shown by examples from proto-industries in France, Spain, Sweden, and many other parts of Europe. Indeed, it is rare to find a corporate group anywhere in Europe, whether of merchants or of workers, which effectively regulated markets without state enforcement. This is one indication of how strongly European proto-industries were influenced by the growing power of the early modern state. Thus we cannot study proto-industries without also looking at state institutions and the political framework.

State institutions

Early modern Europe saw the rise both of proto-industries and of the modern state. Yet the role of the state is one of the least-researched aspects of proto-industrialization. Partly, this neglect is a reaction against interpreting state *policy* as a mirror of reality. Closer empirical research shows that often state economic policies and industrial legislation did not have the intended outcome; but state economic regulations often had serious unintended consequences. Another reason for the widespread neglect of the state was that the original theories viewed proto-industrialization as causing the transition to 'capitalism' and 'market society', concepts which are held (often unjustifiedly) to exclude the notion of state intervention in the economy.

It is now becoming clear that this neglect of the state was an over-reaction. Not only successful economic policies but also those that misfired, and, indeed, state actions undertaken for non-economic purposes (to wage war, for instance, or to gain domestic political support) could have important if unintended economic repercussions. While states' direct attempts to encourage proto-industry saw mixed success, their indirect role, particularly in supporting, changing or challenging other institutions, was substantial.

The little attention which has been directed at the role of the state in proto-industrialization has focussed on the attempts by many European states to set up proto-industries and give them direct support. Yet the vast majority of these attempts failed, and many were damaging to other economic endeavours. Thomson, for instance, describes how many states of central and eastern Europe in which 'corporative economic structures' predominated tried to encourage calico-printing proto-industries through privileges, monopolies, subsidies, state loans, state manufactories and coerced labour from serfs. These were overwhelmingly unsuccessful: 'They contributed to an uncompetitive environment and the policy of granting concessions from, rather than reforming, the corporative system created a situation of yet greater institutional complexity unlikely to favour industrial expansion' (Thomson 1991: 64). Lewis describes how the French state, foiled by provincial resistance to new coal laws in the mid-eighteenth century, began to issue royal mining 'concessions' designed to encourage technological advance and productivity growth. Not only did these attempts fail, but one of the reasons for their failure was the local resistance evoked by the concession holders' privileges enabling them to infringe on local institutional privileges, close down existing producers and charge monopoly prices (Lewis 1993: 24). In Austria, the state-privileged proto-industrial manufactories were granted a wide array of special powers raising costs or destroying the business of other industrial concerns, yet most failed dismally themselves. The Poneggen hosiery enterprise in Upper Austria was founded in 1764 with a wide range of state privileges which proved immensely costly to other producers, yet 'in spite of all the official support it received, the undertaking did not flourish' and eventually went bankrupt (Grüll 1974: 39ff, 49). The Linz manufactory, although it limped along with state support for a much longer period, causing enormous costs to other producers, eventually suffered a similar fate (Freudenberger 1979). Whether they contributed to industrial development is not apparent: certainly this part of Europe was one of the latest to industrialize. It is equally difficult to trace the beneficial effects of most other examples of state assistance, even for successful proto-industries. Although, therefore, state intervention in proto-industry was by no means absent, it seldom had quite the effects desired by its initiators.

By contrast, state activity – often for non-economic purposes such as warfare – had massive indirect repercussions on many European proto-industries. Belfanti has shown how military and strategic considerations led central and north Italian states to grant industrial privileges to remote, frontier, or mountainous parts of their territories, enabling the rise of rural proto-industries in the teeth of urban guild privileges (Belfanti 1993: 260). Military activities also made the state an important customer for proto-industries, and monopolies to produce textiles and metal goods for the army were an important component of political patronage (as well as being essential for many otherwise uncompetitive proto-industries). Monopoly concessions to produce uniform cloth were crucial for the Languedoc woollen industry (Johnson 1982: 2, 4; Thomson 1982). The Eskilstuna iron-working proto-industry only became significant around 1600 'to meet the needs of the Swedish army and navy'; when the famous proto-industrial manufactory was established at Eskilstuna in the mid-seventeenth century, 'the armed forces were the principal customers' (Magnusson and Isacson 1982: 92; Magnusson 1991: 303). The expansions and contractions of the gun-barrel proto-industry in the northern Italian valleys of Brescia were largely caused by fluctuations in military demand (Belfanti 1993: 263). State purchases were essential for many Portuguese proto-industries, and subsequently strongly influenced which proto-industrial regions industrialized and which de-industrialized (Pedreira 1990: 437–8, 536, 543).

The early modern state exerted an even more significant impact on proto-industries by reinforcing (or weakening) *other* social institutions. As we have seen, communities, landholding systems and corporate groups influenced settlement, marriage, work, landholding, resource allocation, access to markets and every form of commerce and trade in most European proto-industrial regions. They were only able to regulate so many activities because of the enforcement they got from the state.

In *territorial states*, government was impossible without the co-operation of local-level institutions, often local communities and land-owners. The central state supported local rules in tacit exchange for local co-operation in implementing taxation, conscription and regulation. The importance of this symbiosis between state and local institutions emerges from every study of the growth of 'social control' on the local level in early modern Europe (Ogilvie 1992). Its importance for proto-industries, as we have seen, emerges from almost every micro-study.

In *city-states*, the community was co-extensive with the state, and often urban guilds and companies played an important role in the government. This was an important factor influencing proto-industrialization in northern and central Italy (Belfanti 1993), the territories of the German Free Imperial Cities (Kießling 1991; Kisch 1981b), and to a considerable extent also the territories of the Swiss Federation (Braun 1978).

In *feudal states*, which existed in different forms in eastern Europe, parts of Italy, and the micro-states of southern Germany, either the prince was also the major landowner, or the great landowners enjoyed governmental as well as tenurial powers over their peasants (Belfanti 1993; Kießling 1991; Kisch 1981b; Klíma 1991; Palairet 1982; Rudolph 1985). The establishment and control of proto-industries by feudal landlords were only possible because in such territories the state and the seigneurial system supported one another.

It was often not until the second half of the eighteenth century (or even later), and thus only towards the very end of the period of proto-industrialization, that most European states became strong enough to begin to try to dispense with the support they obtained from traditional social institutions – whether these were local village communities, towns and cities, guilds and companies, or feudal landlords. Even then, there was almost always a prolonged phase during which these institutions retained significant portions of their traditional powers. Even if they no longer enjoyed complete monopolies, even if they were facing competition from new institutions, they nevertheless retained important privileges, which often enabled them to exercise real economic effects on proto-industries (and other economic sectors) for generations longer. During this phase, production and trading activities which violated these institutions' surviving privileges continued to be persecuted and penalized; at best, such activities constituted a 'black market' or 'informal sector' (as it is called in modern developing economies), not an open and regulated 'market economy'. Moreover, the institutional arrangements with which the state formally replaced the traditional institutions of communities, landlords, guilds and companies were generally not open markets, but rather countervailing structures of privileges and monopolies (such as those of the 'Fabriken' – manufactories – in Austria and Bohemia), protecting the interests of new and favoured social groups, and enforced with new effectiveness by the rationalized administrative apparatus of the 'enlightened' absolutist state.

The emerging modern state thus played a range of roles in European proto-industry. It intervened directly, though not often effectively, to encourage proto-industrial enterprises. It made war, collected taxes, captured and administered colonies, and set up customs barriers, helping to shape the export markets within which proto-industries operated. Above all, however, the state provided support to the other institutions – whether communities, landlords, guilds and companies, or the new structures of privilege and protective regulation emerging from the late eighteenth century on – which had such a wide-ranging impact on most European proto-industries and, indeed, often survived into industrialization proper.

Conclusion

Perhaps the greatest service performed by the concept of proto-industrialization is to have generated so many studies of the *same phenomenon* in such a wide variety of contexts, thereby making comparisons across societies more fruitful than is ordinarily the case. These comparisons have revealed an important common feature throughout early modern Europe: an enduring specialization of production, creating a network of interdependent regions of agriculture and proto-industry linked by urban centres with one another and the non-European world.

Yet such comparisons have also revealed profound differences and divergences among European societies. Some proto-industrial regions – particularly in north-western Europe – experienced economic growth, social transformation and ultimate industrialization. Sadly, many others did not, and this had enduring consequences for their economic and political futures, particularly in the case of eastern Europe. A major factor behind these differences in proto-industrialization – and, by implication, economic development in general – appears to have been the framework of social institutions, which profoundly affected the costs of different economic, social and demographic decisions. Deeper investigation of these social institutions, and closer analysis of their effects, may hold out the best perspectives for explaining differences in economic development, certainly in early modern Europe, and perhaps in pre-industrial societies more generally.

4 Proto-industrialization in France*

Pierre Deyon

Franklin Mendels is to be praised for having inspired a debate twenty years ago whose echoes are still resounding to this day (Mendels 1972). Dozens of historians, from Europe to the United States and from Moscow to Tokyo, have debated his propositions and sought to refute or confirm his hypotheses. As a result, dozens of articles, books and seminars have appeared, enriching our knowledge of rural industries and our understanding of the process of development, but for all that without providing us, as Franklin Mendels appeared to hope it would, with a general theory of the origins and the mechanisms of the industrial revolution.

Even before the work of Mendels as a young doctoral researcher at the University of Wisconsin (Mendels 1969/1981), there was already a certain amount of interest in the diffusion of textile production in the countryside. Well before the First World War, the German Historical School, and especially Werner Sombart, had emphasized the importance of rural industries in the development of capitalism (Sombart 1891, 1900). In France during the period 1910–30 Henri Sée, Emile Tarlé and Emile Coornaert were recognizing the role of rural manufactures in the growth of the mercantilistic economy. But even though these historians had all traced a connection between the growth of this sector and the opening up of distant markets, none of them had attempted to analyse its relationship with the surrounding agrarian economy, nor had they got as far as generalizing it into a general interpretation of pre-industrial development.

Nor, before the birth of historical demography, had any of them foreseen the relations between these economic changes and the biological and mental equilibrium of the populations involved. The way in which Mendels took these relationships into account goes a long way toward explaining the interest inspired by his hypotheses. He had devoted his doctoral thesis to inland Flanders in the eighteenth century, and had showed how the diffusion of linen weaving into the countryside and into areas with the least fertile soils broke down agrarian society,

* This chapter is translated from the French by Sheilagh C. Ogilvie.

caused fragmentation of landholdings and aggravated over-population (Mendels 1969/1981). He described the seasonal activities of these peasant families as they allocated their time between spinning, weaving linen cloths and working in the fields. Furthermore, he connected this development with the growth of commercialized agriculture in neighbouring districts, and pointed out that this complementarity was an influential and enduring factor in economic development.

The results of his own monograph and a revision of the existing historiography devoted to rural industries led him to formulate a general hypothesis about the relationship between this 'proto-industrialization' and the industrial revolution. Under certain conditions, he argued, proto-industrialization was nothing less than the preparatory and creative phase for industrialization itself. In an article which appeared in the journal *Annales* in 1984, he defined proto-industrialization in terms of the following four basic characteristics (Mendels 1984). First, proto-industrialization referred to the rise and development of a type of industry whose final product was destined for export outside the region, thereby bringing this sector under the influence of factors external to the local agrarian and climatic conditions. Secondly, proto-industrialization fundamentally implied the participation of peasant families. In proto-industrial activity, which was often seasonal, peasant populations found the supplementary resources indispensable for their subsistence. Thirdly, proto-industrialization assumed a complementary relationship between commercialized agriculture and subsistence farming. Fourthly, proto-industrialization functioned in a framework of regions formed around one or more towns or cities, and connected by some minimum level of transportation infrastructure and juridical homogeneity.

It was this definition which was adopted in the preparation of the Eighth International Economic History Congress in Budapest in 1982, and those responsible for the relevant session of the congress insisted on the necessity of a comparative approach to the model proposed for discussion (Mendels 1982). Basically, it was a question of understanding why in certain cases proto-industrialization had evolved in the direction of the factory system, whereas in other cases the process was interrupted, and an abortive proto-industrialization left nothing behind it except for poverty, with emigration from the countryside as the only option. Why did what succeeded in Lille, Roubaix, Tourcoing, Lancashire and Yorkshire fail in Lower Normandy, Brittany and East Anglia? Why was it that the capital accumulated by the merchants and putters-out, the skills acquired by the workers and the merchant-industrialists and the markets which had been discovered and conquered did not everywhere and naturally propel the economy toward industrial revolution and industrial concentration?

The Budapest conference itself involved almost fifty contributions (Deyon and Mendels 1982) and in the following years gave rise to even more contributions, but it did not satisfy the fundamental aim of the organizers. Neither the confirmations nor the counter-examples have generated articulated and convincing descriptions of successful chains of events leading in the direction of the industrial revolution, or to miscarriages leading inexorably toward de-industrialization and misery. Thus uncertainty has persisted, and there have been many who have concluded that the model was inadequate, and that the Flemish case was exceptional or at least very limited in its application.

The list of questions which have remained unanswered, and the list of objections, appear in fact to be quite long. The first uncertainty concerns the point of departure, the initial 'engine' of proto-industrialization. At what point in time do the medieval rural industries succeed to the dignity of being termed 'proto-industrial'? The answer which comes naturally to mind invokes the great overseas discoveries and the beginning of transatlantic trade. This answer takes into account an expansion in the volume of exchanges in the sixteenth century, but not in any way a change in the nature of production and its organization. It remains no less the case that the most vibrant regions of textile proto-industrialization were all producing for the distant markets of Spanish America and the South Seas. This is what the studies by J. Tanguy, A. Lespagnol and J. Dloussky have again confirmed for the Breton linen trade and that of the Haut Maine (Tanguy 1966; Lespagnol 1990; Dloussky 1990). The fabrics manufactured around Vitré, Laval, Saint Brieue, Loudéac and Morlais for the greatest part headed toward Cadiz, by way of the ports of Saint Malo and Rouen.

A second objection can be directed at the correlation which Franklin Mendels (1972), and especially the Göttingen team of Peter Kriedte, Hans Medick and Jürgen Schlumbohm (1981), discerned between proto-industry and population growth, through a fall in the age at marriage, and through self-exploitation and over-exploitation of families and domestic workshops. This proposition, in its most general formulation, does not stand up well to a whole series of contradictions and counter-examples. It appears to assume, independently of the cultural context, identical and irresistible forms of behaviour, and a unique response to the vicissitudes of economic trends and the impact of economic misery. On the one hand, setting up a household and establishing oneself as an independent peasant or domestic weaver also depended, to a considerable extent, on customs and practices of inheritance. On the other hand, the impoverishment of households has not been proved for all the very diverse models and all the successive phases of proto-industrialization. Finally, the behaviour of households and couples is not as simple or as primitive as is sometimes imagined. Didier Terrier, in particular, has been able to show that in the weaving families of Cambrésis a certain degree of controlling of births was able to adjust the fertility level to economic fluctuations (Terrier 1994). Terrier has also shown that a reduction in demand did not automatically cause the weavers to reduce their requirements or accept a diminution in piece-rates; instead, it led them to delay marriage and family formation, by remaining in the parental household for longer. G. L. Gullickson has made similar findings for the Pays de Caux where, when mechanization began to compete with domestic industry, the weavers and the spinners married less readily and even, once they were married, adopted Malthusian forms of behaviour (Gullickson 1986).

In a well documented article which appeared in the journal *Annales* in 1980, Pierre Jeannin made two additional critical comments (Jeannin 1980). First, he pointed out that the theory was based much too narrowly on textile industries alone; he argued that any general theory must integrate other sectors of production, such as mining, metallurgy, the wood and leather industries and so on. He also insisted upon the importance of towns and cities in the organization of the pre-industrial regional economy. He reminded us that towns and cities were not only centres for distributing labour, collecting output and accumulating capital, but also the locations of a large number of domestic workshops and manufactories producing luxury goods and carrying out the finishing stages of production. Peter Kriedte has insisted for a long time on the importance of this urban activity by domestic workshops in his work on Krefeld (Kriedte 1982, 1983, 1986, 1991). Line Tesseyre Sallmann has recently confirmed these observations in her thesis on 'Industrial growth: the textiles of Lower Languedoc in the seventeenth and eighteenth centuries' (Tesseyre Sallmann forthcoming). It was, in fact, from Nîmes that wholesale merchants adapted, diversified and organized the manufacturing activity of the whole province, commercializing the production of linen cloths, financing the cultivation of mulberry trees, the raising of silk worms, and the throwing of silk threads, and allocating the making of linen and silk hosiery between rural and urban looms. Analogous findings are reported in Claude Marquié's book on the linen industry of Carcassonne in the eighteenth century (Marquié 1993). The town carried out the organization, financing, distribution and concentration of the industry, but also some of the production and manufacturing itself:

in reality, production resulted from a large number of activities dispersed around the centre of the town in which the most numerous and most powerful manufacturers were located, which was the seat of the main inspection, and where the most delicate activities, finishing and colouring, took place. Around this core there existed a large number of production locations, especially on the south slope of the Black Mountain, with less important clothiers, a large number of fulling-mills, carders, spinners and weavers, who were often also cultivators of the soil, working at linen production in the dead season. (Marquié 1993: 153)

Serge Chassagne analyses both the role of the town of Rouen in initiating and directing the diffusion of proto-industrialization in Normandy, and the participation of urban workshops in the development of the industry of this region (Chassagne 1991). Cotton production began in Rouen at the very end of the seventeenth century. At that time, the merchants allocated the preparation of the yarn and even the manufacturing of mixed cotton–linen and cotton–silk cloths ('siamoises') to the rural labour force. The parliament, the municipal magistrates and the Rouen chamber of commerce in vain protested and denounced this competition by the countryside. The same merchants had the spun yarn warped in their Rouen workshops, in which as many as fifteen or twenty wefters could be employed, and then put the warps into the hands of 'warp carriers'. These had the job of conveying the warps to weavers settled either in the suburbs or in the villages of the province, and of then returning them to the 'staple' ('marque'), which was held every Friday in the weaving hall of the town. This close association between urban and rural manufacturing activities led to a record growth in the weaving production of Normandy during the eighteenth century.

The studies by Gérard Gayot on Sedan, those of Charles Engrand on Picardy and those of Claude Cailly on the Perche confirm these complementarities between rural and urban manufactures (Cailly 1993a, 1993b; Engrand 1979a, 1979b; Gayot 1981, 1995). Between the workers of the countryside and those who were town citizens, there arose a conflictual division of labour, in which the former were allocated the coarser products and the latter the more delicate and costly ones, as well as the operations of dyeing, finishing and dressing. In these conditions, how and why should the decisive impulse be reserved solely for rural proto-industrialization, when the distribution of productive activities, the prospecting of markets, the choice of techniques and the commercialization of the industry had always been mainly controlled by urban elites?

Investigating the origins of industrial entrepreneurs is another unavoidable chapter of all research on the industrial revolution. Serge Chassagne has made an essential contribution to this study. He has shown how the wholesale merchants of Rouen, with the assistance of Trudaine and John Holker, set up the first concentrated manufactories in Darnetal and Saint Sever, gathering together the weaving looms, the jennies, the calendering machines and the chemical processes required for the dye-baths (Chassagne 1991: 38ff). In an article published in *Annales de Bretagne*, he provides additional information, showing that at least one quarter of French cotton entrepreneurs of the generation of 1815–40, and several of the most important individuals, such as Auguste Florentin Pouyer and François Guillaume Vaussard in Rouen, were former proto-industrial merchants (Chassagne 1990). All of this confirms that even if proto-industrialization was only one path toward the industrial revolution, it was at least one of the more privileged forms of access to it.

The relationship invoked by Mendels between proto-industrialization and the developmental structure of the agrarian economy appears much less evident, if not totally doubtful. As the monographs continue to proliferate, the Flemish model turns out to be quite singular. For the Pays de Caux, for example, Gay L. Gullickson has shown that proto-industrialization was not necessarily associated with subsistence agriculture on landholdings which had been excessively sub-divided, but that on the contrary it could co-exist with commercialized arable agriculture and large estates (Gullickson 1986). These large estates did not offer to many inhabitants of the village anything but seasonal employment, and liberated a substantial proportion of the male labour force for textile work, while the female labour force remained available practically all year round for the making of yarn. The case of the Pays de Caux also shows the excessive neglect, up to now, of the role played in such proto-industrial work by women, which sometimes complemented and sometimes competed with the work of the men, and as a consequence conditioned both the behaviour of households and the relations between the sexes.

Less attention should be attached to the arguments of those who point out the large number of proto-industrial regions which fell into decadence in the course of the nineteenth century: they forget that Mendels was not unaware of these failures, and himself urged that they be analysed with care, hoping that they would reveal to us, by their very deficiencies, the basic principle of industrial transformation. In this perspective, a more useful approach would have been to carry out more monographic studies of cases of industrial transformation which were independent of any prior or antecedent proto-industrialization.

In any case, it is true to say that the passage from proto-industrialization to industrialization proper was a function of multiple and complex factors. Inter-regional and international competition, the degree of customs protection and regulatory protection guaranteed by the political authorities, the availability of entrepreneurs and their spirit of initiative, could all play a fundamental role. It is therefore necessary to identify the economic variables, the quantitative facts, which would, at a given moment, direct those responsible for manufacturing either toward over-exploitation of labour power or toward increasing the productivity of labour through concentration and mechanization. But it is also necessary to find out about the representations, expectations and ambitions of the merchants and wholesale dealers who regulated the system. Thus Claude Marquié has shown that in Carcassone, these 'false entrepreneurs' remained fascinated by the prestige of the noble order (Marquié 1993: 430). For them, buying land and seigneuries, and preparing for ennoblement, were the basic objectives of any social advancement. They devoted most of their profits to acquiring these landed and seigneurial rents. This pilfering away of capital, this collective inferiority complex, this new 'treason of the bourgeoisie', were, according to Claude Marquié, the fundamental causes of the decline of the Languedoc textile industry at the end of the eighteenth century (Marquié 1993: 243, 287).

Because Mendels worked on localities and archival deposits near the French–Flemish frontier, and because he had visited Lille several times to present his work and its results, it was natural that he inspired emulation among researchers in northern France in particular. Several issues of the journal *Revue du Nord* bear witness to their contributions. These researchers did not contradict the ideas advanced by Mendels, but they undoubtedly introduced a number of nuances into his model. Didier Terrier, for instance, came to draw a distinction between two contrasting phases in the history of proto-industrialization (Terrier 1994). The first coincided with the prosperity of 'mulquinerie', the making of fine linen cloths. This industry enabled rural artisans, in the more favourable framework of the *Kaufsystem* (artisanal system), to enjoy a comparative security, and even – for some of them – true wealth. Their purchases of land bear witness to their success and their social ascent into the ranks of the middle-sized peasantry. By contrast, in the second phase of proto-industrialization in the region, after the Revolution, this pattern experienced fluctuations. New forms of organization appeared, accompanying the introduction of cotton, the return of linen and the use of mixed fibres. From this point on, weavers, gauze makers ('gaziers'), and tulle makers ('tullistes') became piece-workers, to whom the raw material was put out, for them to turn into woven cloths, paid by the piece. These new arrangements gradually distanced the domestic workers from the peasant world. Soon dispossessed of their small landed inheritances, constrained into a new work discipline, monitored by travelling overseers, they found themselves pushed to the bottom of the village hierarchy. Soon misery and over-population would compel them to join the town and the factory. As for the entrepreneurs, since they themselves delivered the raw material to the gauze makers and weavers, the dispersion of manpower to greater and greater distances in response to the expansion in production became a financial handicap and a cause of retardation. Saint Quentin was eager to repatriate within its walls, and then to mechanize, first the spinning operations and later those of the weaving.

Other monographs have generated additional reasons for puzzlement. Thus Philippe Guignet has pointed out proto-industrial survivals in Cambrésis and particularly in the cantons of Caudry and Carnières, which lasted into the twentieth century (Guignet 1977). Similarly, Michel Hau has described the organization, under the Second Empire, on the initiative of the wholesale merchants of Sainte Marie aux Mines, of domestic weaving in the villages of the Lower Rhine for more than forty kilometres roundabout. It was thus that Richard and Lenoir operated 100,000 spindles in their urban spinning mills, but also employed thousands of dispersed weavers in a hundred villages in Normandy and Picardy. And it was thus that the first captains of industry in the textile sector sometimes retained a constellation of domestic workshops around their modern factories, like a sort of safety belt, enabling them to cushion the shocks of economic fluctuations. In cases of a collapse in demand, orders to the piece-workers and the dispersed workshops were interrupted first of all, in order to maintain in as good shape as possible for as long as possible the activity of the 'new machines', and thus to preserve their profitability and the rhythm by which they were amortized.

Moreover, wholly new constellations of domestic workshops appeared out of nowhere, well into the nineteenth century, leading Pierre Cayez to describe the Lyon region as one of 'a staggered proto-industrialization' (Cayez 1978). Cayez's thesis describes how the looms for weaving the least luxurious sorts of silk moved out of town in the direction of the Loire, the Ain, the Ardèche and the Isère; he analyses both the political and the economic reasons for this migration. The electric motor, the knitting machine and then the miniaturized weaving machine would inspire analogous reincarnations in textiles, cutlery, wood working and plastic products in France and Italy into the present day.

Thus, having lost part of its explanatory force, proto-industrialization has also lost a part of its chronological specificity and hence its identity.

Just when greater attention was being paid to the performance of French industry and the growth rhythms of the nineteenth-century French economy, it was discovered that French-style industrialization had been sustained and supported by the talents of individual workers and the activities of domestic workshops and small firms. The large factory did not put paid to the small workshop, whose advantages – its flexibility and its capacity for innovation and adaption to crisis – are now being analysed much better. At the end of the Second Empire, small industry in urban and rural areas still accounted for two-thirds of all industrial production. In the region of Lille, Roubaix and Tourcoing, weaving remained mainly located in family workshops, dispersed in the midst of a veritable industrial nebula. Moreover, domestic industry was to maintain itself for a long time in sectors which were difficult to mechanize, and in sub-contracting activities: leather working, shoe making, trimmings production, glove making, hat making, ironmongery, clock making, small metal-goods making, handkerchiefs and lace making.

This leads forcibly to the conclusion that the industrial revolution in France, far from making the proto-industrial system disappear, on the contrary solicited, integrated and perpetuated it until the beginning of the twentieth century. This does not invalidate the relationship between the two systems which was described by Mendels, but reveals it to have been much more complex and enduring than he had originally imagined. The Flemish example which he studied appears to be something of an extreme case, and proto-industrialization was capable of taking diverse forms in other places and at other periods. In France, the textile sector alone reveals several different organizational models. The manufacture of cloths in Laval or Saint Quentin, and that of the clothiers of Amiens or of Languedoc, were organized according to different schemas, and the complementarity between manufactories, proto-factories and proto-industrial nebulae are reminiscent of those which can be observed nowadays in less advanced economies between large firms and the small or medium enterprises which surround them and serve them as intermediaries or sub-contractors.

The social consequences of proto-industrialization do not appear to be any more uniform or automatic. The pauperization and the 'self-exploitation' which is supposed to have occurred among domestic workers in the countryside have not been confirmed for all places and all circumstances. Here and there, higher-quality manufactures, tricks of the trade, small technical innovations and clever inventions made it possible to escape from misery. Nor was the domestic workshop socially or culturally uniform. The role played in it by men, women and children varied across countries, types of production, the state of the market and family structures; and demographic behaviour naturally adapted to this diversity of situations. It appears more and more clearly today that the paths to industrialization are multiple, just as are those toward modernization, and that proto-industrialization is only one of those paths. This diversity can be confirmed for Europe in the nineteenth century, just as it can for the countries of the Americas or of Asia in the present day.

Despite these uncertainties and objections, the merits of those who launched the concept of proto-industrialization nonetheless remain substantial. First, they enriched our thinking concerning the interrelationships between the agrarian sector, the industrial sector and the market. Secondly, they inspired a fertile current of international comparisons, and suggested interesting analogies and comparisons between the pre-industrial economies of the west and those of eastern Europe, Mogul India and Tokugawa Japan. Finally, they sought to articulate relationships between agrarian structures and demographic structures, and within ethno-history they illuminated the history of worker and managerial cultures further back in the past. The way of life of the trimmings makers, the songs of the weavers, the custom of 'Blue Monday', practices of fraud and embezzlement, conflicts between employers and workers before the board of arbitration, and the consumption of tobacco and coffee, have all become subjects for historical investigation, and have been integrated into the analysis of economic and social behaviour.

This is one of the aspects of industrial history which has perhaps been least mentioned in the last twenty years. In the zones where proto-industrialization operated, it is now known that modest intermediaries between the wholesale merchants and rural artisans – clever and entrepreneurial farmers, unscrupulous accountants, and tenement builders – all founded dynasties of entrepreneurs and members of the bourgeoisie. Above all, contrary to older ideas which argue that worker consciousness sprang fully armed from the brow of industrial capitalism, it is now recognized that there are elements of cultural continuity and traditions common to domestic workers and the first factory workers. It is thus that the individual and litigious resistance of the domestic weavers before the 'conseils des prudhommes' (boards of arbitration between employers and workers) in Roubaix and Tourcoing armed the cunning and the combativeness of the workers of the Lille region. It is thus that the lace makers, the fine linen cloth makers and the gauze makers of Cambrésis and of the Valencienne area created a tradition of sociability and solidarity in this region which manifested itself again at the beginning of the twentieth century in the multiplicity of co-operatives and festive societies. Nor would it be mistaken to point out that these two regions, which had been locations of dense and wide-spread proto-industry, were among the first to elect socialist municipal governments and parliamentary representatives.

Finally, Franklin Mendels had the merit of having attempted to bring to the economic history of the period before the nineteenth century concepts susceptible of making sense of our thinking and organizing the little information we possessed on this period. Wresting this field of history away from qualitative estimates and toward an accumulation of empirical descriptions, and providing it with the rigour of scientific reasoning, was undoubtedly his ambition. If he did not altogether achieve it, the numerous research studies which he inspired, the diffusion of the concepts which he proposed (sometimes even through abuse of them), and the accumulation of new knowledge which resulted from these debates, all bear witness to the merits and fruitfulness of his ideas and his approach.

5 Proto-industrialization in England

Pat Hudson

Historians of the industrialization process in England have long recognized the importance of industries in the countryside (Mantoux 1928; Heaton 1920; Wadsworth and Mann 1931; Thirsk 1961; Chambers 1957, 1962; Jones 1968; Mann 1971). In the two or three centuries before the coming of increasingly centralized and urbanized manufacturing after 1800, household industries, producing goods for non-local consumption, proliferated. And their existence became concentrated and specialized in certain regions of the country (Hudson 1989). Nevertheless, debates surrounding the concept of proto-industrialization, developed in the European literature from the late 1960s, were rather slow to influence research and writing on the foundation and impact of commercial manufacturing in England. In fact there was entrenched resistance to the use of the term and the ideas to which it gave rise (Coleman 1983; Houston and Snell 1984).

This at first seems surprising given England's early lead in the transition to an industrial society. If any environment were to provide a test case for various hypotheses derived from the work of Mendels and others it was likely to be England. Not only did several proto-industrial regions later become the heartlands of a more fully fledged urban industrial society but they did so without competition from earlier mechanized and transformed industries in other parts of Europe. In addition, the social structure, the expansion of markets and the framework of law and taxation in England were such as to provide every encouragement to the unfettered expansion of commercial manufacturing, proletarianization and wealth accumulation, compared with social and institutional environments in many areas of continental Europe. Thus if, *ceteris paribus*, the process of proto-industrialization contained a series of dynamic elements propelling a region or an entire economy in the direction of centralization and mechanization of industry, expansion of population, proletarianization and urbanization, one would expect English examples to highlight this most forcefully. Furthermore, because industrialization in England was marked initially

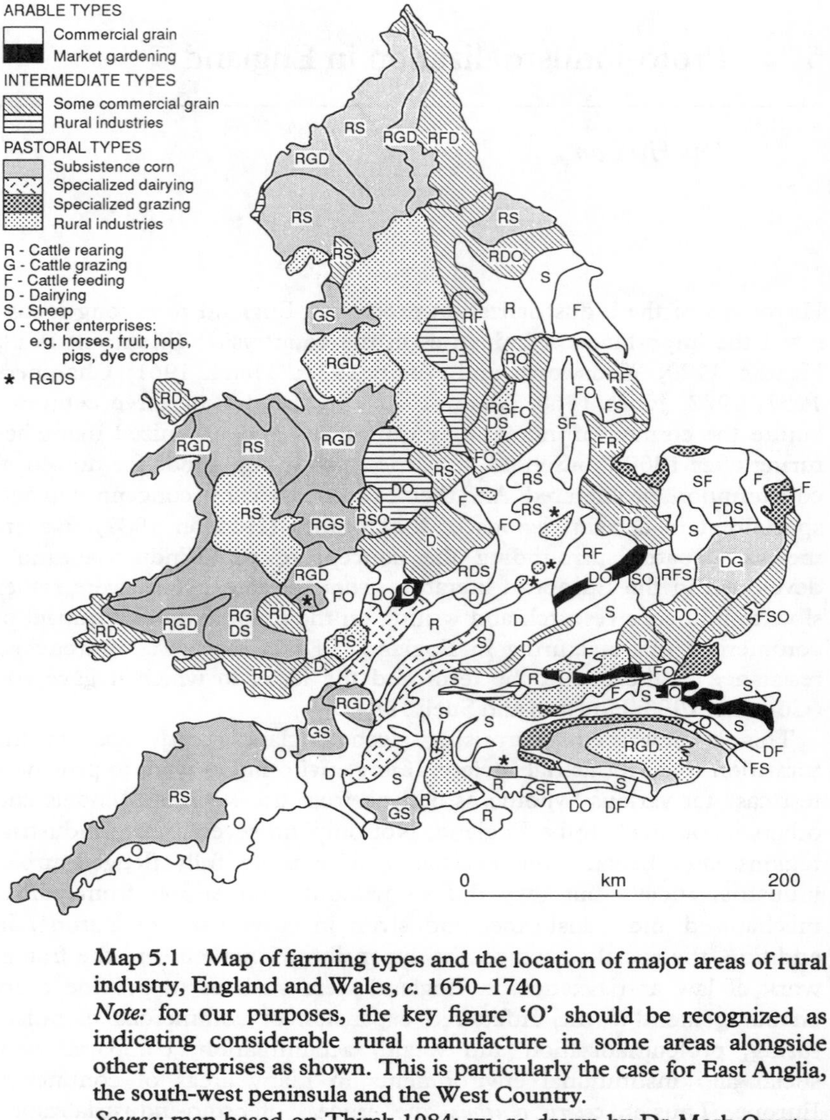

Map 5.1 Map of farming types and the location of major areas of rural industry, England and Wales, *c.* 1650–1740

Note: for our purposes, the key figure 'O' should be recognized as indicating considerable rural manufacture in some areas alongside other enterprises as shown. This is particularly the case for East Anglia, the south-west peninsula and the West Country.

Source: map based on Thirsk 1984: xx, re-drawn by Dr Mark Overton and reproduced here with his permission and the gratitude of the author.

by a revolutionizing of the consumer goods industries (especially textiles) and of the regions where they dominated, one would again expect a close association between proto-industrialization and later developments and thus a considerable attractiveness of the model for studying the English economy as a whole. In many countries of Europe where 'take-off' was achieved later and primarily as a result of expansion in the capital goods/coalfield sectors one would expect greater spatial and temporal discontinuity and more tenuous links between the spread of rural domestic industries and industrialization proper.

One reason why the ideas surrounding proto-industrialization were only slowly accepted by historians in England is that economic history in the 1960s and 1970s was increasingly influenced by macro-economic and econometric techniques dominant in the subject in America. With no counterpart in English historiography to the Annales School or to the Swiss–German folklorist tradition and with a marked separation of economic from social and cultural history, the inter-disciplinary nature of the hypotheses and ideas surrounding proto-industrialization fell at first upon stony ground. There was also a deep suspicion of stage theories of growth, particularly those derived from a Marxist perspective as was prominent in the Kriedte, Medick and Schlumbohm analysis. Finally, the representation of 'traditional' or 'peasant' society in much early continental proto-industrialization literature was regarded as inappropriate in the case of England (Macfarlane 1978). The impact of rural manufacturing was both less obvious than in some European peasant regions and more difficult to disentangle from other forces at work in the economy (urbanization and the commercialization of agriculture in particular).

Thus, with one or two significant exceptions (Levine 1977; Hudson 1981, 1986; Swain 1986), it is only recently that a broader range of studies has appeared addressing aspects of proto-industrial theorizing in regional and local contexts. If we consider these studies alongside the older literature it is clear that we know a great deal more about pre-factory industry in England than we did when Mendels first brought the term proto-industrialization and its connotations into popular use (Mendels 1972, 1975). Early criticism of the concept which concentrated, perhaps unreasonably, on its predictive qualities or on its validity as a stage theory of economic growth (Coleman 1983, Houston and Snell 1984) has given way, as in Europe, to use of the concept as an agenda of interesting questions (Eley 1984; Hudson 1989) to be asked in inter-disciplinary, regional and local studies (see for example King 1993; Zell 1994). This chapter considers research on English proto-industries and the impact of proto-industrial theorizing on English historiography, but first the distinctive character of the economy in the early modern period is surveyed.

The English economy

The early modern economy witnessed many fundamental changes, an understanding of which is essential for the study of expanding commercial manufacturing (for a detailed and referenced account of these changes see Hudson 1992). Population growth was sluggish in the seventeenth century but did not suffer the serious reverses experienced on the continent. The urban share increased markedly with the growth of London and rapid expansion, from the later seventeenth century, of many important provincial centres (Wrigley 1985a). Agricultural production increased and real incomes appear to have been buoyant. This may have provided the growing and increasingly sophisticated home market for English manufactures through to the mid-eighteenth century which has been indicated in the work of John (1961), Thirsk (1978), Spufford (1984) and Weatherill (1988).

Thereafter, a marked acceleration of population growth appears to have been promoted largely by a lowering of the age of marriage and an increase in the rate of marriage in both towns and countryside (Wrigley and Schofield 1981). The agricultural sector was slow to respond, resulting in rising food prices, and historians are still debating whether there was any sustained increase in the purchasing power of the mass of the population before the mid-nineteenth century. Urbanization continued with a speed and intensity unique in Europe. The proportion of the population living in towns over 10,000 by 1800 was 24 per cent compared with 9.5 per cent in the rest of Europe (Wrigley 1985a). Reorganization of agriculture, growth in the number of larger farms, expansion of mixed farming and enclosure coupled with population increase in the countryside resulted in considerable under- and unemployment. This was felt acutely in areas of the country such as the Midlands, which adopted a less labour-intensive pastoral regime in place of earlier arable production, and by women and children, whose income-earning opportunities appear in many regions to have been reduced most dramatically (Allen 1993; Snell 1985).

Thus, in many rural areas a classic precondition for the expansion of domestic manufacturing obtained: cheap under- and unemployed labour at zero opportunity cost. It appears from male occupational ascriptions that the rural non-agricultural population expanded faster and was considerably larger than its counterparts on the continent even in Holland and France (Wrigley 1985a). However, as we shall see, surplus labour was rarely, in itself, sufficient to attract and sustain proto-industry (as opposed to ephemeral sweating). It is clear that proximity to raw material supplies, market links and the supply of capital and entrepreneurship as well as labour were important factors in the location and longevity of proto-industry.

Unlike continental experience, proto-industrial expansion in England in the eighteenth century did not appear to occur at the expense of urbanization (de Vries 1984; Wrigley 1985a). The absence of powerful urban guilds on the continental pattern, together with the size and number of towns themselves, meant that urban industry was by no means faltering as may have been the case elsewhere in the proto-industrial period. Neither was there such a clear division of labour in England (as there may have been in other parts of Europe) between towns (providing mercantile, financial and finishing services) and the countryside (providing cheap family labour for mass production processes). The rapid growth of urban villages, unincorporated towns and suburbs in London and other large towns in the eighteenth century was associated specifically with expansion of employment in the low-wage, unregulated domestic and small workshop trades (Walton 1990; Berg 1990, 1994; Schwarz 1992).

A final factor to consider in providing a view of the economic environment of proto-industry in England is domestic and overseas demand for mass-produced goods (Hudson 1992: 182–200). Between 1750 and 1850 over 50 per cent of the gross output of the English cotton industry was exported and between a quarter and a half of wool textile output. Some regions which specialized in the production of export commodities were even more dependent on overseas demand than this suggests. The Yorkshire woollen textile industry exported about 70 per cent of its production in the 1770s as did the Birmingham and Wolverhampton hardware trades. English exporters enjoyed advantages over their rivals which accrued largely from geographical position, and the market catchment gained from state policy, militarism, colonial expansion and diplomacy. By these means Britain after 1707 became part of a 'quasi common market' with Ireland and the British colonies in the Americas. The dependencies were discriminated against in this market but for British exporters it was a free-trade area, the largest in the world and the fastest growing. Between 1670 and 1770 this area grew in population by 70 per cent and per capita consumption remained stable, at least (Price 1989). In addition, the growing trade with the colonies of European settlement in particular was important in stimulating demand for manufactured goods that could be mass produced: printed textiles, blankets, nails, ropes, buckets, handtools, copper and wrought iron products (including leg irons for slaves), beaver hats, linens, sails, trinkets. Thus many proto-industrial regions of England were very dependent upon the pattern and volume of long-distance and intercontinental overseas trade. Subject to rapid growth spurts, and vulnerable to trade fluctuations, these regions perhaps conform more closely to the classic models of Mendels and Kriedte, Medick and Schlumbohm than do many European examples.

Commercial manufacturing in England was also crucially dependent upon the growth and increasing sophistication of domestic demand (Hudson 1992: 173–81). Considerable debate is in progress about the sources of buoyancy of domestic demand for imported colonial commodities as well as manufactured goods in the late eighteenth and early nineteenth centuries. There was no marked secular trend in real wages sufficient to sustain the increases which occurred in per capita consumption. There is evidence to suggest a shift in income distribution in favour of those whose income derived from commercial profits, land and property rents, at the expense of wage earners, but this cannot explain the consumption and proliferation of new commodities and fashions lower down the social scale. Several authors, notably McKendrick (1982), have argued that increasing income-earning opportunities for women and children boosted family earnings and increased the power of women in consumption decisions sufficiently to account for the significant increase in purchases of household textiles, clothing, pottery, cutlery and furniture. But recent research on the low levels of women's earnings and their contribution to family budgets has undermined this argument (Horrell and Humphries: 1992). Several historians of the so-called consumer revolution in England have called for analysis of the close links between shifts in family labour allocation between subsistence and market activities and the growth of an internal market for mass-produced household items in everyday use (Fine and Leopold 1989). Some time ago Saito emphasized the need to understand the mix of motivations leading women and children in particular to enter into wage earning, especially the importance of decline or interruption in male earning abilities (Saito 1981). And recently de Vries has re-entered this debate arguing that consideration of change in women's household roles is the key to unlocking the riddle of widespread expansion of consumer demand and manufacturing output in England alongside minimal if any growth in real individual earnings. He argues that an 'industrious revolution' predated industrialization: a series of household-level decisions (largely concerning a shift of female labour from subsistence production to commercial manufacturing for wages) altered both the supply of marketed goods and labour and the demand for market-bought products (de Vries 1993, 1994). This stress once again places the impact of proto-industries high on the agenda for researchers interested in the industrialization process, particularly in England, and highlights the need to examine the lives of women and children as much as men.

The location of proto-industries

Early studies of the location of rural industries in England stressed their association with areas of pastoral farming and less fertile soils where growing populations could not be sustained by the agrarian sector alone. Leaning heavily on a theory of comparative advantage, Jones described the emergence of the north and west of England as the prime site of manufacturing industry in the eighteenth century because the improvements of the 'agricultural revolution' gave advantage in agricultural production to the south and east (Jones 1968). The light-soil areas of early enclosure for sheep rearing adapted most readily to rotational techniques of mixed farming and rootcrops. The Midlands and the north could not compete in efficiency of cereal production with the south and thus specialized in pastoral farming. In the Midland clay area this entailed a major shift from arable to grass. Accompanied by enclosure, this generated high levels of unemployment which were only partly soaked up by rural industries including lace making, hosiery and metalwares.

The importance of pastoral settings has also been emphasized because of the degree of seasonal complementarity in labour demands between agriculture and industry, but this was by no means always the case. Often the seasonality of farming, whether arable or pastoral, coincided with the seasonality of manufacture and the division of labour between agriculture and industry was as likely to be determined by gender as by season (Marshall 1989; Whyte 1989; Snell 1985). Proto-industries were also found in areas which were not primarily pastoral or upland: woollen manufacture in East Anglia; linen on the Norfolk/Suffolk border; the silk industry of Essex; knitting in arable parts of Leicestershire; pillow lace and straw plait industries in Buckinghamshire, Bedfordshire, Hertfordshire and Huntingdonshire; cloth making in lowland Lancashire. The variety of agrarian systems in England and the main locations of rural domestic manufacturing for distant markets are shown in Map 5.1.

It is clear that institutional factors were also important in both the location and the longevity of proto-industry. Thirsk argued that rural industry was most likely to flourish where there was no strong framework of co-operative agriculture, where freeholders and customary tenants had firm property rights, and where partible inheritance led to the fragmentation of holdings (Thirsk 1961: 70–2, 86–8). Swain's study of north-east Lancashire in the sixteenth and early seventeenth centuries supports this reasoning although unigeniture was practised there (Swain 1986). The Weald of Kent in the sixteenth century appears to fit Thirsk's model in a classic way (Zell 1994).

Chambers stressed that employers looked for labour in areas of weak manorialism which allowed in-migration and the division of land among small cultivators (Chambers 1963: 428–9) whilst Hey (1972) argued that it was not so much partible inheritance or weak manorialism that was important in attracting rural industry but access to common rights which enabled squatters to settle. In the north-west Midlands cottagers kept cows and sheep on the heath and made up their incomes by work in the metal trades. Thus predominantly (but not exclusively) pastoral areas with unemployed and under-employed labour and particular structures of property rights became major manufacturing areas: the Kentish Weald, north and west Wiltshire, the valleys of the Stour and Colne in Essex and Suffolk, west and south Yorkshire, the West Country and south and east Lancashire. In some areas employment in rural industries was not a reaction to agricultural poverty but 'a vigorous response to additional opportunities for profit' (Hey 1972: 21). In Staffordshire and parts of south and west Yorkshire this was associated with smallholders with some capital who became rural artisans (Hey 1969, 1972; Frost 1981; Hudson 1983). As in France (Gullickson 1983; Vardi 1993), proto-industry was by no means confined to areas of impoverished farming or subsistence agriculture.

Different trades adapted to, or were encouraged by, a variety of types of agricultural context, farming community and institutional history. In the west Midlands many of the varied products and processes of the metalwares trades were in localized enclaves in both towns and the countryside (Rowlands 1975, 1989; Berg 1990, 1993b, 1994). In south Yorkshire, cutlery, scythe and nail making settled in very different contexts (Hey 1972). In Derbyshire, lead mining by small independent producers (free miners) continued in the seventeenth century only in those manors where they were able to preserve their common law rights. Elsewhere they were replaced by more heavily capitalized concerns employing wage labour (Wood 1993). In Lancashire the cotton, woollen, linen and silk industries were all important in different parts of the county each having a different set of relationships with agriculture and landholding (Wadsworth and Mann 1931; Walton 1989).

The organization of manufacturing

Different institutional and agrarian contexts were in turn associated with differences in the way in which trades were organized and financed. In west Yorkshire the putting-out system of worsted manufacture expanded in the eighteenth century where the ownership of land was dispersed, where freehold predominated over copyhold land and where the process of proletarianization was advanced. The rural artisan structure of woollen manufacture, by contrast, endured in more fertile areas where manorialism had been more entrenched, where there was more control over landholding and where the predominantly copyhold land was rented out in plots suitable for the dual occupation of clothier/farmer. These different structures in turn influenced the sources of finance and entrepreneurship involved in the transition to more centralized and mechanized forms of production, with merchants playing a major role in the worsted sector and landowners and small producers playing a more significant role in the building of mills in the woollen branch of the industry (Hudson 1981, 1986). In the Kentish Weald in the sixteenth century landownership was important to the entrepreneurs who financed the rural cloth industry and local gentry provided capital for iron making although significant funds for iron manufacturing also came from outside the region, which may have been in part responsible for the later decline of the sector (Zell 1994; cf. Short 1989).

The sorts of products made and the markets served also influenced the organization of production. When worsted manufacture expanded in Yorkshire it had to compete with established manufacturing in East Anglia and to find its way in difficult, predominantly export, markets. The long turnover time of capital was a further factor necessitating the presence of substantial putting-out merchants as catalysts of the trade. Wilson (1973) and Mann (1971) have argued that in the West Country woollen industry the production of higher-quality woollen cloths than in Yorkshire necessitated a *Verlagssystem* there in contrast to the *Kaufsystem* in Yorkshire which produced (generally, though not exclusively) 'cheap and nasty' products.

Proto-industrialization in England appears to have involved a variety of household structures, divisions of labour and employment relations which bear no simple linear developmental relationship one to another (thus, for example, putting-out did not invariably supercede independent producers). On the contrary variations appear to have been conditioned by the availability and flexibility of labour and by product type. Heaton argued that as it took six people to make a piece of broadcloth in the eighteenth century, many west Yorkshire households were of this size, additional adults being taken on as journeymen or apprentices within a household where men, women and children worked together as an independent production unit, buying raw wool from staplers and selling unfinished cloths at weekly cloth markets in Leeds and elsewhere (Heaton 1920). In the Yorkshire worsted sector whole families were sometimes involved in textile manufacture but individuals were often employed for separate processes (females mainly on spinning and men, predominantly, on weaving or combing) by different employers. It was also very common for proto-industrial workers in Yorkshire, especially women, to live in households in which other individuals were engaged in entirely different sectors such as agriculture or mining. Similarly, in the lace-making areas of the Midlands and south-west and in areas which became centres of straw plaiting in the late eighteenth and early nineteenth centuries, women were engaged in low-wage, labour-intensive domestic industries in households in which men were often under-employed or seasonally employed in agriculture. In the Black Country in trades such as nailing, and the making of chains, nuts, bolts, files and stirrups, expansion was associated entirely with the use of female workers and children from the age of five or six upwards (Berg 1987). Sometimes, here as in other parts of the country, female and child workers were sub-contracted via the male head of household and were paid only through him. In other cases women received their wages independently. Obviously, these very different structures of household employment have important implications when one comes to consider the impact of proto-industry on gender and inter-generational relations, on demographic decision making and on the status and independence of women and children.

Industrialization and de-industrialization

The structure of trade and of manufacturing households is also a factor in considering those proto-industrial regions which later became the sites of successful factory-based and mechanized manufacturing and those which did not. As Coleman rightly pointed out, only four out of ten major English proto-industrial regions witnessed early industrial revolution (Coleman 1983). He argued that coal supplies are more important than proto-industry for our understanding of regional dynamics but the eclipse of the Kentish Weald, East Anglia, the West Country and several other proto-industrial regions occurred before coal became a vital locational influence. Comparative advantage models based largely upon differential natural resource endowments do not explain the considerable spatial shifts which often occurred between proto-industry and 'phase two'. The shift of capital from the textile industries back to the land in Norfolk and Essex in the later eighteenth century, as in the Weald more than a century earlier, is not satisfactorily explained simply by emphasizing the agricultural potential of the area. What prevented these regions changing to new types of cloths? And why, if the comparative advantage of agriculture was so great, did Norfolk and Essex see the growth of other sorts of domestic industries alongside agriculture after 'de-industrialization' (Sharpe 1995a, 1995b)? The answers appear to lie in social and institutional factors concerned with the way in which proto-industry was organized in both town and country. The power of Blackwell Hall factors rather than indigenous merchants over the textile trades of both East Anglia and the south-west have been emphasized as important in contributing to inflexibility and decline in the face of fashion changes and competition from Yorkshire. And the shifting gender division of labour in agriculture in the south and east was important in the drift to female-specific forms of domestic industry such as straw plaiting and lace making alongside agriculture (Snell 1985; Sharpe 1995a).

Social and institutional factors appear to have been most important in accounting for the longevity of proto-industry and its potential transformation. The way industry was organized, regional institutions, financial and commercial practices, social relations and traditions of worker resistance were all important in influencing the sources of capital, entrepreneurship and labour for expanding industry (see, for example, Hudson 1986; Randall 1991). Explanations of the success of the Birmingham area have stressed lack of institutional regulation, religious toleration, skill traditions, artisan mutuality and economies of agglomeration. Conflict and competition between large and small manufacturers and diversification of products and markets (which left a place for smaller firms in the industrial structure) were also important dynamic elements (Berg 1990, 1994; Rowlands 1989; Sabel and Zeitlin 1985). In the West Country, the very success of the large putting-out clothier, commonly employing several hundred workers, led to industrial inflexibility and entrepreneurial decline. In addition, worker resistance added to their problems when attempts were made to introduce new techniques and machinery: 'the advanced specialization of the workforce ... produced stable and craft-conscious communities of workers who drew self confidence and pride from their shared proto-proletarian experience of waged but autonomous work' (Randall 1989: 197, 1991).

Industrial decline in the Weald occurred in the late sixteenth century before the rise of a major iron industry elsewhere and almost two centuries before the establishment in Lancashire and Yorkshire of steam-powered textile factories. This 'failed transition' defies any simple model of comparative advantage. The area did not diversify into New Draperies or metal products but instead saw some shift into agricultural activities and hop growing for the nearby London market. Despite the marked population growth during proto-industrial expansion, at no time did a major landless proletarianized workforce dependent on industrial capitalists arise and the dual economy remained sufficiently strong to facilitate 're-ruralization' (Zell 1994). Although iron and glass making were also present, lack of overlap between these sectors and textiles in mercantile or investment terms meant that there were no external scale economies which might have benefited all the industries. In addition Short has laid emphasis on the lack of indigenous finance and entrepreneurship (especially in iron and glass making) which made these sectors more easily transferable to other locations (Short 1989).

Discontinuities and disjunctures occurred between rural domestic manufacturing and later forms of production even in areas which experienced the later growth of factories and heavy industry. In Cumbria a range of rural industries proliferated in the early modern period but none was powerful enough radically to alter demographic behaviour or to stimulate major social transformation. The different industries, as in the Weald, were not significantly linked together in terms of capital or entrepreneurship, and seasonalities of labour were varied, sometimes even clashing with agriculture. The development of coal, iron, steel, shipbuilding and cotton in the coastal areas of Cumbria in the nineteenth century had little or no connection with earlier proto-industries. Few external economies accrued to the whole region and de-industrialization was its long-term fate. Even in west Yorkshire and Lancashire the transition from proto-industry to 'phase two' was not as straightforward as Mendels' model might suggest. In both counties the first generations of factory entrepreneurs and factory labour were by no means predominantly drawn from those previously engaged in proto-industries. Artisans, putting-out employers and domestic workers were frequently those most resistant to change (Hudson 1981, 1986; Walton 1989).

The long-term survival and success of regions was associated with waves of entrepreneurial renewal and a flexible, cheap labour supply (especially women, youths and children) which had little strong institutionalized attachment to earlier methods of working. Also important was inter-dependent diversity and a certain critical mass (Pollard 1981). Proto-industrial concentrations varied in size from relatively isolated pockets to entire counties, whereas industrial regions in England by the nineteenth century were clearly marked by a size capable of generating significant external economies in terms of service trades, infrastructure and communications, which enabled them to maintain momentum and to keep up with competitors (Hudson 1989). The major industrial regions surviving through to the twentieth century were those which saw a succession of economic bases overlapping and taking over from one another as earlier successful sectors were overtaken by competition elsewhere. Both Lancashire and Yorkshire progressed from textile domination to a broader base which included engineering, services and chemicals. South Yorkshire and the west Midlands had a succession of metal and hardware trades to create balanced growth and in the north-east diversification and a mixed and inter-dependent industrial base created stability quite apart from the existence of coal in all these areas. These conditions eluded the Weald, north Wales, the West Country and East Anglia.

The demographic impact of proto-industries

What effect did household manufacturing have upon demographic development, fertility and mortality, marriage and the family? It is obvious that much theorizing about the social impact of proto-industry, by stressing the putting-out system and the employment of whole families in a single industry (often alongside agriculture) has failed to take into account the great variety of organizational forms which domestic manufacturing could take. The impact which extra-agricultural rural incomes would have upon courtship, age of marriage, family size and inter-personal relations is likely to have been very different in areas where a whole family worked as an 'independent' household unit of production compared with those where putting-out merchants employed only young female workers on piece-rates. And in between these was a varied spectrum of different combinations of domestic manufacturing alongside agricultural and other occupations such as mining; different forms of payment; and different gender and generational divisions of labour.

Most areas of expanding proto-industry in England were already characterized by dense population and proletarianization. Thus the effects of commercial manufacturing on the age of marriage and fertility are difficult to separate from the initial conditions found where much proto-industry took root. The ideal-typical preventive checks of patriarchal control, inheritance and therefore late marriage that are argued to have governed peasant landholding societies were not characteristic of England. Live-in service, long apprenticeships and poverty were more important as regulators of marriage (Wrigley and Schofield 1981). English population growth in the eighteenth century appears to have been more closely linked to proletarianization (occurring both in industrializing and in commercial agricultural regions) and to expanding job opportunities and urbanization than to proto-industrialization. The earliest detailed analysis of the demographic impact of proto-industry in England is Levine's study of stocking knitting in the village of Shepshed in Leicestershire. Levine's findings supported Mendels' hypotheses concerning the demographic 'hot-house' created during periods of proto-industrial expansion. The age of marriage for women fell by five years during the eighteenth century and marital fertility increased. Illegitimacy also rose but Levine argues that this resulted from frustrated marriage plans occasioned by fluctuations in labour demand in the industry rather than by any increase in sexual promiscuity. Levine's most interesting finding related to the period of industrial involution after 1815 when poverty, high mortality, deliberate family limitation and high emigration resulted in a marked fall in population increase. The proto-industrial dynamic was clearly capable of going into reverse. Interestingly, too, Levine found changes in household structure occurring in the nineteenth century in favour of increases in the number of co-resident wage earners and multi-nuclear households. This he attributes to a conscious effort by working people to protect themselves from the precariousness of economic conditions (Levine 1977).

The small-scale nature of the Shepshed study and reconstitution results from similar villages as well as agricultural communities, cast a question mark over any wider or more schematic application of Levine's findings (as can be found in Levine 1987). A lowering of the age of marriage in the Midlands and elsewhere most often preceded industrial expansion and was more likely to have resulted from prior agrarian changes than from proto-industry (Houston and Snell 1984: 482; Wrigley 1983; Carpenter 1994). New work on the demographic history of Calverley in west Yorkshire has also indicated a low age of marriage long before the major eighteenth-century take-off of wool textile manufacturing, and relatively stable ages of marriage through the proto-industrial period (King 1993). The availability of land and small farms in Calverley (as the vital basis of the dual economy artisan structure) influenced marriage and fertility whilst short breast feeding (perhaps necessitated by female labour demands in manufacture) appears to have been an important influence on marital fertility. Zell's work on the Kentish Weald in the sixteenth century gives more support to the models of Mendels and Kriedte, Medick and Schlumbohm. Cloth-making parishes grew more rapidly than others and were characterized by low age of marriage and short birth spacing. Here as elsewhere there was much in-migration which makes it difficult to assess the nature and importance of a proto-industrial demographic dynamic in itself. When the industry became more unstable from the late sixteenth century, out-migration from the Weald, as in Shepshed, acted as a demographic regulator (Zell 1994).

Custom, culture and gender roles

Social and cultural attitudes within the family, social norms and collective discipline in village life often interfered with any straightforward link between the earning capacity of young people and their sexual or social independence. As Braun argued was the case in Switzerland (1960), proto-industry fixed people on the land enabling them to stay near their wider families in established rural communities. These communities had norms of behaviour and informal policing of the social life of young people and women which was largely absent from the growing towns and cities of the proto-industrial period. In Calverley, for example, close co-operation between the generations (including early retirement from economic niches and kinship support structures) appear to have been the forces promoting early marriage and resulting in low illegitimacy levels (King 1993).

Industrial earnings were no straightforward route to economic or social freedom. The earnings of most women and children in proto-industry were too low to promote independence and most regarded their earnings not individualistically but as vital to family viability. Thus the age of leaving home (and, by implication, of marriage) was often high amongst female lace makers, for example, because their earnings were so important to the family unit (Wall 1978). The notion of independence also changes if we consider female perspectives. Proto-industrial theorizing suggests that the ability to earn an income early in life would result in earlier marriage but Sharpe has found that the earnings of young female lace makers in Devon may have been regarded not as a spur to early marriage but as a way of avoiding the economic necessity of marriage (Sharpe 1991).

The work process in different sectors and the gender- and age-specific labour demands of these sectors are likely to have modified the impact of earnings upon family size and intra-family relationships. In some trades ancillary tasks for children and youths proliferated but children were not everywhere prized as an earning asset especially where childbearing and child care reduced maternal earnings. We have little evidence for England that women's involvement in commercial manufacturing released them from their traditional domestic priorities in the manner suggested by Medick (1976a), even where the demand for female labour outstripped that for men. The labour market was segmented so that excess demand for female labour did not result in higher female wages (Horrell and Humphries 1992; Berg 1993c; Pinchbeck 1930). These were conditioned by the notion of income appropriate for female (generally supplementary) earners, rather than by supply and demand. But the limited involvement of men in domestic and household tasks was not just dependent upon differential opportunity costs: it resulted from long-established and little-questioned gender divisions of labour. Most often proto-industrial tasks were added on to rather than substituted for women's work in the home or in agrarian sidelines. Distaff spinning, hand knitting, lace making and straw plaiting remained common in parts of rural Britain well into the nineteenth century because they utilized the cheap labour of older women and children in particular, and they were popular because they could be done simultaneously with other tasks such as child care or walking to and from market or field work.

In areas of England dominated by a proto-industrial structure of independent artisanal family businesses (parts of the West Riding and south Yorkshire, parts of Lancashire and some of the Birmingham trades) opportunities were created for women, especially widows, to take a leading role in business and some blurring of gender roles must have been promoted by market expansion in these areas (Berg 1993a). Technological change also disrupted some long-standing divisions of labour. In Shepshed, for example, in the eighteenth century men knitted and women spun but with the mechanization of spinning and its shift to factories, women and youths got involved in framework knitting. Similarly, the identification of weaving largely as men's work in Lancashire broke down following the removal of spinning from the household but this did not necessarily increase the status or independence of women as wages were driven down by an influx of Irish and agricultural workers as well as of former spinners. Technological change in most sectors produced a re-working of the sexual division of labour such that women were generally employed on processes which were socially defined as less skilled or inferior and hence lower paid than male jobs. On the whole, within putting-out structures it is difficult to sustain the idea that proto-industrial employment enhanced the status and self-esteem of women or children and the existence of proto-industry alongside factory forms of manufacturing in the nineteenth century was often associated specifically with women whose conditions and rates of pay in these sweated sectors were notoriously bad.

Proto-industries could and did contribute profoundly to changes in material culture, ideas, beliefs and everyday life (see for example both

Rollison 1992 and Urdank 1990 on Gloucestershire). They were at the heart of the shift that de Vries has termed the 'industrious revolution'. As women and children as well as men turned from subsistence activities to the production of commodities for the market the primacy given to manufacturing work meant less time to engage in food preparation, growing food and raising cows, poultry or pigs. Families had to enter the market for their needs and industrial villages developed a diversified range of service industries producing and trading in goods for everyday use. Clothing, hats, shoes, pots and pans and candles, for example, were all produced in the rural industrial villages of west Yorkshire by the mid-eighteenth century (most much earlier) despite the proximity of nearby urban centres and markets. These developments increased the number of face-to-face transactions and credit links which helped to cement manufacturing communities together and which acted to increased their local identity and sense of place in a changing world (Hudson and King 1994, 1995). Consumption patterns and habits changed, new tastes were awakened and shifts occurred in diet, clothing and the domestic environment. In west Yorkshire the extended cultivation and eating of potatoes from the 1730s was one result. But diet also expanded to include much more non-local produce including white flour, tea and tobacco. The routines and demands of proto-industrial work itself also promoted new dietary habits (such as tea drinking), leisure activities and architectural styles (Hudson and King forthcoming).

Conclusion

Research on proto-industries in England has highlighted the difficulties of generalizing about the location of commercial domestic manufacturing and its impact upon economic, social and cultural life. In each proto-industrial region the pre-existing nature of landholding and wealth distribution, and the nature of products, markets and technologies, all influenced the extent to which proto-industry affected economic transition, demographic behaviour and social life. Furthermore, not all proto-industry was dynamic and the links between dispersed manufacturing and more centralized, technologically advanced production were rarely straightforward even in those regions which apparently saw a transition from one to the other. Seldom can proto-industry be seen to be a dominant source of fundamental shifts in the mode of production in England in the manner which much theorizing has implied. On the other hand the impact of domestic manufacturing upon mercantile skills and contacts, on commercial infrastructures, in promoting new working and consumption habits and in influencing personal and family life is likely to have been fundamental to the industrialization process in England.

Dispersed forms of manufacturing did not, of course, disappear with the coming of the factory. Some were encouraged and spawned by the factory system via sub-contracting arrangements and others remain viable today as ways of producing certain types of goods, using particular technologies and, generally, avoiding the costs and rigidities of organized labour. Industrial structures in England, as elsewhere, exhibit a complexity and flexibility which cannot be understood solely by using a model which stresses a single organizational form or a unilinear path of development. The concept of proto-industry in English economic and social history has however been extremely valuable in providing an agenda for research and as an approach to industrialization which breaks down the boundaries between economic history and other social sciences.

6 Ireland 1841: pre-industrial or proto-industrial; industrializing or de-industrializing?

L. A. Clarkson

Introduction

When, almost a quarter of a century ago, Mendels coined the term, 'proto-industrialization', he did so to identify a phase of industry possessing specific characteristics which preceded factory-based industry. The crafts concerned were labour intensive and, for that reason, were usually found in country areas where cheap labour abounded. They made goods for markets beyond the regions in which they were located. Production was carried out by cottage workers who combined farming with manufacturing, but their efforts were co-ordinated by merchants whose function was to provide the commercial networks linking producers with distant customers. The populations involved in manufacturing came to depend on food grown outside the region; once again, therefore, trading links were needed, to bring food (and perhaps also raw materials) from distant parts. If conditions were right, this first, or 'proto', phase of industrialization merged into the second phase of modern, capital-intensive industry. The right conditions included, on the demand side, access to expanding markets and, on the side of supply, suitable factor endowments, particularly an amenable labour force, entrepreneurship and capital. If conditions were not right, the proto-industrial stage was followed by de-industrialization and not by industrialization. Mendels never explicitly defined the time-period of proto-industrialization, but its golden age was the 150 years or so between the mid-seventeenth century and the early decades of the industrial revolution (for a survey, see Clarkson 1985).

Since Mendels wrote, the issues outlined above have been resolved into a number of specific questions. These include the relationship between handicraft industries and population growth. There is now a common assumption in the literature that the presence of industrial employments in the countryside provided an alternative or supplementary source of income to farming, and hence contributed to more frequent, younger and more fertile marriages. Historians have also

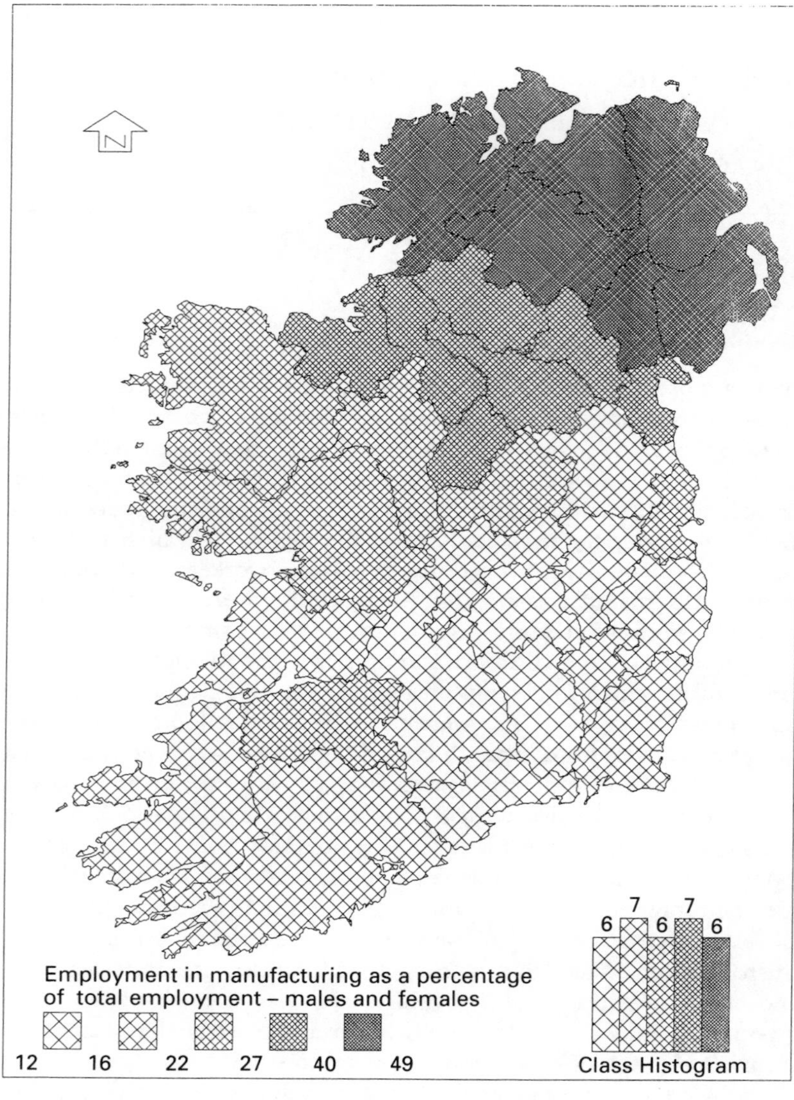

Map 6.1 Employment of males and females in manufacturing in Ireland, 1841

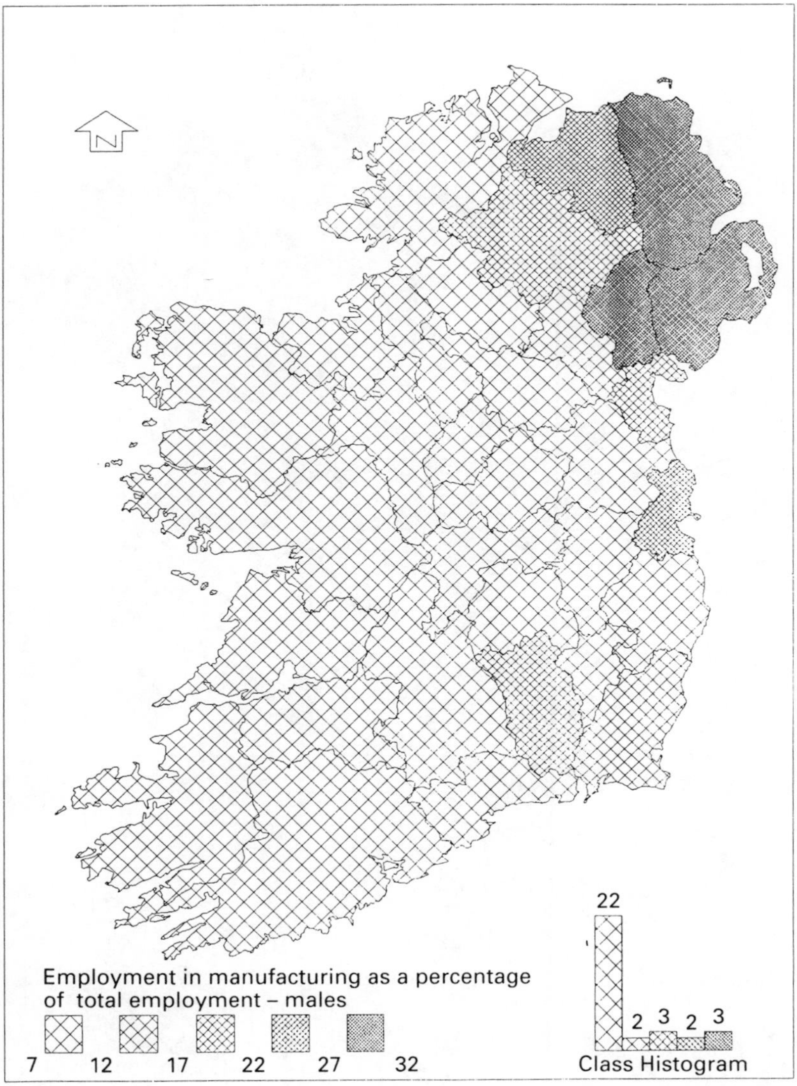

Map 6.2 Employment of males in manufacturing in Ireland, 1841

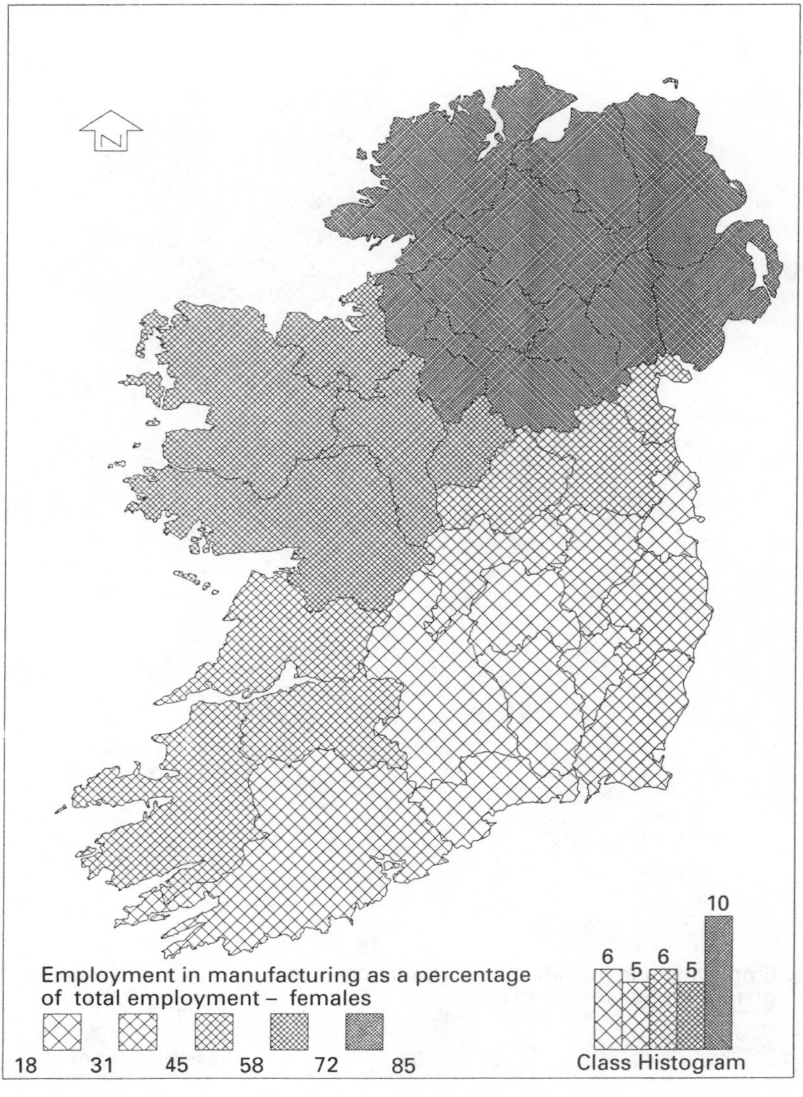

Map 6.3 Employment of females in manufacturing in Ireland, 1841

examined the nature of industrial organization, drawing attention to the distinction between independent domestic craftsmen working on their own account, although relying on merchants to dispose of their products in distant markets, and wage earners working on raw materials supplied to them on a putting-out basis by capitalist employers. Either way, production was directed to markets outside the region and often beyond national boundaries.

A further set of questions has been concerned with the institutional and dynamic aspects of industrialization. These have been analysed at two levels. At the local level, scholars have attempted to tease out the relationships between particular types of family and farming structures – for example, whether families were nuclear or extended, whether cultivators were property-owning peasants or tenant farmers – and the emergence of industries in the countryside. At the regional and national level, they have examined whether the state or urban guilds or powerful landlords have assisted or retarded industrial development. And, finally, there is the over-arching Mendels theme: was proto-industrialization followed by a subsequent stage of factory industrialization? If so, how was a population increasingly absorbed in manufacturing supplied with the food that it required for its well being?

The original focus of Mendels' work was the Low Countries, but there have since been many empirical studies extending proto-industrialization to other parts of Europe and to regions outside Europe. In the process, more and more industries have been caught in its net. The thesis was originally based on a study of the textile crafts, but progressively metal extraction and metal working, leather manufacturing, wood working, mining – in fact almost anything that did not use equipment requiring heavy investment in plant – has come to be regarded as 'proto-industrial'. Since most manufacturing before the industrial revolution made only limited use of fixed capital, virtually every craft could be cast in the proto-industrial mould by a careless use of the term. In such manner, proto-industrialization has almost ceased to be a concept embracing a distinctive stage of industry and has become, instead, a polysyllabic description of almost every craft before the nineteenth century.

To re-establish some analytical power to the Mendels thesis, we need to remember that he drew a clear distinction between urban craftsmen satisfying local and restricted markets, and producers geared to national and international markets. Before the nineteenth century, towns swarmed with small-scale craftsmen normally working with locally produced raw materials, although sometimes depending as well on supplies coming from some distance away (for a recent discussion see

Corfield and Keene 1990). Such craftsmen were vitally important for the well being of their localities but they did not have the same functional role as those producers who were linked to a subsequent stage of factory-based industry. Indeed, during the late eighteenth century and the first half of the nineteenth, the tide of industrialization often left local craftsmen unaffected. These pre-industrial craftsmen should not be confused with that type of industrial organization in which cheap labour was harnessed by enterprising merchants to the production of goods for national and international markets, and which was sometimes the prelude to the growth of factory industry.

Proto-industries in Ireland

The theory of proto-industrialization has rarely washed over the extreme western fringe of Europe, even though before 1841 the population of Ireland grew at a pace unparalleled in western Europe and even though Ireland had possessed major textile industries during the eighteenth century which, with the exception of the linen industry in east Ulster, suffered painful contraction during the nineteenth. Ireland, that is, demonstrated two important features that have elsewhere attracted the attention of historians of proto-industrialization: rapid population growth and stark de-industrialization.

This chapter is not much concerned with the demographic aspects of proto-industrialization, since it is unnecessary to invoke proto-industrialization to explain the growth of the Irish population during the eighteenth century – and its eventual decline after the famine of 1845–9 – when more obvious explanations are readily to hand (but for some discussion see Almquist 1979, and Collins 1982). Although the presence of rural industry stimulated the growth of population, for example in south Ulster, the most important influences were the peculiarities of a land system that permitted continual sub-division, and the widespread adoption of a diet dominated by potatoes that sustained a healthy and fertile population. Inasmuch as youthful and fertile marriages required an economic base, in Ireland it was amply supplied by the ubiquitous potato. After the disaster of the Great Famine, radical changes in the land system and a rapid retreat from a potato diet profoundly changed the population history of Ireland (for the most recent discussion see Kennedy and Clarkson 1993). Neither is this chapter concerned with the problems of feeding the industrial regions. There was a vigorous inter-regional trade in foodstuffs, and towns such as Dublin, Cork and Belfast offered growing markets for commercially minded farmers. Everywhere, the normally high-yielding and nourishing potato provided food in abundance.

The focus of this study is industrial development from the late seventeenth century to the mid-nineteenth century. For much of this period the north-east of Ireland, comprising much of the province of Ulster and the more northerly parts of the province of Connaught, was the home of one of the most important linen-producing regions in Europe, with large markets in England and Scotland, North America and western Europe. The great bulk of production came from farmer-weavers scattered throughout the countryside who, with their wives and children, were responsible for everything from growing the flax to the manufacture of unbleached cloth. The development of the industry has traditionally been explained in the terms established by Gill, writing in the early part of this century. Gill stressed the role of Huguenot refugees who were encouraged by the English government to settle near Lisburn, County Antrim. He also emphasized the importance of protected markets for Irish linens in England provided by legislation of the Westminster parliament. More recently, historians have emphasized the importance of indigenous skills, an abundant labour force, and the efforts of local landlords to foster linen manufacture by establishing markets where flax, yarn and cloths could be bought and sold. The high-point of the domestic linen industry was the early years of the nineteenth century, when perhaps two-thirds of Irish linen production was sold overseas. Thereafter, the domestic industry declined, principally in the face of competition from cheaper, factory-produced cottons (Gill 1925; Clarkson 1989a; Crawford 1988). When the industry revived during the 1830s it was as a factory-based industry confined to Belfast and the Lagan valley.

It is less well known that from the 1660s to the end of the eighteenth century, the south-eastern segment of Ireland possessed a flourishing woollen industry that generated employment and wealth throughout the southern province of Munster. It was a rural industry, although there were substantial numbers of urban craftsmen in the towns of Cork, Kilkenny and Carrick-on-Suir, making high-grade fabrics such as ratteens for the Dublin fashion market. The markets for woollens were principally within Ireland, where the rapidly growing population generated a demand for cheap frieze and similar cloths. There was also a considerable demand for Irish yarns in England where they were used in the manufacture of serge and worsteds. Opportunities to compete in continental markets were restricted by legislation enacted in London and designed to protect English producers.

During the late eighteenth and the nineteenth centuries the woollen industry largely failed to make the transition into factories. This failure can be explained by rising costs of wool, as farmers switched away from sheep into cattle and arable production, and by competition from English woollens and cottons which were available ever more cheaply from the new factories (Clarkson 1989b). The woollen industry, nevertheless, does not deserve the neglect it has received from Irish scholars. For more than a century its importance in generating employment and incomes for people living in the south-east of Ireland was, arguably, as important as the linen industry was to the inhabitants of the north-east. Furthermore, the trading restrictions imposed by the English parliament on the Irish woollen industry at the end of the seventeenth century, and which some historians used to blame for the eventual demise of the industry a century later, remain a contentious issue in political history (for a discussion see Kelly 1980).

The third strand of the Irish textile industries – cotton – is probably better known than the woollen industry, but is not well understood. It began modestly in the Cork area in the 1740s, but from the 1770s until about 1840 cotton became an important industry concentrated in and around Belfast. This was an area already specializing in the manufacture of linen, and the upstart industry attracted labour and capital away from the older industry (Dickson 1977). The spinning branch of cotton manufacture was mechanized from an early stage along the lines familiar in England, although weaving remained primarily a hand process – as it did in England – for most of the period. Recent research has demonstrated that the Belfast cotton industry was as competitive and as well organized as its counterparts in Manchester and Glasgow. Its eventual contraction was caused, not by inefficiency, but by changes in relative factor costs brought about by the introduction into the linen industry of wet flax-spinning techniques at the end of the 1820s. Wet spinning shifted the comparative advantage in east Ulster towards the production of linen and away from that of cotton (Geary 1989).

The history of these three industries – linen, woollens and cotton – seem to conform to the broad patterns suggested by the theory of proto-industrialization. All made use of cheap country labour. The precise location of the woollen industry in Munster still awaits investigation; it was found in the countryside, but it was also an important employer of labour in some towns. In the north of Ireland, the linen industry generated employment across a wide swathe of the countryside. Some of this area was pastoral or poor arable, but the heartland of the industry was in the rich farming country of north Armagh (Clarkson 1989a). Production in both the woollen and linen industries was usually carried out by independent producers, and within the household there was a

Table 6.1. *The employed workforce in Ireland, 1841*

	Total employed	Percentage of population employed
Males	2,342,225	58.2
Females	1,169,635	28.1
Total	3,511,860	43.0

clearly defined division of labour, with men weaving and women and children engaged in spinning and related processes. Marketing was firmly in the control of urban-based merchants who linked producers with distant customers. From the 1770s the prosperity of both woollens and linens was threatened by the rise of the cotton industry. The emergence of the Belfast cotton industry was a local example within the British Isles of factors of production moving from domestic manufacture into factories. In this process, entrepreneurs switched from the spinning of flax, which was difficult to mechanize, to the spinning of cotton.

Irish occupational structure in 1841

The remainder of this chapter is concerned with the transition from the first, or 'proto', industrial phase to the second stage. In many parts of Europe this second stage was factory industry, but in Ireland, with a few exceptions, it was industrial decline. The occupational statistics contained in the magnificent census of 1841 offer an opportunity to survey the industrial landscape of Ireland (Census, 1841). The date 1841 is rather late in the context of the proto-industrial debate, but it can be justified on two grounds. First, for earlier periods there is a shortage of direct evidence relating to industrial development in Ireland; for example, few business records survive. Secondly, such evidence as does exist suggests that factory-based industry came late to Ireland.

Table 6.1 shows that 43 per cent of the population thought of itself as being in gainful employment in 1841, with males outnumbering females in a ratio of 2:1. There are major problems in interpreting the census data, but these do not detract from their value. The commissioners depended on the perceptions of householders who completed the census forms. By relying on the judgement of mainly male heads of households, the commissioners probably understated the involvement of women and juveniles in economic activity, although, for reasons discussed below, they may have exaggerated the involvement of females in manufacturing in country areas.

The problems of occupational classification are greater still when we

Table 6.2. *Occupational distribution in Ireland, 1841 (total employed population) (%)*

	Agriculture	Building	Mining	Manufacturing	Other
County Antrim	38.72	1.42	0.61	46.77	12.48
County Armagh	40.63	1.40	0.73	46.21	11.04
Belfast	3.48	4.14	0.89	53.11	38.38
County Carlow	59.86	2.19	1.25	16.28	20.43
Carrickfergus	31.64	1.65	0.95	42.71	23.05
County Cavan	52.79	0.97	0.47	35.58	10.19
County Clare	63.45	1.05	0.49	21.60	13.39
County Cork	63.25	1.76	0.75	16.24	7.99
Cork City	6.42	3.92	1.22	32.37	56.07
County Donegal	51.04	0.76	0.33	39.81	8.06
County Down	35.51	1.40	0.85	49.35	12.89
Drogheda	6.25	3.56	0.93	44.29	44.97
County Dublin	42.71	3.01	1.43	15.14	37.70
Dublin City	1.56	5.01	0.38	33.51	59.51
County Fermanagh	48.96	0.93	0.69	39.15	10.27
County Galway	63.22	1.10	0.38	24.31	10.99
Galway Town	13.36	3.25	1.25	31.22	50.91
County Kerry	62.53	1.07	0.52	20.46	15.43
County Kildare	60.43	2.12	0.61	15.74	21.09
County Kilkenny	70.49	2.04	1.40	10.48	15.59
Kilkenny City	8.29	3.97	1.54	31.83	54.37
King's County	62.72	1.90	0.71	16.83	17.85
County Leitrim	54.24	0.57	0.42	36.29	8.49
County Limerick	61.07	1.45	0.50	19.91	17.07
Limerick City	7.33	3.71	1.38	33.16	54.43
County Londonderry	40.97	1.33	0.56	44.60	12.53
County Longford	58.71	1.22	0.59	27.32	12.16
County Louth	50.56	2.06	0.85	25.17	21.35
County Mayo	63.84	0.54	0.34	26.29	8.99
County Meath	59.17	1.97	0.80	19.39	18.66
County Monaghan	50.38	1.10	0.72	37.56	10.23
Queens' County	65.19	1.81	1.17	16.00	15.84
County Roscommon	65.87	0.92	0.53	21.92	10.76
County Tipperary	63.67	2.02	1.01	13.72	19.58
County Sligo	57.49	0.62	0.49	28.75	12.65
County Tyrone	44.52	1.01	0.63	44.66	9.17
County Waterford	67.81	1.89	1.17	11.16	17.97
Waterford City	6.19	3.85	1.68	29.86	58.42
County Westmeath	58.84	1.81	0.59	21.73	17.02
County Wexford	56.31	2.33	0.88	20.92	19.52
County Wicklow	58.53	2.29	2.61	14.91	21.66
Average	47.24	1.95	0.87	27.11	22.82

consider the distribution of the workforce across the various sectors of the economy.

Of the total workforce, 47 per cent worked in agriculture and 28 per cent in manufacturing and mining. These proportions are almost the reverse of those in Britain, where 22 per cent of the workforce was employed in agriculture and 41 per cent in industry (Deane and Cole 1962: 142). On this showing, only the Ulster counties and towns of Antrim, Armagh, Down, Londonderry, Tyrone, Belfast and Carrickfergus, and Drogheda in County Louth reached British levels of industrialization. At the other end of the spectrum, the counties of south-east Ireland were very lightly industrialized. (See Map 6.1; in this, and all the maps, the towns have been incorporated into their respective counties: Belfast and Carrickfergus into Antrim, and Drogheda into Louth.)

The occupational categories in Table 6.2 are those used in the census, re-arranged by Charles Booth in 1886, and modified by Armstrong many years later (Armstrong 1972). The commissioners identified over 900 occupations and, as C. H. Lee has pointed out, it is trusting a great deal to the accurate reporting by householders to accept this level of detail (Lee 1979). Still, the broad picture is clear, even though Table 6.2 distorts the degree of manufacturing in a number of ways. The category 'other', for example, includes dealing and industrial service. The distinction between dealing and manufacturing was hazy in the mid-nineteenth century, while 'industrial service' included a large number of general labourers; whether they worked in farming, in building, or as industrial labourers is impossible to say. If we add all dealers and everybody employed in industrial service to 'manufacturing', the proportion rises to 32 per cent.

Then there is the problem of dual occupations. Many men described in the census as farmers spent part of their time in manufacturing (and in dealing, for that matter). The most obvious examples were farmer-weavers engaged in the linen industry. Some of these no doubt described themselves as weavers rather than farmers when they completed the census forms; others probably thought of themselves as farmers, particularly if they occupied very small farms but aspired to the higher social status implied by the label 'farmer'. Conversely, many weavers, as well as blacksmiths, saddlers and other manufacturers in rural areas, spent part of their time working as farmers or farm labourers. It is impossible to say whether the importance of labour devoted to agriculture would increase or decrease if we had evidence about the time that people spent on one activity rather than another.

Thirdly, there are the difficulties caused by female occupations. Women and children were seldom recorded as employed when working

Table 6.3. *Male and female manufacturing employment in Britain and Ireland, 1841*

	Great Britain	Ireland
Per cent of employed males working in all manufacturing	34.0	16.0
Per cent of employed males working in 'revolutionized' industry	19.0	10.0
Per cent of employed females working in all manufacturing	32.0	44.0
Per cent of employed females working in 'revolutionized' industry	19.0	42.0

for husbands and fathers. For this reason, N. F. R. Crafts and others have endeavoured to measure the degree of manufacturing in Britain during the industrial revolution by concentrating on male employments, in the process earning the opprobrium of Berg and Hudson for undervaluing the contribution of women and children (Crafts 1985; Berg and Hudson 1992: 35). It is useful, nevertheless, to follow Crafts' methodology to make comparisons between Britain and Ireland.

The 'revolutionized' industry sector identified by Crafts includes chemicals and allied products, metal manufactures, mechanical engineering, vehicles, transport and – especially – textiles (Crafts 1985: 5). As explained above, Crafts does not give the proportion of females employed in total manufacturing; these are taken, instead, from Armstrong, whose occupational classifications are slightly different (Armstrong 1972). However, the categorizations are robust enough to yield some interesting contrasts.

The proportion of males engaged in manufacturing occupations of all kinds in Britain was double that prevailing in Ireland. The female proportion, on the other hand, was substantially higher in Ireland than in Britain. Furthermore, virtually all females working in manufacturing in Ireland appear to have been concentrated in the sector defined by Crafts as 'revolutionized' industry, whereas, in Britain, only a little over one half the females in manufacturing were so employed.

These contrasting patterns can be explained in two main ways. The first is the way that female employments were registered – or not registered – by heads of households. In total, twice as many males as females were recorded as employed in 1841 (see Table 6.1), but in manufacturing, females outnumbered males by three to one. There was a difference, though, between town and countryside. Only in the former did the number of males in manufacturing employments exceed the number of females; urban male householders did not attribute occupations to their wives and children, even when their labour was essential to the domestic economy. This is clearly demonstrated by the unofficial census taken in the woollen manufacturing town of Carrick-on-Suir, County Tipperary, in 1799. Not a single carder or spinner was recorded, even though there were close to 1,300 wives and daughters of weavers working at these occupations (Clarkson 1989b; Clarkson and Crawford 1991). The same thing happened with the nation-wide census in 1841. In the countryside, female employment in farming was under-recorded, but this time it was agricultural labour that went unnoticed. On the other hand, wives and daughters of farmers and farm labourers who supplemented the family income by spinning, carding, combing, embroidering and similar tasks were entered on the census forms by their farming husbands and fathers. These female textile workers were the survivors of the once-prosperous handicraft linen industry.

A second explanation of the contrasts in Table 6.3 is the definition of 'revolutionized' industry used by Crafts, which included textiles. But textiles were the great employers of female labour in the countryside. They were the archetypal proto-industrial occupations, the gateways both to modern factory industry and to the slippery slope of de-industrialization. Crafts' 'revolutionized' industries possessed a Janus-like characteristic of marking the end of the pre-industrial past and looking forward towards the golden, if smoky, future of factory industry; or, alternatively, to the less prosperous land of industrial decline. The Irish census of 1841 is, outside the narrow region of Belfast and its hinterland, a monument to de-industrialization and not a milestone on the way to the creation of a factory-based economy.

Two pictures of Ireland thus emerge. If we restrict our attention to males, Ireland in 1841 was a very lightly industrialized economy; such manufacturing as existed was concentrated in east Ulster, with a thin trickle down the east coast, reflecting some clustering in towns such as Drogheda, Dublin, Cork and Kilkenny (see Map 6.2). By focussing on females, Ireland can be made to look more industrialized than Britain. Female manufacturing was much more broadly distributed than was the case with males; there was a large presence in the north-east, from where manufacturing employment stretched across a broad sweep of the countryside in a south-westerly direction (see Map 6.3).

In 1841, many industrial workers in Ireland laboured to satisfy merely local demands. Except in east Ulster, textile workers, together with thousands of craftsmen and women working as boot and shoe makers, tailors and dress makers, saddlers and harness makers, cabinet makers and coffin makers, tobacco twisters and toy makers, constituted the 'non-revolutionized' industries. In the nine cities and towns distinguished separately in the census (Belfast, Carrickfergus, Cork, Dublin, Drogheda, Galway, Kilkenny, Limerick and Waterford), such crafts accounted for the majority of the industrial workforce. In Galway, for example, half the manufacturers worked as boot and shoe makers, dress makers and milliners, brewers and distillers and similar trades. In Cork City, two-thirds of all workers in manufacturing were employed in local trades, with the largest concentrations in boot and shoe making, tailoring and dress making. In Dublin, with a population of 250,000, there was an even greater concentration in the non-'revolutionized' industries. The census commissioners recorded 180 different manufacturing occupations employing 33,741 people. Of these trades, 140, involving 26,000 people, existed mainly to satisfy the wants of the Dublin population. Only in Belfast was the picture different. Even there, nearly 40 per cent of manufacturing craftsmen in 1841 worked in manual handicrafts connected with clothing, leather working, milling, distilling and brewing, watch making and the like.

The prevalence of the 'non-revolutionized' industries in Ireland in 1841 is summarized in Table 6.4.

In the provinces there was a marked contrast between the two northern and western provinces of Ulster and Connaught, and the two southern and eastern provinces of Leinster and Munster in 1841. The former had been the home of the linen and cotton industries whose markets lay well beyond the borders of Ireland. There remained a large degree of handicraft working in 1841, as well as an embryonic factory industry in east Ulster. The south-eastern provinces had at one time supported a flourishing woollen industry, most of which had vanished by 1841. Despite a few exceptions, the history of this region was that of industrial decline.

Examples of Irish industry

The census of 1841 provides no more than a generalized picture of Irish industrial activity. The picture can be enhanced by looking at two areas of Ireland in a little more detail. In the south of the country, Cork City offers a revealing vignette of the diversity of industrial activity. In 1841 Cork had a population of 81,000 and was still a major urban centre, although it no longer enjoyed the pre-eminence it had held during the eighteenth century. Cork City had possessed an important food-processing industry during the eighteenth century, producing salted meat and butter for export. County Cork also enjoyed a modest reputation as a linen-producing area, although it was always subordinate

Table 6.4. *Proportions of manufacturing workforce employed in 'non-revolutionized' and 'revolutionized' industries in Ireland, 1841 (%)*

Province and towns	'Non-revolutionized' industry	'Revolutionized' industry
Leinster	42	58
Munster	45	55
Connaught	21	79
Ulster	20	80
Nine towns	59	41

to Ulster and, from the 1750s, labour and capital moved from linen into the cotton industry. But the woollen industry was always more important than linen. Domestic spinning and weaving of wool had been a thriving activity up to the 1780s, when competition from the rapidly developing industry in Yorkshire undermined its prosperity. The French wars, nevertheless, generated a healthy demand for military cloth that saw the industry through the next three decades, until the coming of peace in 1815 sent it into chronic and almost terminal decline. Some investment in factories and machinery powered by water and steam took place in Cork City and other towns such as Bandon, Blarney and Fermoy. Many of these ventures were small and short-lived and in 1839 there were just five mills in the county, employing 188 people. In 1850 there was only one, with 187 employees and 5,638 spindles. During the second half of the century there was an increase in factory production, and in 1897 there were twenty-seven woollen mills employing between 2,000 and 3,000 operatives (Bielenberg 1991: 8–40). Mill workers producing for markets in Britain, however, were set within a sea of miscellaneous local crafts producing for local markets.

A similarly diverse pattern of industrial organization existed in Ulster. Cotton and linen vied for dominance in the 1820s and 1830s, and factory production and domestic workshops existed side by side, more often in a complementary than in a competitive relationship. The mechanization of flax spinning at the end of the 1820s led to a decline of cotton production and an increase in linen. In 1839 there were thirty-five power-driven factories throughout Ulster engaged in the wet spinning of flax, employing nearly 8,000 workers; in 1850 there were sixty-two factories, with 500,000 spindles and 19,000 employees. The great majority of these factories were in the east of the province. Domestic flax spinning consequently contracted in the west. So, too, did handloom weaving for, although power weaving did not become significant until the end of the 1850s (there was only one power loom factory in 1850, employing 138 operatives and containing thirty-four looms), handloom weavers clustered around the factories that supplied the yarn. Cottage production, nevertheless, remained important. Hand spinning, as well as hand weaving, continued to cater for local needs. and thousands of one-time cotton weavers and domestic linen spinners turned to the embroidering of muslin and the manufacture of shirts as their traditional pursuits declined. At the same time, the demand for textile machinery generated by the new factories laid the foundations of an engineering industry in Belfast (Kennedy 1985: 1–16; Ollerenshaw 1985: 66–76).

Returning to the general questions raised by examining the industrial pattern in Ireland in 1841, we are confronted by a substantial amount of manufacturing, but much of it was highly localized and contracting. Manufacturing activity weakened throughout the nineteenth century – with one important exception. Linen, shipbuilding, engineering, distilling and food processing transformed Belfast into one of the great industrial cities of the British Isles (Ollerenshaw 1985: 86–96). By contrast, at the other end of the country, the industrial base of the region centring on Cork City was shrinking (Bielenberg 1991: 116–26). Cork was more typical than Belfast.

Looking at Ireland as a whole, industrial employment in 1901 accounted for 32.6 per cent of total employment, a modest but misleading increase since 1841. In Ulster, the proportion was 43.1 per cent, in Leinster, 32.8 per cent, in Munster 25.5 per cent, and in Connaught only 14.0 per cent (Census: 1901). The relatively high proportion of the workforce engaged in manufacturing in Leinster is explained more by the decline of the rural population outside the city of Dublin than by any substantial growth of industrial activity. Even in the city of Dublin, both the numbers and the proportion of males employed in manufacturing declined in the second half of the nineteenth century, while the numbers and proportion of females remained stable (Daly 1984: 50–1).

Irish economic development and the theories of proto-industrialization

To describe nineteenth-century Ireland as a region undergoing de-industrialization does not explain why the process occurred. There was clearly no direct progression from proto-industrialization to de-industrialization. Even in the woollen industry, there was some limited development of factory production from the 1780s. The story in the linen industry was even more complicated. There was an uncomfortable period at the beginning of the nineteenth century when the handicraft industry experienced severe competition from factory-made cottons. But even in these years a few manufacturers, assisted by the Linen Board, attempted to set up dry-spinning factories for manufacture of sail cloth; these efforts did not survive the coming of peace in 1815 (Takei 1994). Flax spinning eventually moved into factories with the innovation of wet-spinning techniques, albeit in a geographically much more confined area than the old handicraft industry. But the route into factory production was a roundabout one, via a detour of capital and labour into the factory spinning of cotton, which was the industrial basis of Belfast's prosperity from the 1780s to the 1820s.

The collapse of much of Irish industry cannot be ascribed to a lack of entrepreneurship. Individual woollen manufacturers in towns such as Carrick-on-Suir and Cork invested in modern power-driven machinery without, however, arresting the decline of the industry (Clarkson 1989b; Bielenberg 1991). In Ulster, manufacturers moved resources readily from flax spinning to cotton and back to flax as the technology became available. Early nineteenth-century Belfast, too, abounded with businessmen possessing enterprise and capital that they used to develop the harbour and lay the foundations of the shipbuilding and engineering industries that dominated the late nineteenth-century city (Moss and Hume 1986: 1–35).

Many years ago, George O'Brien argued that the Act of Union of 1800–1 'proved disastrous' for Irish industry by removing the protectionist duties that Irish industries – particularly cotton – had enjoyed during the eighteenth century and by making Ireland part of a free-trade area embracing the whole of the United Kingdom (O'Brien: 1921). We cannot say for certain what would have happened had Ireland remained an independent political unit during the nineteenth century with its own parliament. But Geary's work suggests that the decline of the cotton industry from the 1820s had little to do with the removal of the modest protectionist duties that it had enjoyed, while Ó Gráda has written, 'given the massive secular drop in the prices of British industrial staples', the retention of a tariff in favour of Irish manufactures would have had little effect unless set at very high levels (Geary 1989; Ó Gráda 1989: 144).

The most plausible explanation of Ireland's industrial decline during the nineteenth century, outside eastern Ulster, was that it was a region within a United Kingdom where all regions were specializing according to their comparative advantages (for a discussion see Othick 1985). We have seen how, in and around Belfast, industrial capital moved from cotton to linen as wet flax-spinning techniques became available from the late 1820s. Half a century earlier, farmers in south-east Ireland had switched land from pasture into tillage to satisfy the demands of the British food market, in the process pushing up the price of wool, thus weakening the ability of woollen manufacturers to compete with more favourably endowed regions of the British Isles. Throughout the nineteenth century the creation of a system of cheap transport enabled Ireland to specialize in agricultural produce for the British Isles. That same cheap transport exposed local industries such as shoe making, tanning, tailoring and dress making to goods produced in England (see Bielenberg 1991; Daly 1984).

Industrial decline was made all the more probable by demographic changes: the retardation of population growth after 1820 and its rapid decline after 1845. The dramatic and sustained fall in population after the Great Famine tilted the comparative advantage of Irish agriculture – always a country endowed by nature as a grass-growing region – towards the production of meat and dairy produce for the British market. On the evidence of the 1841 census, industrial development in many counties in Ireland lagged behind the United Kingdom as a whole. But Ireland was not unique. In England and Scotland industrial employment contracted in several counties as the 'revolutionized' industries took root in a few. The problem for Ireland was that in a free-trade nation where regional specialization was king, the counties whose future lay in agricultural specialization were more numerous than those whose future lay in manufacturing.

So, does the industrial landscape of Ireland that emerges from an examination of the occupation data contained in the 1841 census tell us anything about the validity of the model of proto-industrialization? The question is, perhaps, incorrectly posed. As is so often the case in history, it is the hypothesis that throws light upon the empirical evidence rather than the other way round. In considering the industrial profile of mid-nineteenth-century Ireland, we should remember the distinction made by the original proponents of proto-industrialization between local handicrafts and those identified as precursors of modern factory industry. We should also remember that factory-based industry was accompanied by regional concentration and specialization based on comparative advantage.

Acknowledgements

This chapter is based on data taken from the Database of Irish Historical Statistics being created in the Department of Economic and Social History, Queen's University of Belfast, with the support of the ESRC and the University. I am grateful to my colleague, Dr Margaret Crawford, for her assistance with coding the occupations and to Dr Paul Ell for preparing the maps.

7 Proto-industrialization in Spain

J. K. J. Thomson

A broad definition for proto-industry has been adopted in this chapter, that of all forms of pre-factory industrial activity, but my analysis of the Spanish experience of such industry will be far from complete. I have chosen to survey in some depth the position of textile proto-industry in two key phases of Spanish modernization – the industrial expansion in Castile between the fourteenth and sixteenth centuries, which ended in decline, and that in Catalonia between the seventeenth and eighteenth centuries, which concluded in a successful transition to industrialization – rather than attempting to describe all industrial activity which would correspond to this definition. I hope thereby to provide a sense of process concerning the position of proto-industry in Spanish industrialization, as well as fulfilling a more straightforward descriptive purpose. Following these surveys I shall provide a summary of the existing Spanish literature on the subject.

Industrialization and de-industrialization in Castile in the golden age

The picture that emerges from recent work on the Castilian medieval and early modern experience is somewhere in between the polarized positions which used to characterize interpretations of Spain's industrial past. On the one hand some of the wilder claims made concerning the extent of industrial specialization in Castile in the 'golden age' have been discredited and on the other the scepticism shown by some historians about Castile's ever having had an industry meriting comment has been shown to have been misplaced (Vicens Vives 1972: 237). Castile did have an industrial history, indeed one whose character serves to throw considerable light on the causes of Castilian decline as well as illustrating the varied manner in which proto-industrial development can relate to modernization.

It would have been surprising if this had not been the case. There was a range of factors which gave rise to exceptionally favourable conditions for industrial expansion in Castile from the thirteenth to the sixteenth centuries. A first of these was the Reconquest: Christian Spain doubled its territory in the space of fifty years between 1212 and 1264 and this represented a massive extension in markets for industrial producers, a one-off enrichment on the basis of the spoils of war and access to the superior technical expertise in textile production – particularly marked in dyeing techniques and silk production – possessed by the conquered Muslim population. In addition the industry had the prospect of expanding into the neighbouring Portuguese market. Supply-side circumstances were also favourable: the situation with respect to wools, already good, was enhanced by the Reconquest for the finest wools were those of southern Spain – around Cuenca, which was to emerge as the capital of the Castilian industry in the fifteenth century, and in Andalusia. In addition, the increasing specialization of the Castilian economy in sheep farming – less labour intensive than arable farming – and the buoyant demographic circumstances provided favourable conditions with respect to labour supply (Iradiel Murugarren 1974: 36, 103; 1983: 107–12).

These circumstances, historians have now established, provided a basis for a steady growth in the Castilian industry from the fourteenth to the sixteenth centuries. Initially, rural and small-town production predominated. It was a primitive industry at this stage, characterized by minimal division of labour (Iradiel Murugarren 1974: 19–23). This did not, however, necessarily imply a disadvantage with respect to the industries of northern Europe. The fourteenth and fifteenth centuries were marked (unusually for textile industries) by rapid technological and organizational change in woollen production. Both the invention and diffusion of the fulling mill and the need to escape high urban production costs and restrictive guild practices were stimulating the diffusion of industry in rural areas (Miller 1965). Castile's industrial expansion thus commenced at a time when market and technological circumstances were favourable to the type of predominantly rural industrial structure which it possessed. 'Backwardness' may even have been an advantage allowing Castile to adapt more readily to the new trends (Bilbao and Fernández del Piñedo 1988: 126).

Iradiel Murugarren distinguishes between two principal zones in the Castilian industry – the northern and the southern Mesetas. The capitals of the former were in Palencia, Soria, Segovia and Avila. Its quality of production ranged from low to medium (cloths with 2,000 threads to the warp being the finest made) reflecting the quality of the local wools and demand patterns. Production was not concentrated. The centres of the second zone were in Cuenca, Toledo, Ciudad Real, Murcia,

Córdoba and Baeza. Production here was of higher quality, using the finer Merino wools available from the local transhumant herds, while markets were more developed – capitalist practices were extensive in the agriculture of the area, causing both landowners and labourers principally to depend on the market for their purchases, and levels of urbanization were among the highest in Europe. These circumstances generated an early tendency for the industry to be dominated by large urban centres of production. The contrast between the two zones was not by any means total, on the other hand – there were areas of rural industry in the southern zone (Iradiel Murugarren 1974: 39–40; 1983: 110) and significant examples, too, of large-scale urban cloth-making concerns in the northern Meseta before the sixteenth century when this format was to become the predominant one (García Sanz 1987: 69).

These north–south distinctions in fact emerged gradually during the period which we are analysing. Initially there were a great many common features in the development process of both areas. From the late fourteenth century, and especially during the fifteenth century, a process of incorporation of the industry occurred, with the spread of guilds. This development attested to improvement in quality of production, enforced by guilds' apprenticeship rules and monitoring of the final product, and growing division of labour – different guilds exercised monopolies over particular stages of the production process. Division of labour was taken furthest in the largest centres. In Cuenca, for example, in 1468 the office of dyer was separated from that of *pelaire* (derived from the Catalan word *paraire*, meaning to prepare – card – wools, and a profession which extended to the finishing processes generally and was often the predominant one in the production process) (Iradiel Murugarren 1974: 82–90).

As early as 1436 the towns of Cuenca and Baeza in the southern zone had emerged as the leaders of the industry. There, and in other southern centres, high-quality production and success in export markets were achieved as well as some significant innovation with respect to cloth types – in particular, the so-called *escarlatinas* and *granas*, which were high-quality broadcloths (up to 3,000 threads to the warp), using cochineal as a dyeing substance in the case of the former, designed to respond to the late fifteenth-century demand for brightly coloured cloth, and selling at double the price of normal broadcloths. Precise details are lacking, but the concentration of production in these larger centres by the early sixteenth century was considerable – in excess of 4,000 pieces per annum in Cuenca, where the industry's dyeing and fulling operations caused strains on local water resources (Iradiel Murugarren 1974: 83, 130, 209–10).

The principal political agents in this industrial expansion were local town councils, but the process was presided over, too, by the monarchy with respect to matters requiring a national policy. Two of these were the issues of wool exports and cloth imports. In the case of both, the response was supportive. A measure taken by the Cortes held at Toledo in 1462 gave the national industry the right of 'tanteo' (first option) on up to one third of the product of the annual wool shear and until the first half of the sixteenth century the national market was protected from foreign imports (Iradiel Murugarren 1974: 68–9, 82–5).

The fates of smaller production centres in the southern Meseta varied and information on them is by no means complete. Some may have been relatively unaffected by the trends just described. Others managed to adapt to the modernizing trends by introducing guilds, increasing quality and standardization of production, and incorporating the finishing processes – centres which achieved this include Agreda, Oña, Sigüenza and Valdena. A frequent experience of smaller-scale producers, however, was to succumb to the power of the major centres or to that of merchant capital (Iradiel Murugarren 1974: 104–9).

The general trend was certainly in the direction of an industry increasingly dominated by merchant capital, characterized by a *Verlagssystem* organization of production. Various factors lay behind this shift – the high cost of raw materials; the predominance of production for distant rather than local markets, which favoured a standardization of product which was more easily achieved by the larger concern and required, again, a larger input of capital; and finally the need for more attention to the finishing processes for such production, in the provision of which economies of scale applied. The finishing tended to be concentrated in the urban centres (Iradiel Murugarren 1974: 39, 82–9, 109–10; 1983: 110).

The trend towards capitalist structures in the industry was further enhanced by the growing efforts of the monarchy, from 1494, with mercantilist ambitions, to enforce uniformity in cloth types and ensure good quality of production. It tended to be on the basis of the practices of the large concerns that regulations were modelled (Bilbao and Fernández del Piñedo 1988: 127). The extent of direct control exercised by such concerns over the production process was, on the other hand, limited: a rapid expansion in the number of guilds from the late fifteenth century created structures opposed to innovation in cloth types and to cutting costs by, for example, expanding rural employment (Iradiel Murugarren 1974: 89–90). The industry was later to pay the price for this inflexibility.

If the Cuencan industry peaked during the first half of the sixteenth century, this was not the case for the Spanish industry as a whole. The commercial conjuncture was more favourable than ever at this point; with continued population growth and the expansion in the American trade, state policy was still mainly favourable to the national industry, and from 1550 the religious wars in France and the fighting in the Netherlands sheltered the Spanish market from competition. It was the industry of the northern Meseta, this time, which benefited from these trends and that of Segovia in particular – the industry there was employing 20,000 people in 1515 and producing 16,000 pieces of cloth per annum in the 1580s. If not as predominant as in the fifteenth century, some southern centres continued to grow, in particular the Cordoban and Baeza/Ubeda areas where production also peaked in the 1580s at some 18,000 and 8,000 pieces respectively (Fortea Pérez 1981: 268ff, 335ff). The Segovian industry was also distinguished by the quality of its production – the range extended to cloth with 2,400 to 3,600 threads to the warp (Ruiz Martin 1965: 275; Bilbao and Fernández del Piñedo 1988: 130–1).

As had been the case with the Cuencan industry, changes in the organization of production in the industry, and state intervention, encouraged tendencies which in the long run were to prove pernicious. The power of merchant capital gradually grew, and the *Verlagssystem* became predominant, with merchant manufacturers carrying out their own finishing processes and increasing pressure on formally independent workers both by purchasing their equipment – loom, spinning wheel, or whatever – and by advancing money (García Sanz 1977: 215; 1987: 65–79; Ruiz Martin 1965: 269–71). The same commercial and technical factors were at work as in the concentration of the Cuencan industry in a small number of hands slightly earlier.

The contribution of state policy was first, as already emphasized, the bias towards large concerns in the general regulations adopted for the industry, and secondly the decision made in 1566 to abolish the requirement that foreign merchants use their trading profits to buy Spanish products (principally wools and silks), allowing them to export bullion. As Spanish merchants had been the principal intermediaries in the provision of these goods, this change in legislation left them with large, redundant sums of capital which were transferred to cloth production. The extent of the shift was considerable. Le Flem documents an increase in the percentage of notarial contracts devoted to the cloth industry from 40 per cent in 1550 to 80 per cent in 1570 (1976: 532–3). (Such contracts recorded most mercantile transactions.) It was not the case that the small-scale producer had been entirely eliminated from the Castilian industry. As Bilbao and Fernández del

Piñedo show, there was resistance by the guilds to the dominance of commercial capital and smaller towns avoided the pressures and secured changes in the general regulations permitting the production of lower-quality cloth (1988: 135–6). In addition, the relatively large number of clothiers in Segovia (eighty-one in 1584) suggests that cloth-making concerns of all sizes must have continued to exist (Ruiz Martin 1965: 271). Commercial capital, on the other hand, clearly had a variety of ways of involving itself in the production and marketing processes (Iradiel Murugarren 1983: 107–10), and of the overall direction of the trend – a growing predominance of urban commercial capital over out-workers – there can be no question (Bilbao and Fernández del Piñedo 1988: 135).

The fragility of this industrial structure revealed itself fully during the seventeenth century. If the circumstances confronting Spanish industry had been favourable during the sixteenth century, the reverse was the case from 1600. The end of the wars first with England in 1604 and then with the Low Countries in 1609 not only terminated that artificial protection consequent upon warfare from which the Spanish industry had been benefiting, but also resulted in treaties which opened Spanish markets to foreign exploitation. The policy of industrial protection which, with some ups and downs, the Spanish monarchy had been attempting to pursue since the Reconquest was interrupted: no longer did Spain have the political strength to enforce such a policy, and its markets were to suffer a deluge of imports. The domestic industry could not compete against these – its guilds refused to accept the necessary changes, and the merchant manufacturers, on the one hand confronted with these difficulties, and on the other presented with the new possibilities of participating in the export–import trade, introducing foreign cloth and exporting raw materials (principally wool), chose the latter course, disinvesting from the industry on a major scale. The percentage of Segovia's notarial contracts relating to cloth production had dropped to a mere 5 per cent by 1630 (Le Flem 1976: 535).

Some rural production stood up better – there were some gains to be made from the collapse of the urban industry – but not in Segovia's hinterland which had experienced commercial capitalism at first hand. Overall there is again no question of the direction of the trend: de-urbanization and de-industrialization, as a free-trading policy effectively took over from a mercantilist one. Segovia's production had fallen to some 3,700 pieces of cloth per annum by the end of the century and three-quarters of Toledo's silk looms had been lost (Bilbao and Fernández del Piñedo 1988: 137–42).

Iradiel Murugarren's verdict is that there had been a progressive aristocratization of the industry from the first half of the sixteenth century, and that the industrial initiatives had aggravated the misery of the productive classes rather than fomenting a genuinely capitalist system (1974: 246–50).

Catalonia from the seventeenth to nineteenth centuries

If there have been some grounds for doubting the value of relating the proto-industrial model to Castile in view of the area's unsuccessful transition to industrialization, such has clearly never been the case for Catalonia. The region's industrialization was precocious within Europe; it was led by textiles; and it followed a long period of prosperity in the eighteenth century which had at its source an expansion in overseas trade in which both agriculture and industry shared. Finally, demographic conditions were buoyant during this period of growth, the Principality's population nearly doubling during the eighteenth century. The correspondence to the 'proto-industrialization' paradigm is clearly close (Nadal 1975: 188–225).

The exclusion of the area from my analysis up to this point has been determined by limitations of space and a decision to prioritize the experiences of the region during the key period of its transition to industrialization. To provide a background to later developments, however, a brief summary of the Catalan experience from the Middle Ages is of some assistance.

Both Catalonia and Aragon participated in some of the trends which have been described in the last section. A primitive, predominantly subsistence cloth industry, concentrated in mountainous areas of the region's interior, where water power and wool supplies were abundant and where the skills of the more advanced French industry could be drawn upon, progressed during the thirteenth and fourteenth centuries into a large-scale, predominantly urban industry (centred in Barcelona, Gerona and Perpignan), producing principally for Mediterranean markets and the Levant. From the fifteenth century, in contrast, the Catalan performance was less favourable, and although there was some recovery in the sixteenth century, medieval levels of prosperity were not re-attained (Vilar 1962: I, 544–53; Riu 1983: 208–13).

Two aspects of the early Catalan experience were, however, it would seem, distinct, and thus merit emphasis, insofar as they provide potential clues to the causes of the later successful Catalan transition.

The first of these concerns the relationship of commercial capital to industrial development. As in Castile, involvement took the form of the provision of credit, raw materials and the selling by merchants of the final product. However, apart from a short period during the first half of the fourteenth century, when conditions in the cloth industry were exceptionally favourable on account of opportunities for rapid import substitution, and another in the fifteenth, when the silk industry was introduced, merchant capital did not involve itself in the basic production processes (Carrère 1967: I, 522). This characteristic has been accounted for first in terms of the better returns which were to be made in the very wide range of other types of investment in Barcelona, particularly in the importing trades, and secondly in the opposition to the trend from the guilds, which enjoyed rights of political representation on Barcelona's Consell de Cent. In the absence of mercantile investment, the *paraire* became the predominant figure of the Catalan industry and, unusually, had the prospect of effectively rising to merchant status and, consequently, involving himself in mercantile transactions in his own, and other, trades (Carrère 1978: 37–57). This development ensured, in contrast for example to the situation in Cuenca, that the Catalan industry remained an avenue for social mobility and accumulation of capital by individuals from artisanal backgrounds (Vilar 1962: I, 426–7).

The second characteristic of the early Catalan experience meriting emphasis concerns the extent to which the area weathered the crisis of the seventeenth century with its potentially mixed implications for different types of industry, with rural and small-town production possibly standing to gain where urban industries lost. Catalonia's experience would appear to have been distinct from the average: not distinct to the extent that the losses of the urban centres were completely compensated for by a growth in rural or small-town production, but it would certainly seem that the industrial deficit was smaller than elsewhere. From the very inception of the Catalan expansion of the fourteenth century, although the industry had been dominated by the merchant centres of the plain, there had been a tradition of small-town production in the interior which had been maintained and consolidated. Substantial centres, such as Vic, Olot, Berga, Ripoll and Sant Joan de Les Abadesses, concentrated in the Lower Pyrenees, had retained their autonomy during these years with respect to the capitals of the industry, and had experienced a parallel process of 'modernization' with respect to achieving incorporation for their industries, with the advantages which that implied for cloth standardization and quality of production, establishing their own fulling and finishing processes and, equally important, their own sales and wool supply networks. Not only were such smaller centres better placed to survive the crises experienced by the large-scale urban producers but also their existence ensured that when a secondary phase of 'ruralization' of industry began during the sixteenth and seventeenth centuries – one induced by falling demand and a consequent need to cut costs and escape guild restrictions – it had many sources from which to diffuse.

This industrial recovery, led by the Catalan interior, began to make some impact on the regional economy during the second half of the seventeenth century. It is to this period that Pierre Vilar traces the roots of Catalonia's modern growth process (1962: I, 646–53). The expansion was halted by the War of the Spanish Succession but revived after 1714, and continued throughout the eighteenth century. It has been studied by the Catalan historian Jaume Torras who argues that the initial stimulus to the growth did not come from growth in export markets for cloth, but rather from agricultural expansion – the export of agricultural products, above all of wine and eau-de-vie, from south-eastern Catalonia. The consequent higher agricultural earnings and levels of employment on the one hand drove out local proto-industry and on the other stimulated that of those mountainous areas of the Principality which were deficient in agricultural resources. There was, consequently, an increasing agricultural-industrial specialization within the Principality, with gains in efficiency. The contribution to industrialization proper, Torras argues, did not consist so much in capital accumulation and technical or managerial expertise, but in the indirect benefits accruing from higher levels of employment, and thus higher incomes and demand, and the creation of a labour market (Torras 1984: 113–27).

Those areas benefiting from this division of labour produced, principally, low- to medium-quality cloth. In addition, another sector of the regional cloth industry was in expansion, the sector concentrating on higher-quality cloth. This was concentrated principally close to the coast – in Barcelona itself and in the neighbouring towns of Igualada, Terrassa and Sabadell. More recent work by Torras on one of these centres, Igualada, provides additional insights into the character of the Catalan growth experience. Such centres experienced a development into a *Verlagssystem* organization of production, with a handful of families emerging from relative obscurity to positions of dominance. In this process three elements were fundamental: close collaboration between the family members of the ascendant entrepreneurial class, the undermining of traditional guild restrictions on such concentration by means of lengthy court cases, and the building up of extensive market networks by clothiers within the national market. The growth dynamic was, thus, distinct from that previously analysed, with industrial concentration developing on the basis of success in penetrating the peninsular market. In addition, the potential impact on industrialization was different.

Capital accumulation and the gaining of entrepreneurial expertise were clearly significant, enabling these towns to maximize the advantages to be obtained from the more liberal economic regime which came into existence after 1789 and from the beginning of the mechanization process. The extensive market networks which were established also served the following industrialization process (Torras 1987: 145–60).

Following this pioneering work, other local studies have been carried out. Josep-Maria Muñoz has demonstrated that the successful nineteenth-century industrialization of Sabadell and Terrassa was anticipated by eighteenth-century 'pre-industrial' growth (1984: 399–410). By contrast, Asumpta Muset has discovered that although the industrial development of Olesa and Esparraguera in the eighteenth century conformed to the principal elements in Mendels' model, it was not followed by industrialization: the two industries experienced structural problems and decline, and their contribution to industrialization was limited to the provison of labour forces for the textile factories elsewhere (1989: 45–68). These diverging studies express well the complexity of 'proto-industrialization' in Catalonia. The political turbulence of the period, and the fluctuating advantages between rural and urban industrial location which this, and mechanization, occasioned, caused repeated geographical shifts in industrialization, and thus total continuity between proto-industrialization and industrialization was not to have been expected. The complex nature of the relationship has been most fully explored in a thesis by Enriqueta Camps on labour migration during the industrialization process. The textile industry was characterized by high rates of labour mobility, she shows, but this did not result in the labour market's being disorganized and characterized by discontinuity. On the contrary, there were strong links between proto-industrial and industrialized employment, with labour migration tending to take place at specific points in the family life-cycle when the economic burdens on textile workers were greatest. Family networks, and the possession of industrial skills, were as important to textile workers in ensuring their survival in the unstable conditions which characterized the industry, as they were for the employer class in its drive for enrichment (1990: 82–183).

Putting these various studies together, a picture emerges about links between proto-industrialization and industrialization in the area. Camps' and Muset's research confirms the emphasis placed by Torras in his earlier work on the importance of the industrial expansion of the Catalan interior in the establishment of a labour market, while that of Muñoz confirms the other thread in Torras' interpretation – the centrality of the entrepreneurial and financial role in industrialization played by the proto-industrial centres along the Catalan Littoral. A further, challenging study, that of Gabriele Ranzato on Sabadell, indeed suggests that the extent of capital accumulation achieved by some industrial families in these centres in the vicinity of Barcelona during the eighteenth century was such that it enabled them to dominate the towns in which they lived, both politically and financially, throughout the nineteenth century. In this case, a link with proto-industry is shown, but one which was not necessarily optimal (1987: 7–16).

There is a central element missing, on the other hand – cotton, the industry which was to dominate Catalonia's industrial revolution. Its omission, it has been argued, is justifiable as it was a new industry, which could not thus have been contributed to by proto-industrialization (González Enciso 1984a: 26). A preliminary step must thus consist in clarifying the relationship between cotton and the process which I have been describing.

In a variety of ways the experience of cotton did not conform to the proto-industrialization paradigm: the expansion of the industry was not a consequence of a gradual shift to respective industrial and agricultural specializations; production was initially urban rather than rural and concentrated in large manufactories; sales were in the home market, rather than for export. This is not to say, however, that the early development of this industry was not important for the later industrialization process. Its experience needs to be considered.

The source of the industry lay in prohibitions in 1717 and 1728 against the import of Asian, and later European imitations of Asian, calicoes and the granting of privileges (*franquicias*) to manufactories founded to substitute for these imports. From the start, commercial capital was extensively involved in the industry. The large scale of production can be explained partly by the exceptional size of the investment which wholesale merchants were in a position to make (Thomson 1991: 57–89). The growth of the industry was rapid but confined almost entirely to Barcelona – the city contained over 100 manufactories by the 1780s, the largest concentration of such concerns in Europe (Thomson 1990: 86). It limited itself almost entirely to the weaving and finishing processes up to this point, with the consequence that its social and economic impact was reduced, but from the 1780s, again with encouragement from the state, there was a rapid extension into spinning, with the introduction of manual techniques being rapidly followed by that of mechanical ones (Thomson 1992: 235–67).

On the basis of this short summary, some assessment of the contributions made by the pre-factory cotton industry to the later industrialization process is possible. The growth of the industry, it is clear, represented a means of accumulation and preparation in all sorts of spheres – capital accumulation, technological progress, the development of managerial and entrepreneurial expertise and the establishing of supply and marketing networks. That these changes were principally concentrated within Barcelona does not mean that their impact was restricted to the city – Barcelona was a pole of attraction to migrant labour from the Catalan interior, and the influence of its merchant capital radiated throughout the Principality. Besides, from the 1780s both calico-printing and, on a bigger scale, spinning and cotton weaving began to diffuse rapidly outside the city walls and in the case of the latter it did so in the form of the domestic production unit.

An apparently stronger ground for questioning the link with the industrialization process has been that the industry experienced a severe crisis in the late 1790s and the early nineteenth century as a consequence of the disruptions to economic life following the French Revolution. The extent of discontinuity was such that the most generally accepted viewpoint has been that industrialization effectively had to start again from scratch in the 1830s. Such an interpretation, it is clear, would leave little place to the legacies of proto-industrialization in the industrialization process. Recent research, however, has established that the discontinuity was not total – some of the eighteenth-century achievement survived to act as a permissive factor facilitating the recovery after 1830. Most affected were the large calico-printing manufactories, whereas the expanding spinning industry and a new sector, the weaving of cotton cloth outside the large manufactories, suffered less. Although trading circumstances were difficult during these years, technological change, the incorporation of spinning into the industry and the greater industrial freedom with respect to guild restrictions and rural working provided economic opportunities to those flexible enough to take advantage of them. Those in this position were predominantly the small production units, operating according to the domestic system. This sector of the industry expanded and its proliferation ensured continuity with respect to the eighteenth-century development of cotton on the basis of the 'proto-factory'.

There were indeed some improvements in the character of the contribution made to industrialization by this second phase in the growth of the cotton industry. The ease with which cotton-manufacturing skills could be learnt, the compatibility of the industry initially with the domestic unit of production and the fact that it was a new industry in which there were no vested interests or guild restrictions to oppose its diffusion had the consequence that it spread rapidly throughout

Catalonia, becoming Catalonia's first 'national' industry and achieving a rapid breakthrough with respect to the types of restrictions which had previously confined industries to particular towns (Thomson 1992: 235–319; Sánchez 1992: 65–114).

Studies of Spanish proto-industrialization

Rafael Aracil and M. García Bonafé were responsible for the first, general studies on 'proto-industrialization' in Spain. In these they emphasized the extent and variety of proto-industrial activity, documenting the existence of some 3,000 localities with some form of proto-industry in the early nineteenth century. On the basis of an analysis of industrial surveys for the regions of Castile, Estremadura, Galícia and Salamanca-Zamora at the end of the eighteenth century, they showed the existence of 34,000 looms producing some 15 million meters of cloth, amounting to one loom for every 130 inhabitants and production of 3.34 meters of cloth per inhabitant at this stage.

On the other hand, by means of maps showing the density of industrial activity at various stages of the eighteenth and nineteenth centuries, they demonstrated that, with the exception of the Catalan region and some areas of Valencia, industry became more, rather than less, dispersed over this period. There are two aspects to their explanation for this relative failure. Comparing the Castilian textile developments with those of the rest of Europe for the early modern period, they argue that the form of development was 'Florentine', rather than 'English', by which they mean that it was characterized by that combination of strong guilds and a predatory merchant capital, restrictive of capital accumulation, which was noted in the first section of this chapter. With respect to the eighteenth and nineteenth centuries, they attribute the diverging performances to agricultural systems and to the strength of commercial capital. Market developments in the Catalan area stimulated industrial change, whereas the low productivity of agricultural production elsewhere gave rise to a continued need to supplement agricultural earnings with by-employment in industry; proto-industry, in these conditions, served as a prop to the survival of feudalism (1978: 113–29; 1983: 83–102).

Agustin González Enciso has taken a more literalist approach in his use of proto-industrial terminology, arguing that the term can only be applied legitimately to Catalonia and Galícia. Elsewhere, he points out, there is lack of evidence of that type of fruitful interaction between agriculture and industry, followed by industrialization proper, which characterizes the proto-industrial model. In addition, he argues that the market element of the model does not appear to have corresponded to the Spanish case generally. Commercial involvement there was, in numerous industrial centres, but it was relatively weak, with manufacturers very often carrying out their own marketing, and there was a significant lack of towns purely specializing in commerce (as did Liverpool, for instance, in England). Barcelona, for example, combined commerce with industry. Finally he attaches importance to guilds: these were restrictive, possibly more restrictive than elsewhere (1984b: 51–82; 1984a: 11–46).

Behind González Enciso's arguments lies the fact that Spain was an industrial 'late-comer' and, in view of this, industrialization was largely imported rather than being, as is the premise for the proto-industrial model, consequent upon a gradual change in the pre-industrial economy. Despite this characteristic, Torras has argued in a paper which extends his work on the Catalan region to a consideration of the performance of the Spanish economy as a whole, that an analysis of the Spanish experience of the eighteenth century provides clues as to the causes of the diverging regional experiences of industrialization in the nineteenth century. The premise of his approach is that the eighteenth century, with rapid population growth, generally favourable agrarian conditions and the Bourbon monarchy supporting industrial change in a variety of ways, was a particularly favourable period for industrial growth: consequently there is the possibility of comparing regional responses to this favourable situation and also assessing the extent to which these varied responses influenced the industrialization process of the following century.

A first and important point which he emphasizes is Spain's political weakness, which barred it from protecting its markets fully from foreign products. Throughout the eighteenth century, it remained the principal European destination for English cloth exports. There was one exception to this impotence, however: cotton. In the case of cotton, Spain enjoyed *carte blanche* with respect to industrial policy, and responded to this situation with the restrictions summarized in the previous section. In other industrial sectors, however, the import-substitution effort had to be confined to items of lower to medium quality, for which the high ratio of transport costs to value provided a natural protection to the Spanish product.

Torras makes various distinctions about the types of response to this market situation. Galicia's linen industry had all the appearance of being optimal. Expansion in production was such that the industry was forced to rely increasingly on imported yarn and by the end of the century a significant industrial specialization had developed, the total number of looms involved in linen production in Spain (most of them in Galicia) having risen to some 15,000. The industry conformed to the proto-industrial model insofar as much of its product was 'exported' to other parts of Spain, but from other points of view it barely qualifies for consideration, since the capital accumulation to which it gave rise was minimal – the main consequence of its growth was a rise in the density of local population – and, rather than encouraging a reciprocal industrial-agricultural specialization, it was characterized by joint agrarian and industrial activity, both on a very small scale (1989: 1–13).

Since Torras wrote this paper, a study by Joám Carmona Badía has further added to our understanding of the failure of this industry to generate an industrialized successor. In addition to stressing the particular inertia of the Galician agrarian sector, he emphasizes first that the practice in the local industry of bleaching its cloth in the yarn, rather than in the piece, meant that it was done by the producer, rather than as elsewhere by the merchant, occasioning less possibility for accumulation of capital. Secondly, there was little in the way of a local merchant class involved in the commercializing of the final product: this was done on a very small scale, by pedlars and the producers themselves. What mercantile involvement there was tended to be based in the receiving areas for the cloth: the industry was deprived again of a local mercantile accumulation of capital (1990: 233–6).

A second important response to the favourable demand situation, but one again which only occasioned short-term growth, was the establishment of a range of state manufactories or state-supported manufactories, most notably that of Guadalajara. Research has shown, however, that these were never competitive, but depended throughout on income from the Treasury. Their impact on local industry was, if anything, negative, and their demise was not followed by spontaneous industrialization (La Force 1965: 28–50, González Enciso 1975: 41–64). Positive development was thus restricted first to the success of a number of wool-producing centres in achieving growth and capital accumulation on the basis of medium-quality production – some of the centres already mentioned in Catalonia, others, like Alcoi, in neighbouring Valencia, Antequera in Andalusia and Bejar in Castile (García Sanz 1994) – and secondly to Catalonia's urban cotton industry. Other textile producers did no more than follow the fluctuations in the agrarian cycle, expanding and contracting production.

Although these areas which responded successfully to the opportunities of the eighteenth century, and thus experienced 'proto-industrial development', were scattered throughout Spain, there was an overwhelming concentration of them in Catalonia and Valencia. The greater flexibility of these areas' economies is attributed by Torras to their having developed market economies, with agrarian-industrial specializations, and consequently achieving capital accumulation and economies of scale in their industrial sectors. He also reiterates the importance to the Catalan success of the building of marketing networks throughout Spain during the eighteenth century, a development which was encouraged by the gradual removal of customs restrictions between Castile and Aragon from 1717 (1989: 1–13).

Conclusion

In this chapter I have shown how an early period of industrial expansion in Castile was brought to an end, and probably had negative consequences on the region, because of a combination of too great an intrusion by commercial capital, which did not permit accumulation of capital in rural industry, restrictive guilds and a failure to provide protection, which was soon followed by large-scale industrial disinvestment.

Catalonia, I have argued, was spared the worst of these trends insofar as its commercial capital generally avoided industrial investment, permitting regular accumulation of capital within the industry, and in that it developed a successful and competitive small-town and rural industry which showed greater staying power than its urban counterpart.

This represented a promising base, it was shown in the second section of the chapter, for a response to the eighteenth-century opportunities provided by the growth in the regional and national markets. By contrast, the relative lack of response in Castile and other Spanish regions to these opportunities suggests that the flaws in their economies created by the character of their responses to the economic opportunities of the fifteenth and sixteenth centuries had endured. A sign of this was the need to resort to royal manufactories to stimulate industrial growth – not that they were successful – whereas responses to market opportunities on an individual and private basis had been multiple before the sixteenth century.

Catalan eighteenth-century industrial growth, I have argued, both in the wool and cotton industries, represented an important contribution from many points of view – the establishment of a labour market, capital accumulation, the development of managerial and entrepreneurial skills, an increase in technical skills and the creation of marketing networks – to the area's successful industrialization in the nineteenth century. It has been seen that the principal reason for this having occurred was the development of a market economy in which there was a fruitful interaction between industrial and agricultural change.

In contrast, it has been seen that the abundant, traditional rural industry in other parts of Spain, according to some scholars barely deserving of the epithet of proto-industry, which survived well into the twentieth century in many cases, acted as more of a barrier than a stimulus to industrialization, because it consolidated subsistence agricultural economies and deflated the national market for consumer goods.

An additional, negative characteristic of Spanish proto-industry was its exceptional concentration in one region, Catalonia. Torras has argued that this, while consolidating the identification of the Catalan personality with hard work, contributed to the creation of 'an additional barrier to the diffusion of the social values associated with the rise and development of modern capitalism' in other parts of Spain (1989: 10).

8 Proto-industry in Flanders: a critical review

Christiaan Vandenbroeke

The problem is well known. At the beginning of 1972, Franklin Mendels formulated a theoretical concept of domestic industry, or proto-industry, based on the example of Flanders. From this followed a plethora of publications. The Eighth International Economic History Congress, held in Budapest in 1982, was a landmark event for the study of proto-industry, which was one of its main themes (Mendels 1982).

From the very start, this theoretical model was subjected to very severe criticism (Ogilvie 1993a). The concept was based on demographic as well as socio-economic premises which Mendels believed were present in Flanders. In more ways than one, however, these premises have been refuted, and quite often even utterly contradicted, by in-depth investigations (Vandenbroeke 1981, 1984). The following survey of proto-industry in Flanders will seek to illustrate this.

It is important to get one thing straight right from the start. It is clear why Mendels concentrated on Flanders in his study. After all, this region was characterized, long before the eighteenth century, by very high population density, enormous fragmentation of landholdings, rapid population growth and sensational expansion of the linen industry. Far-reaching disparities among regions can also be distinguished, with predominantly agrarian areas on the one hand, and on the other, areas in which more than a quarter of the population was active in the linen industry (Mendels 1972, 1981). Participation in the linen industry was particularly high in southern and central Flanders, both areas characterized by the largest degree of fragmentation of landholding (but also very high proportions of the population owning land), and the fastest population growth. This suggests the existence of a positive relationship between proto-industry and demography. The causal relationship between the two, however, differs a great deal from the one proposed by Mendels and later supported by David Levine and Hans Medick (Medick 1976a; Levine 1976). We will return to this question shortly, but first let us examine more closely the regional disparities in rural organization in Flanders, and the level of activity in domestic industry.

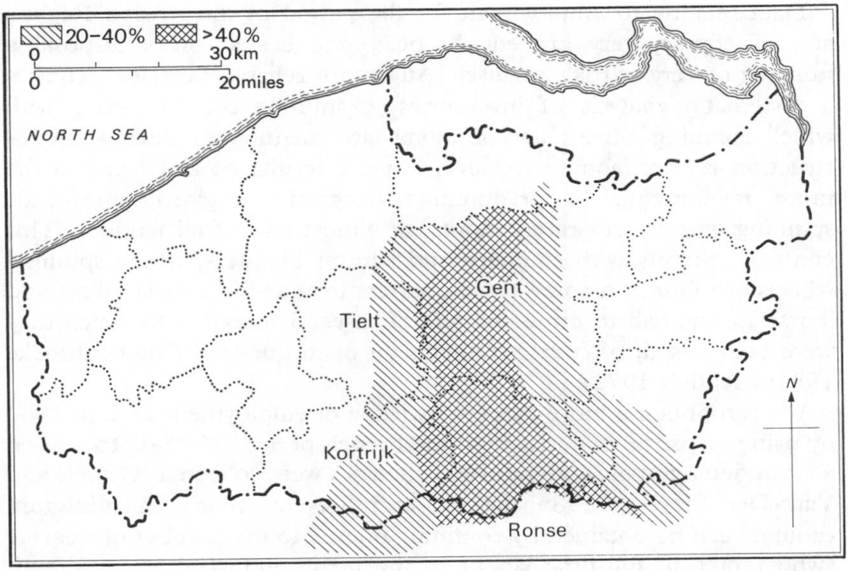

Map 8.1 The textile industry in Flanders, *c.* 1765: the proportion of households active in the textile industry

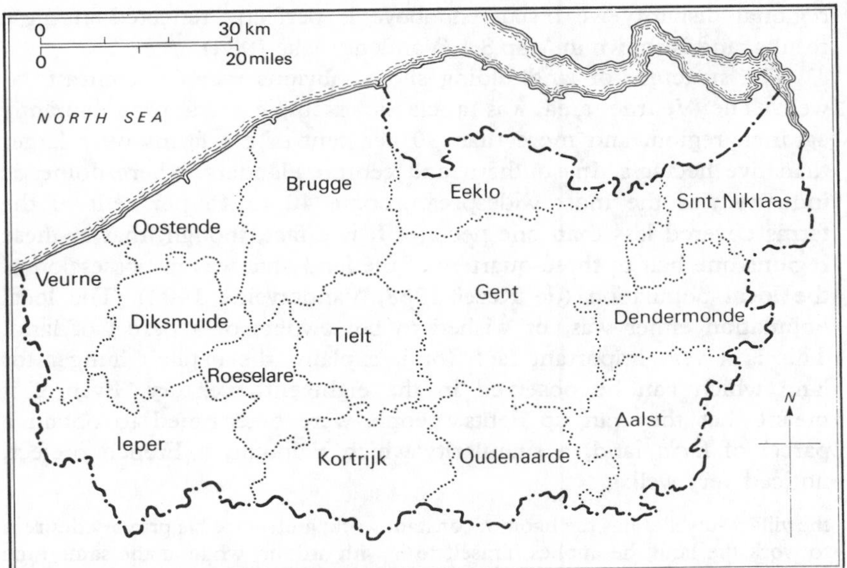

Map 8.2 Map of Flanders

Data relating to employment for the period of the Ancien Régime are, of course, very limited. At best, one has at one's disposal a number of very partial censuses. Any more reliable overview requires a systematic analysis of inventories, examining the frequency with which spinning wheels and/or looms are mentioned. Such a reconstruction is very labour intensive, but the results obtained are all the more meaningful. In predominantly agrarian regions, one finds spinning wheels, but rarely looms, in almost half of all families. This contrasts sharply with southern and central Flanders, where spinning wheels are found in some three-quarters to four-fifths of families, and looms in one half to three-quarters of cases. The extent to which they were being used, of course, remains an open question (Vandenbroeke 1984; Mendels 1972).

We can obtain a more exact knowledge of employment around 1800 by using statistical material from the French period (1795–1815), when a lot of demographic and industrial statistics were collected (Gyssels and Van Der Straeten 1986; Jaspers and Stevens 1985). A minimum estimate can be obtained by confining oneself to the number of weavers (who represent full-time labour in the textile industry). A maximum estimate can be obtained by also taking into account agricultural workers and day-labourers, and assuming that they were active part of their time in agriculture and part in domestic industry. In any case, the regional disparity we discussed above is perfectly reflected in these results, and is shown in Map 8.1 (Vandenbroeke 1984).

The structure of landholding shows obvious regional contrasts as well. The Veurne area was a classic example of a predominantly agrarian region, and more than 90 per cent of the farms were larger than five hectares. In southern and central Flanders, where domestic industry was the most widespread, some 40 to 45 per cent of the farms covered less than one hectare. It is a fact, though, that in these regions one half to three-quarters of the land area was in possession of the local population (de Kezel 1988; Vandervelde 1902). The local population either was, or wished to be, owners of a parcel of land. This is a very important fact, for it explains the explicit hunger for land which can be observed in the eighteenth century. Even if it meant that they ran up debts, people were determined to obtain a parcel of farm land, a singularity which Faipoult, a French prefect, noticed very well:

> the village-dweller has the habit of constant work; and, since his primary desire is to work the land, he applies himself to it with ardour, while at the same time devoting to the work of weaving or spinning of flax and wool all the moments which he cannot employ in cultivation. Many of the village-dwellers achieved

some affluence from this advantageous regime, and desired to become farmers and not merely day-labourers. The land holdings have been divided up astonishingly. (Faipoult 1800: 103)

Recent micro-studies cannot but confirm this. Local residents, including small farmers and agricultural workers, monopolized some three-quarters to four-fifths of all land sales (de Kezel 1988; Van Isterdael 1980).

There are also some striking differences in the development of population in Flanders. These differences are both chronological and geographical. It has been shown that population growth was most remarkable during the first sixty years of the eighteenth century. Compared to the rest of the world, southern and central Flanders attained a very high population growth rate at that time. Yet by the end of the Ancien Régime there occurred a clear slow-down, a logical result of increasing difficulties in these regions (Vandenbroeke 1981).

Geographically, a clear distinction in population growth can be drawn between areas with a rapid expansion of domestic industry, areas which were predominantly agrarian, and urban centres (Deprez 1965). An advanced process of ruralization was typical of the eighteenth century, and especially of the middle of that century. This process has been described by Eckart Schremmer as a 'territorialization of craft industry' (Schremmer 1976). We can therefore speak of a process of de-urbanization. This can be illustrated by showing, in Figure 8.1, the population of Ghent relative to the total population of eastern Flanders. These regional contrasts are further illustrated in Figure 8.2 (Vandenbroeke 1984).

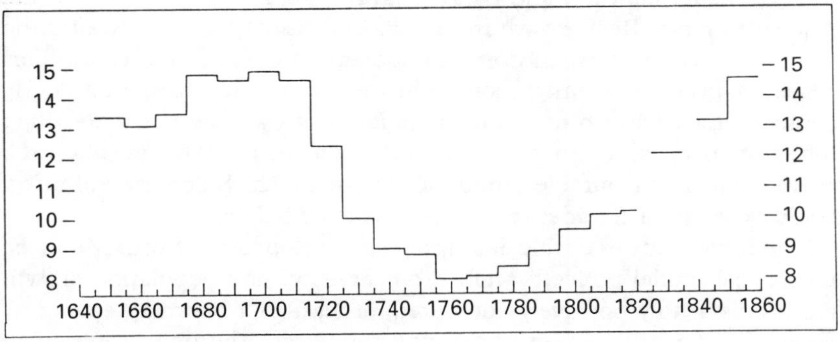

Figure 8.1 The population of Ghent as a proportion of the total population of eastern Flanders, 1640–1860 (%)

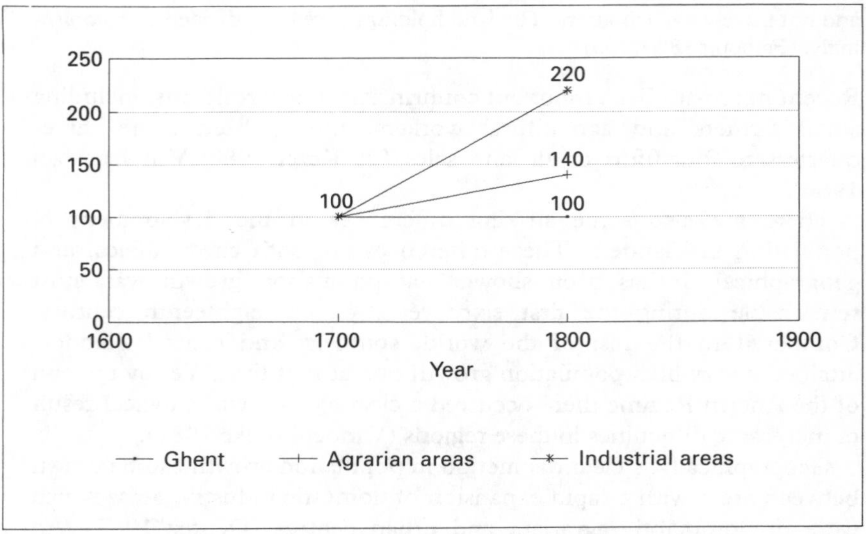

Figure 8.2 Index of population growth in southern and central Flanders, 1700–1800 (1700 = 100)

In real terms, southern and central Flanders more than doubled their populations during the eighteenth century in those dynamic areas in which a booming domestic industry offered plenty of employment. There were also the agrarian areas, which – logically – had a very limited growth of population. Lastly, there was the development of population in urban areas, which was characterized by decline during the first half of the eighteenth century, and by gradual recuperation by the end of the Ancien Régime. Real growth in the urban areas appeared only after the turn of the century, when domestic industry entered into a crisis. This caused a process of emigration from the countryside to the cities. By contrast, the eighteenth-century population growth figures were quite different, because there was no 'rural flight' at all. This suggests the prevalence of a favourable economic climate in which domestic industry could develop for decades (as will be discussed below).

The basic features of this demographic development fit with Mendels' theoretical model perfectly well. Proto-industry and population growth are unmistakably positively correlated, at least in a booming economy. However, the explanation underlying this is not the one proposed in Mendels' model. For one thing, population growth in proto-industrial areas certainly cannot be related to a more intensive nuptial pattern and higher fertility. Moreover, both Mendels and later Levine conclude that – by definition – proto-industry led to impoverishment, one of the results being that mortality increased. Each of these starting points of the proto-industrial model is completely contradicted by empirical studies.

This can easily be demonstrated by an abundance of evidence. Fairly rough indicators, such as birth and marriage rates, show virtually continous decline between the late seventeenth and the mid-nineteenth century (Vandenbroeke 1984). Around 1700, the birth rate in the Flemish countryside was 45 per thousand, while around 1840 it was about 30 per thousand. Within that same period, the marriage rate fell by an average of 12 per thousand, to barely 6 per thousand. Permanent celibacy increased by one quarter, with all of the attendant consequences: in the early nineteenth century, one fifth to one quarter of the population were completely renouncing marriage. That is, parallel to the expansion of domestic industry was created a more restrictive marriage pattern, not a more intensive one. The same also applies to a large number of other areas on the European continent (Wrigley 1985b; Gutmann 1987). Not surprisingly, this resulted in an ageing age structure, and certainly not in a younger one. As can be seen in Table 8.1, this contrasted with the situation in Great Britain, where a more intensive marriage pattern did emerge, resulting in a younger age structure (Floud and McCloskey 1981). Mendels and Levine completely ignored this distinction between Great Britain and the continent.

A restrictive marriage pattern, with average ages at first marriage of 26–8 for women and 28–30 for men, has been found in family reconstitutions for about thirty localities in Flanders (Vandenbroeke 1981, 1984). The implications of this finding for proto-industrialization can best be seen by relating them to a comparative survey. The 1796 census (Gyssels and Van Der Straeten 1986; Jaspers and Stevens 1985) allows us systematically to compare nuptial behaviour by geographical area by defining an index of nuptiality (Im). At the same time, this indicator can be subjected to a Spearman correlation test, to investigate its relationship with the degree of participation of the population in domestic industry (see Table 8.2).

The resulting coefficient of correlation between participation in the textile industry and the index of nuptiality is $R = -0.196$. This confirms that the relationship between proto-industry and nuptiality was not only non-existent, but actually negative. We have already explained the deeper reason for this: to engage in spinning and/or weaving, even though they might at times be lucrative businesses, was only an alternative. The real fulfilment was to set up in business as a farmer and to own a parcel of land (even a very small one); nothing else was so

Table 8.1 *The age structure of the population in Flanders and Great Britain at the end of the eighteenth and the beginning of the nineteenth century (%)*

Age group	Flanders			Great Britain		
	1796	1815	1846	1791	1821	1842
0–19	43.0	45.3	40.2	42.3	49.0	46.1
20–39	29.0	27.4	30.6	26.7	27.5	29.0
40–59	19.0	18.7	20.4	19.1	15.9	15.8
60+	9.0	8.6	8.8	11.8	7.3	7.2

Table 8.2 *Arrondissements of Flanders according to participation in the textile industry in 1796 and various demographic indicators, 1750–1850*

Arrondissement	Proportion of population active in textile industry in 1796	Index of nuptiality (Im) in 1796	Index of fertility (Ig) in 1796	Infant mortality (<1 year) in 1800	Illegitimacy 1750–1800 (%)	Illegitimacy 1840–50 (%)	Pre-nuptial conceptions 1750–1800 (%)
Veurne	2	0.494	1.032	32.5	1.46	2.51	6.7
Oostende	1	0.529	0.999	21.7	2.44	4.23	2.9
Brugge	6	0.522	0.969	20.2	1.61	4.18	3.5
Diksmuide	3	0.450	1.242	30.4	2.37	3.35	11.4
Ieper	8	0.451	1.029	20.7	2.26	5.26	25.0
Roeselare	27	0.473	0.887	20.1	1.73	4.66	5.5
Tielt	17	0.479	0.884	15.9	2.54	4.32	9.0
Kortrijk	15	0.477	1.025	17.9	1.69	4.61	20.5
Eeklo	22	0.484	0.878	17.7	2.26	4.10	6.4
Gent	21	0.463	0.917	17.7	2.79	4.15	24.1
Oudenaarde	25	0.466	0.924	15.1	4.10	6.70	26.0
Sint-Niklaas	7	0.421	1.055	26.1	1.63	3.70	25.5
Dendermonde	11	0.438	0.924	21.7	2.40	4.30	19.3
Aalst	12	0.485	0.898	13.9	3.01	5.70	30.5

important. This also explains the very sharp rise in the price of land throughout the eighteenth century, which was more than the rise in land rents. Thus the land rent declined from about 4 to 5 per cent of the value of the land around 1700 to barely 1 to 2 per cent around 1800 (Mendels 1972).

For the most part, it was the native population which tried to get possession of a piece of land, a finding which immediately refutes the assumption that there occurred a continuous process of impoverishment. Impoverishment and expropriation are typical of the nineteenth century, when both agriculture and domestic industry went through a severe crisis – but the situation was totally different in the eighteenth century. Around 1800, Faipoult, a contemporary who was a particularly sharp observer, was still describing the material situation of the population in very favourable terms: 'all the villages present an appearance of affluence and neatness which astounds the traveller, whose glance is met in other districts, which have already been denuded of such resources and employment, by very different scenes' (Faipoult 1800: 110). Around 1780, the French traveller Dérival had evaluated the situation in similar terms: 'All the inhabitants of the towns of the Low Countries live, if not in opulence, at least in the greatest of affluence; but this affluence is even greater in the countryside ... the population that lives there is a fortunate population' (Dérival 1782–3: I, 9–10). A few years later, in 1788, Shaw made the same remark: 'the face of the labourer, his healthful nourishment, and his clean dwelling, all show that he shares in that abundance which his industry propagates in his fields' (Shaw 1788: 82). It is thus not surprising that the theoretical model which postulates the existence of proletarian demographic behaviour is contradicted by reality.

The same applies to fertility. Whereas the theoretical model postulates that fertility was higher in areas characterized by strong expansion of domestic industry, empirical studies for Flanders show exactly the opposite. A comparative analysis of fertility, based on the 1796 census, generates very clear results. A test of the correlation between participation in proto-industry and fertility (expressed by the index of marital fertility (Ig)) yields a very high negative value ($R = -0.740$). In other words, fertility was highest in very agrarian areas, and lowest in areas with a great deal of domestic industry!

The reasons behind these regional contrasts have to do with nursing habits and women's position in the production process. A high degree of domestic industry implies home labour, and a long lactation process (twelve months or more). In most cases, lactation causes temporary sterility, with the result that there are longer intervals between births. A side effect of this long and frequent nursing is lower infant mortality. In other words, in southern and central Flanders, where proto-industry was most highly developed, there were fewer births, but also fewer children's deaths (Vandenbroeke 1984). Again, a correlation test illustrates this perfectly. There is a strong negative correlation ($R = -0.749$) between proto-industry and infant mortality and, turning it around, a strong positive correlation between marital fertility and infant mortality ($R = +0.774$).

Before ending this examination of correlations between proto-industry and demographic behaviour, let us examine the relationship between participation in proto-industry on the one hand and illegitimate births and pre-nuptial conceptions on the other. These two indicators provide an indirect way of characterizing the conduct of young people in courtship and choice of partners. The proto-industrial model assumes that in predominantly agrarian areas courtship and marriage were closely supervised, while in areas of domestic industry there was more freedom (Levine 1977; Medick 1976a). Correlation tests indeed point in this direction; however, the results obtained turn out to be weak. The correlation between proto-industry and illegitimate births in the late eighteenth century is positive, but rather low, at R = +0.377. By the middle of the nineteenth century, the correlation is higher, at R = +0.516.

The correlation between proto-industry and pre-nuptial conceptions turns out to be totally different. For the late eighteenth century, we get a weak positive correlation, at R = +0.248. Half a century later, by the middle of the nineteenth century, this has completely reversed itself, and we obtain a somewhat stronger *negative* value, R = −0.442. This was a result of the desperate crisis through which proto-industry passed in this later period. When women got pregnant, they no longer got married, and this resulted in a sharp increase in numbers of illegitimate children during the first half of the nineteenth century.

Rounding off this analytical section on demography, it turns out that a positive relationship between population growth and proto-industry in eighteenth-century Flanders is the only thing that can be corroborated. But the reasons behind this positive relationship are totally different from the theoretical model put forward by Mendels and Levine. The interaction between proto-industry and nuptiality, fertility and mortality turn out to be completely different to that proposed in the proto-industrial model. The positive relationship between population growth and proto-industry is to be explained mainly in terms of a lack of push factors, resulting in ruralization of the population, and this in turn was because for a considerable period of time employment in agriculture and domestic industry provided relatively favourable perspectives. The fact that we observe this in eighteenth-century Flanders also means that it is necessary to subject the thesis of proto-industrial pauperization to a significant nuancing. A process of pauperization did not become a reality in Flanders until the nineteenth century. In the eighteenth century, particulary in the second and third quarter of the century, proto-industry experienced a period of relative prosperity (Jeannin 1980). The implications of this fact will be further explored in the remainder of this chapter.

According to the theoretical model, proto-industry is logically related to a phase of over-population, and can be labelled as a continuous self-propelling process of pauperization. We have already shown that it is possible to refute this causality in terms of demographic factors. The relationship between proto-industry and the material environment must also be evaluated more subtly than proposed by the theoretical model. For Flanders, in particular, it is necessary to distinguish three phases in the development of proto-industry. When we do this, we find that the starting period (from the sixteenth to the seventeenth century) and the final period (the nineteenth century) did indeed see a direct relationship with socio-economic crises and pauperization. However, this is by no means true of the intermediate period, the eighteenth century, when proto-industry combined with employment in agriculture was associated with relative comfort (Vandenbroeke 1981, 1984).

The deeper background for the emergence of semi-industrial activities in rural Flanders remains vague. It is clear, however, that it dates back to as early as the thirteenth and fourteenth centuries, and thus is situated much earlier than the demographic revolution of the early eighteenth century (Gullickson 1983). Furthermore, it is now clear that the more systematic expansion of domestic industry can be quite precisely dated to around the middle of the seventeenth century. At that point in time, any exaggerated population growth was out of the question. Taxes and fiscal extraction were considerably increased at this time, and this resulted in an increased dedication of the population to work (Vandenbroeke 1984).

This resulted in the realization of a higher 'worker productivity' throughout the year. In summer, there was work in the agricultural sector, in winter in textiles. Particularly the small farms characteristic of southern and central Flanders worked in this way.

The further development and growth which took place throughout the eighteenth century simply indicates the existence of a particularly expansive economic climate, with favourable conditions for work in many sectors. There are various causes for this: the high degree of involvement of the local population in land transactions and the rapidly increasing consumption of so-called luxury items (including coffee, tea, tobacco and chocolate) which boosted domestic buying power (Vandenbroeke 1975). A large number of contemporaries confirm this development in purchasing power and buying behaviour. We can quote Bacon (1765) as an example: 'one is no longer interested in home-made products [linen], it is necessary that it be muslin, cotton or other fabrics of the Indies ... there is not one woman nowadays who wears anything but stuffs of the Indies, even down to the village-women' (Hasquin 1978).

Micro-studies, of the type carried out over the past few years, of the

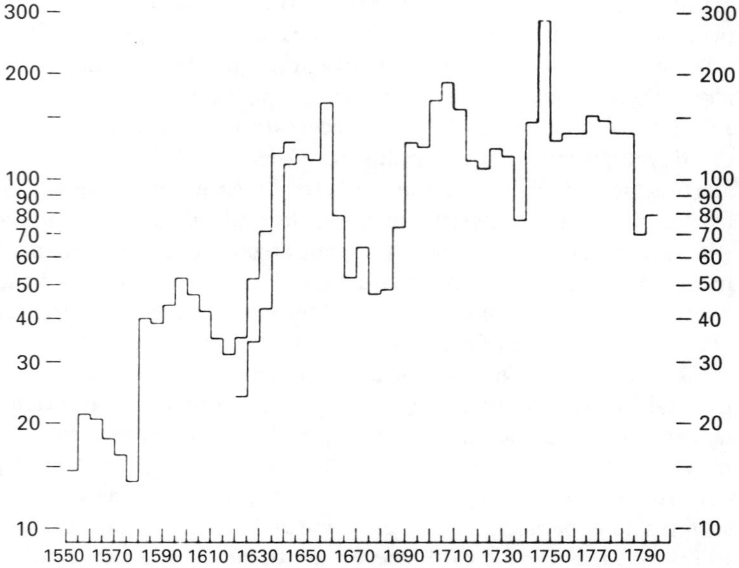

Figure 8.3 Land tax in Flanders, 1550–1800 (in litres of rye per capita)

income and/or earnings of small farmers, day-labourers, agricultural workers and spinner–weavers, wholly confirm the extent to which the mid-eighteenth century should be labelled a 'golden age'. This was a period of enrichment, not of pauperization. The reality of life at this period can be represented in three different sets of findings, each of which consolidates the implications of the others. First, we will examine how many days a full-time weaver had to work to support a (theoretical) family (see Figure 8.4). Then we will follow the development over time in the real wages of a day-labourer (in Figure 8.5), and finally that of the wages of a linen weaver (in Figure 8.6) (Vandenbroeke 1981, 1984).

Naturally, in each case we are dealing with reconstructed estimates; however, these do confirm the favourable socio-economic climate which prevailed in the second and third quarters of the eighteenth century. These findings cast serious doubt on Mendels' assumption that domestic industry, whether as a self-employed activity or in combination with part-time work in agriculture, inevitably led to pauperization. What was crucial was the competitiveness of the sector, an especially important factor in domestic industry, given that some three-quarters to four-fifths of production was destined for the export market. In a period

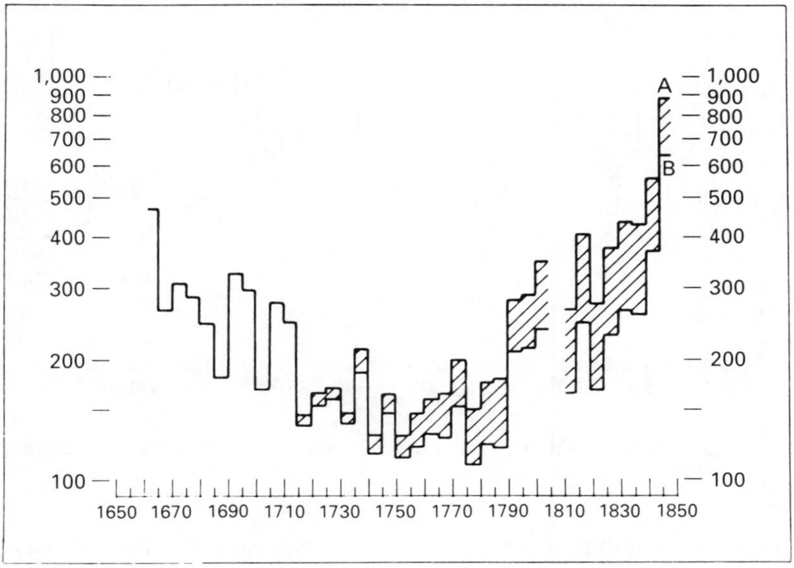

Figure 8.4 The number of working days required by a weaver to support a family, *c.* 1660–1850 (A = without potato consumption; B = with potato consumption)

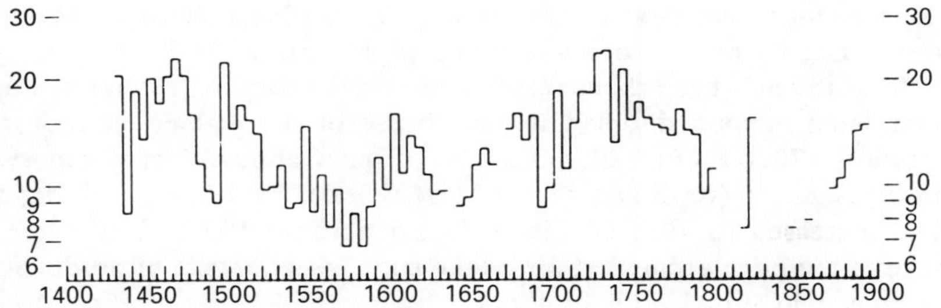

Figure 8.5 The real income of a day-labourer, 1400–1900 (in litres of rye)

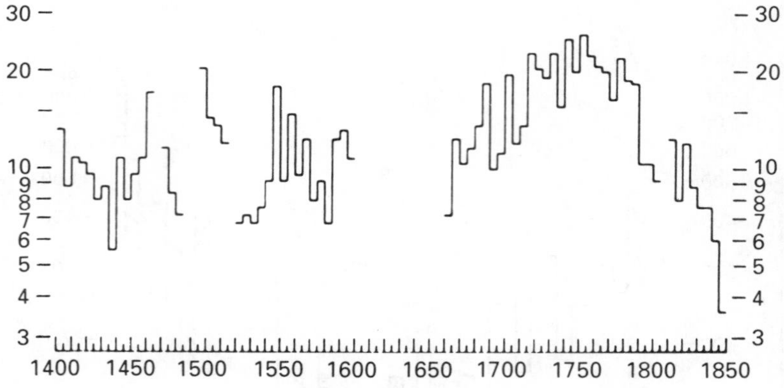

Figure 8.6 The real income of a linen weaver, 1400–1850 (in litres of rye)

with no mechanization or other way of increasing the productivity of labour, competitive advantage is particularly determined by the level of pay. This, indeed, was the reason that domestic industry was mainly located in the countryside, and only commerce in the cities. That competitive advantage was determined by the level of pay is also mentioned by D. C. Coleman (1983). Morineau has explained the success of proto-industry by the end of the Ancien Régime in similar terms: 'it is too often forgotten that the cost of living and, as a consequence, wage-rates were lower in northern Europe, thereby decreasing the net cost of manufacturing' (Morineau 1985: 544).

In Flanders, these characteristics are very apparent. It is no wonder that linen exports doubled in the course of the eighteenth century. Around 1700, about 120,000 pieces of linen annually were exported from Flanders (via Spain to the New World); by 1780–5, this figure had increased to 195,000 pieces (Vandenbroeke 1984). The percentage of the price accounted for by the costs of each stage of production is known in broad outline: about 30 per cent for flax, about 30 per cent for spinning, and 30–5 per cent for weaving (Vandenbroeke 1979). Hence, profit margins were quite low. By the end of the eighteenth century, increasing competition from abroad and from substitutes was pushing down these profit margins. This immediately raises questions about the theoretical proposition according to which proto-industry created a large pool of capital for traders and entrepreneurs, which could subsequently be used for investment in new, modern industrial sectors. Continuity in entrepreneurship between proto-industry and, for example, the cotton industry seems questionable (Mendels 1972).

We can now round off this section on socio-economic developments. The estimated figures quoted above for separate sectors (agriculture, domestic industry, etc.) can be completed by a macro-analysis. The first step in this involves calculating the physical product per head of population in the late eighteenth and the beginning of the nineteenth centuries. These figures can then immediately be compared with those for France and Great Britain, as shown in Table 8.3 (Vandenbroeke 1987).

Given that there were differences among the three countries in rates of inflation, we need to restrict our comparisons to real values, expressed in terms of litres of wheat or kilograms of meat, for example. In any case, the result of such a comparison is self-explanatory. It is a striking finding that Flanders had approximately the same physical product per capita as the two neighbouring countries, even though in several areas of Flanders one quarter of the population was active in domestic industry! This same result still appears for the period around 1800, when domestic industry was past its peak and already fading away owing to competition by mechanized industry.

In other words, the idea that proto-industry saw a continual process of pauperization, as assumed by Mendels, is completely contradicted by the empirical reality. For decades, and especially in the second and third quarters of the eighteenth century, Flanders experienced a period of relative prosperity, thanks to the expansion of the linen industry. Admittedly, this domestic industry was to perish in the course of a particular severe crisis during the first half of the nineteenth century: from the years 1840–5 onwards, the social history of Flanders can indeed be accurately described by the phrase 'poor Flanders'. However, this is another story, a story of loss of competitiveness and a losing battle between low wages in domestic industry and high productivity through mechanization. At that stage, it had already been a long time since the pay level had played a decisive role, as in the pre-industrial situation of the eighteenth century. Nominal wages in Flanders were indeed considerably lower than those in neighbouring countries, 25 per cent lower than in France and 50 per cent lower than in Great Britain. This was of major importance to sectors which specialized in exports and earned profits by competing on international markets. This is also the reason why domestic industry did poorly in the United Provinces of the Netherlands: 'the relatively high wages in the Republic made competition ... more difficult. After 1750, the Dutch textile industry was no match for its rivals in Brandenburg, Prussia, Münster, Ravensberg,

Table 8.3 *Physical product per capita in Flanders, France and Great Britain, 1760–1824 (in francs)*

	Flanders	France	Great Britain
1760–80	(245)	—	—
1780–90	—	192	—
1801–10	235	247	293
1811	—	—	302
1815–24	—	252	266
Litres of wheat	1,282	1,140	857
Kilos of meat	255	230	254

Silesia, the Southern Netherlands and Ireland' (Slicher van Bath 1982: 34).

But this was not relevant to the question of domestic spending power and the level of subsistence in Flanders. Lower levels of pay in fact resulted from lower prices of foodstuffs (Morineau 1969). This was another facet overlooked in Mendels' model. Thanks both to very intensive farming and to the early diffusion of potato cultivation (beginning in the late seventeenth century), Flanders succeeded in keeping down the prices of provisions, and maintaining them at a stable level for decades. Around 1750, corn prices in Flanders were one fifth to one half lower than in France or Great Britain. This explains why it was possible to pay lower wages in Flanders, enabling profits to be earned through successful competition in international trade. Domestic purchasing power, on the other hand, was similar in Flanders to the other two countries, at *c.* 10 litres of wheat a day per capita (in real terms) (Vandenbroeke 1987)!

The conclusion of this survey can be expressed in very formal terms. The great virtue of the theoretical model devised by Mendels was that it generated an abundance of publications concerning domestic industry. However, critical investigation of the model itself, based on in-depth empirical research on particular areas, has brought to light obvious gaps and inaccuracies, both in its demographic and in its socio-economic components. We have seen that this is the case precisely for Flanders, where domestic industry saw such enormous expansion that Mendels was led to base his theory on this region. As a result, however, the international literature on proto-industrialization has held a very distorted demographic and socio-economic picture of Flanders for far too long.

This contribution has sought to provide some necessary revisions to this erroneous picture. Eighteenth-century Flanders was characterized by a restrictive marriage pattern, relatively low fertility, and relatively low infant mortality. In socio-economic terms, it was a thriving region, with a relatively high purchasing power and a large volume of profits deriving from competitive success in those economic sectors which specialized in exports. Indeed, this is the image of eighteenth-century Flanders depicted by contemporaries, both at home and abroad.

9 Proto-industrialization in Germany

Sheilagh C. Ogilvie

German historians began to be interested in 'proto-industries' more than a century before the theory of proto-industrialization. In 1857, Karl Marx was already emphasizing the importance of a 'period of manufactures' before the industrial revolution, and stressing the role of rural domestic industries in the genesis of capitalism (Marx 1857–8 (1973): 277f, 505ff). From 1870 on, the Older and Younger German Historical Schools of Political Economy sought to illustrate the 'debt which economic theory owes to domestic industry' (Sombart 1891, 1900: 1141). By 1930, they had concluded that 'the history of domestic industry is the history of capitalism', and had proposed many of the ideas which would later be built into the theories of proto-industrialization – among them that the 'ruralization' of industry in early modern Europe contributed to the rise of capitalism; that the 'penetration' of merchant capital into the production process played a central role; that industry progressed through a series of stages from *Kaufsystem* to *Verlagssystem* and then to factory; that agrarian by-employments and the 'family economy' were crucial features; and that this process caused social classes to polarize, economic relationships to become impersonal, landownership to contract and wage work to expand, and workers to become impoverished and vulnerable to international market fluctuations (Bücher 1927: 985–9; Schmoller 1900/4: 482–7; Sombart 1916: 708, 723–5, 803; Sombart 1900). This theoretical tradition also inspired numerous case-studies of German rural industries, although almost exclusively in Saxony, the Rhineland and the south (Thun 1897; Gothein 1892; Troeltsch 1897; Furger 1927; Aubin and Kunze 1940; Kunze 1961; Heitz 1961; Aubin 1967; Kisch 1959, 1964, 1968, 1972, collected in Kisch 1981b).

Partly as a consequence of this long existing tradition, both West and East German historians greeted the proto-industrialization theories of the 1970s with scepticism (Kuczynski 1981; Linde 1980; Schremmer 1980, 1981; Schultz 1979, 1983). They questioned the very term 'proto-industry', arguing that Marx and the German Historical School had

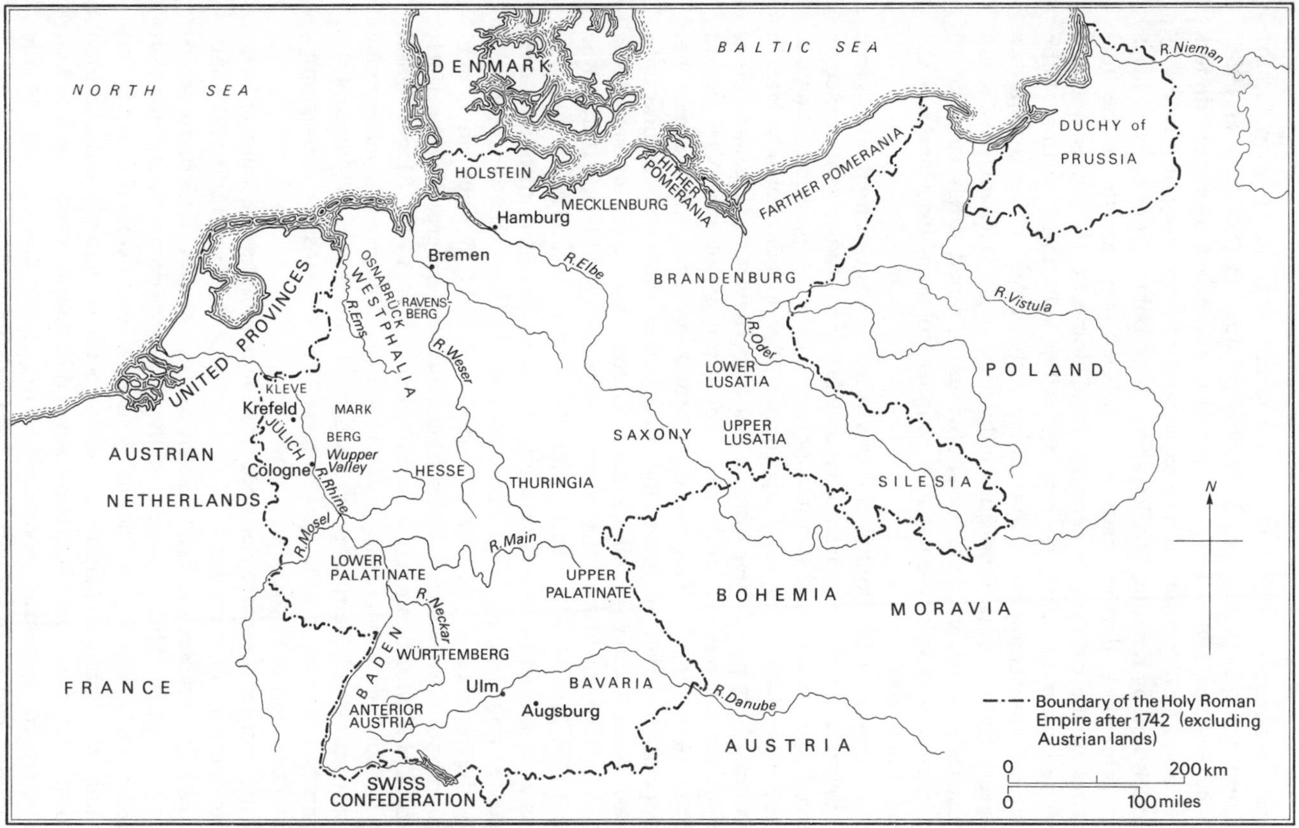

Map 9.1 Map of the Holy Roman Empire of the German Nation after 1742 (excluding Austrian lands)

already generated a rich and precise terminology in German for the different types of pre-factory industrial production (Schremmer 1980: 422–3; Schultz 1983: 1091). They also expressed profound doubts about almost every aspect of the explanatory framework put forward by Mendels and by Kriedte, Medick and Schlumbohm. At first sight, this is surprising, given that in many parts of Germany, as late as the final decades of the nineteenth century, rural domestic industries were no mere remnants of a bygone era, but rather substantial sectors of the economy, co-existing and co-operating with factories. The continuities between these rural domestic industries and mechanized factory industries seemed, in some ways, obvious, and had surely lain behind the important developmental role assigned to them by Marx and the Historical School.

One reason for the doubts of German historians was methodological: the theories relied on community and regional studies, and concepts derived from demography, anthropology and development economics. These new historiographical approaches developed relatively late in Germany, because of their associations with *Heimatgeschichte*, as well as the village genealogies and racial anthropology of the Nazi period (Pfister 1994: 59–60). Even more important, however, was the view that European theories of proto-industrialization imposed assumptions drawn from western (and eastern) Europe on to a fundamentally different German historical reality (Kuczynski 1981: 105, 119ff; Linde 1980: 107, 110–13, 116–18; Schultz 1983: 1081–2, 1089).

As a consequence, empirical case-studies of German proto-industries appeared only rather slowly. There are outstanding exceptions, particularly the regional studies by Kriedte on Krefeld, Medick on Urach, Schlumbohm on Osnabrück and Mager on Ravensberg (Kriedte 1991; Medick 1992/forthcoming; Schlumbohm 1991, 1994; Mager 1982, 1983). But only very recently have there begun to appear a wider range of case-studies of German proto-industries, which not only discuss the traditional themes of industrial history, but also consider demography, agriculture and rural social structure.

This chapter therefore does not provide a complete account of every proto-industry in every territory in Germany between 1500 and 1850. Instead, it discusses the light thrown by case-studies of German proto-industries on the different aspects of the European proto-industrialization debate: on demography, family structure and women's work; on agricultural commercialization, rural social structure, and agrarian institutions; on industrial organization and industrial institutions; and on the German industrial revolution. First, however, it looks at the distinctive features of the early modern German economy.

The economy of early modern Germany

Two features of German economic development are crucial for understanding proto-industrialization in Germany. The first is that Germany industrialized quite late by European standards. While industrial 'take-off' occurred in Britain between 1760 and 1780, and in Belgium, Switzerland and France over the next few decades, in Germany it did not take place until 1835–50 (Spree 1977; Tilly 1979). Although some German regions, especially the Rhineland and Saxony, experienced a phase of 'pre-industrialization' from about 1780 onward, with scattered establishment of mechanized factories, industrialization proper did not begin even here until about 1815, and many other areas, especially in the north-east and the south, failed to industrialize until the late nineteenth century or even later (Hoffmann 1931; Kiesewetter 1980).

This illustrates the second main feature of German economic development: its enormous regional variation (Fremdling, Pierenkemper and Tilly 1979; Kiesewetter 1980; Tipton 1976). During the entire period we associate with proto-industrialization, Germany did not exist. What we now call Germany was a conglomeration of some 384 separate sovereign jurisdictions – indeed, almost 2,500, when the sovereign estates of Free Imperial Knights are also taken into account. This conglomeration included 85 dominions of Free and Imperial Cities; 136 ecclesiastical territories, belonging largely to bishops and religious houses; and 173 secular territories ruled by princely dynasties, some small and relatively enclosed, but many larger and interspersed with the territories of others, and some (such as Brandenburg-Prussia) scattered across Europe from Poland to the Netherlands. Almost all they had in common was that they spoke the same language, and were loosely organized (along with what are now Austria, the Czech Republic, and parts of western France, northern Italy, northern Slovenia and Croatia, and southern Poland) into a constitutional entity called the Holy Roman Empire of the German Nation. Although the imperial constitution meant that until 1804 all Germans were in theory subject to the Habsburg Emperors in Vienna and could appeal against their own princes to the various imperial courts, diets and circles, in most everyday matters German states were independent sovereign countries. It was not until 1814–15 that this plethora of German principalities was reduced to a mere 39 (including Austria), not until 1834 that they even formed a customs union, and not until 1871 that all (except the Austrian lands) were unified into a single state, the German Empire, headed by the King of Prussia (Gagliardo 1991).

Political fragmentation and the two-level structure of imperial and territorial government created on the one hand considerable social and economic diversity, but on the other a number of shared pressures and experiences which gave rise to common features in all German societies. Diversity arose because the German economy was segmented, over very small geographical areas, by trade barriers, economic policies, currency, weights and measures, transportation infrastructure, the level and distribution of taxation, warfare, diplomatic alliances, religion, education and law. Above all, each German state possessed a different legacy of social institutions, and thus a different framework for economic activity. The common pressures were created by the two-level structure of imperial and territorial state, and by Germany's geographical location in the centre of Europe. Together, these helped to generate a situation of almost continual warfare in many areas of German-speaking central Europe from 1618 until 1814. This warfare induced – or compelled – German princes to expand the size of their armies and bureaucracies, the level of taxation and the intensity of social and economic regulation (Fiedler 1972; Klein 1974; Ogilvie 1992). To achieve this, they were forced to obtain the support of traditional social groups and institutions: noble landlords, privileged cities and towns, village communities, guilds and merchant companies. Almost all German states did so by issuing and enforcing corporate privileges to these institutions and social groups, privileges which ultimately came to cover almost every sector of economic activity – including proto-industry. Only within the framework of corporate privileges enjoyed by favoured social groups were markets able to operate (Ogilvie 1992). Thus early modern Germany was characterized by enormous social and institutional variation over very small geographical distances, yet an over-arching common pattern of powerful corporate institutions surviving in symbiosis with strongly interventionist states. This combination of diversity and shared structures emerges strikingly from the economic geography of German-speaking central Europe.

The single most important demarcation in German historical geography is the river Elbe, which rises east of Prague on the Silesian–Bohemian border, and flows north-west through Bohemia, Saxony and Brandenburg to Hamburg on the North Sea. At least in theory, the Elbe divided the 'advanced' German societies of the west from the 'backward' ones of the east. In most parts of western Germany – as in England, the Low Countries and France – the institutional powers of feudal landlords over the rural population had greatly weakened by the sixteenth century at latest. But in many areas of eastern Germany – as in Poland, Bohemia and Hungary – landlords' powers declined little, if at all. Indeed, after roughly 1600, in a process sometimes referred to as the 'second serfdom', the great noble landlords began to intensify their institutional powers, and the expanding early modern state enforced them in exchange for fiscal and military support.

But this is a simplified picture, and even within east Elbian Germany there were important variations. In some areas, soil and climate favoured large-scale grain cultivation to such an extent that landlords monopolized the entire rural labour surplus for forced work on their own demesne estates – as in East and West Prussia, Brandenburg, Pomerania, Mecklenburg and Holstein. Industry was restricted largely to the towns, partly because of feudal restrictions on rural labour, and partly because the state could only tax craftsmen in towns, and thus tried to keep them there (Kisch 1981a; Reininghaus 1990: 9, 32, 72; Schultz 1979: 211).

But in other parts of eastern Germany, conditions were much less suited for grain cultivation on large estates, or indeed for any kind of agriculture. In such areas, the landlords saw more profit in extorting feudal payments from rural industrial work than in enforcing labour services in agriculture. A prime example is Silesia, a large German-speaking territory north-east of Bohemia and Moravia, first ruled by Austria, captured by Prussia in 1742, and part of Poland since 1945. Here, a dense linen proto-industry arose in the seventeenth century, at the same time as the so-called 'second serfdom' enormously increased landlords' powers. It was dominated by the great feudal landlords until well into the nineteenth century, and although it ultimately stagnated and de-industrialized was one of the most important and longest-lasting German proto-industries (Kisch 1981a).

Finally, there were important eastern German states, such as Saxony, where although landlords enjoyed wide institutional powers, so too did towns. The conflict between the two, and the failure of the Saxon princes to enforce the privileges of either consistently, created considerable freedom of manoeuvre, particularly in rural non-agrarian activities. This encouraged a wide variety of successful proto-industries, and one of the highest industrial densities in Germany by 1800 (Quataert 1985; Reininghaus 1990; Schöne 1981, 1982; Wolff 1979). Thus even within eastern Germany, there were wide variations in institutions and social structure, some altogether preventing the rise of proto-industry, but others merely channelling its development in different directions.

The same can be said of the German south, which was dominated by three substantial territorial entities – Bavaria in the east, Württemberg in the middle and Habsburg-ruled Vorderösterreich (Anterior Austria) in the west. Apart from these territories, southern Germany, particularly toward the west, was highly fragmented, with a complicated patchwork of Free Imperial Knights, Free Imperial Cities, sovereign religious houses, prince-bishoprics and secular principalities (especially the various margraviates of Baden). The societies of most larger south German principalities were characterized by quite strong peasant communities. The autonomy of these rural communities, combined with territorial fragmentation (aiding smuggling) and export markets in nearby free city-states, enabled the rural population to move massively into industry in the early modern period (Schremmer 1981). But although town–country distinctions became very weak, rural communities themselves strictly regulated proto-industry as well as farming. The proto-industrial population was also regulated in Bavaria by strong landlords, and in Württemberg and the Baden margraviates by networks of 'regional' (rural–urban) guilds enforced by the state (Gothein 1892; Medick 1983a; Ogilvie 1985; Schremmer 1970; Troeltsch 1897). Throughout the German south, therefore, proto-industry co-existed with strong rural institutional controls.

The presence of the great south German trading cities of Ulm, Nuremberg and Augsburg, and their importance in the trade between southern and northern Europe, also stimulated the rise of rural industry in smaller south German principalities, especially the East Swabian micro-states between Bavaria and Württemberg. In the sixteenth century, competition between different cities created a situation reminiscent in some ways of the Low Countries: that is, no single city was able to restrict the rapid growth of rural industry, even in its own dominions. But the seventeenth century saw industrial stagnation, as the Thirty Years War disrupted exports, and the economic centre of Europe shifted away from the Mediterranean toward the north Atlantic. The south German cities responded to decline by increasing political restrictions on rural industries, setting up rural and regional guilds, and trying to limit production and exclude new techniques. Although not wholly successful, the partial implementation of these strategies imposed costs which made the east Swabian textile proto-industries much less competitive (Kießling 1989, 1991; Reith 1986; Zorn 1988).

The west of the Empire, along the river Rhine, was another area of great political fragmentation and high industrial density. The Rhineland contained not only great Free Imperial Cities such as Frankfurt and Aachen and their rural dominions, but also the ecclesiastical Electorates of Cologne, Mainz and Trier, the fragmented Lower Palatinate, and a plethora of miscellaneous principalities, including the highly industrial county of Mark and duchies of Berg, Jülich and Kleve, situated close to the Netherlands border. Some were ruled by tiny independent dynasties, others by monarchs with larger possessions elsewhere, especially the Electors of the Palatinate and of Brandenburg-Prussia. In most parts of the Rhineland, landlord powers declined early, entrepreneurial peasants practised commercial agriculture and social institutions were quite flexible, creating a cheap, mobile and plentiful labour supply (Kisch 1981a: 188–9; Kriedte 1983: 249–50, 256–7). Guilds and merchant companies still exerted more power over rural industries in most parts of the Rhineland than, for example, in neighbouring France or the Netherlands (Kisch 1981b, 1972; Reininghaus 1990: 62). However, territorial fragmentation meant that proto-industries – like proto-industrial workers – could easily cross state boundaries to locate themselves where political and institutional conditions were least oppressive (Kisch 1981a: 187–8). As a result, the Rhineland was the most economically advanced part of Germany, even more than Saxony, and harboured many of the most dynamic and successful German proto-industries (Kisch 1972; Kriedte 1982b, 1983).

North-western Germany was less fragmented than the south and the west (although more so than the east), and from 1648 on increasingly came under Prussian rule. Landlords and village communities retained greater institutional control over rural society than in the Rhineland, but much less than in Prussia's eastern possessions. Guilds remained strong in the towns, but lost most of their rural powers by about 1700. However, towns themselves were strong enough to force rural proto-industrial producers to sell their output through urban staple markets, and these rights were enforced by the state into the nineteenth century, especially in the great Westphalian linen proto-industries (Mager 1982, 1983; Reininghaus 1990; Schlumbohm 1983, 1992). To the north-east of Westphalia lay the important Hanse cities of Bremen, Hamburg and Lübeck which, like the great south German cities, were important centres of trade – for proto-industrial as well as agricultural output – between east and west. To the south-east of Westphalia, in the centre of Germany, lay Nassau, Hessen and Thuringia, all with quite strong rural institutions and significant textile and metal proto-industries (Reininghaus 1990: 19, 25f, 28; Schremmer 1981; Göbel 1988).

Even a simple geographical survey of the early modern German economy thus reveals enormous institutional variations, and obscures an even greater number of smaller-scale differences. Yet proto-industries arose almost everywhere in Germany, illustrating an important finding which has emerged from European research more widely: the fact that proto-industry was an economic sector which could co-exist with a wide variety of social and institutional conditions. However, research on German proto-industries has also contributed to another important finding: that the differing social and institutional contexts for different proto-industries played a crucial role in how they developed.

Demography, the family and women's work

This can be seen quite clearly in demographic studies of German proto-industrial regions. Rapid population growth, as predicted by the original theories of proto-industrialization, has been observed in a number of German proto-industrial regions, at least in some periods: in the linen- and silk-weaving city and rural district of Krefeld in the Rhineland, in the linen-weaving prince-bishopric of Osnabrück in Westphalia, in the neighbouring Prussian-ruled linen area of Ravensberg, in the cotton- and linen-weaving areas of Upper Lusatia in Saxony, in the variegated textile trades of the Wupper valley in the Rhineland and in the worsted-weaving Black Forest of Württemberg (Ebeling and Klein 1988; Kisch 1972; Knieriem 1986; Kriedte 1986; Mager 1982; Ogilvie 1985, 1995; Quataert 1985; Schlumbohm 1992; Troeltsch 1897).

But there is considerable doubt about whether proto-industrialization *caused* population growth, or whether both were caused by underlying characteristics of the regions in question. Proto-industry was certainly not *necessary* for rapid population growth in Germany, since population also grew fast in a number of purely agrarian areas (Harnisch 1979: 287ff, 303–20; Knodel 1988; Lee 1979; Sabean 1990: 40–1, 60–2, 256–7, 454–8; Thümmler 1977). Nor was proto-industry *sufficient* for population growth, as is shown by the fact that population only began to grow fast in areas such as the Wupper valley and Ravensberg in the mid-eighteenth century, although proto-industry had arisen in the sixteenth century (Knieriem 1986: 169; Kisch 1972: 338–40; Ebeling and Klein 1988: 31). In the Württemberg Black Forest, some worsted-weaving villages grew fast while others did not; the same was true of agrarian villages (Ogilvie 1985: 233–8). Even to say whether proto-industry was more *frequently* associated with fast population growth than were other economic activities would require systematic comparisons of population growth in areas with different economic bases, holding other factors constant, and such studies are difficult and rare. In a sample of sixteen Württemberg villages and small towns, pooled cross-section time-series analysis showed no statistically significant effect of proto-industry on population growth rates between 1672 and 1784, although villages grew faster than towns (Ogilvie forthcoming). Thus proto-industry was associated with population growth only in some regions and some periods, and was not the only source of demographic growth in early modern Germany.

The demographic behaviour underlying population growth also varied across German proto-industrial regions, according to social institutions and economic trends. In Osnabrück, where landlords and villages strictly regulated settlement, marriage ages stayed high, fertility was moderate and in-migration was minimal; population growth was due almost entirely to the fact that almost everyone was able to marry, however late in life (Schlumbohm 1992: 189–90). In neighbouring Ravensberg, where agrarian institutions were liberalized in the 1770s, one third of population growth was caused by in-migration (Ebeling and Klein 1988: 32; Mager 1981: 143). In-migration also played an important role in the rapid growth of population in the Wupper valley and in Krefeld, because of liberal social institutions which offered not only work in proto-industry but also freedom from conscription and religious oppression (Kisch 1972: 338–9; Knieriem 1986: 169ff; Kriedte 1986: 260ff, 275f). In the Württemberg Black Forest, where communities and rural guilds rationed settlement and niches in proto-industry, there was high out-migration of young men, high female celibacy, and universal (though quite late) marriage for men who obtained community citizenship and guild mastership (Ogilvie 1985, forthcoming). Mendels' 'ratchet mechanism' – whereby proto-industrial upturns increased the marriage rate but downturns had no effect – does not appear to lie behind population growth in any German proto-industrial region studied so far. Statistical tests have established its absence in the proto-industrial region around Hagen in Westphalia (Hohorst 1977: 208–27), and in other regions, such as Krefeld, downturns in proto-industry were followed by declines in both marriage rates and population growth (Kriedte 1986: 260, 280, 288).

Marriage ages, too, varied according to the particular institutional context. In liberal Krefeld – at least in the 1820s and 1830s – proto-industry was associated with lower marriage age for both sexes, although more for men than women (Kriedte 1991: 36–8). In Ravensberg, the *Heuerlingssystem* (cottager system) made it easier to obtain a niche as a cottager than as a peasant, so cottager men (whether linen producers or agricultural labourers) married slightly earlier than peasant men; however, savings from service remained important to finance marriage, so cottagers married much older women (Ebeling and Klein 1988: 35–7). Osnabrück, with a *Heuerlingssystem* but stricter community and landlord regulation, showed the same pattern but later marriage for all (Schlumbohm 1992: 189ff). In the Württemberg Black Forest, guild and community regulation meant that proto-industrial worsted weavers married at the same age as other craftsmen, but the stagnation in their industry meant they married older women (Ogilvie 1985: 238–50).

These variations in marriage age were reflected in fertility and family size. In Ravensberg, later female marriage meant fewer children born to proto-industrial families; birth intervals were high for all, but higher for proto-industrial cottagers than for peasants (Ebeling and Klein 1988: 42–3). Industrial organization also influenced family size: in Ravensberg, linen production stages were divided *among*, rather than within, households, so that proto-industry – unlike agriculture – did not require a complete family. Consequently, cottagers wholly dependent on proto-industry had smaller households, fewer children and more solitaries and single-parent families than cottagers dependent on agricultural labour (Mager 1984: 156–61). In Osnabrück, the division of labour was *within* the household, so both peasants and cottagers produced linen; the peasants, who lived from farming and proto-industry, had higher fertility than the cottagers who lived from labouring and proto-industry (Schlumbohm 1992: 192). In the Württemberg Black Forest, late female marriage age meant that proto-industrial households had fewer children; guild restrictions on work and output, combined with proto-industrial stagnation, meant that weavers exported their children early in life to work in other, non-proto-industrial households (Ogilvie 1985: 265–6 and *passim*).

Proto-industry is supposed to have increased women's work and overall independence (Medick 1976: 280–1; Kriedte, Medick and Schlumbohm 1981: 61–3). However, empirical research for Germany does not bear this out. The position of women was influenced by many factors, including technology and social institutions, but proto-industry had no consistent effect on it. Technological influences on the sexual division of labour are illustrated by the various Westphalian linen proto-industries. In eastern Westphalia, the technology of coarse linen production made it optimal to unite all production stages in the same household, resulting in a clear sexual division of labour. The technology of fine linen production in Ravensberg, by contrast, encouraged different households to specialize in different stages of production; within the household, men and women worked at the same small set of proto-industrial tasks (Mager 1982: 453–6; 1983: 64; Mooser 1984: 48–52, 62–7; Schlumbohm 1979: 280–5, 290–2). In southern Upper Lusatia, too, women did the same tasks as men in the production of linen and cotton, partly because new tools introduced around 1800 meant that all the preparatory steps were done by outside specialists (Quataert 1986: 10, 15–17). But 'a critical variable in the ability of women to assume such broad productive roles', according to Quataert, was 'the absence of guild control and state regulation of labour' (Quataert 1986: 11–12, 19–20). The Württemberg Black Forest shows the dark side of the same coin: women were very active in worsted weaving when it first arose in the 1580s, but were gradually pushed out by strong rural guilds, corporate communities and state regulation, and were ultimately restricted to spinning (at below-market rates fixed by the rural guilds) (Ogilvie 1990, 1993b). It was social institutions, not proto-industry, which expanded or contracted women's economic role.

Agriculture, rural social structure and agrarian institutions

Originally it was thought that proto-industry was associated with part-time subsistence farming within the proto-industrial region, and commercial farming in neighbouring regions, to supply it with food and raw materials. But in Germany, the organization of agriculture – which varied widely from region to region – affected its relationship with proto-industry. Thus in Ravensberg, fine linen production, commercial grain farming and part-time flax cultivation were all practised in the same region, because proto-industrialization in neighbouring regions and remoteness from trade routes made food and flax imports too costly (Mager 1982: 442, 444–6, 465). In Württemberg, by contrast, proto-industrial areas lived partly from their own farming and partly from grain surpluses produced elsewhere in Württemberg (Ogilvie 1985; Troeltsch 1897). The Silesian variant on the 'second serfdom' produced yet another pattern, whereby the proto-industrial population was hardly at all involved in farming, but rather depended for food on feudal – not commercial – agriculture before the coming of the potato in the early nineteenth century (Kisch 1981b: 179, 182–3, 197–8).

By-employment in agriculture, initially regarded as an essential element in proto-industrialization, was present in some German proto-industries but absent in others, depending on how both agriculture and industry were organized. Thus in the coarse linen industry of eastern Westphalia, proto-industrial workers cultivated the raw flax and hemp as well as processing, spinning and weaving it. In the higher-quality linen proto-industries of Bielefeld, Upper Swabia and Silesia, by contrast, weavers did not cultivate the raw material, but bought ready-made yarn from specialized spinners and yarn dealers (Harder-Gersdorff 1986: 204–7; Kaufhold 1986: 136f; Mager 1982: 453f; Schlumbohm 1979: 180–5, 290). The Westphalian *Heuerlingssystem* meant that proto-industrial cottagers worked part time in grain cultivation, although the reform of agrarian institutions in Ravensberg after 1770 enabled a group of full-time proto-industrial cottagers to arise, while in Osnabrück the survival of the traditional institutional structure maintained agrarian by-employments for all (Mager 1982; Schlumbohm 1992). In Württemberg, strong communities and strict partible inheritance meant that a majority of rural worsted weavers continued to live partly from their own land (Ogilvie 1985). In Silesia, the 'second serfdom' enabled noble landlords to influence access to land, as well as to other opportunities to work in agriculture (Kisch 1981a: 180–1). Both industrial organization and agrarian institutions thus influenced the nature and extent of agricultural by-employment in proto-industrial regions.

Agrarian institutions also decided whether the potential which proto-industry (like other non-agrarian activities) created for expansion in the land-poor or landless 'rural sub-stratum' would in fact be realized. In Silesia, as we have seen, the increasing institutional powers of landlords enabled them to determine land supply after the Thirty Years War, affecting the number of land-poor and landless who turned to proto-industry (Aubin 1942: 162f; Kisch 1981a: 180–1). In Westphalia, strict enforcement of one-heir inheritance into the nineteenth century combined with population growth to create a growing group of *Heuerlinge* (cottagers) who lived not only from proto-industry but also from labouring in commercial farming (Mager 1982: 440, 448; Schlumbohm 1992). But in parts of Westphalia, such as Osnabrück, the landed peasants *also* participated in proto-industry and, indeed, produced more linen than the landless cottagers, because their land enabled them to marry younger women and maintain a larger household labour force (Mager 1981: 143f, 157ff, 165; 1982: 486ff; Mooser 1984: 234ff; Schlumbohm 1991: 43, 52). Indeed, some proto-industries, such as the metal production in Berg and Mark in the Rhineland, required substantial capital, which kept them in the hands of the landed peasants (Engels and Legers 1928: I, 56–70, 171–6; Kaufhold 1976: 42–71; Wagner 1986, 1993). In other cases, such as Upper Lusatia, Württemberg and Bavaria, rural social institutions ensured that most of the population, including proto-industrial producers, continued to own land (Ogilvie 1985; Quataert 1985; Schremmer 1981: 670).

Differences in commercialization of agriculture, agrarian by-employments and rural social structure all reflected differences in rural social institutions. Seigneurial systems and communities were originally believed to have been weak in all proto-industrial regions (Kriedte, Medick and Schlumbohm 1981: 8, 16–17, 40; Mendels 1982: 80), but the German evidence shows enormous diversity. In areas such as the Rhineland, landlords and communities had already become weak long before proto-industry arose in the sixteenth century (Kisch 1972: 299–304; 1981b: 94–6; Kriedte 1983: 225). In Saxony, village communities were relatively weak, and landlords could not control settlement, although they could and did demand feudal 'loom taxes' from rural weavers into the nineteenth century (Gröllich 1911: 9–11; Kunze 1960: 20; Quataert 1986: 8–9). But the Rhineland and Saxony were exceptional. In Württemberg and Baden, landlords were weak before proto-industrialization, but local communities remained strong – in proto-industrial as well as agrarian regions – until well into the nineteenth century (Gothein 1892; von Hippel 1977; Ogilvie 1985; Tipton 1976). In Westphalia, the communal 'Markenwirtschaft' and the powers of landlords survived until 1770 in Ravensberg and until 1806 in Osnabrück, deeply influencing the entire course of proto-industrial development (Mager 1982: 443, 447–9; 1984: 162–3; Schlumbohm 1982: 334; 1991: 47; 1992: 187, 197). In Silesia, the linen proto-industry was controlled by powerful feudal landlords, whose powers actually expanded during the proto-industrial period (Kisch 1981a: 179, 180–3, 185, 198; see also the contribution by Myška in the present volume). Although there was thus wide variation in agrarian institutions across German proto-industrial regions, the majority were regulated by rural communities, or powerful landlords, or both, until the late eighteenth century, and many to an even later date.

Industrial organization and industrial institutions

Research on German proto-industries does not generally support the view of a stage-like progression from *Kaufsystem* to *Verlagssystem* to factory. Although some German proto-industries were purely artisanal and others purely putting-out, it was not uncommon to find a 'conglomeration' of different organizational forms existing side by side (Bräuer 1983: 58; 1987: 31; Mager 1993: 187–8). In the Ravensberg linen proto-industry, for instance, putting-out dominated in one stage of production, an artisanal system in another stage, and the finishing processes were carried out in centralized manufactories (Mager 1982: 453–6; Mooser 1984: 48–52, 62–7; Schlumbohm 1983: 290–2). In the Württemberg worsted industry, some weavers accepted raw wool from putting-out merchants, while others operated as independent rural craftsmen; this was the case from *c.* 1580 until the industry declined around 1800 (Ogilvie forthcoming; Troeltsch 1897). In many German proto-industries, large centralized manufactories co-existed with and were supplied by extensive putting-out or artisanal systems (Flügel 1993; Henderson 1985; Knieriem 1986; Schöne 1979). State-enforced monopolies over certain stages of production, and state-enforced monopsonies over input and output markets, were the rule, not the exception in the organization of proto-industry – a factor widely neglected in the theories of proto-industrialization.

The theories argued that proto-industrialization led to the breakdown of the traditional institutions regulating industry: urban privileges, guilds and merchant companies (Mendels 1981: 16, 26; Kriedte, Medick and Schlumbohm 1981: 7, 13, 22, 106, 115, 128). In Germany, however, this was far from true. Indeed, in many regions, proto-industrial profits created an incentive for powerful social groups to try to capture them by extending their existing institutional privileges to the new economic sector, or obtaining new ones; the desire to tax and regulate the new sector, and to obtain domestic political support, led states to grant such privileges. In Krefeld, certainly, guilds and merchant privileges were always unimportant, owing partly to Krefeld's quasi-village origins and partly to the development of its industrial institutions under 'laissez-faire' Dutch rule from 1601 to 1702 (Kisch 1981b: 100–3, 116, 130ff; Kriedte 1983: 221ff, 241ff, 258; 1986: 260–1). But Krefeld was an exception, even for the Rhineland. The Wupper valley proto-industry was dominated from 1527 to the end of the eighteenth century by a privileged merchant company, and from 1738 to 1783 was also regulated by a rural guild; both were formed with encouragement from the state, which also enforced their privileges (Kisch 1972: 307, 351–3, 400ff). Rural guilds also regulated the small iron goods industry of Berg and the scythe industry of Remscheid (Kriedte, Medick and Schlumbohm 1981: 115; Mager 1993: 188; Thun 1897).

In Saxony, although most rural proto-industries were guild-free after about 1650, some – such as the trimmings and lace making of the Erzgebirge-Vogtland – had rural guilds (Quataert 1986: 8, 14–15; Schöne 1981, 1982; Wolff 1979: 33–5). In others, urban guilds retained significant privileges, as in Lusatia, where the urban guilds obtained a state ban on ribbon mills, whose repeal in 1765 released enormous growth in rural production (Schöne 1979: 178–9). In almost all Saxon proto-industries, urban merchant guilds obtained state privileges forcing rural producers to sell their products through them; black-market rural traders operated, but with high risks and costs, and were not legalized until after 1800 (Quataert 1986: 8, 14–15; Wolff 1979: 33–5, 38).

In Westphalia, rural producers were unregulated by the urban guilds after about 1700, but were compelled to sell to merchants in the local town through the *Leggen* (state inspection offices), which were strengthened by the state in the 1770s. Although there was some rural smuggling, records for Osnabrück suggest that most rural linen output was sold through the *Legge*, enabling the urban merchants to form an oligopoly (Mager 1982: 444; 1983: 67; Schlumbohm 1982: 331).

In Württemberg, all proto-industrial linen and worsted weavers were placed by the state under the 'Bann' of privileged merchant companies, to whom they were legally obliged to sell their output, at fixed quotas and prices, until the companies dissolved – along with the industries – around 1800 (Flik 1990; Medick 1983a, 1983b; Ogilvie 1985; Troeltsch 1897). Although there was some smuggling and illegal rural trading, the company monopolies were largely effective, as is shown by their successful maintenance of prices lower than the 'free market' price in neighbouring Free Imperial Cities (Flik 1990: 92–3; Medick 1983b: 301). Proto-industrial linen and worsted weavers also formed 'regional' (rural–urban) guilds, whose privileges and regulations were enforced by the state (Flik 1990; Medick 1983a; Ogilvie 1985; Troeltsch 1897). Surviving records for one of these guilds reveal intense and effective regulation of all aspects of rural production (Ogilvie 1985, 1995). Although there was thus wide variation in institutions across German proto-industries, the majority were regulated by guilds, merchant companies or other corporate privileges and monopolies, until at least 1800.

The German industrial revolution

In 1800, a number of areas of Germany had more than sixty rural industrial producers per 1,000 inhabitants: the Lower Rhine, Saxony, Thuringia, Westphalia, Baden, Württemberg and Bavaria (Reininghaus 1990: 9). Yet during industrialization these regions developed in widely different directions: Saxony and the Rhineland were the earliest parts of Germany to industrialize, by about 1815; parts of Westphalia industrialized, but only in the 1850s, while others returned to agriculture; Baden, Württemberg and Bavaria stubbornly resisted industrialization until after about 1870 (Hoffmann 1931; Kiesewetter 1980; Tipton 1976). Whether a German proto-industrial region made the transition to factory industrialization was therefore an open question, which was decided by many of the same factors that had shaped its proto-industrialization.

It was in the Rhineland and Saxony, where there had been fewest social and institutional obstacles to growth and flexibility during proto-industrialization, that factory industrialization was accomplished earliest and with greatest ease. Even here, however, corporate monopolies and urban privileges survived to a later date than in the Low Countries or England, and were direct obstacles to industrialization. For instance, when Brügelmann, a Wupper valley merchant, tried to set up the first English-style spinning mill in Germany in 1782, he met huge opposition from the proto-industrial merchant company and rural weavers' guild; eventually he obtained a state monopoly concession, but built the mill outside the Wupper valley. As late as 1792, the Wupper valley merchant company prosecuted one of its members who attempted to set up a ribbon manufactory in Alsace (Kisch 1972: 394–8, 399–401).

In Saxony, too, industrialization could only take place in the interstices left by privileges granted during the proto-industrial period (Wolff 1979: 35, 38–41; Tipton 1976: 30–8). In Lusatia, it was not the privileged proto-industrial merchants of Zittau and Löbau, but illegal village traders who promoted the shift from linen to cotton in the 1770s, and introduced mechanical cotton spinning after 1800 (Wolff 1979: 35). In the Vogtland, the shift to cotton saw the foundation of compulsory guilds of cotton 'merchants' and 'manufacturers' in 1764, which were still competing for each other's privileges when the merchants' guild was abolished in 1843. Calico printing developed under guild regulation and a state monopoly which was still in force in 1805. As late as 1786, two-thirds of muslin workers in the region around Plauen were still guilded (Tipton 1976: 32). Mechanization began around 1800, but found it hard to compete until the state began to remove 'the prohibitions, monopoly rights and restrictions' in 1817 (Wolff 1979: 39–41; Tipton 1976: 30ff). Thus even in the Rhineland and Saxony, early industrialization was delayed by a proto-industrial institutional legacy of corporate privilege, which was only gradually broken down through state action.

In Westphalia, nine out of ten proto-industrial linen regions de-industrialized. In the Osnabrück region, for instance, proto-industrial merchants turned to other wares, large peasants shifted to market farming and small peasants and cottagers emigrated or became agricultural labourers (Mager 1982: 441; Schlumbohm 1982: 330–4). Industry survived and mechanized only in Ravensberg. Not proto-industry but institutional factors made the difference, according to Mager and Schlumbohm: the early reform of Ravensberg's agrarian institutions in the 1770s created a proletarianized labour force before international linen demand fell, and the less thorough enforcement of the Bielefeld *Legge* permitted some black-market rural trading (Mager, 1982: 441; 1983: 71; Schlumbohm 1982: 330). Even so, there was no direct continuity between proto-industry and factory industry: the black-market rural traders played no role in mechanization; the urban proto-industrial merchants delayed mechanization for decades, and boycotted the first spinning mill in 1852; the second mill was established only with state assistance and foreign managers; local proto-industrial flax cultivation ceased, so the mills had to import costly Russian flax; local proto-industrial spinners refused to work in the mills, so workers had to be brought in from Silesia, East Prussia and Bohemia; and proto-industrial weavers resisted mechanization until

1870 (Mooser 1983: 75–82; Schlumbohm 1982: 330; Wolff 1979: 30–3).

In Silesia, too, proto-industrial institutions proved inimical to industrialization (Kisch 1981b: 182–7; Tipton 1976: 18–20; Wolff 1979: 20–3). The institutional powers of the landlords had forcibly kept labour costs low, creating a comparative advantage for proto-industry, but they also generated feudal dues on proto-industry, which were threatened by mechanization; to protect the landlords' feudal revenues from proto-industry, the Prussian state prohibited technological improvements to linen production (Kisch 1981a: 182f, 185; Wolff 1979: 20–3). The enormous legal privileges of Silesian landowners also meant that capital did not accumulate in proto-industry, but flowed into landownership and noble consumption (Kisch 1981a: 184–5). As Kisch concludes, 'In many ways the Silesian linen trades corroborate the contention ... that domestic industry was not always, as might be generalized from the English case, an agent of progress; rather, where domestic trades have been appendices of the feudal order they have had the opposite effect' (Kisch 1981a: 187).

In Bavaria, Württemberg and Baden, too, the institutional legacy of proto-industrialization proved an obstacle to factory industrialization (Schremmer 1981). In the Württemberg Black Forest, both merchant company and worsted weavers' guilds opposed any change in technology or organization that would threaten their privileges; after the dissolution of the company in 1797 (against state protests), the worsted industry collapsed and found no resilient successor (Flik 1990: 241–308; Ogilvie 1995; Troeltsch 1897). In the Urach linen proto-industry, the company monopoly and state regulation meant that neither privileged merchants nor illegal rural traders were willing or able to become industrial entrepreneurs; the district remained heavily proto-industrial, lost markets to mechanized competitors after about 1800 and was only industrialized in the 1860s by outside entrepreneurs (Medick 1983b: 306–10). It was Heidenheim, the least successful of the Württemberg linen districts, which was the only one successfully to industrialize, possibly because the repeated company bankruptcies from the 1760s on created greater flexibility; yet even here, the proto-industrial linen-weavers' guild violently opposed the shift to cotton in the 1780s (Flik 1990: 117ff, 142–3).

Conclusion

No systematic link can be found, therefore, between proto-industrialization and changes in the demography, society or economy of early modern Germany between the late medieval period and the nineteenth century. Rather, the empirical evidence suggests that social and economic developments (whether in proto-industry, agriculture or other sectors) were shaped by underlying factors – particularly the social and institutional framework – which varied widely from one German region to the next. But in all parts of Germany – even the most advanced – both proto-industries and factory industries were characterized by a long survival of traditional institutions, whose corporate privileges constituted direct and enduring obstacles to economic and social change.

The causes of this survival are the subject of lively debate, but it may be ascribed partly to the enormous growth of the powers of most German states in the early seventeenth century, in the 'institutional hothouse' of the Thirty Years' War. Local and regional studies are making increasingly clear the way in which, in order to gain the fiscal and military resources to survive decades of continual warfare, German states had to grant extensive corporate privileges to traditional social institutions (see the survey in Ogilvie 1992). The continued demands of the perpetual central European warfare of the seventeenth and eighteenth centuries, which resulted in enormous state indebtedness, made it impossible to provoke domestic social unrest by attempting to withdraw these privileges (Klein 1974; Fiedler 1972). The corporate privileges of traditional institutions could only be weakened, beginning in the late eighteenth century, by the issuing of countervailing state privileges issued through new institutions to favoured social groups. Even then, the new institutional regime tended simply to overlay the older one, rather than replacing it, and corporate privileges remained a ubiquitous feature of most German economies well into the nineteenth century (Tipton 1976).

Research on German proto-industrialization therefore makes clear that the 'corporative' and 'statist' features so often emphasized in accounts of German industrialization did not originate, as frequently argued, in nineteenth-century Prussian militarism (Spree 1977; Tilly 1979; Fremdling, Pierenkemper and Tilly 1979; Kiesewetter 1980). Rather, these features, like industrialization itself, had their roots much further back in German history, and can already be observed in the economy and society of early modern Germany.

10 Proto-industrialization in Switzerland*

Ulrich Pfister

The area of present-day Switzerland saw the emergence in the early modern period of a differentiated industrial landscape which has stimulated studies by historians and social scientists since the eighteenth century. As a result, Switzerland possesses a rich tradition of research into the social and economic history of rural industries. Despite both this background and the fact that two important exponents of research into proto-industrialization, Rudolf Braun and Franklin Mendels, taught at Swiss universities, no explicit engagement with the concept of proto-industrialization has taken place in more recent scholarly debates. A considerable number of regional studies of domestic industrial regions, however, have been carried out in the last two decades.

By proto-industrialization is meant a process of regional growth in heavily export-oriented industrial production, in which no role is played by increases in the productivity of labour and capital through technological change (Pfister forthcoming). As a consequence of the comparatively minor importance of material technology in the production process, centralized plants are rare, and most stages of production are carried out by individual producers as domestic work. At the same time, the absence of technological change is connected to certain conditions and problems, which distinguish proto-industrial from industrial growth. In particular, given the constant factor productivity, economic growth is limited to that which can be achieved through increases in inputs of labour and/or capital. In addition, relative prices, especially in the foreign trade of a proto-industrial region (exported manufactured goods, imported foodstuffs), must remain constant, since otherwise factor yields and thus factor inputs can change unfavourably (for instance, labour may turn back to subsistence agriculture when real wages decrease).

* This chapter is translated from the German by Sheilagh C. Ogilvie.

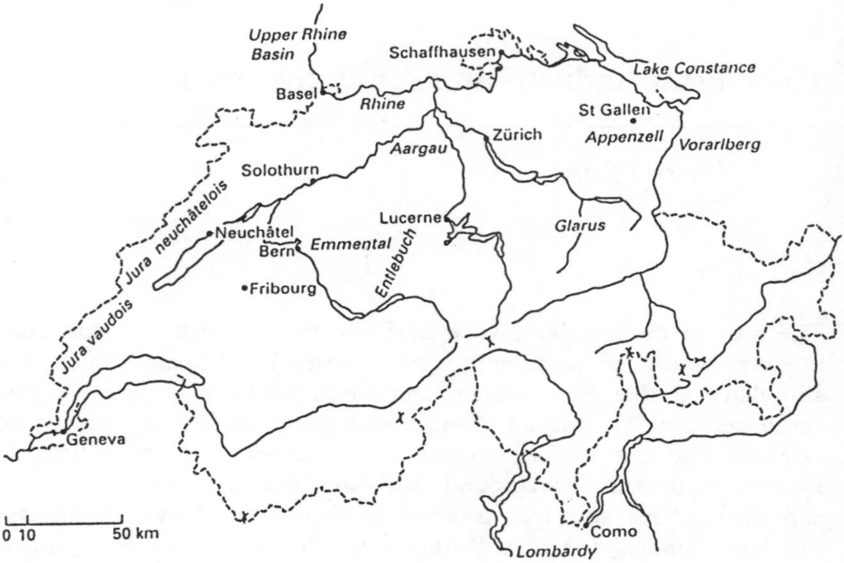

Map 10.1 Map of Switzerland

The development of industrial regions and new forms of production

On the eve of the industrial revolution, Switzerland was interspersed with regions of dense industry. In particular, the area circumscribed by the trapezoid whose corners are Basel, Emmental, Glarus and Vorarlberg can be described as an integrated industrial countryside with a partial division of labour; cotton and silk industries were settled here, as was the processing of linen cloths. In western Switzerland, the Jura regions of the cantons of Vaud and Neuchâtel must be mentioned, and the agglomeration around Geneva where both clock making and various textile industries were practised. In the Jura, the clock industry followed upon older metal-processing and lace-making trades. Finally, from the second half of the eighteenth century, southern Switzerland was integrated into the periphery of the silk-processing zone in the Lombard hills whose local centre was Como (see Map 10.1; Bodmer 1960).

This picture contrasts markedly with the situation at the beginning of the early modern period. The industries of the fifteenth and sixteenth centuries, such as the woollen cloth industry in Fribourg and the various textile industries in Geneva, were still concentrated in the towns or were subject to urban control, at least as far as quality maintenance and end processing were concerned (Peyer 1975: 81–2; Mottu-Weber 1987: 49–53, 236–41, 315–18). The early modern period can thus be described as a phase of ruralization of export-oriented industry. Following a general European trend, the period around 1650/70, namely the 'crisis of the seventeenth century', appears to have been the decisive phase: in this period occurred the emergence of putting-out based on rural labour forces, the introduction of advanced Dutch techniques in the silk-ribbon making of Basel, the establishment of linen markets in Appenzell Ausserrhoden and the beginnings of the struggle of the Zürich authorities against rural cotton putters-out (Fink 1983: 26–44; Tanner 1982: 12–13; Pfister 1992a: 65–7, 210–14). In Geneva in this period, the guilds began to decline, in woollen manufacturing the town retained only the end processing of woollen cloths from the surrounding French countryside, and non-guilded silk-stocking weaving saw its first beginnings (Piuz and Mottu-Weber 1990: 407, 423–6, 450–2).

Parallel to this, there were also changes in the products and the dominant forms of organization. Beginning around 1600 with high-quality articles such as the Geneva 'serges' (heavy woollen cloths) made according to the 'façon de Florence', the palette of products developed by the late eighteenth century into mass-market articles such as the printed handkerchiefs produced in Zürich out of coarse, small Aargau cotton cloths. The earlier high-quality production was heavily dependent on urban guilds, with their capacity to maintain skill qualifications and production quality. An example of this is Geneva which, with its transformation into an industrial city in the second half of the sixteenth century, saw a massive expansion in its guilds (Piuz and Mottu-Weber 1990: 396–400). Less demanding products, by contrast, were produced outside the guild framework, in small businesses operated by female entrepreneurs. The Zürich cotton industry, for example, had its origins in such urban businesses operated by women (Pfister 1992a: 38–48; 1993).

These seventeenth-century processes of ruralization and transformation in the palette of products were accompanied by changes in organization. Some branches of industry (such as linen cloth production) and some work processes (such as cotton spinning) which were not very demanding in terms of raw materials and processing techniques were organized as a *Kaufsystem* (artisanal system). Yarn was purchased by partly itinerant traders; the inspection of the finished cloths in fixed market locations was the only instance of quality control in the production of linen. In other sectors (such as the silk industry) the putting-out system dominated. In this system, an entrepreneur provided the raw materials, half-finished products (yarn) or working tools, and paid the workers a piece-rate for processing them. Finally, in some areas (such as wool combing in Zürich, or calico printing in the eighteenth century) centralized manufactories arose, which now and then employed more workers than the early industrial businesses (Caspard 1979: 114). It should be stressed that a particular branch of industry could display several different forms of organization. In the Zürich cotton industry, for instance, spinning was organized mainly as a *Kaufsystem*, while weaving was organized as a putting-out system under the control of small rural entrepreneurs, and cotton printing took place in urban manufactories.

Preconditions for the development of proto-industries

Local raw materials

Especially in early phases, the local availability of raw materials appears to have played a role in the development of industrial regions. The Fribourg woollen industry profited from sheep raising in the neighbouring pre-Alps and Alps, and several early industrial regions arose in areas whose soils suited them for the cultivation of flax: this was true of the Appenzell country, the Zürich highlands and the area extending from the border between the Aargau and Lucerne into the Emmental (Peyer 1975: 80; Tanner 1982: 9; Pfister 1992a: 250–1, 406–7). However, as soon as industrial development expanded to such an extent that imported raw materials (Spanish or German wool, silk, cotton) could be processed, i.e. particularly from the seventeenth century on, the significance of this factor declined.

Entrepreneurial potential

The whole region of the Alps was probably never autarkic; exchanges of goods with lower-lying regions early formed an important basis for full-time settlement. This explains why small traders were noticeably widespread in many parts of the Alpine region during the early modern period. In several cases, this factor was an important starting point for the development of rural industries. In the Fribourg woollen cloth industry, traders from the Aosta Valley appear to have played a certain role, and in the Appenzell country it is noticeable that there was a dense infrastructure of (often itinerant) yarn traders at a very early date (Peyer 1975: 84; Tanner 1982: 12). The rapid development of the cotton industry in Glarus, too, can hardly be explained without taking into consideration the older table-making industry and the wadding industry (the production of wadding from silk waste) controlled by travelling pedlars who journeyed across half of Europe (Stauffacher 1989: 40–2, 161). In the Zürich countryside, finally, a close relationship can be observed between the activity of small entrepreneurs in the textile industry, and other activities directed toward provision of the basic needs of a population which was far from autarkic. This group of rural entrepreneurs consequently developed in the higher-altitude southern zones of the canton in particular. The relevance of this group of small Alpine traders for industrial development can be seen from the fact that the Zürich lowland underwent a process of de-industrialization in the early eighteenth century, when there was a decline in the wool industry organized into a putting-out system by urban merchants. In the southern parts of the canton, by contrast, where a local infrastructure of small and itinerant traders already existed, there occurred a re-orientation toward the local cotton industry, which was partly organized into a *Kaufsystem* operated by existing rural entrepreneurs (Pfister 1992a: 118–24, 130–2, 251).

The significance of the group of small and itinerant traders for the development of proto-industrial organizational structures can be explained partly by the fact that these groups linked urban with rural markets, thereby providing a basis, in terms of information and transportation infrastructure, for spatially wide-ranging forms of organization for industrial production. Secondly, the integration of small trading with the textile industry enabled an optimization of the circulation of capital, in that trade wares, through the practice of payment in kind (the 'truck system'), could at the same time serve as proto-industrial circulating capital. This was especially the case where work performed in the framework of the domestic economy (such as baking by women) was incorporated into the values of wares used for payment in kind (such as bread). This phenomenon of capital formation linked to payment in kind should, despite all the contemporary criticisms directed at its exploitive character, not be neglected (Pfister 1992a: 218–22).

As a consequence of lack of capital, the rural entrepreneurs mainly became involved in branches of industry or work processes relying on local raw materials and simple technologies. The introduction of more complex processes and foreign raw materials took place mainly through urban merchants. This required that urban elites have some interest in commercial activities. These groups' most lucrative alternatives lay in administrating rural dominions, i.e. in political careers, and in supplying mercenaries, which also partly relied on the labour force potential of the subjects. It was therefore particularly the elites of cities which lacked any rural dominions worth mentioning (such as Geneva, Basel and St Gallen), or whose states were prevented by their religious policies from furthering the mercenary trade for a long time (such as Zürich), which developed into promoters of proto-industrialization.

Insofar as ruralization of production was linked to the rise of rural entrepreneurs, there arose a competitive relationship between these and urban groups of entrepreneurs. But since the two groups frequently belonged to different political bodies (e.g. St Gallen and Appenzell, or Geneva and Jura), as a rule the possibilities for the urban merchants to take action were modest. An exception was Zürich, where in 1670 there began a long chain of restrictions on rural entrepreneurs. Successful exponents of this group often operated illegally, and repeatedly became objects of state sanctions. Since most production processes in the cotton industry were controlled by rural entrepreneurs, state obstacles to their activity at least partly explain why the mechanization of cotton spinning, i.e. the transition to industrialization, took place somewhat later here than in other important industrial centres in Europe (Pfister 1992a: 99–100, 210–17).

Agrarian structure

The largest part of the proto-industrial labour force lived in the countryside, carrying out domestic work for export industries but at the same time being active in agriculture. The rise of a group of proto-industrial workers is thus closely connected with the agrarian structure. In a population which divided its work between agricultural and industrial activities, the allocation of labour to both sectors in principle depended on the reciprocal relationship between the marginal productivity of labour and capital in both proto-industry and agriculture. On the regional level, this meant that in areas in which many households subsisted on small landholdings or ones which required only an extensive labour input, an especially large potential labour force was available for proto-industry.

This general relationship also explains why proto-industrial regions were especially able to develop in higher-altitude locations. The nature of the soil, the low temperatures, and the high volume of precipitation meant that these zones were poorly suited to arable farming and demanded labour-extensive forms of exploitation (such as ley farming, i.e. tilling and pasturing in succession, or alpine animal husbandry). In the context of the intensification of supra-regional integration, this zone underwent a transition, especially in the fifteenth and sixteenth centuries, to export-oriented cattle raising and dairy farming which (probably especially among women) led to structural under-employment, which was compensated for by industrial activities. The combination of extensive agriculture and domestic work also enabled new areas of settlement to be opened up (Tanner 1982: 8–9; Braun 1960: 157–61; Pfister 1992a: 424–5).

In addition, in many parts of the lowland area of Switzerland between the fifteenth and the eighteenth centuries, a process of pauperization took place, with the result that numerous agrarian holdings in time became unable to feed their owners. Here, it was less physical preconditions than social processes which created a proto-industrial labour potential. The origins of this development can be seen in the varying degree to which the right of disposal over land shifted from the feudal powers to the rural population in the fifteenth and sixteenth centuries. This greatly weakened the mechanisms fixing the size of holdings and restricting opportunities to set up a household. Where partible inheritance prevailed, there arose an intense fragmentation of holdings (Tanner 1982: 10, 69–70; Pfister 1992a: 416–20). In areas with impartible inheritance, by contrast, the non-inheriting offspring with their families took in marginal new land (Bietenhard 1988: 244–5, 275–81). Both led to the rise of a large lower class dependent on non-agrarian by-employments.

Admittedly, the speed and extent of this pauperization process was also partly dependent on agrarian structure. It went further where a farm could be set up with very few initial resources and could be gradually extended over the course of the life-cycle with the assistance of savings from proto-industrial activities, i.e. where a strategy of incremental accumulation was possible. In areas with a pure 'three-field system' (a communally organized crop rotation in a three-year rhythm) this was scarcely possible, since setting up a farm required higher initial investments (arable land in all three rotation categories, draught animals and tools). Where agrarian capital could be traded in small units, i.e. in areas with a high proportion of pasture land, extensive animal husbandry and arboriculture, the necessary preconditions were more available. In this, an important role could be played by large village commons. They could be used as a basis for animal raising, and the fruit which grew on them made an important contribution to feeding land-poor households. The practice of taking savings from proto-industrial activity and investing them in agriculture supported an early transition to ley farming (an agricultural system of tilling and pasturing in succession) in areas which were suited to it (Mattmüller 1983; Abt-Frössl 1988; Head 1986: 89; Pfister 1992a: 389–2, 433, 440–1).

Finally, one aspect of agrarian structure should be mentioned, which created preconditions for the rise of a proto-industrial labour force which went beyond the narrow framework of an individual industrial region. The processes just described implied an increase in the number of households whose agrarian yields were not enough for feeding themselves. A stable proto-industrial growth path required, as mentioned at the beginning of this chapter, that an industrial region be able to import an increasing quantity of foodstuffs at constant relative prices. In turn, this required a highly developed transportation system and the existence of commercial agriculture outside the area.

Given the modest development of transportation, which was often further hindered by territorial fragmentation, grain markets in early modern Europe were mostly very small-scale in nature. Under these circumstances, geographical proximity to a region producing grain surpluses was a prerequisite for the development of regions of dense industry. In this context, Mendels (1980) developed an ideal-typical model of a division of labour between two complementary neighbouring regions: one region located in a low-lying alluvial area and having a grain surplus confronts another, higher-lying region which specializes in extensive agriculture, temporary migration (harvest work, service) into the low-lying region and proto-industrial activity. A town located in the centre provides the grain market and the entrepreneurial potential.

In the areas surrounding Switzerland, a pair of complementary regions can be seen in the northern foothills of the Alps and in a strip extending from the Upper Rhine plain through the upper Danube valley to the northern hinterland of Lake Constance. Although as early as the late Middle Ages there is evidence of a dependency by northern Switzerland on grain deliveries from areas north of the Rhine, after the Thirty Years War, and thus parallel with the ruralization of the textile industry, we observe a deepening of supra-regional integration. The dependency of the great grain markets of northern Switzerland on grain deliveries from southern Germany was intensified, and several areas north of the Rhine increasingly oriented themselves toward commercial grain cultivation and grain exporting to the south. In the second half of the eighteenth century, the degree of self-provision of northern Switzerland has been estimated as being no more than two-thirds. A specific feature of this upper Rhine system, which distinguishes it from Mendels' ideal-typical model, is its segmentation into at least three sub-systems: in the west the pair consisting of the upper Rhine plain and Basel, in the centre the region between Schaffhausen and the upper Danube valley in the north and Aargau and Zürich in the south, and in the east the Lake Constance region broadly defined. The cause of this situation probably lies in the already-mentioned territorial fragmentation of the country (Pfister 1992a: 413–24).

Where the agrarian structure favoured the adoption of non-agrarian activities, but other factors such as remoteness from a town and a consequent lack of entrepreneurial potential made proto-industrial development impossible, an alternative existed in dense industry of a local nature. By this is meant products requiring simple raw materials and undemanding production techniques, which were sold over a limited geographical range by the producers themselves or small pedlars. Examples of this were the straw plaiting of the area around Wohlen and the stocking knitting of several northern areas of the canton of Zürich (Dubler and Siegrist 1975: 531–44; Meier 1986: 309–49). Finally, there was an osmotic relationship between local industries and proto-industries: local industries could provide the foundation for proto-industrial development (thus probably in Glarus the wadding and joinery industries), and when the latter failed a reverse development could occur, into local industries (as, for example, into stocking knitting in parts of the Zürich lowlands).

Family economy and demography

Rudolf Braun argued for the Zürich highland that the growth of a land-poor stratum living mainly from proto-industrial activities led to a change in the subsistence basis. Consumption needs were increasingly satisfied through the market, and less through domestic production. The livelihood was now not only used to still hunger, but also served for self-representation and consumption to compensate for monotonous and deadening work. Since domestic work required less strength than it did continual concentration, there was greater demand for stimulants and luxuries, and less for nutritious food. Increases in female earning capacity, finally, meant that foodstuffs were favoured which could be prepared quickly. For all of these reasons, white bread, meat, coffee and tobacco entered into consumption. A leisure culture arose, mainly involving young adults, with specific forms of sociability and conspicuous consumption (such as 'fine attire'). The fact that new households could be set up without an agrarian basis worth mentioning also led to a change in marriage patterns. The influence of parents and other relatives declined, and marriage decisions became more individualized. Since household foundation now depended on proto-industrial earning capacities, marriage could take place as soon as adult years were reached and the economic situation permitted. This caused the age at marriage to fall, and there was rapid population growth (Braun 1978, 1990).

Although similar familial, demographic and cultural patterns have also been documented for other textile regions of Switzerland (Tanner 1982, 1986), nevertheless by no means all proto-industrial areas manifested such a development. While population growth is a generally undisputed phenomenon, Markus Mattmüller in particular has argued that proto-industrial regions were distinguished less by low marriage ages and high fertility, and more by low mortality. This was caused by the phenomenon which has already been mentioned: the fact that domestic industrial households took their savings from proto-industrial activity and invested them in agriculture. Depending on the agrarian structures which made such strategies possible, this led to a differentiation in the nutritional basis (grain, fruit, milk products, later also potatoes), making it richer and more resistant to crises than the exclusive dependence on grain usual in a pure three-field economy. Proto-industrial populations were consequently less vulnerable to mortality crises than were purely agrarian populations, and life expectancies increased (Mattmüller 1983: 51–2).

The existence of a variety of demographic patterns in proto-industrial regions is linked to the position of industrial activities in the rural domestic economy. In general, as mentioned above, the principle is true, that in a population which divides its work between agricultural and industrial activities, the work done in the two sectors depends on the relative marginal productivities of labour and capital in the two sectors. On the level of individual households, three ideal-typical patterns of demographic behaviour can be derived from this (Pfister 1992b: 210–14).

(1) If poorly paid industrial activities dominate, domestic work remains closely linked to the agrarian subsistence basis. It forms nothing more than a supplementary source of earnings pursued only by some family members and often only in winter time. Accordingly, lace making, and the spinning of wool, floss-silk and cotton before the boom in cotton processing which set in in the course of the eighteenth century, were activities mainly carried out by women and children. The men worked as mercenaries, as farm-servants in large peasant households in the surrounding area, or in the rich agrarian areas north of the Rhine as small farmers or day-labourers. Disposing of a minimum agrarian subsistence basis remained a prerequisite for setting up a household. Proto-industrialization could lead to an increase in carrying capacity at most via the already-mentioned investments in agriculture, and the resulting improvements in nutrition. One would therefore expect to observe particularly those demographic changes which result from a healthier population. An example is the canton of Zürich in the late seventeenth and early eighteenth centuries, where proto-industrial areas

grew faster than purely agrarian areas only owing to temporarily lower mortality (Pfister 1992a: 471–9). A similar pattern is observed in the Entlebuch which saw linen and cotton spinning in the eighteenth century, and in the Val de Travers in Neuchâtel in the decades before about 1760, when lace making was still the most important industrial employment (Bucher 1974: 106–7, 227–33; Sorgesa Miéville 1992: 120).

(2) Many proto-industrial activities required training, equipment and suitable working rooms. This was the case for weaving in a whole range of textile industries, but also for parts of the clock-making industry, for instance. Frequently, the required investments could not be found by the poorest, landless or land-poor households. Accordingly, in the canton of Zürich, weaving was more widespread in zones of extensive agriculture among the rural middle stratum of the 'half-peasants' and small peasants, than among the landless households (Pfister 1992a: 280–9, 1992b: 202–6). In the Basel countryside, as well, the silk ribbon makers appear not to have belonged to the poorest stratum of the population, and there was a close connection between weaving and small farming (Fink 1983: 82; Mattmüller 1983: 55). This meant that setting up a household could not take place as a direct reaction to proto-industrial market relations, but rather depended to a considerable extent on small peasants' capacity to save and their disposal over inherited resources. Here, too, proto-industrialization expressed itself mainly in investments of saved income in agriculture, and similarly the population grew mainly through mechanisms which can be associated with improved nutrition. As a consequence of the considerably higher productivity of industrial activities, compared to the first constellation described above, a proto-industrial boom could increase saving capacity, and thereby enable earlier establishment of a household, so that comparatively high fertility caused by a higher marriage rate could emerge as a secondary growth factor. A constellation of lower mortality and higher fertility can be found, accordingly, in the areas of the Basel countryside pervaded by silk ribbon weaving in the eighteenth century (Mattmüller 1983: 50–1) and also during the final upswing of linen weaving in Appenzell Ausserrhoden in the last third of the seventeenth century (Tanner 1982: 127–8). The two Jura communities of Vallorbe with its iron-working trades and the Val de Travers where clock making developed from about 1760 on show this type of demographic pattern (Hubler 1984: 273–82; Sorgesa Miéville 1992: 120, 168, 222).

(3) High sales prices in industries whose practice required only a small amount of capital enabled the rise of a fully landless group, for whom an investment of proto-industrial income in the agrarian sector hardly came

into question any longer. Especially consequent upon the cotton boom from the mid-eighteenth century onward, a category of households can be observed in the affected areas which were hardly at all connected with agriculture any longer, and in which not only women but also men practised spinning (Pfister 1989b, 1992a: 316–26, 386–9). It was above all these social groups which developed an early proletarian mode of life, as described above, through differentiation of their particular sub-culture. For demographic development, this meant that frequency of marriages increased in close connection with proto-industrial real incomes – measured by the relationship between proto-industrial conjuncture and grain prices. Insofar as this relationship developed favourably, the marriage rate increased, and the population grew. Because this pattern was linked to the availability of a large and mainly landless sub-stratum, mortality did not decrease; the agrarian innovations which set in in the late eighteenth century, especially potato cultivation, hardly touched such areas. This pattern of development can be seen most clearly in the spinning areas in the south of the canton of Zürich during the second half of the eighteenth century, where the increase in nuptiality and fertility rates can be explained very well in terms of developments in real proto-industrial incomes (Pfister 1989a, 1992a: 483–9). In Mollis in Glarus, as well, the age at marriage varied in the medium term according to proto-industrial–agrarian fluctuations, and in Cortaillod on Lake Neuchâtel the setting up of a calico-printing plant caused a massive decline in marriage age within a few decades (Head 1986: 393–4; Caspard 1979: 124). It should also be mentioned that the expansion of silk spinning in the eastern border area of the Italian Comasco, in combination with metal working, led to a rapid decline in marriage age and a greater frequency of nuclear families. By contrast, the spread in the eastern neighbourhood of Como of small silk mills in combination with silk reeling, which was practised purely by women and was as a rule a very poorly paid activity (constellation 1 or 2), resulted in no changes worth mentioning in the marriage pattern (Merzario 1989: 157–75).

The existence of a variety of different relationships between proto-industrialization and the demographic situation had serious macro-economic implications. In the introduction it was mentioned that proto-industrial growth was limited to that which could be achieved through increases in proto-industrial labour inputs. As long as work organization and sales prices do not permit any emancipation of household formation from the agrarian basis, proto-industrial labour has only a low elasticity of supply. An increase in demand thus does not automatically lead to an increase in the labour force in a specific region. Given the minor relevance of productivity growth, a geographical expansion of production locations is an indispensable precondition for long-term expansion in industrial production. The expansion, which was mentioned earlier, of proto-industry from Appenzell Ausserrhoden into the Rhine valley and into Vorarlberg, or from Zürich into the Aargau, central Switzerland and Glarus, in the course of the seventeenth and eighteenth centuries, had its structural roots to some extent in this fact. However, in the long term, i.e. until the late eighteenth century, this led to a rise in overhead costs (payment of middlemen, problems in supervising the labour force) and in sales prices. This created a situation which made investments in labour-saving tools, and in centralized production workshops which shifted the work process out of the domestic economy, appear profitable. The disposition of rural households, which was inflexible as far as the proto-industrial production process was concerned because it also took into consideration the situation in the agrarian sector, thus represented one reason for the transition to industrialization.

Two additional general points must also be expanded upon here. First, it must be stressed that in proto-industrial regions it is hardly possible to distinguish agrarian and industrial households precisely from one another. The relationship between social stratification (as measured, for example, by landownership) and the proportion of the family labour force pursuing proto-industrial activities is fairly continuous. As mentioned earlier, the relationship between the productivity of labour in agriculture and earning capacities in proto-industry is the most important determinant of the family economy in industrial regions. This is true not only of the demographic patterns which have been mentioned, but also of differences between social strata with respect to the sexual division of labour and the age at which children leave home and participate in local or supra-regional agricultural labour markets.

Secondly, it must be pointed out that proto-industrial activities are embedded in a life plan which also includes non-proto-industrial industrial activities and the building up of agricultural property. Detailed material on the canton of Zürich concerning the age- and sex-specific occupational structure, age-specific earning capacities of female spinners, and sex-specific inter-generational mobility, reveals the existence of a characteristic life-cycle dependent on the region's agrarian structure and on available proto-industrial employment. Where the agrarian structure was such that the agrarian subsistence basis could be enlarged with small sums of money, a strategy of incremental accumulation became visible, through which the proto-industrial earning capacity of wives and children was exploited for the purpose of gradually building up an agricultural holding. While in this way the men advanced from domestic workers to craftsmen and finally to small peasants or full peasants, for wives this kind of family cycle could bring with it a move from full-time proto-industrial activity into proto-industrial work which could be practised as a seasonal by-employment. Insofar as a demographic differentiation of the population developed in proto-industrial regions when particular preconditions prevailed (Kriedte, Medick and Schlumbohm 1981: 58–60), this was connected with a close interlinking of various economic sectors, which was dependent on the life-cycle (Pfister 1992b, 1992a: 280–392).

Political conditions for proto-industrial growth

Whereas the demographic situation and, to a somewhat lesser extent, the structures of the domestic economy in industrial regions have been relatively thoroughly studied, the political conditions which ensured the long-term profitability of proto-industrial enterprises are a theme which has been relatively little explored in the existing literature. Given the low level of technology in most industries and the minor significance of technological progress for proto-industrial growth, which have already been mentioned, efficiency and the ability rapidly to adopt technological innovations played a minor role in international competition between industrial regions. On the one hand, constant relative prices were a precondition for a reasonably stable proto-industrial growth. Therefore, proto-industrial success assumed an unsaturated demand for manufactured goods, and thus a constant expansion of the market. On the other hand, corresponding to the low level of production technology, competing supplier regions confronted comparable production functions and factor costs, generating the possibilities of conflict over access to markets. It is thus to be expected that in this sort of world economy, strategies of coercive control aimed at protecting markets will play a large role (Lane 1979). With these framework conditions as a background, two state strategies for ensuring proto-industrial growth can be observed in Switzerland.

Protection of market areas

If simple, internationally largely standardized goods (such as half-finished products) are produced, the control of market areas through political and military means becomes decisively important in securing longer-term market success. Already in the older literature on the history of trade, it is widely agreed that Swiss customs privileges in

France in the sixteenth century were an important precondition for the upturn in the linen processing of eastern Switzerland and the woollen and silk industries of Zürich (Pfister 1992a: 170–9). These privileges were supplemented by a similar agreement concluded in 1615/18 between Bern and Zürich on the one hand and Venice on the other. For Venice, the Swiss cities served to weaken Habsburg encirclement, and in return the contract guaranteed Zürich secure access to markets for raw materials (silk, cotton) and for its own output in Venetian Lombardy. While securing access to external markets through contracts based on the position of Switzerland as a supplier of mercenaries must have been of substantial significance for the proto-industrial upswing of the late sixteenth and early seventeenth centuries, the rising tax requirements of France, which went hand in hand with a growing autonomy from external suppliers of mercenaries, led in the course of the seventeenth century to the loss of most privileges. This development partly explains the crisis which can be observed in the decades around the mid-seventeenth century.

Securing of monopoly rents

Where a more complex palette of products in terms of technology and work processes dominated, there arose the possibility of a strategy which was less vulnerable to the incalculabilities of international trade policy: the setting up of a monopoly and the exploitation of the resulting rents. For this, on the one hand production standards and production processes had to be precisely laid down, and their maintenance monitored. On the other hand, any sort of transfer of technology in the form of out-migration of skilled workers or exports of working tools had to be prevented as much as possible. A core element in this industrial policy became the fight against embezzlement, a basic problem of proto-industrialization resulting from the rarity of formal enterprises in the *Kaufsystem* (artisanal system) and *Verlagssystem* (putting-out system). Emanating from this, there developed a range of further strategies through which the state sought to secure proto-industrial production relations (Fink 1983: 115–33; Mottu-Weber 1987: 49, 236–41, 344–52; Pfister 1992a: 180–99).

Both sorts of measure assumed the existence of an active state, and required a close relationship between proto-industrial entrepreneurs and the political powers. Thus in early modern Switzerland successful development into an industrial region went hand in hand with the rise of proto-industrial entrepreneurial strata to influential positions in the relevant state structure. This included the take-over of political offices by merchants, and the forming of kinship relationships with other, prominent families not involved in proto-industry. In addition, in order to institutionalize the relationship with the state, special organizations of a corporative nature were formed from the seventeenth century on. The German Swiss cities were among the first cities in which so-called 'merchant directorates' and 'manufactory commissions' developed. These corporate groups were as a rule made up of selected committees of merchants and members of the city government. They supplied an institutionalized representation of interests outside the established guild framework, through which proto-industrial merchants could influence state policy (Röthlin 1986: 63–6; Fink 1983: 109–11; Tanner 1982; Stauffacher 1989: 156–72; Pfister 1992a: 150–70).

Ultimately, around the middle of the eighteenth century, both of these strategies for state securing of proto-industrial growth were exhausted. For the small Swiss states governed by notables and devoid of a professional administrative apparatus, external trading areas were difficult to control, and both embezzlement and transfers of production practices could hardly be prevented, given the rudimentary nature of the bureaucratic apparatus. The cotton boom of the second half of the eighteenth century was thus based less on support by state structures, and more on a wide-ranging and efficient transaction system linking financial activities and a well-developed postal system with industrial involvement. This enabled the beginnings of a flexible palette of products to be marketed in large volumes in ways that were responsive to customers (Pfister 1992a: 91–8). Parallel to this, in some localities such as Glarus and Zürich, the interest of entrepreneurs in political activity declined (Stauffacher 1989: 168–70; Pfister 1992a: 199–204). The relative autonomy of the industrial sector in this phase was the second element in Swiss proto-industry – the first consisted of the bottle-necks in the labour supply – which led toward industrialization and ultimately to modernization more widely.

Implications for the concept of proto-industrialization

With regard to the chronological development of proto-industrialization, Switzerland corresponds to an ideal-typical pattern: ruralization of export-oriented industrial production in the 'crisis of the seventeenth century', and transition to mechanization in the early nineteenth century. Insofar as a substantial continuity can be shown to exist between proto-industrial and industrial entrepreneurial groups (Jäger *et al.* 1986: 69–72), the argument of Mendels, that proto-industrialization favoured the accumulation of the human and physical capital necessary for the industrial revolution, is correct (Mendels 1984: 993). Similarly, the classical thesis that the industrial revolution at least partly represented a reaction to rising labour and overhead costs (Landes 1973: 65–8) can also be substantiated. Here, this rise in costs was caused in particular by the inelasticity of the proto-industrial labour supply. The argument concerning rising labour and overhead costs, however, points to further determining reasons for an early and relatively successful transition to industrialization, which in the end have to do with the age of a proto-industrial system. First, sustained growth must have increased the size of the industry to the point that both overhead costs and recruitment of additional labour at constant real costs became severe problems. Secondly, it is noticeable that by the late eighteenth century the Swiss proto-industries had already lived through various models of state protection. As a result, they had achieved a maturity which led to an increasing differentiation of the political and entrepreneurial spheres, and which, owing to a strong international presence, enabled a rapid adoption of technological innovations. Thirdly, it must be pointed out that in the late eighteenth century, in contrast to the situation of the early seventeenth century, when the separate isolated production locations were still very strongly oriented toward international trade-fairs, a national market for selling industrial half-finished products had developed. On the eve of the industrial revolution, Switzerland thus already had at its disposal a differentiated and integrated industrial basis (Bernecker 1990: 435–6; Pollard 1991: 44–6).

Among the most-discussed aspects of the concept of proto-industrialization is undoubtedly the family economy of the rural labour force and the demographic behaviour which accompanied it. As the discussion above has shown, Swiss material on this theme is large and full of contrasts. The Zürich highland is the only area to which Mendels' statistical model of the relationship between marriage behaviour and proto-industrial real incomes has been applied with even partial success (Mendels 1972: 205–6; Pfister 1989a), and there are other cases in which proto-industrialization caused population growth mainly through lower mortality, or in which the population hardly increased at all. The classical thesis that proto-industrialization led to a breakdown in agrarian family forms and demographic behaviour through the creation of possibilities for household formation without an agrarian resource basis (Mendels 1984: 993) thus certainly does not apply as a general rule. By contrast, a more general model based on an analysis of the allocation decisions of rural households can adequately explain the observable differences (Pfister 1992b).

The agrarian preconditions for proto-industrialization also count among the most frequently discussed themes. It must be stated that northern Switzerland, together with a belt of neighbouring south German regions which specialized in grain production, correspond very well to a model of regional allocation, as Mendels ultimately formulated it (1980). According to this view, the development of proto-industrial regions is linked to the existence of numerous households whose agricultural holdings provide for only limited employment. This situation can come into being either through a labour-extensive system of cultivation or through a high degree of social inequality with a large group of people poor in land. Peasant inheritance law and a low degree of control by landlords can play a supplementary role in the rise of population pressure. Beyond these well-known arguments, the current discussion also stresses factors linked only peripherally to agrarian structure, namely the local availability of raw materials and the existence of an infrastructure of rural itinerant traders and urban merchants.

Finally, the current discussion takes into account political variables, whose analysis has been described, in one of the most lucid criticisms of the concept, as an 'open flank' in the theory of proto-industrialization (Schremmer 1980: 434–41; Ogilvie 1993a). The present chapter has argued that, given the absence of technological progress as a motor of growth, state protection, through maintenance of unsatiated export markets or constant relative prices which represented a basic condition for stable proto-industrial growth, was connected in the closest possible way with proto-industrialization. Based on the Swiss material, it has been shown that state protection encompassed various strategies, depending on the technological content of the goods being manufactured, and that it went hand in hand with various patterns of relationship between the state and entrepreneurs.

To sum up, the interpretation offered here of recent Swiss literature in the framework of a concept of proto-industrial growth stresses the great variability in proto-industrial development. The comparative examination of several regions which were not enormously different in terms of their system of agrarian exploitation or political framework has already brought to light an array of contrasting patterns. This fact makes ideal-typical development models of proto-industrialization, as aimed for in the classical studies of the proto-industrialization debates, seem problematic. By contrast, they provide an incentive to develop more rigorous formal models which can explain the differences which existed between the numerous proto-industrial regions now known to us (Pfister forthcoming).

11 The proto-industrial heritage: forms of rural proto-industry in northern Italy in the eighteenth and nineteenth centuries

Carlo Marco Belfanti

Introduction

In the traditional historiography, the seventeenth century is represented as the century of economic decline in Italy. This negative image is by and large justified because during the seventeenth century the urban economies of northern Italy, which had made this region one of the richest in Europe, were indeed affected by a profound crisis (Cipolla 1968). However, in recent times historians have not only described the seventeenth century in terms of crisis, but also pointed out the positive elements that were emerging from the transformations which had been caused by the difficult economic slump during the period (Sella 1979; Aymard 1991).

The crisis of city-based manufacturing produced effects which were heterogeneous, varying from place to place. In the broadest sense, however, the crisis may be said to have had two types of consequence. On the one hand, we witness a consolidation of activity around the manufacturing of those luxury goods which still maintained their competitiveness on international markets (Aymard 1991: 116–19). On the other hand – and this is the aspect which interests us most – the decline of city-based manufacturing industries, which were controlled by guilds, made possible the diffusion of industrial activity into the countryside (Aymard 1991: 98, 117).

The rigidity of the guild system and the high cost of labour which it imposed were among the principal causes of the de-centralization of some manufacturing into rural areas (Cipolla 1968: 137–41; Aymard 1991: 117). This development represented an important innovation to the pattern of division of labour between city and countryside which had been established in Italy since the time of the Communes. Cities had in fact gained a monopoly over manufacturing activity, which was strictly controlled by the urban guilds, while the inhabitants of the surrounding countryside were allocated the task of producing the basic foodstuffs necessary for supplying the city. The crisis of the seventeenth century shifted this balance, favouring a rural re-location of manufacturing industry.

Although known to historians, the importance of this phenomenon has for a long time been misunderstood, because it was considered a marginal change, unable to compensate for the decline of the rich urban industries (Ciriacono 1983: 58). This assessment is in large part founded in fact; however, it has prevented rural manufacturing from being accorded the attention it deserves.

In the last two decades, due partly to the debate aroused by the theories of Franklin Mendels (Mendels 1972), historians have begun to examine rural manufacturing more closely, and have discovered that its growth represented a positive transformation of the production system, a change generated by the seventeenth-century crisis (Aymard 1991: 98). In fact, it is to the growth of manufacturing activity in the countryside that we must look in order to find the most efficient long-term response to the decline of the city industries. The choice of relying on the manufacture of luxury goods in order to overcome the crisis was an option endogenous to the traditional organization of work, in that it accentuated the characteristics of the urban guild system, and it enjoyed only a very short-term success.

If we look at the situation of manufacturing in northern Italy in the later eighteenth century, we find that the majority of the traditional urban industries were in serious difficulties, while the most flourishing industries were those located in the countryside. In fact, the largest part of the traditional urban manufacturing did not survive beyond the end of the Ancien Régime. By contrast, some of the rural industries which made names for themselves between the seventeenth and the eighteenth centuries were remarkably long-lived, to the point of forming a not insignificant component of the industrial scene in the nineteenth century. This is why the rural industries represent a sort of 'proto-industrial heritage' from the pre-industrial age which maintained its vital role in nineteenth-century Italy.

The spread of rural manufacturing, triggered by the crisis in the urban economy, took place owing to a combination of variables, which differed from place to place. The diverse factors which determined the location of proto-industry were the presence of low-cost labour, abundance of water power, availability of raw materials, 'institutional particularism' or greater freedom from guild and state control thanks to the privileges enjoyed by these areas, and state support (Belfanti 1993).

In some cases we are observing manufacturing activity which already existed in the late Middle Ages because it was located in territories which, thanks to the privileges they enjoyed, were not subject to the direct dominion of a city and thus of the urban guilds. This particular legal status, which made the birth and survival of manufacturing outside the city walls possible, can be found in some mountain areas such as the Brescia and Bergamo valleys. In these territories the income earned in domestic industry enabled the peasants to supplement the meagre profit yielded by poor soil. Elsewhere, the beginnings of rural manufacture were more closely linked to the decline of urban industry, and it was the urban merchants themselves who, in the transfer of manufacturing to rural areas, found a solution to the high cost of labour within the city walls. In yet other cases, we find manufacturing activity created *ex novo* through the ability of an individual entrepreneur with the support of the state (Belfanti 1993).

Such a variety of combinations produced diverse forms of rural manufacturing. Depending on the situation, the families involved in domestic industry belonged to different social groups: small landowners, tenant farmers or farm labourers. In some cases, the work was carried out at home, while in others the seasonal employment practised by some members of the household was performed in a primitive factory. Furthermore, there were situations in which there was little or no integration between agricultural activity and industrial work, and the principal occupation was the production of manufactured goods. Finally, it is necessary to distinguish between the rural industries which declined and disappeared and those which transformed themselves into forms of rural proto-industrialization. It is these, and their respective characteristics, which are discussed in this chapter.

Above all, we will be examining the most important form of proto-industry present in the northern Italian countryside: the manufacture of silk. But domestic industry – as we will see – had had a fundamental role in the production of other sorts of textiles, such as cotton and wool, in which the passage to the factory system took place at different rates during the nineteenth century. There were also forms of rural proto-industry which retained their original character of domestic work up to the beginning of the twentieth century; for example, the manufacture of hats from straw in Tuscany and of the same article from plaited willow shavings at Carpi.

The peasants and silk

From the first half of the seventeenth century, the cultivation of mulberry trees, the breeding of silk worms and the reeling and throwing operations in silk production appear to have spread into the countryside throughout the Po valley. This progress must be seen as particularly significant when compared to the less brilliant development of the urban silk textile industry.

The reason for this growth was an expansion of the market which began in the second half of the seventeenth century (Sella 1976: 375–7). It was in this context that, in the following century, some important silk textile production centres elsewhere in Europe set up in business and became the strongest competitors for the Italian silk textile industry (Poni 1976: 495–6). But, although it is true that the silk-weaving sector suffered the consequences of strong foreign competition, it is also true that the production of raw and thrown silk benefited from an expanding international demand for semi-manufactured products (Moioli 1981).

In the seventeenth century, and even more in the eighteenth century, northern Italy consolidated its position as the principal production area in Europe for raw and thrown silk, and the semi-manufactured Italian silk products were exported to France, Switzerland, Germany, Holland and England (Poni 1976: 495–6; Moioli 1981: 94–7).

From the seventeenth century, the cultivation of mulberry trees and the breeding of silk worms played a leading role in the economy of Lombardy, especially in the highland and hilly areas lying to the north of Milan. In the area of so-called 'dry farming', where the estates were lacking in water, and grain cultivation had poor yields, arboriculture was very popular (Cafagna 1989: 88–112). In this context, the strong impetus given to the cultivation of mulberry trees and to the breeding of silk worms – in the form of a shared contribution between the landowner and the peasant – was an attempt to find a solution to the problems afflicting farming. The increasing international demand for raw silk and semi-manufactured silk products gave the landlord a source of cash, which operated as a safeguard against any decline in his agricultural income, while the greater demand for silk also enabled peasant families to diversify agricultural production as part of an integrated system (Moioli 1981: 39–41, 83–5). This ensured the survival of these peasant families, despite a context of worsening contract relations and indebtedness (Merzario 1989: 43).

However, during the eighteenth and nineteenth centuries, the living conditions of the peasant families who lived in the hilly areas of the Brianza and Como rapidly worsened, due to radical changes in agrarian contracts and a progressive proletarianization of the rural classes (Merzario 1989: 93–107). The traditional sharecropping contract had a term of several years, and was formed between the landowner and a patriarchal-type peasant household consisting of several family units and owning its own tools and ploughing team. This type of relationship allowed the sharecropping family a certain margin for negotiation, since it offered itself as a labour force suitable for the cultivation of fairly ample estates (Corner 1993: 39–40).

But the sharecropping contract was progressively abandoned in these areas in the course of the eighteenth century and replaced by a rental contract which was much more onerous for the peasant: payment consisted of a fixed quota of grain, to which was added half of everything else the peasant produced, including raw silk (Merzario 1989: 39–42). This change was brought about at the desire of the landowners, who aimed at increasing the share of the harvest due to them and raising the productivity of cereal production by imposing highly labour-intensive cultivation systems on their tenants. The landowners were in fact induced to break up their estates into small units which could be leased out on annual contracts to small family units belonging to the so-called 'pigionanti' (Corner 1993: 40–4). The latter thus became wage-earning dependants totally subject to the will of their master the landlord (Merzario 1989: 107; Corner 1993: 44–5). In addition, the number of such small households of poor peasants was expanded by the break-up of the patriarchal sharecropping families who succumbed under the weight of the new contractual forms (Merzario 1989: 106–7).

Not even the activity of silk-worm breeding succeeded in alleviating the poverty of the peasant families: they were forced to turn to the landowner for the purchase of their basic stock and even for the leaves on which the silk worms fed, thus getting themselves heavily into debt. This debt was then paid off with a quota of cocoons, which otherwise would have remained the property of the peasant. In this vicious circle the peasant family became ever poorer and the landowner could dispose of the entire product from the cocoons (Corner 1993: 47–8).

The cumulative effect of this process was increasingly to proletarianize the peasants, but without causing them to leave the land and emigrate to the cities, since the members of the peasant family – above all, the women and children – were offered the possibility of carrying out complementary work which allowed them to survive. Women and children were in fact employed in the reeling of silk, and in the operations preliminary to the throwing. Thus, while Italian silk continued to find a profitable place on international markets (Cafagna 1989: 281–3), the silk merchants could utilize at a derisory cost both the raw materials and a sizeable labour force which was employed in the early stages of the production process.

In many cases, it was the landowner himself who utilized this low-cost labour force to carry out the processing of the raw silk (Cova 1987: 138). This stage was often carried out at home since it did not require any particularly complex equipment (Caizzi 1968: 98; Merzario 1989: 109).

However, even where larger numbers of women were collected together to work in a primitive factory, the tie with the land was not broken and the activity of reeling continued to be a seasonal job which represented a source of extra earnings with which the peasant family would supplement the meagre yield from the land (Caizzi 1972: 42; Cova 1987: 138–50).

Towards the middle of the nineteenth century the reeling operations lasted seventy to eighty days a year and were carried out by several thousand workers: around 17,000 in the territory of Como, 8,000 around Bergamo, and 7,000 in the province of Brescia (Caizzi 1972: 42). This workforce was largely female: in 1844, according to statistics for the territory of Como, women made up 98 per cent of the workforce employed in the reeling; roughly half of them were under fifteen years of age (Merzario 1989: 115). It was only after the modernization of the plants, which followed the grave crisis in silk-worm breeding in the middle of the nineteenth century, that the processing of raw silk began to lose its character as seasonal work.

However, in the succeeding stage, the throwing, the organization of work was very different, and was no longer reconcilable with agricultural activity (Caizzi 1972: 36). From the end of the seventeenth century this stage of the production process was already concentrated into primitive factories (Poni 1976), the water silk mills, and it was less subject to seasonal fluctuations. In these factories, where the thrown silk was processed, the work, though not continuous in every case, lasted for several months a year (Caizzi 1968: 100; Cova 1987: 170–2). Thus, despite being almost all located outside the principal urban centres, the silk mills took on the shape of an early factory system (Poni 1976), where the workforce depended almost exclusively on a wage (Caizzi 1972: 41).

The 'proto-industrial' cycle which involved the peasant family was thus interrupted on the threshold of the silk mill, where the workforce was predominantly masculine: this was the situation until the middle of the nineteenth century. However in the second half of the century, in many cases the men were replaced with women, even in the silk mill, because a female workforce was regarded as more submissive than a male one (Corner 1993: 58).

In the countryside of the Brianza, around Como, and in the Lombardy highlands, there had therefore come into being, beginning around the middle of the eighteenth century, proletarianization without concentration into urban centres: the peasant family remained tied to the land, with the head of the family responsible for cultivating the land while the women and children sought, in the physically demanding work of silk reeling and throwing, the indispensable additional earnings needed for survival. This meant that the landowners and silk entrepreneurs (sometimes combined in one and the same individual) had at their disposal a low-cost labour force which – unlike a factory proletariat – could be evicted or sacked without creating dangerous social tensions (Corner 1993: 56–7).

We are dealing with a 'proto-industrial form' – or, as Cafagna defines it, an 'industry in equilibrium' (Cafagna 1989: 370–1) – in which the peasant family and the factory co-existed without there being, at least until the last decades of the nineteenth century, either a process of de-industrialization and return to agriculture, or the complete proletarianization and emigration to the cities of the peasant families. This socio-economic system remained in some measure static for almost a century (Corner 1993: 79–82).

The equilibrium which had lasted for so long began to show its first symptoms of crisis in the 1880s (Dewerpe 1991: 32–8), when the Italian economy went through a difficult phase of transformation (Cafagna 1989: 293–7). Starting from the last decade of the century, in fact, even the males of the peasant family – especially the younger ones – began to show an interest in the attractive salary offered by work in urban industry (Corner 1993: 83–7). But this was a slow evolution and did not become generalized until the outbreak of the Great War: according to Paul Corner, the land never ceased to be a fundamental reference point in the economic strategy of these peasant families (Corner 1993: 105).

Cottage weavers and cotton mills

In the north-west area of Lombardy, the cotton industry developed in an agrarian context almost analogous to that of the adjacent territory in which the manufacturing of silk was common. The peasants who lived on the moorlands of this zone mostly belonged to the same class of 'pigionanti' also found in the territory of Como and in the Brianza. They were crushed between back-breaking work on small, meagre plots of land in the search for subsistence, and the weight of onerous rent contracts (Romano 1990: 16–17). Here, too, the peasant often found himself irredeemably caught up in a vicious spiral of debt. Here again, the survival of the peasant family was tied to supplementary earnings, which in these areas came not from working silk, but from weaving lengths of cotton and mixed cloth.

This activity was particulary extensive around the communities of Gallarate and Busto Arsizio: a public official visiting there in 1767 observed that 'there are very few houses without a loom' (Caizzi 1968: 89). At the same date in these areas roughly 9,000 weavers produced about 100,000 lengths of cloth a year: this cloth, of medium quality, was sold in the neighbouring regions (Caizzi 1968: 89).

In the course of the nineteenth century the manufacture of cotton was to undergo considerable growth in these regions, until they became the principal production centre in Italy. The consolidated tradition of working in this fibre, the abundance of water power, and, naturally, the availability of low-cost labour, were the most significant factors which determined the location of the industry, and which underlay the diffusion of the numerous operations of mechanized spinning into the highlands of Milan beginning in the first half of the nineteenth century. The weaving of the cloth, by contrast, remained for much of the nineteenth century within the confines of a domestic industry practised at irregular intervals by the peasants (Caizzi 1972: 126–7; Romano 1990: 86–7).

Here, therefore, we observe a 'proto-industrial form' which presents analogies with, but also differences from, the situation in the silk-producing territories. The mechanical spinning of cotton, like the reeling of silk, absorbed a workforce which was predominantly made up of the women and children belonging to the peasant families (Romano 1990: 103–5, 197). But in these areas, unlike in the silk industry, the males of the family were also involved in manufacturing activity as weavers working at home, probably in order to supplement agricultural earnings which were particularly meagre (Caizzi 1972: 129). It was precisely for these reasons that weaving was mechanized and centralized in factories much later than spinning. In the 1860s, 90 per cent of the looms of Busto and Gallarate were still located in the home (Romano 1990: 129–31). For most of the nineteenth century, in fact, the entrepreneurs preferred to use the services of cottage weavers, which came at very low cost, rather than invest enormous sums in the mechanization and centralization of weaving. Only in the last twenty years of the century was significant progress made in the centralization and mechanization of weaving (Romano 1990: 154–70).

The manufacture of cotton therefore involved, although in different modes and at different phases, both the males and the females of the peasant family in the Milanese highlands. In this area, the participation of members of the peasant family in manufacturing activity, both 'proto-industrial' and fully industrial in the strict sense of the word, was higher than was the case in the silk-producing zones. In the cotton-producing zones, higher participation in manufacturing activity may have facilitated the absorption of the male workforce into the complete unfurling of the factory system, starting in the last twenty years of the nineteenth century (Romano 1990: 209–10). This did not mean, however, that the figure of the peasant factory worker now belonged to the past – it persisted at least until the wage was raised to the point at which it allowed the peasant to break every residual tie with the subsistence quota which came from agriculture (Romano 1990: 262–4).

The weaving of wool from cottage industry to factory system

The proto-industrial origins of wool manufacturing in the Biella territory, which became the most important wool-textile-producing district in Italy in the course of the nineteenth century, go back to the eighteenth century (Ramella 1984: 27–8). The spinning and, above all, the weaving of this material represented a fundamental source of income to supplement that earned from agriculture, which enabled the survival of numerous peasant families of small landowners who lived on these poor mountain soils, providing them with an alternative to emigration.

Weaving based in the home was a predominantly masculine activity, while women were employed principally in the spinning (Ramella 1984: 39–41). The early mechanization of this latter stage of the production process – which took place in the first decades of the nineteenth century – reinforced this sexual division of labour. In fact, following the centralization of spinning, many women accepted the non-specialized work and the wages offered by the factory. But work in the factory offered harsh conditions for women who were married and had children, so it was principally single women who were involved in this activity. Such a situation had significant consequences for the age at which couples married, causing it to rise in parallel with the increasing use of female workers in the factory (Ramella 1984: 43–9).

Weaving remained a cottage industry until about the middle of the nineteenth century, when the definitive closure of the independent market outlets which the weavers had previously enjoyed left them at the mercy of the entrepreneurs. The cottage weavers became principally dependent on the commissions they received from these merchants, and turned into almost an annexe to the factory (Ramella 1984: 43–4). Thus, when in the 1850s the necessities of production induced the entrepreneurs to abandon the putting-out system in favour of a centralized system, the weavers were forced to transfer their labour to the factory (Ramella 1984: 125–7).

This happened at a cost of acute tension in the workplace, partly because, while the times of industrial work in the home had been reconcilable with traditional agricultural activity, the discipline and working hours of the factory were no longer compatible with work in the fields (Ramella 1984: 132–4). Thus the commitment of men to agriculture had to change: it was now predominantly the women of the household who did these tasks (Ramella 1984: 154–5).

The manufacture of woollen cloth developed in the following decades and with it the opportunities for work in the factory increased. The small landholding, which most of the weavers still possessed, still played an important role in providing for the family's food needs, but the wage had by now taken on a decisive importance in the family budget. This meant that the hereditary transmission of land was no longer the determining factor for young people who wanted to marry and form families of their own. It is in this light that the increase in the number of marriages, the lowering of the age at which people married and the increase in population which are observed in the 1860s and 1870s must be interpreted (Ramella 1984: 157–60).

The breakdown of the social conditioning of demographic growth, which in Mendels' model characterizes the 'proto-industrial' phase, seems to have happened in the case of the Biella district, instead, when the production structure was already decisively directed towards the factory system.

Straw hats and willow plaits

In 1878 the Academy of Brescia, the city's principal cultural institution, announced a public competition for the best dissertation on the following title: 'Light industry suitable for agricultural labourers, especially women and children, in the intervals of work in the fields'. The work which won the prize and was published was by Bortolo Benedini, an accurate observer of the economic situation of his time, who had analysed the manufacturing activities carried out at home by Italian peasants (Benedini 1880). He pointed out, as the most typical and interesting form of domestic activity, 'the industry of plaiting and making hats from straw' (Benedini 1880: 26), which was widespread in the territories of Vicenza and Bologna, in the Marche, and above all in Tuscany.

The starting point of this Tuscan industry can be dated to the beginning of the eighteenth century, with the spread of a particular species of grain ('March corn'), from which the straw was obtained (Malanima 1990: 101). From the first half of the eighteenth century, straw hats, although initially destined for the regional market, began to be exported to England, France, Germany and eventually America. This industry expanded in several areas of the Grand Duchy of Tuscany and the labour force increased from 25,000 to 100,000 workers in the period between 1800 and 1861 (Malanima 1990: 102). The golden age of straw hat production was the nineteenth century, when this became the principal Tuscan manufacture thanks to the success it achieved on the American market (Pescarolo and Ravenni 1991: 69).

The workforce employed in this cottage industry was predominantly female, but, although we are dealing with a rural population, they did not belong to the peasant class, which in Tuscany was made up almost entirely of sharecroppers. In Tuscan sharecropping, the size of each estate was exactly proportional to the number of members of the peasant family; the labour provided by the family unit was completely dedicated to work in the fields. Moreover, these peasant families also had to provide a range of services and labour without pay (corvée) for the landowner. Furthermore, we must bear in mind that in Tuscany mixed agriculture prevailed, with corn associated with olive trees, vines and the like, which required attention throughout the year (Malanima 1990: 105–7). In Tuscan agriculture – which was unchanged by any radical transformation of the sharecropping contract analogous to that in Lombardy – the vine, the olive and, later, stock breeding probably absorbed the work which elsewhere was dedicated to proto-industrial activity (Giorgetti 1974: 294–301).

In such an agrarian context there was no place for complementary activities, except for some secondary tasks carried out by women (Pescarolo and Ravenni 1991: 26–7). Tuscan rural manufacturing of straw hats therefore found low-cost labour in another social group, the so-called 'pigionali' (Malanima 1990: 104–7). This was a rural class which grew contemporaneously with the expansion of the rural population that occurred during the second half of the seventeenth century and in the eighteenth century (Malanima 1990: 146–51).

The 'pigionali' were substantially wage-earning occasional labourers who mainly found employment as field hands, but also worked at other seasonal or sporadic activities (Pescarolo and Ravenni 1991: 76–7). The women of these families made up the largest proportion of the workforce active in the manufacturing of straw hats (Pescarolo and Ravenni 1991: 28–9).

The first great growth in this domestic industry, which took place in the first decades of the nineteenth century, necessarily modified the demographic behaviour of the labour force employed. The relief brought to the family budget by the wages earned in industry favoured an increase in the number of marriages and a lowering of the age at which such marriages were undertaken: the families of the 'pigionali' multiplied rapidly under the astonished and anxious eyes of contemporary observers. Only the increase in emigration and the recurrent and aggravated high incidence of infant mortality defused the danger of this demographic trend (Pescarolo and Ravenni 1991: 78–96).

In the second half of the nineteenth century, the succession of periodic crises to which this manufacture was subject, combined with the surplus in the available labour force caused by the increase in population, produced a progressive decline in the level of the wages offered and a consequent deterioration in the living conditions of the families employed (Pescarolo and Ravenni 1991: 89–96). However, this dynamic, which culminated in the crisis of the last years of the century, did not lead to the eviction and uprooting of the 'rural proletariat' which had been formed around the manufacture of straw hats, but rather to its survival through the organizational re-structuring of the industry in the first decades of the twentieth century (Pescarolo and Ravenni 1991: 31–4, 125–76).

In the course of the nineteenth century, the manufacture of straw hats also spread to other areas, where it achieved a certain volume, even if this was never comparable to the importance of the Tuscan trade (Benedini 1880: 24–5). The industry established in the area of Carpi, near Modena, was analogous in some respects. Its most notable product was a hat for which the raw material was willow shavings.

The production of willow plaits was already widespread in the sixteenth century, employing thousands of people, especially women and children. During the eighteenth century this industry developed significantly, due to the success of these hats on the English market. The commercial success of the hats from Carpi was also to increase in the course of the nineteenth century. The marketing outlets had expanded conspicuously and the hats began to be exported all over Europe and to America. This phase of expansion lasted until the 1870s, and after the crisis of the 1880s had passed, a new phase of growth began which continued until the first decades of the twentieth century (Cappello and Prandi 1973: 56–64).

Around 1870 this industry employed up to 12,000 people at home and at the beginning of the twentieth century, when the recruitment area for the workforce was further enlarged, the number of women employed reached as many as 40,000 (Cappello and Prandi 1973: 61, 67). The workforce employed in the production of willow plaits and hats was largely made up of women and children, and was recruited both from the peasant families resident in the countryside and from those resident in the villages. It is, however, certain that this was a cottage industry which was complementary with agricultural work, and which could be set aside when the work in the fields was particularly intense or remunerative. In 1856, one entrepreneur in this industry complained of the lack of available workers for the processing of the willow shavings, following a favourable year for agriculture, and wrote: 'The peasants have grown rich and this means enormous damage to our production!' (Poni and Fronzoni 1979: 18).

The domestic processing of willow shavings did not produce proletarianization or an expulsion of the workforce from the rural world, but rather contributed to avoiding the break-up of the social fabric, by offering a supplementary source of income to the peasant families living in the area. The situation changed only after the Second World War, when the manufacturing of hats, which was by then in decline, was replaced by the domestic production of knitwear. Hosiery production – which was established on the old network created by the hat merchants (Cappello and Prandi 1973: 117–41) – was no longer an activity complementary with agriculture, but instead a form of widespread light industry based on small business (Capecchi 1991).

Forms of rural proto-industry in the age of industrialization

One of the major merits of the theory proposed by Franklin Mendels is probably that of having pointed out that rural proto-industries represent a strong element of continuity in the passage from the pre-industrial age to the phase of industrialization, of which they are without any doubt a component. This does not mean, however, that proto-industrialization was an essential prerequisite for the process of industrialization, nor that rural proto-industry necessarily evolved towards a factory system or towards de-industrialization.

Examination of the Italian cases presented in this chapter, which were significant examples of forms of rural proto-industry which played a role in the process of industrialization, seems to me to demonstrate that rural proto-industry was a very fluid phenomenon.

Certainly, every 'proto-industrial form' was necessarily based on the availability of a cheap rural labour force, which needed to supplement agricultural earnings which were insufficient for the family's subsistence. But this labour force belonged to different social classes, depending on the specific situation. Thus in Lombardy the reserve of labour for the manufacturing of silk was provided by the families of the 'pigionanti', poor peasants who had meagre smallholdings for which they paid rent, while in the Biella territory it was the owners of small pieces of land who supplied their work to the wool merchants. In Tuscany, the proto-industrial workforce was made up of the 'pigionali', a poor class which lived in rural districts – above all in the villages – but had no land to cultivate.

As far as the patterns of development of these various proto-industrial forms are concerned, here too diverse paths can be observed, depending on the context. In the case of wool textile manufacturing in the Biellese territory, the passage to the factory system was quite rapid, despite the reluctance of the weavers to accept this new work discipline. It was only following this transformation, and consequent upon the increasing role of the wage in the family budget, that the social ties which bound the formation of a new family to the hereditary transmission of land broke down. In the cotton-producing districts of the Milanese highlands, the passage to the factory system was slower, perhaps because, in comparison with the Biellese area, the wages for domestic weaving were lower and therefore the proportion of the family budget which derived from agriculture was still significant. This may be regarded as the main reason for the reluctance of the domestic worker to move to working within the factory. In the silk-producing districts, such as the Brianza and the Comasco, the proto-industrial family survived side by side with the factory up to the beginning of the twentieth century. The family budget benefited both from the contribution made by the wages the women earned from manufacturing and from the proceeds of the men's work in the fields. Finally, the picture is completed by those forms of proto-industry, such as the manufacturing of straw hats in Tuscany or hats made from willow shavings at Carpi, whose organization remained based on a putting-out system up to the beginning of the present century.

The lack of uniformity among the various experiences of proto-industry in Italy is very significant, and this is why, at least as far as Italy is concerned, we cannot speak of 'rural proto-industry' *tout court*, but must instead refer to 'proto-industrial forms'. However, the interpretative category 'rural proto-industry' – although a more restricted definition than that of Mendels' model, being understood simply in the sense of a mode of production based on the use of the peasant family as a workforce for manufacturing – represents a useful concept, which can help us to understand an important component of the process of industrialization. The proto-industrial experiences described in this chapter demonstrate, in fact, that in vast areas of northern Italy and in important branches of industry – above all, the silk industry – the peasant family was a factor in a method of production which, despite the multiplicity of forms it manifested, continued to be vital for almost the whole of the nineteenth century (Dewerpe 1985).

This situation was evaluated positively by many contemporary observers (Dewerpe 1986: 46–8), who were aware of, and were anything but enthusiastic about, the social degradation created by the first great industrial concentrations in England. In the middle of the nineteenth century, for example, Giuseppe Sacchi wrote of the peasant weavers of the Milanese highlands:

For all of these workers who live in their own homes it has been possible to maintain the family order established by Providence. Allow us this expression, which will perhaps seem poetic to those economists who count men only as numbers, for we will always persist in believing that the worker without family, or outside of it, will never be a man of whom it is possible to say that he lives in a civil society. (Caizzi 1972: 129)

He was echoed by Giovanni Frattini, who, with no less emphasis, underlined the advantages to be derived from the condition of the peasant weaver compared to that of the factory worker:

Here it never happens that the worker is reduced to living on potatoes alone; instead, he also feeds himself with rice and maize and various other products which are supplied to him by life in the fields, in the midst of which he lives, and in which he can find refuge when he lacks work. (Caizzi 1972: 132)

Leaving aside these observations, which are beyond doubt guilty of painting far too rosy a picture, in the proto-industrial reality which has been examined here the factory system did not represent a drastic alternative to cottage industry, but in many cases existed side by side with it, without causing it to disappear. In many cases, as we have seen, the two types of production were integrated and complementary: some phases of the production process were carried out at home, while others were centralized in the factory. The land continued for almost the whole of the nineteenth century to represent a significant point of reference for the proto-industrial family, although in different measures according to the particular situation. In some cases, as in the Brianza and Comasco, agricultural activity never completely disappeared, while elsewhere, as in the Biellese, the small landholding owned by the peasant was principally important for the satisfaction of the family's food needs. In the first factories, in fact, the imposition of work discipline and fixed hours clashed with the exigencies of seasonal work in the fields (Ramella 1984: 132–4; Romano 1990: 200–1).

In general, however, it was the women who first confronted the experience of work in the factory, precisely in order to safeguard the ancient tie with the land, thus maintaining the division of labour within the peasant family. The achievement of this objective, however partial, represents a common feature of the proto-industrial experiences presented in this chapter. In fact, although there were situations of extreme poverty, and, at times, proletarianization of the families involved, at least during the nineteenth century proto-industry did not issue in the extreme consequences described by Mendels, namely social disintegration and the uprooting of rural society. Nor does it seem that there was wild demographic growth to such an extent as gravely to prejudice the existing social equilibrium. The area of straw hat manufacturing, in Tuscany, was involved in phases of population growth which reached high levels, but thanks to the action of safety valves such as emigration we do not observe an uncontrolled boom (Pescarolo and Ravenni 1991: 87–96).

The proto-industrial areas of northern Italy therefore maintained the characteristics of their origins for a long time without being precipitated into the critical, transformational spiral described by Mendels. Moreover, in the areas where the proto-industrial family managed to resist most tenaciously the allurement or necessity of moving to the town, according to some authors in some chronological phases there were created forms of industrialization which were alternatives to the large factory, and instead were based on the small business (Cappello and Prandi 1973: 117–41; Pescarolo and Ravenni 1991: 23–34; Corner 1993: 163–79).

12 Proto-industrial development in Austria*

Markus Cerman

Introduction

The concepts of proto-industrialization (Mendels 1972; Kriedte, Medick and Schlumbohm 1981) have been taken into account in a variety of ways in the economic and social history of the Austrian area. They range from applications of the theories to the economic development of the whole Austrian half of the Habsburg monarchy before the actual industrial revolution (Good 1983; Komlos 1983b), to detailed case-studies of proto-industrial regions concentrating to varying degrees on the economic, social-structural and demographic effects of proto-industrial domestic production (Berkner 1973; Fitz 1981; Komlosy 1988; Zeitlhofer 1995). In the context of research into changes in family structures, too, the effects of domestic industry have been subjected to a more detailed analysis (Ehmer 1980; Mitterauer 1986, 1992). In accordance with the approach adopted by the theories themselves, what follows will take regional developments as a point of departure, in order subsequently to examine the structural characteristics of proto-industries in Austria.

Owing to geographical preconditions, the economic structure of the area occupied by present-day Austria – in both the Alps and the plains – has been marked by specialized forms of agrarian economy since the early modern period. Consequent upon mining activities (especially salt and iron, but in the early modern period also precious metals), industries and early industrial production forms developed locally, including within the Alps themselves, for example in Salzburg, Styria and southern Upper and Lower Austria. In addition, in the extreme western and northern parts of the country, from the sixteenth century at latest, there developed proto-industrial regions which were initially characterized mainly by the cultivation and processing of the domestic raw material, flax. By and large, in the economic area of present-day Austria one observes a relative multiplicity of geographical conditions and ecotypes, and considerable regional specialization (Hassinger 1986: 945ff; Knittler 1993: 906; Mitterauer 1986, 1992; Sandgruber 1995).

* This chapter is translated from the German by Sheilagh C. Ogilvie.

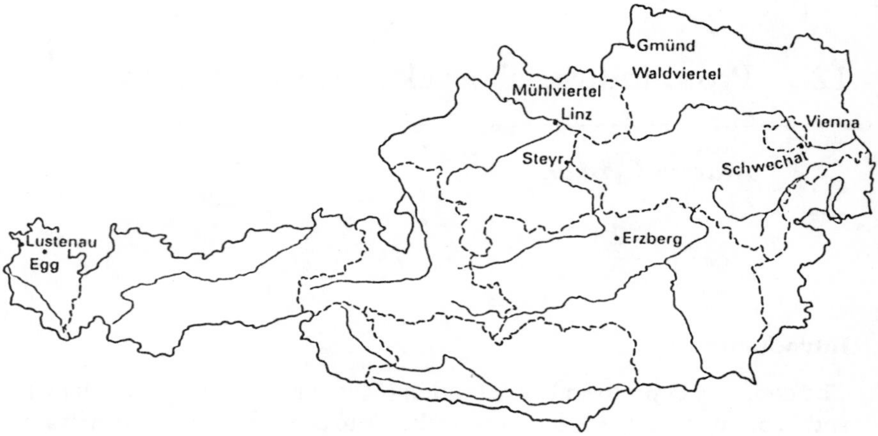

Map 12.1 Map of Austria
Source: Mitterauer 1986: 199.

The textile industry

The very variety of agrarian activities led to a certain degree of involvement by some groups of the population, especially those belonging to sub-peasant groups, in seasonal domestic work with a wide variety of raw materials and products. However, these domestic industries, even when they expanded in times of agrarian crisis, did not attain the status of primarily export-oriented proto-industries. Owing to the absence of a complete permeation by industry in the sense of a dominant source of earnings, it can be assumed that the demographic and social consequences postulated in the theories played no role for such regions (Mitterauer 1986: 236, 252; 1992). For testing the theory, it is thus important to distinguish in the Alpine countries between the widespread domestic industrial by-employments (with a wide variety of combinations of main occupation and by-employment, sometimes also in combination with peddling), which were not considered in the theories, and actual proto-industrial activities, which will be the focus of attention here.

As in other countries, so too in Austria the textile industry played the most significant role. The production and processing of linen had been widespread since the late Middle Ages, especially in north-west Vorarlberg and in the Upper Austrian Mühlviertel. While the former region limited itself mainly to production of the high-quality raw material, and partly also spinning for the Swiss-German linen-processing area around Lake Constance, and thus did not enter into complete proto-industrial production relations in this phase, the Mühlviertel became the centre of linen processing in Austria.

The Upper Austrian Mühlviertel

Although the production and preparation of the raw material took place in rural regions, the actual processing began with the handing over of the yarn to the small-town weavers' guilds which began to form in Upper Austria at the turn of the fifteenth into the sixteenth century. However, the frequent complaints of the urban guilds are evidence of the existence of non-guilded rural weavers at latest in the sixteenth century (Hoffmann 1952: 103).

At the same period, merchants from Salzburg and Germany (especially Nuremberg) appeared, and organized exports of linen to Germany and Italy. By the beginning of the Thirty Years War, the linen industry had reached a peak. Although after the interruption of the war, strong export relations are also observable for the second half of the seventeenth century, they did not attain the intensity of the pre-war period (Halmdienst 1993: 61ff; Hassinger 1986: 952ff; Hoffmann 1952: 181ff).

It was the initiative of foreign merchants which led to an expansion in linen production. As their partners in production, they selected the linen weavers' guilds, which had formed a dense network of organization, not least owing to the stimulus of exports. Not only were most urban weavers incorporated into a regional guild, but in 1578 the territorial prince granted their demands for a general 'Landeshandwerksordnung' (provincial craft ordinance for the province of Upper Austria). This was renewed repeatedly until 1777, and functioned almost as a framework for a unification of all linen weavers' guilds in the province (Hoffmann 1952: 103ff). A guild organization of this size in a proto-industry, which was able to retain real influence until the final years of the seventeenth century, was not frequently found in Europe.

The export merchants pushed ever more forcibly into the production process, in that they provided individual craftsmen with cash for obtaining yarn, or even provided yarn directly. This situation was gradually regulated through putting-out contracts which, in the form of a 'Zunftkauf' ('guild purchase'), could also involve an entire guild. A 'guild purchase' was mentioned for the first time in Upper Austria in a linen weavers' ordinance of 1506. The institutionalization of putting-out relations as early as the period of guilded production makes the borderlines between this and non-guilded proto-industrial production indistinct; it laid the basis for the inclusion of a growing number of rural weavers into putting-out relations in the course of the seventeenth and eighteenth centuries (Hoffmann 1952: 181ff).

It is undoubtedly the case that rural weaving also developed early on. Many rural weavers worked for wages for their landlords, who obtained the flax which they provided to the weavers from their own peasant subjects. The finished linen cloth was then sold to the landlord at a wage agreed upon in advance, and sent on for further processing by the landlord. The landlords often protected the rural weavers vis-à-vis the territorial prince, when they were subject to attacks by the guilds, which were particularly directed against the permanent scarcity of yarn and the resulting competition. In 1709 the rural weavers were made *de facto* equal to the guilded producers, until around the middle of the eighteenth century the Theresian Reforms got rid of the excessive influence of the guilds in proto-industries (Halmdienst 1993: 42, 71; Hoffmann 1952: 79, 134f; Mosser 1981: 400ff; Otruba 1981). It was the rural weavers who, in the course of the eighteenth century – after the loss of the Silesian linen industry – became the agents of renewed expansion in the industry. The putting-out link remained in existence – mainly under other putters-out – and the *Verlagssystem* (putting-out network) of the Linzer Wollzeugmanufaktur (Linz Worsted Manufactory) founded in 1672 dominated large sections of the industry. With the decline of the influence of the guilds, however, linen merchants also pushed more forcibly into production, and in the course of the eighteenth and early nineteenth centuries they established themselves as a dominant factor (Halmdienst 1993: 95ff; Hoffmann 1952: 310ff).

The Waldviertel

Large manufactories enjoying privileges from the territorial prince also played a role in the proto-industrial cotton processing in the Lower Austrian Waldviertel in the eighteenth century. With the putting-out systems of the great cotton manufactories in Schwechat near Vienna (founded in 1724), Fridau (founded in 1752) and Šastín in Slovakia (founded in 1736), the permeation of rural areas with domestic industry attained a higher intensity, but also showed a certain continuity with linen processing from the seventeenth century on. The main region of domestic textile industry was the north-west Waldviertel, whose climate and soil were quite harsh and barren – consequently, agricultural production for the market did not come into question (Berkner 1973: 25ff; Mitterauer 1986: 233f; 1992).

In the second half of the eighteenth century, weaving was to a greater extent added to the spinning of cotton which had already been established previously. Because mechanization was only very gradual, and because of its role as a structural supplement to factory weaving, domestic weaving endured into the late nineteenth century, to some extent even into the early twentieth century. In addition to manufactories, an important role in export-oriented cotton processing was also played by the 'regional' (urban–rural) weavers' guilds (Berkner 1973: 123ff, 146ff; Komlosy 1988: 26ff, 137ff; 1991; Matis 1991).

The social structure of the Waldviertel area did not correspond to the classic social polarization in proto-industrialization, because peasant groups were in a relative majority. This was linked to the impartible inheritance system and the strict control over new settlement and use of the commons, which was exercised by landlords and village communities. As a result, until the second half of the eighteenth century it was hardly possible for sub-peasant groups to erect their own houses. Inmate families became a widespread social form in the peasant households of the Waldviertel, where they leased a piece of potato field and were available to the peasants as day-labourers. Only from the 1780s on did village communities permit the building of new houses, which meant that inmate families could become independent in houses of their own. But a 'social revolution' did not occur in this stage, either, for the proportion of the population made up by the peasant strata hardly changed – thus no unrestricted growth of sub-peasant groups occurred as a result of proto-industrialization (Berkner 1973: 172ff; Komlosy 1988: 11ff).

Despite the fact that proto-industrial domestic work developed into an important branch of earnings, it was integrated into the traditional social structure, instead of transforming it. This may also have been linked to the fact that the industry was practised by all social strata, and that proto-industrial activities among the peasant groups were to a large extent seasonal and life-cyclical in nature. No divorce from agricultural resources came into question. Berkner has shown unambiguously that mentalities and everyday culture remained within traditional paths, too (Berkner 1973: 194ff).

Although the new earning possibilities led to a substantial increase in the number of married inmates in the course of the early nineteenth century, at no period was the social framework broken open. There occurred merely a quantitative expansion in the number of people in what was a traditional social form. A qualitative change took place to the extent that, in the course of the nineteenth century, the inmate families may have become economically more independent from the heads of the farmer households in which they lived, particularly since, after the collapse of the putting-out of the great cotton manufactories during the beginnings of the industrial revolution, the latter withdrew from industry. In the phase of domestic weaving as a supplement to the factory, domestic industry really became an exclusive activity of sub-peasant groups (Komlosy 1988: 146ff; Mitterauer 1986: 234f; 1992).

Studies on the marriage ages of domestic workers in the area of Gmünd for the period 1791–1843 have found that the age at marriage of men and women employed in domestic industry was clearly lower than the average for all other groups in the population (Zeitlhofer 1995). However, the marriage age of all groups showed a tendency to rise in the first half of the nineteenth century. In the case of those employed in domestic industry, this development was connected to the economic crisis consequent upon the abolition of the Continental Blockade.

Vorarlberg

The structure of domestic work in Vorarlberg displays an even more complex inter-penetration with agriculture and with other forms of earnings. The land offered favourable conditions for flax cultivation, and seasonal spinning of yarn was one of many supplementary forms of earnings for a population with only relatively scarce land resources at its disposal. Already in the early modern period, the partible inheritance customary in Vorarlberg led to considerable fragmentation of land-holdings and a dependency of the inhabitants on exploitation of the commons. This development was linked not least to a weakly developed seigneurial system which, until the seventeenth century, failed to exercise strict control over division of holdings and new in-migration; through the abolition of the 'Flurzwang' (communal system regulating cultivation of the fields) and the three-field system, this also favoured more intensive forms of cultivation (such as maize and, in the eighteenth century, potatoes). From the sixteenth or seventeenth century on, limited land resources led to an expansion of mercenary service and seasonal labour migration. Re-orientation to a highly specialized animal husbandry and dairy farming freed additional labour (Fitz 1981: 59ff; Mitterauer 1986: 234ff; 1992; Weitensfelder 1991: 12ff, 39ff).

Similar to the involvement of parts of Vorarlberg in flax production in the early modern period, cotton spinning was also established, under the influence of neighbouring eastern Switzerland, where the putters-out and merchants of St Gallen had an interest in extending the production basis. The expansion of putting-out cotton spinning from the mid-eighteenth century on created an additional source of earnings, especially for women and children, and did not place the traditional social framework into question. Only with the emergence of weaving and embroidering in later phases did men become involved more intensely. But as in the Waldviertel, here too it was not an actual 'landless class' which became involved in domestic work, but rather a group of small peasants, whose attitudes and primary economic interest were, now as ever, concentrated on the land, even when the agrarian resources might not suffice for survival (Fitz 1981: 110ff; Mitterauer 1986: 234f; 1992; Weitensfelder 1991: 73).

The market structure for embroidery products required greater flexibility, which could not be guaranteed by rigid and excessively large putting-out organizations or large plants. By contrast, in the spinning and weaving of cotton the putting-out system was from 1764 on gradually surpassed by manufactory-like large plants; this was an important organizational parallel to the textile regions discussed earlier (Fitz 1981: 133ff; Weitensfelder 1991: 40ff).

Demographic development, which has been investigated in selected regions, shows two distinct patterns. In Lustenau, in the area with the greatest expansion of domestic work in Vorarlberg, a considerable rise in population had already taken place before the intensive beginnings of the domestic industry; this can primarily be traced back to the expansion in available foodstuffs through the introduction of maize and potatoes, which continued in the proto-industrial phase. In the marginalized regions of the Bregenzerwald which experienced proto-industrialization later, however, domestic industry appears to have been responsible for a considerable growth of population in the late eighteenth century. The income possibilities which proto-industry initially improved for women caused them in particular to marry and form households earlier in life. While for Lustenau a constant and low female marriage age can be observed for the duration of the entire proto-industrial period from 1765 onward, the marriage age of women in the region of the Bregenzerwald fell swiftly under the influence of domestic work, and then rose again rapidly after the end of the boom around the turn of the century. In this case it emerges that proto-industrial demographic trends were wholly reversible. In the 1850s the Bregenzerwald underwent a re-agrarianization, and the non-agrarian population migrated out of the region (Fitz 1981: 188ff, 327ff).

Changes in family structure under the influence of proto-industrialization can hardly be observed. Especially in the first decades, this was linked to the inter-penetration with agriculture, which made a small farmstead a precondition of family formation and a core element of family structure. Such a strong tie to the land was created by the system of partible inheritance, which meant that each heir automatically received a piece of land. However, a change in mentalities and everyday culture (such as status-oriented consumption, for example) and a certain loosening of the tie with the agrarian basis (a neglect of cultivation of the fields in periods of favourable industrial conjunctures) can be observed.

From the early nineteenth century on, a strengthening of the 'political consent to marriages' (*politischer Ehekonsens*) made marriage in Vorarlberg dependent on the agreement of the local government. This agreement was unambiguously connected to property, and in turn town citizenship was linked to married status, as for example in Lustenau. Rules of this sort, and the traditional mode of conduct according to which marriage was the sole legitimate form of sexuality, represented a developing counter-current to liberalization, which excluded 'social revolutions'. Despite the observed demographic consequences, Vorarlberg, too, saw no complete break with traditional rules (e.g. in the area of marriage behaviour or the maintenance of peasant smallholdings) (Fitz 1981: 253ff, 293ff, 371ff).

Iron and metal processing

The 'textile bias' of the theory of proto-industrialization has often led to disagreement about whether other branches of industry should also be regarded as proto-industries. When one takes into account the two main factors for designating proto-industries, namely export-orientation and the specific organizational form which relies on domestic work and the family economy, metal processing in Austria corresponds to the narrow definition of proto-industrialization only in the first of these two respects. In addition to this, it apparently did not lead to changes in demographic behaviour in the affected regions.

Certainly, it is repeatedly pointed out in the debates that the neglect of centralized forms of production represents an inadequacy in the original theories (Hudson 1986: 59). In the early modern metal industries, we are dealing with production which was export oriented and tied to a particular location, and which relied partly on centralized or guilded workshops; it is, however, not always easy to distinguish these workshops from small, family-operated production units (Hassinger 1986: 950).

The development of this industry since the Middle Ages was characterized by numerous acts of regulatory intervention on the part of the Austrian territorial princes. Around the middle of the fifteenth century, these were directed above all at the availability of fuel (wood) and at providing industrial areas with foodstuffs, both of which were ensured by setting up 'Widmungsbezirke' ('dedicated districts', which were not allowed to sell their wood and food production anywhere but to the iron-manufacturing regions). However, in the Middle Ages the territorial princes already also regulated the market. The towns of Judenburg (in 1277), Steyr (in 1287) and Leoben (in 1344) were designated as distribution centres for the most important iron-mining locations, Vordernberg and Innerberg on the Erzberg (also on what follows: Hassinger 1986: 950ff; Knittler 1986: 6ff; Pickl 1986: 18ff; Sandgruber 1995).

The production process can be divided first into the actual production of iron in the smelting works directly at the sites of extraction, and secondly into its further processing in forges; because of the availability of water power and the increasing scarcity of wood on location, these also shifted to more remote locations. In the fifteenth century, differentiation of production and technical innovations led to an increased need for capital, which could not be provided by the individual works; these were often operated on a very small-scale basis, or by former peasants. At this point, provision of capital by merchants became important; these also took on the intermediary functions between the actual iron production and the further processing. The merchants of the town of Steyr who exercised influence on the Innerberg side of the Erzberg became putters-out to the forges, and these in turn put out to the smelting works. Without exercising direct putting-out over the Vordernberg side of the Erzberg, Leoben had become the other centre of trading activities. As early as 1416, the traders there united into an iron-trading association. The putting-out relations were also partly regulated by the territorial prince.

The high point of production in the early modern period may have been reached around the middle of the sixteenth century, while the Thirty Years War represented a low point. The largest customers for the Styrian industry were the Nuremberg and Augsburg merchant houses, and it is held that their departure was partly responsible for the crisis. Increasing difficulties in the last years of the sixteenth century led to state measures for improving infrastructure, and Innerberg in particular was supported through capital inputs from Steyr traders, who had since 1583 been unified into an iron-trading association. Its failure in the crisis of the 1620s led to the establishment in 1625 of the Innerberger Hauptgewerkschaft, i.e. a company similar to modern joint-stock companies, which from then on dominated both production and sales. On account of the crisis, the producers in Vordernberg joined together in 1626 merely into a purchasing association, which – like guild organizations – also determined wages and work organization. This strong export orientation was also present in the next upswing in the course of the seventeenth century. Some 40 to 50 per cent of the Innerberg production went to Germany, but this share was falling. Further increasingly important export areas for the Austrian iron regions were Italy and western Hungary.

With respect to the further processing of iron, which was similarly export oriented, in particular the production of blades in Steyr and the processing of scythes in Lower and Upper Austria came to the fore in the early modern period (Fischer 1966). Spatially, this industry was tied to particular locations by supplies of both fuel (wood and water power) and raw materials. These features combined with the insufficiency of agricultural land in these areas to generate a necessity for industrial production (Fischer 1966: 15f; Hassinger 1986: 951f; Sandgruber 1995).

Setting up water-driven forges also permitted the scythe-processing areas their own production of scythe billets, half-finished metal scythe cores which still had to be smithed and finished. In the course of the sixteenth century, this branch of production led the previously primarily urban industry to shift to the surrounding countryside. The favourable upturn in agriculture in the sixteenth century ensured demand for this expansion of the industry. Not only the actual workshops themselves, but also the supplier industries (such as transport services and collieries), which are not explicitly considered by the theories of proto-industrialization, created numerous earning possibilities for peasant groups in the sixteenth and seventeenth centuries. Regional studies in southern Upper Austria have revealed an increase in the number of sub-peasant smallholdings in this period. For the landlords, the settlement of new scythe smiths also created increased employment possibilities for the sub-peasant group, as well as an increase in their own rent revenues. In this way, despite the expansion in sub-peasant groups, the expansion of the industry contributed to fortifying the traditional seigneurial order (Hassinger 1986: 951f; Fischer 1966: 8ff, 76, 81f).

As a consequence of the substantial intervention by the territorial prince in the iron-producing industry, which provided the scythe smiths with their raw material, it was important for the scythe producers to organize themselves, in order better to represent the interests of the industry. Thus by the beginning of the seventeenth century almost all scythe producers in the various production areas successfully petitioned for the establishment of regional guilds. Through formulating and granting the actual guild privileges, the territorial princes secured influence over this branch of industry (Fischer 1966: 19ff).

Not least through this interest on the part of the territorial prince, the scythe industry was also tied into the putting-out system which encompassed the whole of iron production and iron processing (Fischer 1966: 104ff). For the producers, the functionality of this system was based on its ensuring the raw material supply and guaranteeing the market. From the early sixteenth century at latest, the scythe putters-out distributed raw materials for processing, to both the forge smiths and the scythe smiths. In addition, associations of these scythe traders arose on a regional level, as in 1653 in Waidhofen. In other production areas, although the scythe smiths' guilds still retained their autonomy, in matters of putting-out and trade they relied exclusively on the iron putters-out of Steyr. When it appeared that the scythe smiths were threatened by excessive dependency, the guilds obtained from the territorial prince an emancipation from their obligation to sell in Steyr. Thus in the late seventeenth century, the putting-out framework was replaced by a production and trading framework organized by the state.

Real structural changes in the production and processing of iron in Austria were brought by transformations in iron-production techniques around the middle of the eighteenth century. The most essential organizational innovation was the withdrawal of the state from regulation of the industry, and ultimately the complete liberalization of production in 1781 (Knittler 1986: 24f; 1993: 908). In the course of the nineteenth century, large industrial plants arose. The small-scale iron industry of the Eisenwurzen region in south-western Lower Austria declined, but in iron production itself, by contrast, Styria survived as the main location until the twentieth century. Thus in the core regions of this industry there was a direct continuity with the industrial revolution, connected not least with its being tied to the sites of ore deposits. In the late nineteenth century the Innerberger Hauptgewerkschaft was incorporated into the largest Austrian iron and steel company.

The political economy of proto-industrialization

From the late Middle Ages on, the economy of the Habsburg monarchy experienced a high degree of state and princely intervention, which affected both the general framework (trade, legal infrastructure) and the organizational regulation of particular sectors of the economy and branches of industry (cf. for example iron processing).

At latest from the seventeenth century on, the economic policy of the central state repeatedly came up against the structural opposition of the local seigneurial administration and the feudal state structures, which were based on provincial particularism. After the end of the Thirty Years War, in the attempt to strengthen the political stability of the Habsburg monarchy, the Austrian territorial princes relied on the seigneurial system. With differing rights and duties in the different provinces of the monarchy, the landlords fulfilled all the functions of state administration in complete autonomy: tax collection, jurisdiction, social control and so on. The enormous power of the noble and ecclesiastical landlords with their control of gigantic domains (e.g. in Bohemia or Moravia) created large structural obstacles to the implementation of economic policy measures. Provincial particularism – by which is meant the fact that the separate lands of the monarchy were autonomously administered, although they had the same territorial prince – intensified these difficulties and in particular prevented the market from being integrated (Baltzarek 1979: 353ff; Freudenberger 1981: 375ff; Matis 1981a; Sandgruber 1995).

The interest of the Austrian rulers in the economic performance of the population was connected exclusively to their need for taxes, especially for warfare, which increased the financial requirements of the state to an enormous extent (Berger 1981: 126ff; Dickson 1987; Knittler 1993: 895ff; Otruba 1981: 77). Mercantilistic ideas are linked with the names of several Austrian theorists, but found entry only slowly into Austrian economic policy, and then often encountered difficulties of implementation. However, the territorial prince's exclusive right to grant guild privileges (asserted in laws of 1689, 1708 and 1731), and the practice of granting monopolies over production and trading in the form of privileges (exclusive rights of production and trade, 'Fabriksprivilegien'), secured for the state at least a certain amount of influence on industrial development in the late seventeenth and early eighteenth centuries (Knittler 1993: 900f, 907f).

Not least because of external threats, there began a new phase of economic policy with the reign of Maria Theresia (1740–80) and the administrative reforms she instituted. The structure of government was re-organized, in the Haugwitz Reforms. State administrative organs, the 'Kreisämter', were created and strengthened. Export industries were freed from restrictions imposed by local authorities. A distinction was drawn between 'Polizeigewerben' (industries for sale to local markets, which were made subject to local and state authority) and 'Kommerzialgewerben' (export industries, which were placed directly under state administration without interference from the local authorities). Later the textile industries were liberalized. The development of new branches of industry was actively pursued: the linen and cotton industries were supported in both Bohemia and Austria, and the immigration of skilled labour from abroad was encouraged. Manufactories were issued with privileges (i.e. monopolies over production and selling) and subsidies. Finally, the integration of the population into industrial occupations was furthered through educational measures, such as the establishment of spinning schools (Freudenberger 1981: 357ff; Good 1983; Knittler 1993: 893ff, 907f; Mosser 1981: 401ff; Otruba 1981).

The growth of central state power created the possibility for further reforms. In particular, these improved the framework for industry through prohibitive customs duties toward the outside and the creation of a single customs area internally, through the customs ordinance of 1775 (Knittler 1993: 908ff; Otruba 1981). The boom in manufactory foundations from the 1780s indicates the upswing which the industry experienced under these conditions. This new concentration of power now for the first time permitted the implementation of a state agrarian policy vis-à-vis the landlords, and the 'Leibeigenschaftspatent' ('Serfdom Patent') which was consequently issued in 1781, the Raab Reforms (1775) and the Land Tax Reform (1783) led to real improvements in the legal, economic and social position of the rural subjects (Knittler 1993: 903ff; Matis 1981b; Otruba 1981). The shock of the terrible famine of 1771 certainly contributed to the acceleration of such measures.

As a consequence of the late beginning of these reforms, the market for mass consumption goods, which recent studies in economic history assign an important significance for the industrial revolution, remained relatively limited in the Austrian monarchy until well into the nineteenth century (Mosser 1981: 406; Sandgruber 1982).

The large number of reforms and acts of state intervention in the second half of the eighteenth century, which favoured proto-industries and coincided with their upturn (although this sort of 'progressive' economic policy was interrupted in 1792; Knittler 1993: 909), have long attracted the interest of Austrian economic historians. Their importance in helping to create the preconditions for the beginnings of factory production in Austria is assessed as being very great, and precisely for the Austrian example the neglect of such factors in the original theories of proto-industrialization appears problematic.

Proto-industrial forms of production and the transition to industrialization

A structural feature of the Austrian proto-industries was the multiplicity of their organizational forms, which deviates from the main organizational form named by the theories. Only in the sixteenth and seventeenth centuries were the agents of the putting-out system merchant houses or bourgeois merchants (as in the production of iron and linen). The newly arising cotton industry and the silk proto-industry in Vienna display a completely different putting-out organization. The minor role played by domestic work in the narrow sense of the word and the dominance of centralized production forms in iron processing, which was determined by technical requirements, as well as the inclusion of the guilds in putting-out work, represent a further structural difference.

In several branches of industry the state, too, appeared directly as an industrial entrepreneur, whether by establishing manufactories (e.g. the Vienna porcelain manufactory, the Neuhaus mirror manufactory) or by seeking to rescue, through nationalization, businesses which had got into financial difficulties despite numerous advances of funds and premiums (e.g. the Linz Worsted Manufactory in 1754, Nadelburg in 1763). In the cotton industry, large enterprises relying on early forms of joint-stock company dominated, such as the Schwechat cotton manufactory. The seigneurial system led to a relatively large accumulation of capital in the hands of the feudal nobility, which also caused them to become involved in industry (Freudenberger 1981: 365ff).

In the urban proto-industrial silk production in Vienna in the eighteenth century, by contrast, a production organization developed which relied on a conflictual side-by-side existence of guilded producers and guild-free, privileged manufactory operators. The conflicts arose above all over the recruitment, payment and training of the labour force. Larger and smaller centralized workshops arose, initially in the area of finishing and refining the product, but after 1800 also to a greater extent in silk weaving. The individual guilded master entered increasingly into dependency on putting-out, and the boundaries between the independent guilded master and the putting-out weaver, as well as between centralized forms of production, guilded workshops and putting-out, began to dissolve (Ehmer 1980: 22ff, 66ff).

For the proto-industrial regions in Upper and Lower Austria, by contrast, there were three manufactories or 'proto-factories' in the eighteenth century (Freudenberger and Redlich 1964; Freudenberger 1981) which were of decisive importance: the Linz worsted manufactory, and the cotton manufactories in Schwechat and Šastín (the latter was permitted from 1754 on, despite the monopoly of the Schwechat manufactory, to operate in the Austrian market). All three disposed of gigantic putting-out systems (in 1791 Linz and Schwechat together employed *c.* 80,000 persons in manufactory and putting-out), and concentrated most stages of the end processing and finishing in a large central plant, which employed *c.* 1,000–2,000 workers. Despite the numerical preponderance of the domestic workers, we must speak here of a combination of a putting-out system with centralized production forms (Matis 1981c: 415ff; 1991: 17ff; Mosser 1981: 407f; Sandgruber 1995).

After the abolition of the monopoly of the Schwechat manufactory in 1763, Lower Austria experienced a real boom in manufactory foundations. All the newly founded manufactories also disposed of putting-out systems. As a consequence of proximity to the important consumer market of Vienna, most of these manufactories – even those in other branches of industry – were set up in southern Lower Austria, where the putting-out was organized. Numerous manufactories arose in Upper Austria and Vorarlberg, as well (Hassinger 1964; Kropf 1982; Matis 1991: 21ff; Sandgruber 1995).

It was in cotton processing that mechanization began, and its whole development displays continuities with preceding proto-industrialization. Despite the fact that the first mechanical spinning plants were set up in 1803 and 1813, the industrial upswing in the cotton industry actually began only in the 1820s. With the fall of the Continental Blockade in 1815, the higher-quality English textile products came on to the market, creating a severe crisis for the Austrian textile industry, from which it was only able to recover after 1820. The two largest manufactories, however, in Linz and Schwechat, were not able to reorient themselves to mechanical production, and in the course of the first half of the nineteenth century were compelled to cease production. Of the other large manufactories, Kettenhof and Himberg completed the transformation with success, as did the manufactory in Ebreichsdorf, although with discontinuities (Good 1983; Komlos 1983b; Matis 1991; Sandgruber 1991).

After the establishment of the first mechanical spinning plants, production locations and putting-out regions in Vorarlberg and Lower Austria show a clear continuity. Putting-out now turned almost exclusively to domestic weaving, which was able to continue to exist for a long time even alongside mechanical weaving.

In the first half of the nineteenth century, the Upper Austrian linen industry confronted severe competition from cotton products. In the Mühlviertel there was no real continuity with industrialization. The dominance of the putting-out entrepreneurs and the adherence to putting-out domestic industry meant that technological innovations entered into production only gradually. Both the newly established end-processing plants and the linen merchants relied on domestic spinning and weaving organized into a putting-out system. Mechanization began relatively late (1851 or 1854), and linen production had already lost ground compared to other textile industries which it had previously surpassed (Hoffmann 1952: 310ff; Kropf 1982: 299ff).

Conclusion

With respect to the points discussed in international debates about the theory of proto-industrialization, Austria offers a relatively differentiated picture (Clarkson 1985; Kriedte, Medick and Schlumbohm 1993; Mendels 1982; Ogilvie 1993a). With regard to production forms, the Austrian examples display a multiplicity of them, with a strong dominance of large centralized concerns, especially in the cotton industry. In the silk industry, there emerged no comparably unambiguous pattern; at the beginning, small-scale structures dominated, and these were then increasingly supplemented and pervaded by putting-out and manufactories, so that ultimately a clear demarcation could no longer be established. In the metal industry the preconditions were completely different, partly because of its production techniques.

With regard to the concepts of the original theories of proto-industrialization concerning demographic changes, the Austrian proto-industrial textile regions reveal a twofold picture. Although demographic consequences in the sense of the theories (faster growth of population, differences in age at marriage) can be identified without doubt, proto-industrialization does not appear to have caused any wider social transformations. Based on the example of the Waldviertel, Berkner (1973) put forward the thesis that the dimensions of the changes brought about by proto-industrialization depended very strongly on local social traditions and legal conditions, and that the theory should therefore be further differentiated with respect to this question.

A last point relates to subsequent industrialization. For several industries, continuities with industrial development (the cotton industry of Lower Austria, parts of Vorarlberg, the iron industry of Styria) can be observed, but for others one finds discontinuities and regional de-industrialization or re-agrarianization (the Bregenzerwald in Vorarlberg, the Mühlviertel in Upper Austria).

Structurally, the Austrian experience shows a long-term domination by a feudal governmental and social order, which was decisively changed by state reforms in the second half of the eighteenth century, creating the basis for a proto-industrial expansion. These conditions played a decisive role both for the nature of proto-industrialization and for the industrial revolution in the Austrian regions.

Overall, the region-centred approach of the theories of proto-industrialization proves to be useful for the study of Austrian development.

Such an approach demonstrates how regional factors (in the Austrian case landlords and communities), together with structural conditions, influenced the course and effects of the process of proto-industrialization in particular regions; this provides an explanation for deviations from the postulates of the theoretical model.

13 Proto-industrialization in Bohemia, Moravia and Silesia*

Milan Myška

Introduction

Twenty years after the introduction of the proto-industrialization paradigm, it has still not become part of the set of concepts used in the Czech historiography. This is somewhat paradoxical, in that a number of historians regard – quite justifiedly – the two core countries of the Czech state (Bohemia and Moravia) as components of the important proto-industrial triangle of Saxony, Bohemia and Silesia. In those cases in which Czech historians did use the concept, it was neither in the sense proposed by Mendels (1972), nor as the 'system concept' put forward by Kriedte, Medick and Schlumbohm (1977), nor in the meaning adopted by Freudenberger (1981); rather, 'proto-industrialization' was simply a term to designate the development of industry before the industrial revolution. Czech historians have used the concept of proto-industrialization mainly as a chronological framework, therefore, not as a substantive description of a specific stage in the formation of capitalism (Novotný 1983: 19).

There are several reasons for this. A not insignificant role was played by the relatively low degree of information about the proto-industrialization debate (Myška 1989: 47ff). For the last forty years, the writing of Czech history has been methodologically oriented toward 'Historical Materialism', which approached questions about the formation of the capitalist system using the Marxist theory of original accumulation and the 'period of manufactures'; this was the framework applied by the historians of the 1950s, Arnošt Klíma (1955), Anton Špiesz (1961) and František Mainuš (1959, 1960), to Czech and Slovak economic development. Furthermore, the actual development of Bohemia, Moravia and Silesia differed so forcibly from the model proposed in the 'system concept' of proto-industrialization that doubt arose about whether they constituted an example of proto-industrial development in the sense used by the theory, or perhaps instead a distinctive path of development. The question arose, whether

* This chapter is translated from the German by Sheilagh C. Ogilvie.

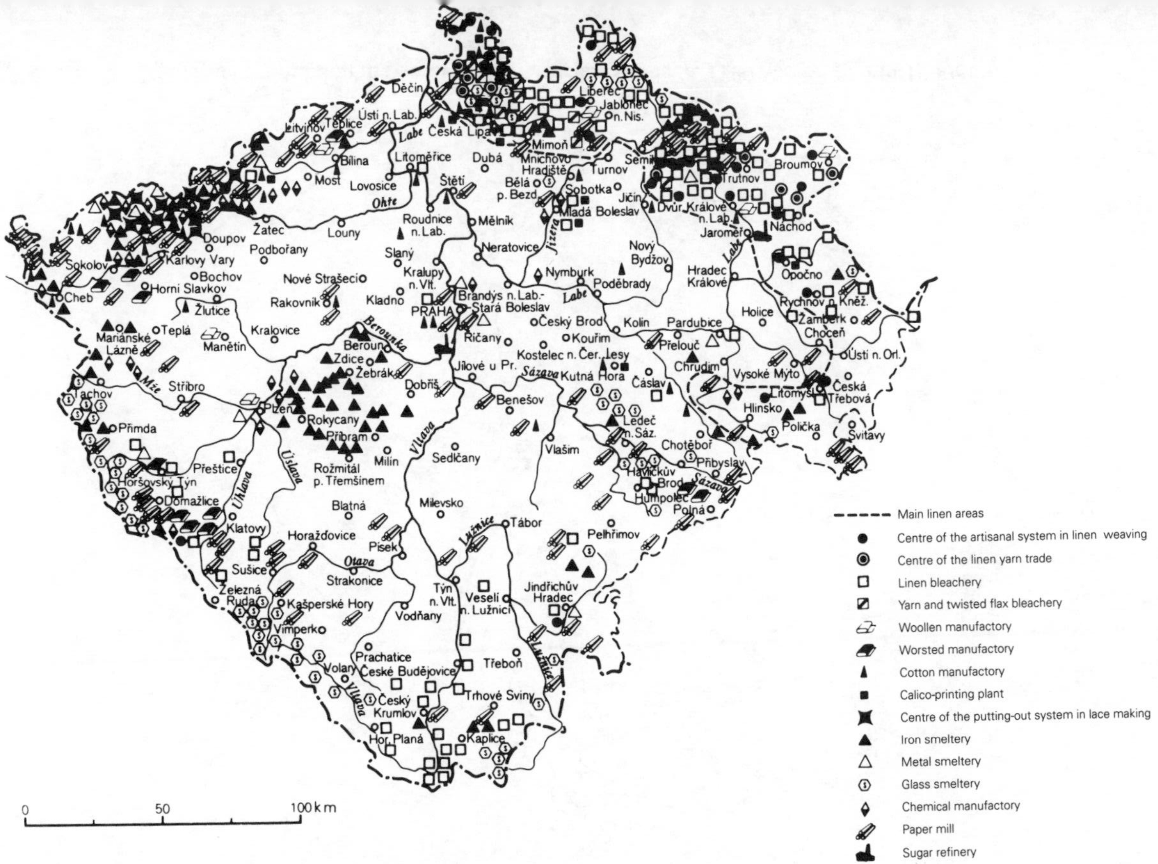

Map 13.1 Industrial production in Bohemia, *c.* 1790 *Source:* Petřan 1990: 56.

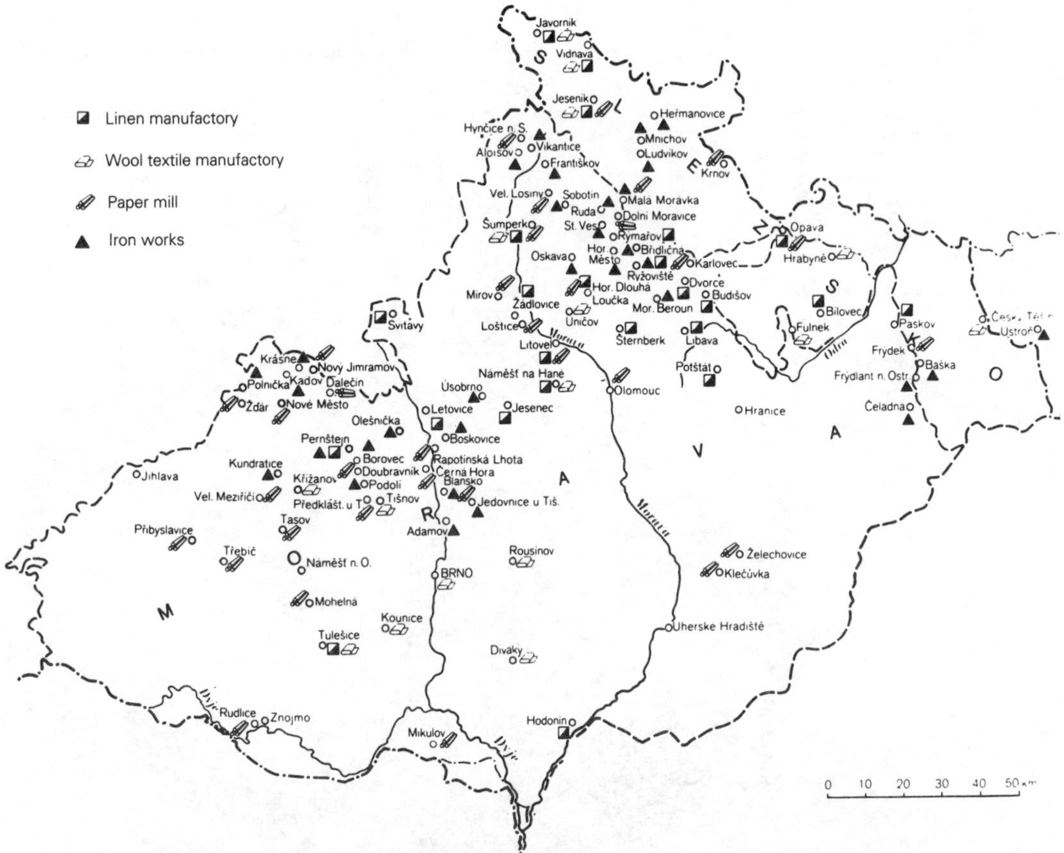

Map 13.2 Industrial production in Moravia and Austrian Silesia, *c.* 1790 *Source:* Petřan 1990: 68.

the 'system concept' of proto-industrialization could be at all helpful, given that it regards many aspects of the transition from feudalism to capitalism as being concentrated in the non-agrarian sector, even though this was a subordinate sector during the transition. The concept of proto-industrialization is only partially suited to covering this set of problems in regions of Europe in which capitalism developed under the conditions of the so-called 'second serfdom' (in the sense of an intensification of hereditary subjection), *Gutswirtschaft* (an economic system characterized by extensive demesne activities) and a patrimonial system whose dominance was for a long time unshaken (Myška 1979: 44f; Válka 1982: 289ff). Moreover, long before the appearance of Mendels, Czech historiography had already been concerned with the basic problems which would later form the core of the 'system concept' of proto-industrialization. In 1932, for example, Jan Klepl had argued that the first signs of capitalistic industrial production developed in regions of rural industry (Klepl 1932: 261f). And as early as 1965, Ludmila Kárníková had pointed out the relationship between the growth of rural industrial regions before the industrial revolution, and its specific demographic consequences (1965: 29ff).

For all of these reasons, not many attempts have been made to engage with the question of proto-industrialization in the Czech lands. Leaving aside John Komlos, whose works suffer from ignorance of the Czech historiography and from seeking to draw very general conclusions from isolated findings torn out of context (Komlos 1980: 198ff; 1983a: 129ff; 1986: 65ff; 1990: 104ff), only Arnošt Klíma (1985: 273ff) and Milan Myška (1979: 44f; 1991, 1992) have attempted to apply the theory of proto-industrialization to Czech development.

The Czech lands are numbered among that group of societies whose development was clearly influenced, from the seventeenth century on, by the so-called 'second serfdom', in the sense of an intensification of feudal burdens (Wallerstein 1974: 346ff; Topolski 1963: 141f). There can be no doubt that the course, nature and dynamic of proto-industrialization in these societies was profoundly determined by this fact.

The periodization of proto-industrialization

Proto-industrialization in the Czech lands can be clearly distinguished into three phases, although unambiguous demarcations cannot be drawn between them.

Phase 1: the formation of the preconditions for proto-industrialization (early sixteenth century – c. *1650)*

It is impossible to determine the precise beginning of this phase, but it can be seen as extending back into the first half of the sixteenth century, and lasting until just after the end of the Thirty Years War. This phase saw the emergence of several elements which were only later transformed into a 'system': production for supra-regional and foreign markets (especially in the textile sector); the linking of industries consisting partly of guild production and partly of rural domestic work through forms of *Kaufsystem* (artisanal system) or *Verlagssystem* (putting-out system); organizational functions performed by foreign merchant capital (Aubin and Kunze 1940: 326ff; Seibold 1977: 312ff); and the beginnings of centralized manufactories in the iron and glass industries (Myška 1992: 46ff) and of de-centralized manufactories (Klíma 1955: 192ff) as typical proto-industrial production forms.

*Phase 2: 'actual proto-industrialization' (*c. *1650 –* c. *1830)*

In this phase, individual elements from the preceding period were formed into a functioning system capable of exercising the transformational functions of proto-industrialization. This phase of 'actual proto-industrialization' occurred despite the fact that at the same time, after the Thirty Years War, feudal hereditary subjection was entrenching itself. This phase lasted until the 1820s or 1830s, when the beginnings of modern capitalistic industrialization appeared on the horizon. The special characteristics of this phase were the formation of proto-industrial regions, the complementarity between various forms of production (especially between the artisanal system or the putting-out system and centralized manufactories), and a specific demographic development in regions densely permeated by industrial mass production for supra-regional markets. This stage can be divided into two sub-periods, according to the degree of intensity of these central processes.

In the first sub-period, running from *c.* 1650 approximately to the accession of Maria Theresia in 1740, development occurred very much within the constraints of the continuing system of 'Leibeigenschaft' (serfdom or villeinage), by means of which the local feudal landlords were able to insinuate themselves into the ongoing process of proto-industrialization and subject it to their own interests and requirements. The dissolution of feudal socio-economic relationships and the development of capitalistic ones was for a time burdened with various forms of extra-economic coercion and monopolies issuing from the power of the feudal authorities (Myška 1984: 258ff). Although proto-industrialization functioned as a system, and the landlords furthered its growth by financing and organizing putting-out industries and centralized manufactories, its effects were slowed down and crippled by the ubiquity of monopolies and extra-economic coercion.

The beginnings of the second sub-period reach back into the era when Maria Theresia and Joseph II were introducing 'rationalist' economic policies formulated by mercantilists and 'populationists'. During this second sub-period (*c.* 1740 – *c.* 1830) the proto-industrialization process was freed (although by no means instantly and completely) from the previous obstacles, and became more similar to the development in western Europe (Klíma 1991: 99ff). Only in this phase could the effects of proto-industrialization prevail without distortions and constraints. Despite the intense entrepreneurial activity of the nobility, this period saw a massive emergence of entrepreneurs from the urban bourgeoisie and the better-off rural strata, as well as large numbers of entrepreneurs of foreign origins.

Phase 3: co-existence between proto-industry and modern capitalistic industry

This phase lasted from the 1820s and 1830s (when the industrial revolution began in the Czech lands) almost to the end of the nineteenth century. The question of whether this phase can be categorized as proto-industrialization deserves to be considered. Kriedte, Medick and Schlumbohm (1992: 243ff) surmise that the original proto-industrial production forms changed function after the beginning of modern industrialization, becoming a 'supplement to the factory'. However, the Czech experience of industrialization shows that in a number of branches of industry, growth was attained not only through modern mechanized industry displacing proto-industry, but also through both sectors developing in parallel. As late as 1891, 52 per cent of those employed in the textile industry in Moravia and Silesia worked in non-factory enterprises using manual techniques; in 1901, it was still 49 per cent (Myška 1988b: 59ff). Regions and branches of industry arose which still lived from proto-industrial types of production in the second half of the nineteenth century, without any firm dependence on, let alone subordination to, modern factories. In the Silesian area of the Silesian–Moravian proto-industrial region, as late as 1869/70 a full 82 per cent of those employed in the textile industry were working with manual techniques and within a non-factory organization (i.e. in an artisanal or putting-out system linked with a manufactory) (Myška 1992: 23).

Until the 1870s the expansion of iron working in the Czech lands also for the most part consisted of manufactory-like enterprises (Myška 1970: 123). This was not a specifically Czech phenomenon; it can also be observed in other countries in which the progress of modern industrialization was delayed or slow. Witold Kula (1963: 3ff) described it as the 'co-existence of anachronisms'.

The regional distribution of proto-industries

Proto-industrialization is defined as a regional phenomenon. In the Czech lands, the proto-industrialization process did not occur over the whole area of Bohemia, Moravia and Silesia from the seventeenth to the ninteenth century. Only gradually did there emerge regions densely pervaded by rural small industrial producers, and these regions consisted not of large areas compactly filled with domestic industry, but rather of mere agglomerations of communities, ranging from a handful to a few dozen, and linked with one another only to a certain extent. Well into the second half of the eighteenth century, these regions were co-extensive with the domains ruled by particular feudal landlords. With the decline in the landlords' influence on the process of proto-industrialization, there occurred an increase in the economic importance of rural towns (which were market centres and the seats of putting-out systems) and of communities in which finishing manufactories were located.

At the turn of the eighteenth to the nineteenth century, when proto-industrialization reached its peak in the Czech lands, rural industrial production for extra-regional markets showed the following spatial distribution.

The west Bohemian proto-industrial region (Matějček 1987: 64f) was made up of the smaller agglomerations of the area around Aš (Asch), the area around Cheb (Eger) and the western Krušné hory (Erzgebirge). At the end of the eighteenth century, the cotton industry predominated here; there was also a group of weaving communities in the Ohře (Egertal) and the Slavkovský les (Kaiserwald) which mainly produced woollen cloths; and finally there was the eastern Krušné hory (the area around Kraslice (Graslitz) and Přísečnice (Preβnitz)), where lace making was widespread. Alongside rural domestic industry, there also existed guilded small industrial production, and Karel Novotný (1983: 89) has identified eleven textile manufactories in the region. In addition to textile production, there was also a manufactory-organized iron-working industry fuelled by charcoal (which included ore mining and the collection of wood for charcoal piles), and a growing paper industry.

Neighbouring on the west Bohemian region was the proto-industrial region of the Krušné hory (Erzgebirge), with highly developed cotton and woollen textile industries, organized into both artisanal systems and putting-out systems, and six textile manufactories. This region, too, saw the development of charcoal-fuelled iron production and paper making.

The north Bohemian proto-industrial region began originally as a homogeneous linen region, but transformed itself into a heterogeneous region producing linen, cotton and wool textiles, and containing important iron and glass manufactories, including glass refining (glass painting, glass cutting and the making of glass jewellery). In the west, this region was bordered by the areas of Rumburk (Rumburg) and Šluknov (Schluckenau), and in the east by Liberec (Reichenberg) and Jablonec n. N. (Gablonz) (Jahn-Langen 1961). The linen industry was organized into both artisanal and putting-out systems, with centralized finishing plants; cotton cloth production was concentrated into twenty-six manufactories.

The eastern Bohemian proto-industrial region ran from Semily (Semil) through Broumov (Braunau) to Náchod, and extended as far as the towns of Litomyšl (Leitomischl) and Česká Třebová (Böhmisch Trübau). It was a homogeneous linen-producing area, and only in the first half of the nineteenth century did it see an invasion of cotton. This area was a classic example of domestic industry subordinated to merchant capital (Šůla 1985: 37ff). Proto-industrial characteristics survived here well into the second half of the nineteenth century. Especially in yarn production, this region had direct and close contact with the Silesian–Moravian proto-industrial area.

A notably dispersed region of proto-industrialization, essentially only a scattered group of a few centres and their immediate hinterlands, extended along the southern border of Bohemia from Tachov (Tachau) to Lužnice (Oberfluβ). In this strip was concentrated the production of linen cloths, worsteds, glass and charcoal-fuelled iron. Worsted production was organized into a manufactory from the second half of the eighteenth century on, while linen was produced by domestic workers and was finished in bleacheries concentrated in three centres. In addition, in the first half of the 1760s, 10,000 domestic spinners in this area worked for nine trading posts of the Linz woollen manufactory in Austria (Hoffmann 1952: 323).

The only proto-industrial region in Bohemia which was a homogeneous area of iron production was the forested area of Brdy between Plzeň (Pilsen) and the river Vltava (Moldau). The charcoal-fuelled production of iron was based on the mining of local iron ores and employed several thousand workers. From the 1780s on, there also emerged a small iron wares industry in the area of Hořovice (Horschowitz), organized into a putting-out system.

The Silesian–Moravian proto-industrial region, which lay in the borderlands between Moravia and Austrian Silesia in the foothills of the mountainous district of Kłodzko (Glatz), had a mixture of different industries. It was primarily an area of linen production oriented toward yarn production until the second half of the eighteenth century; to a lesser extent, cotton was also produced. There was also extensive production of iron goods, and a less important glass industry. Until the end of the nineteenth century, the artisanal system predominated, followed by the putting-out system.

The proto-industrial region of Brno (Brünn) was very dispersed: besides the provincial capital of Brno itself, it consisted of scattered centres located mainly north-west of Brno on the Bohemian–Moravian hills. Industrial production was very mixed, with not only woollen cloths, but also linen, cotton and iron working. There was a very high proportion of centralized manufactories. Because these manufactories were operated by bourgeois entrepreneurs, the transition to factory production occurred very early in this region (Freudenberger and Mensch 1975; Janák 1983). Foreign investors also participated as entrepreneurs, especially in Brno itself.

The proto-industrial region of Frýdek-Místek (Friedeck-Friedberg) emerged in the first half of the eighteenth century (Myška 1991). The area originally specialized in the production of low-value linen cloths destined for export to the not very demanding markets of Galicia and Hungary. In the 1830s and 1840s, it re-oriented itself to cotton production. Until the late 1860s, the region was exclusively dominated by proto-industrial forms of production, in the sense of domestic work within an artisanal or putting-out system; the only exceptions were a few centralized manufactories for finishing. Machine production began only after 1870. In addition to textile production, this region also had an iron-working industry.

In the rest of Bohemia, Moravia and Silesia there existed scattered islands of domestic industry or manufactories. In Prague and the neighbouring towns, there were calico manufactories; and in Prostějov (Proβnitz) and its rural hinterland, a clothing industry organized into a putting-out system developed in the second half of the eighteenth century (Sommer and Gímeš 1970: 17ff). As far as the process of proto-industrialization was concerned, however, these scattered domestic industries had little importance.

The Czech lands were part of an extensive central European proto-industrial area, which also included Saxony and Silesia. Several of the Czech proto-industrial areas immediately bordered on these countries, and there arose a co-operation in production, which exploited the production capacity of the Saxon and Silesian bleacheries and survived until the end of the eighteenth century. The production capacity of the Czech proto-industrial areas was particularly intensely exploited by foreign entrepreneurs. In the eighteenth century, the Silesian–Moravian proto-industrial region was a yarn store-room for the Silesian and Saxon linen industry; and in the 1780s, 10,091 spinners in Bohemia and 2,172 in Moravia worked for the Linz woollen manufactory in Austria (Schlötzer 1782: 212–14).

The majority of the Czech proto-industrial regions arose on the basis of a domestic supply of raw materials: flax, wool, glass sand, iron ore and wood. Unlike other countries such as Austria, Flanders and Russia, most of the Czech proto-industrial regions developed in the foothills or directly in the mountains, where the soil and climate were unfavourable for agriculture and part of the population had been compelled to seek a living outside the agrarian sector since as early as the seventeenth century. At the peak of proto-industrialization, rural industrial regions producing for supra-regional markets comprised no more than one tenth to one eighth of the land area of Bohemia, Moravia and Silesia. In this rather small area, the population density far exceeded the average for the country as a whole. In 1762, the average population density was 35.6 persons per square kilometre in Moravia as a whole, but 55–65 in the proto-industrial areas, one and a half to two times as high (Kárníková 1965: 43).

The proto-industrial regions experienced a proletarianization, which on the one hand was a precondition for proto-industrialization, and on the other hand was furthered by it. In the Moravian part of the Silesian–Moravian industrial region, self-subsistent peasants (i.e. those who did not need to seek any additional source of subsistence outside agriculture) made up as many as 90 per cent of households around 1600, while cottagers made up only 1 per cent. A century later, the proportion of peasants had fallen to 35 per cent, while the proportion of cottagers had risen to 50 per cent (Dohnal 1966: 46). In 1781, according to Raab's estimates, 47 per cent of the total population of Bohemia were rent-paying inmates in the households of others, and 20 per cent were cottagers. Of a population of 17,376 feudal subject families, living in 483 villages in Bohemia, 61 per cent possessed no land. The majority of these were concentrated in the areas with dense rural industry (Svoboda 1957: 452; Klíma 1979: 58ff).

A detailed quantification of the main socio-economic differences between the rural industrial and agricultural regions of Bohemia is made possible by the first modern land cadaster of the Habsburg monarchy (the so-called 'stabile Kataster') drawn up in the early 1840s. The average number of inhabitants per community was 1,064 in proto-industrial regions, compared with 589 in areas of commercial agriculture. The average number of separate landholdings per community was 175.6 in proto-industrial regions, compared with 81.0 in areas of commercial agriculture; the number of inhabitants per holding was 6.1, compared to 7.3; and the area of arable land per holding was 4.9 *Joch* in the proto-industrial regions, compared with 12.2 in the areas of commercial agriculture. The proportion of families obtaining their livelihoods exclusively from agriculture was 41.2 per cent in rural industrial regions, compared with 77.7 per cent in agricultural ones. In the proto-industrial regions, 29.9 per cent of families lived exclusively from domestic industry, compared with only 11 per cent in areas of commercial farming. Significantly, in proto-industrial regions 28.2 per cent of households were by-employed in agriculture and industry, compared with only 6.9 per cent of households in areas of commercial agriculture (Vondruška 1984: 383ff).

Distortion of the pattern or separate model?

It is an orthodoxy among historians that from the sixteenth century onward, Europe experienced a transition from feudalism to capitalism, and in this process divided itself into two distinct socio-economic areas, whose border was the river Elbe. Arnošt Klíma and Josef Macůrek distinguish three different variants of the transition to capitalism within Europe (Macůrek 1960: 329). The Czech lands are included in the central European variant, in which the transition to capitalism took place under the conditions of the so-called 'second serfdom', in the sense of intensified burdens inflicted by landlords on their subject populations. In these countries, the 'second serfdom' was not incompatible with the development of capitalistic relations within the embrace of feudal society. However, it did complicate this process, and gave it a special character.

The distinguishing features of the central European model, as Josef Válka (1972: 181ff) sought to formulate it, was that the nobility and large feudal estates monopolized all economic, political, administrative and judicial functions. The large feudal estates remained the crux of economic, political and cultural activities, to the noticeable disadvantage of the towns. In Bohemia, Moravia and Silesia, the feudal estate retained the medieval functions which it lost in the west, but at the same time adapted to the expanding production of commodities, and oriented itself toward economic activities. This manifested itself not only in feudal landlords establishing their own industrial enterprises, but also in their seeking to shape the framework within which the economic activities of their subjects had to take place, since in the 'second serfdom' the latter contributed significantly to the revenues of the landlords. The landlords sought to further the development of production, but at the same time they made a feudal privilege out of commodity production, using 'extra-economic coercion'. These were the circumstances which determined the late feudal economy in the Czech lands, and at the same time profoundly complicated it. Naturally, these special conditions, which are not found in western Europe, cannot fail to have influenced the development of proto-industrialization in central Europe.

Some proponents of the 'system concept' of proto-industrialization have argued that stronger feudal relations diminished the chances of proto-industrialization. In the case of Bohemia, Moravia and Silesia, by contrast, we witness a very intensive development of export-oriented industrial production. In 1735, goods to a value of nearly six million *Gulden* were exported from the Czech lands, of which half consisted of industrial products. Linen and yarn accounted for two million *Gulden*, woollen textiles for half a million, and glass and iron wares also contributed. Traditionally, linen cloth was sent via merchants in Lusatia and Silesia to merchant houses in Nuremberg, and from there, as early as the seventeenth century, to England. By way of Vienna and Trieste, linen was also transported to Spain, and from there to America and Mexico. The woollen cloths produced by Bohemian, Moravian and Silesian manufactories went to Poland, Russia, Transylvania, the Balkans, Hungary, Germany and Switzerland. The centre of woollen cloth production around Jihlava (Iglau), for example, exported up to 75 per cent of its production in the eighteenth century, and the other woollen centres 50–60 per cent of theirs. The products of Bohemian and Moravian glass works were successfully exported to England, Denmark, Sweden, Russia, Italy, Turkey, Egypt, India and Mexico. Almost to the end of the eighteenth century, Bohemian iron and iron goods were exported even to such a highly developed country as England. The cotton industry, by contrast, was oriented almost exclusively to local or national markets, the only significant branch of proto-industry in Bohemia to be so, even though it undoubtedly had an extraordinary importance for the development of proto-industrialization.

The quantitative expansion of proto-industry in the Czech lands is shown by the number of people employed in it. In 1754 the population of the Czech lands was *c.* 3 million, by 1781 it had increased to 4 million and by 1854 it had reached 6.64 million (Kárníková 1965: 327ff). In the Czech lands (Bohemia, Moravia and Silesia) in the late 1760s more than 300,000 spinners and almost 32,000 weavers' looms were in operation in the linen industry, which was organized predominantly into an artisanal system, with putting-out only in exceptional cases and centralized manufactories only in the finishing stages. By the end of the eighteenth century, the number of looms producing linen in the Czech lands had increased to more than 61,000. Half a million people worked in the linen industry either full time or part time, and the total value of production was estimated at 4.5 million *Gulden*. In the woollen cloth industry, in which urban guilds were still substantially involved alongside centralized manufactories and the mass of domestic workers, 59,000 people were employed in 1780 in Bohemia alone, rising to 87,000 by 1789. In Moravia and Silesia another 7,000 people were recorded as active in the woollen cloth sector in 1783. These figures must, however, be regarded as incomplete and minimum estimates. Klíma estimates that approximately 120,000 people were employed in producing woollen cloths in the Czech lands at the end of the eighteenth century (1993: 711). A further 30,000 persons were active in the cotton industry in the late 1780s.

The iron-working industry was conducted, for technological reasons, exclusively in centralized manufactories. Most of these manufactories were in the possession of feudal authorities (nobles, ecclesiastical institutions or towns). Bourgeois entrepreneurs established themselves only exceptionally, mainly as tenants (Myška 1992: 31). In 1700 there were seventy-seven charcoal blast furnaces in the Czech lands; by 1780 there were ninety. The number of people employed in iron works were, at an estimated 3,500 persons, only a small fraction of the number employed in textile production, but many times the number, mainly village-dwellers seeking work outside agriculture, found employment in auxiliary activities, namely in mining iron ore and additives, cutting and transporting wood for the forge hammers, burning charcoal piles and so on. These tasks were seasonal and were, in end effect, similar to seasonal spinning and weaving. Into the first half of the nineteenth century, feudal corvée labour and forced wage labour were used for such tasks in a number of iron-working areas of the Czech lands.

Thus in the Czech lands proto-industry expanded in a situation of 'second serfdom' (in the sense of an intensification of feudal burdens) and heavy involvement of the nobility in non-agrarian economic activities.

The confrontation of these findings with the thesis that countries with strong feudal relations provided unfavourable conditions for proto-industrialization raises an important question. Is the Czech case a distortion of a proto-industrial 'ideal type', or does it represent a different model altogether, one which corresponds to its special characteristics?

The special features of proto-industrialization in the Czech lands arose from two causes: from the so-called 'second serfdom' on the one hand, and from the intensive involvement of the feudal nobility in the financing and organization of rural domestic industry on the other. While in western Europe the shift of industry from the towns to the countryside represented an emancipation from the fetters of the guild system, in the countries of the 'second serfdom' it meant entering into dependency on the local feudal authorities.

The heavy involvement of the nobility in entrepreneurial activities in the Czech lands has been frequently noted (Redlich 1964: 289ff; Myška 1988a: 169ff; Klíma 1991: 127ff). The largest textile manufactories and the putting-out enterprises linked to them, which in the literature are often incorrectly referred to as 'de-centralized manufactories' (Myška 1985: 84ff), but in actuality were 'manufactories with a putting-out component' (Kocka 1990: 229), could not arise in the seventeenth and eighteenth centuries without the participation of the nobility. The 'second serfdom' laid down unequal conditions for different social strata in accumulating capital and making industrial investments. Entrepreneurial ambitions could only be realized by members of non-noble social groups with the consent of the noble feudal authorities (Myška 1984: 261ff).

It is impossible to make a quantitative assessment of the proportion of proto-industrialization in the Czech lands represented by entrepreneurial activities on the part of the feudal nobility before the end of the eighteenth century, because the statistical evidence is lacking. For the very end of the eighteenth century – i.e. already at the point at which bourgeois entrepreneurs were emerging and noble entrepreneurs were gradually re-orienting themselves toward other sectors (foodstuffs, building materials, mining and iron works) – Jiří Matějček estimates noble participation in 'large textile enterprises' in Bohemia at about 21 per cent, in Moravia at around 18 per cent. By the beginning of the 1840s, the proportion had fallen to 4 per cent in Bohemia and 11 per cent in Moravia and Silesia (Machačová and Matějček 1992: 452). By comparison, 59 per cent of iron works and 65 per cent of the total production were in the hands of the nobility, and 30 per cent of collieries and 50 per cent of coal output. As late as the 1830s, noble entrepreneurs owned 60 per cent of all sugar factories in Bohemia. However, in assessing the participation of noble entrepreneurs it is not enough merely to examine the proportion of enterprises owned by them, given that it is known that the textile enterprises of the nobility were among the largest as far as the number of employees and the volume of production were concerned, even at the end of the eighteenth century (Myška 1983: 106ff).

The feudal nobility made use of the development of rural industries in two ways: first, through their own entrepreneurial activities in organizing and financing trade in the products made by rural industrial producers, or in the manufactories they themselves operated; and secondly, by granting to third parties the monopoly right to purchase the products of their subjects. The latter option can be observed at the beginning of noble involvement in proto-industrialization, with the first known examples found in the north Bohemian lowlands in the mid-sixteenth century and the feudal domains of Frýdlant (Friedland) and Liberec (Reichenberg) in the seventeenth century. These feudal landlords granted large merchant houses in Nuremberg, Saxony, Lusatia and the Netherlands a monopoly right to purchase linen from their subjects through factors, in exchange for a fee for each piece of linen cloth (Aubin and Kunze 1940: 326ff; Seibold 1977: 230). In the Silesian–Moravian proto-industrial region, there is evidence of similar practices around 1670. Whereas in Bohemia this sort of contract was usually concluded between the merchants and linen weavers' guilds (in the so-called *Zunftkäufe*, or 'guild purchases'), in Moravia and Silesia the feudal authorities themselves concluded such contracts with the merchants (Myška 1984: 257). In 1737 and 1738 the Bruntál (Freudenthal) domain of the Teutonic Order concluded similar contracts with a local merchant. The feudal authorities promised not to allow anyone else to purchase yarn in their domain, and the merchants promised to accept the entire output of yarn, to pay the prices customary in the area and to pay the feudal authorities a commission fee proportional to the size of the purchase. In some feudal domains, the landlord permitted the merchants to employ middlemen to buy up yarn, normally members of the local village courts. In exchange for ceding their monopoly rights to purchase proto-industrial output to the merchants, the feudal landlords obtained a profit in the form of a commission fee.

In addition to the economic necessity of selling the product so that the spinner or weaver could earn a living for his family, extra-economic coercion arising out of the relationship between the feudal subject and the feudal lord played an important role in the acts of selling and buying. Thus in the area of Liberec (Reichenberg) in 1619, weavers petitioned the noble landlord at least to be allowed to sell linen cloths to another buyer when they were turned down by the firm Viatis-Peller which had the monopoly. The feudal authorities of Janovice u. R. (Janowitz), Velké Losiny (Groβ Ullersdorf) and Vízmberk (Wiesenberg) set up watchmen around the town on the days the Šumperk (Mährisch Schönberg) yarn markets were held, to prevent their subject spinners from bringing in yarn to sell secretly. Although in this form of organizing production the participation of the feudal authorities was a parasitic one, on the other hand the fees paid by the merchant houses for the grant of monopoly purchasing rights motivated the feudal authorities to create the conditions for the expansion of rural industrial production, and thus did in fact contribute to the proto-industrialization process.

The second form of participation of the feudal authorities in the production and trade in yarn and linen was also based on the principle of the purchasing monopoly. In this second variant, however, the landlords did not grant the monopoly over purchasing to their trading partners, but exercised it themselves. In this way, they began to undertake economic activities of their own in the non-agrarian sphere as well (Šůla 1985: 37ff; Myška 1984: 262ff). There are many references to this form of activity from the seventeenth and eighteenth centuries, mainly from the feudal domain of Orlice (Adlertal), and the Silesian–Moravian region (Šůla 1985: 37–82; Myška 1984: 262ff). Essentially this was an artisanal system organized by the feudal authorities; the landlords set up in their domains a network of yarn and linen purchasers, who bought up output from domestic workers among the subject population, at prices set by the feudal authorities, and brought the wares into the landlords' storehouses, where they were sorted by quality, sometimes also finished, and sold to domestic and foreign merchant houses in large batches. This practice spread immediately after the Thirty Years War in several feudal domains in the Silesian–Moravian proto-industrial region, and in a large number of domains in eastern Bohemia.

This form of proto-industrial entrepreneurial activity by the feudal authorities should not be over-estimated; nevertheless, it generated significant profits. In 1646 the revenues 'from making linen cloth' amounted to 16 per cent of the total revenues of the feudal domain of Nové Město n. M. (Neustadt an der Mettau), and in 1660 the net profit from buying linen cloths provided 11.8 per cent of the landlord's revenues in the domain of Častolovice (Castolowitz) (Šůla 1985: 48). In the second half of the seventeenth and the first half of the eighteenth century, the yarn trade provided about 10 per cent of the revenues of the north Moravian domain of Janovice u. R. (Janowitz) (Mainuš 1955: 233).

In the relationship between the feudal authorities as sellers and the merchants as buyers, clear elements of capitalistic market relations began to prevail. But the relationship between the feudal authorities and their subject spinners or weavers was quite different. The rural producers were only permitted to sell their output to the official collectors; otherwise they were threatened with penalties. The prices of yarn and linen cloth were not the result of a mutual agreement, but were dictated by the feudal authorities. In the relationship between subject spinners or weavers and the feudal authorities or the purchasers, there prevailed a complicated linking of economic necessity and extra-economic coercion.

It must be emphasized that the spinner or weaver was not forced by the feudal authorities to engage in proto-industrial production. Rather, in the absence of other sources of supplementary earnings, producing yarn and linen cloth in the non-growing season represented the only possibility of adding to the subsistence of the family. To this extent, economic motivation played a role, just as it did when a weaver worked for a bourgeois merchant or putter-out. The extra-economic coercion made its appearance only at the point at which the domestic industrial producer sought to sell his output. Through a system of coercion, the feudal authorities restricted him to one single option: selling to their official collectors. There are no documented cases in which the feudal authorities forced their subjects to work as spinners or weavers by means of extra-economic coercion; only exceptionally, in some feudal domains in eastern and northern Bohemia and in Silesia in the second half of the seventeenth century, was linen-yarn spinning required by the feudal authorities as a form of corvée labour services. The extra-economic coercion functioned in the sphere of money exchange: it underlay the monopoly purchasing and the non-voluntary exchange of goods at prices fixed by only one of the parties. In this way, the feudal landlord became a monopoly entrepreneur in his domain, entered into the market as a 'large producer', and set up trading contacts with representatives of large merchant capital.

The forms of proto-industrial noble entrepreneurial activities analysed here disappeared in the course of the second half of the eighteenth century because they were in contradiction to the mercantilistic policy of the absolutist monarchy. This policy sought to free industrial activity from any kind of restriction as much as possible, forbidding forced sales of yarn, declaring the weaving craft to be a free occupation, issuing patents abolishing serfdom and so on (Bělina 1983: 7–36; Urfus 1955: 122–55).

Proponents of the 'system concept' of proto-industrialization found in their concept no place for centralized forms of proto-industry, i.e. for manufactories or proto-factories. However, manufactories played an important role in proto-industrialization in the Czech lands, because by central European standards they were very widespread here, because they employed quite large numbers of workers, and especially because it was they which organized the de-centralized rural domestic industries until the rise of modern industrialization and sometimes even alongside it. The majority of manufactories did not involve any division of labour and did not own equipment of their own: they were in actuality no more than very extensive trading posts for merchants or putters-out, functioning as a supplement to centralized manufactories. In the textile sector, these centralized manufactories were usually oriented around the finishing stages of production (bleacheries, presses, dye-works and mangling plants), while in the iron and glass industries they were oriented around the production of half-finished products (wire and nails, needles, raw glass and glass wares for glass cutting, glass painting and jewellery) (Myška 1985: 84ff). There are numerous examples of this form of organization for the Bohemian area. The linen cloth manufactory of Podtštejn (Pottenstein) established in 1755 was a centralized finishing plant, employing at highest ebb 150 persons, and obtained its raw linen by purchasing it through agents from domestic weavers in market centres in Trutnov (Trautenau), Police n. M. (Politz), Broumov and Žacléř (Schatzlar). A whole array of additional 'manufactories' functioned similarly. Although 2,526 persons worked in the linen cloth manufactory founded in 1775 in Sloup (Bürgstein), only 562 of them worked directly in the workshops of the manufactory, while the remainder were domestic weavers in the domains of Brandýs (Brandeis) and Bělá p. B. (Biela). The manufactories of bourgeois entrepreneurs were similar. Although in 1786 Johann Joseph Leitenberger set up a calico-pressing plant in Zákupy (Reichstadt) as a manufactory in which 400 pressers and assistants worked, the plant obtained its cotton yarn and cotton cloth partly through purchases and partly through a putting-out system involving nearly 5,000 domestic industrial producers.

Iron-working manufactories produced qualitatively similar effects. They were not very numerous in the Czech lands, and the number of employees participating directly in producing iron ore was not large. But when one includes those carrying out the preparatory tasks, i.e. felling and transporting the trees for the forge hammers, burning charcoal and obtaining ore and additives, the number employed reached into the thousands, for several of such iron-working centres. These supplementary tasks performed the same function as, for example, the domestic work of spinners: they provided a non-agrarian source of additional earnings for a rural population which could not live exclusively from agriculture. In addition, these tasks were sometimes seasonal. The demographic consequences of this sort of manufactory industrialization were similar to those in areas of rural textile production (Čermáková-Nesládková 1979).

In this context, the little-known fact should be mentioned that in some charcoal-fuelled iron works belonging to the feudal authorities at least some of these supplementary tasks were carried out through a form of corvée labour services. In fact, this occurred from the beginning of the seventeenth century practically until the abolition of corvée labour services and the patrimonial system in 1848. For some iron works in the Bohemian–Moravian highlands, and for the arch-episcopal iron works in Frýdlant nad Ostravicí (Friedland an der Ostrawitza) in the feudal domain of Hukvaldy (Hochwald) there were even so-called 'forge villages', whose subject populations carried out prescribed corvée labour services for the forge. As late as the end of the eighteenth and the beginning of the nineteenth centuries, the bourgeois entrepreneurs now operating these iron works as tenants made use of these corvée labour services, in exchange for lump-sum payments to the feudal authorities (Myška 1992: 76). To date, this is the only known form of exploitation of labour services for proto-industrial production in the Czech lands.

However, a further form of extra-economic coercion was a distinctive characteristic of textile, glass and iron manufactories owned by feudal nobles. This was forced labour for wages which were not voluntarily agreed, which Wallerstein termed 'forced wage labour' (Wallerstein 1974). There is evidence of this sort of forced labour in the 1740s and 1750s, for example, in the linen cloth manufactories of the counts of Harrach in Janovice u. R., who took experienced master weavers from their northern Bohemian domain of Šluknov and forcibly re-settled them in the weaving villages of Janovice, in order to establish the production of high-value varieties of linen cloth. The count of Harrach also forced the remainder of the linen weavers to work for the manufactory, at wages set by him (Mainuš 1959: 177ff). Similarly, various forms of 'forced wage labour' are known for a whole series of iron works in the areas of the Bohemian–Moravian highlands, the Sudetic Mountains and Carpathia (Myška 1992).

Conclusion

The 'second serfdom', in the sense of an intensification of hereditary subjection, which was experienced by the Czech lands in the period of late feudalism, and the heavy involvement of the feudal nobility in financing and organizing proto-industry, naturally meant that in this part of Europe proto-industrialization proceeded differently than predicted by the 'system concept' of proto-industrialization. But despite the difference in development paths, in general the same results can be observed. Regions densely pervaded by proto-industry were formed, and these manifested a high density of population which resulted not from in-migration, but rather from higher fertility, caused by declining ages at marriage. These areas produced overwhelmingly for supra-regional markets, and they saw a comparatively rapid advance of social differentiation.

Capitalistic relations of production developed not only in proto-industrial enterprises operated by bourgeois entrepreneurs, but also in those of the nobility. The development of capitalistic relations was slowed down and complicated, however, by a dense network of feudal and semi-feudal restrictions, which affected not only the domestic workers employed by the landlords, but also those working for bourgeois merchants, putters-out and manufactory operators. These restrictions included corvée labour services in kind, 'Reluition' (money dues paid in lieu of dues in kind) and various sorts of rents and dues paid on industrial activities, such as spinning fees and weavers' dues.

From the mid-eighteenth century onward, the hindrance to economic development represented by these restrictions declined, at a rate which varied according to region and industry. In the Czech lands, however, proto-industrial forms and relations of production were distinguished by their extraordinarily long survival. Especially in the textile and clothing industries, they survived until well into the second half of the nineteenth century, becoming dependencies or supplements to modern factories only to a partial extent. Because mechanization spread very slowly in some stages of production and some regions (as in the weaving industry), proto-industry retained a significant share in the total volume of industrial growth. The successful, although specific, development of proto-industrialization in the Czech lands created preconditions for modern industrialization, with the result that the Czech lands came to occupy first place in the Habsburg monarchy as far as the degree of industrialization was concerned.

14 Proto-industrialization in Sweden

Lars Magnusson

Introduction

Swedish industrialization during the nineteenth century has generally been regarded as an example of a 'big spurt'. As Gerschenkron's model suggested, Sweden can be looked upon as a late-comer in the industrialization race. Therefore, for successful 'take-off' to occur, a high rate of growth during a relatively short period was pivotal. Furthermore, according to this view a rapidly increasing demand from abroad was a necessary precondition for industrial breakthrough. Thus in his survey on the industrial breakthrough in Sweden, the Swedish economic historian Lennart Jörberg depicted the conventional wisdom: 'Sweden's industrial development was in high degree a process of adaptation to events outside the country's frontiers. Only to a lesser extent was it an independent process of economic expansion' (Jörberg 1975: 439; Isacson and Magnusson 1987: 1f).

According to this view, three distinct periods of accelerated growth have been particularly emphasized: the 1850s, the 1870s and the 1890s. Growth during the 1850s is supposed to have been caused by the expansion of agricultural production as well as by increasing foreign demand for Swedish timber and saw-mill products. Industrialization in the 1870s, which extended into several sectors, was triggered off mainly by a growth in exports, but also to some extent by a growing home market for consumption goods and industrial products: iron and steel, engineering products, timber and planks and so on. Moreover, rapid growth occurred during the 1890s over an even broader range of sectors. To the industries already mentioned were added wood-pulp production and mining. An increasing volume of exports was a specific and distinctive feature of the 1890s. From this, it was easy to draw the conclusion that the industrial breakthrough in Sweden was triggered off and also largely caused by increased demand from an industrializing Europe (Jörberg 1975; Montgomery 1970; Heckscher 1954; Schön 1982).

However, in recent years this interpretation has been challenged. In its place, a different version of Swedish industrial development as a more gradual process of change has been put forward in the debate (Isacson and Magnusson 1987; Schön 1979, 1982, 1985a).

First, this new interpretation suggests that the expansion of the domestic market after the Napoleonic Wars was a major factor behind the take-off in Sweden from the 1850s on. Accordingly, a rapid increase in agricultural productivity is regarded as having been a crucial factor underlying the later industrial breakthrough. It has been estimated that agricultural productivity per capita rose at a rate of at least 0.5 per cent annually during the period 1750–1850. Without doubt, this rising productivity had important income effects which enlarged demand for both consumer and capital goods (Magnusson 1987a; Schön 1985b). Hence, from the 1820s on, growing agricultural incomes encouraged rapid growth in proto-industries in sectors such as textiles, wood working, metal handicrafts, tanning, tile production, brick making, shoe making and so on, as well as the establishment of new processing industries, such as breweries, aimed at the consumer market (Isacson and Magnusson 1987: 18f; Schön 1985a, 1985b). Thus, in Sweden a stage of proto-industrialization preceded full industrialization, and may indeed be seen as an important factor behind the emergence of the latter in the late nineteenth century. Such industrial production located in the countryside was in fact – as we will see – a characteristic feature of many regions of Sweden from the early nineteenth century onwards.

Secondly, this picture is reinforced by the revision of national income data for Sweden recently undertaken by Krantz and Schön. These two scholars argue that growth was more gradual and that it started out from a much higher level than acknowledged by older estimates. One consequence of this revision is that figures on growth per capita during the following period seem distinctly less dramatic than they did previously (Schön 1985a, 1985b; Krantz and Nilsson 1975).

Thirdly, in recent years an institutional interpretation of nineteenth-century Swedish industrial development has been proposed. According to this view, the Swedish 'take-off' was a long-term consequence not only of proto-industrialization and the development of an important home market. Rather, the emergence of production for the market must also be regarded as a consequence of processes of socio-economic and political innovation during the eighteenth century, which created the institutional framework both for a flowering of agrarian capitalism and for the development of a market economy. In this, the loosening of the strict regulation of the Swedish economy according to cameralist principles, which had previously prevailed, was a crucial factor.

Previously, in accordance with the principle of 'Nahrung' ('livelihood'), each occupation and sector in the economy had been protected against competition and interference. At the beginning of the nineteenth century, however, reforms and de-regulation created property rights in land and forests, loosened old restrictions which had inhibited the free flow of goods and labour both within the country and as far as exports were concerned and made a number of other changes (Eliasson 1988; see also Frohnert 1993; Kyle 1987; Ågren 1992; Magnusson 1994). An additional necessary condition for the creation of suitable 'rules of the game' for further economic expansion was without doubt the changing political and social situation in Sweden during the eighteenth century, which curbed the power of the great landlords and placed more political and social power in the hands of the peasants (Fridholm, Isacson and Magnusson 1976; Kyle 1987; Herlitz 1974). As a consequence of the great wars during the seventeenth century, manorial power had been strengthened. However, this tendency toward 're-feudalization' was curbed once and for all through the so-called 'reduction' instituted by Charles XI. This drastic measure undertaken by the new absolutist king involved the appropriation of the bulk of the lands which had been granted to the nobility during the seventeenth century.

Without doubt, these historical revisons have increased our understanding of industrialization in Sweden as a more protracted process of change than was once perceived. In this brief survey, I will attempt to do two things. First, I will present a brief summary of the 'state of the art' concerning what we know of the development of proto-industry in Sweden from the eighteenth century onwards. Secondly, as we go along, I will make some brief remarks about how the Swedish case fits in with the original theory of proto-industrialization as it was formulated by Mendels and others. As we will see, there are at least three general comments to be made in this context.

First, proto-industrial activities in the countryside oriented toward selling to a wider national or international market were not confined merely to a single organizational model, namely the putting-out system. In Sweden, as elsewhere, proto-industry was organized in a number of different ways: as a 'Kaufsystem' or artisanal system, in which peasant artisans sold independently to the market; and as a 'Verlagssystem' or putting-out system. It was mainly in textiles (wool, linen and, from the early nineteenth century, cotton) that production was organized in the form of a putting-out industry. Still, however, the important linen proto-industry of Hälsingland and Ångermanland in northern Sweden was mainly organized by the peasant-producers themselves, or alternatively in the form of a 'Kaufsystem' (Isacson and Magnusson 1987:18f;

Ahlberger 1988; Schön 1982; Isacson 1988; Palmqvist 1988; Haraldsson 1989; Jonsson 1994).

Secondly, the demographic consequences of proto-industrialization were much more complex than suggested by Mendels' simplistic formula. The extent to which population increased as a consequence of variations in fertility caused by different ages of marriage was to a large extent determined by the differing social structures and household structures within which proto-industrial activities took place (Jonsson 1994; Ahlberger 1988). Thus if proto-industry was socially integrated within the peasant household, a different demographic pattern would emerge than if it was undertaken by free crofters or landless labourers, and so on. As we will see shortly, intermediate forms also existed, and in some regions dominated.

Thirdly, there was no deterministic relationship between proto-industrialization and the subsequent rise of 'full industrialization' in the same geographical region. The pattern of development was much more complicated. For some regions we can certainly detect such a direct link. With others, we must rather speak of a process of de-industrialization, in which proto-industries were out-competed by other activities, such as agriculture or forestry. In the latter case, capital, labour and craft expertise often migrated geographically. This would subsequently make industrial progress possible elsewhere (Andersson and Haraldsson 1988).

Proto-industrialization and agrarian development

Without doubt, the development of proto-industry must be related to prevailing conditions in the agricultural sector, and especially to the rhythm of expansion and stagnation in this sector during the eighteenth century. It was Heckscher who first launched a Malthusian interpretation of Swedish agrarian development during this period. He pointed to the rapid increase in agrarian production which occurred from 1720 to the mid-1760s, and the sharp decline thereafter which manifested itself in declining harvests. According to this interpretation, a series of good harvests from the 1720s onwards led to rapid land clearance, population increase and an increased ratio of labour to land. Over time, population pressure led to stagnating productivity – most pertinently because the proportion of arable decreased, which created a shortage of manure. This Malthusian crisis was made manifest in a number of poor harvests, especially in the 1770s. However, the crisis became endemic and was not overcome until the second decade of the nineteenth century. When production increased again after 1820, it was accompanied by agrarian reforms and the introduction of innovations. As a consequence, productivity and production rose simultaneously. From this point on, the threat of a Malthusian crisis seemed to have been removed once and for all (Heckscher 1935–49: I; 1954; for opposing views see Utterström 1954, 1957; Winberg 1975; Ericsson and Rogers 1978; Fridholm, Isacson and Magnusson 1986).

Without doubt, the agrarian decline during the last quarter of the eighteenth century which intervened between the two periods of agrarian expansion was very significant indeed. However, the early expansion during the eighteenth century was so strong that it admitted a slight increase of per capita production over the whole period from 1720 to 1815 – thus production rose by 75 per cent, while population most probably expanded by considerably less than 50 per cent. Certainly, however, the per capita increase after 1815 was much more marked. Until 1860, agrarian production increased by perhaps 75–100 per cent, which was considerably higher than the growth of population during the same period. Thus, contrary to the popular belief, the period 1720–1860 was characterized by rising per capita incomes (Magnusson 1987a; Schön 1985a, 1985b). However, available evidence seems to suggest that incomes may have become more unevenly distributed. Thus the share of the rural population with little or no land increased considerably over time. The number of peasant households was kept constant between the mid-eighteenth century and 1860, while the army of crofters and landless people more than quadrupled (Wohlin 1909; Winberg 1975:16f).

Thus, according to most observers, Sweden experienced an agrarian expansion from the 1720s onwards which issued in rising production, productivity and income. It was good harvests and increased land clearance in particular which triggered off this growth process. However, piecemeal technological innovations (better ploughs, increased use of horses, etc.) which increased total factor productivity (the productivity of labour plus land) also played some role, as did institutional factors such as agricultural reforms (enclosures) and improved property rights which increased the security for peasant investment. These factors were of especially great importance after 1825. However, it is clear that they had already contributed to the growth process in the eighteenth century.

Rising per capita production certainly had important consequences. By way of income effects, it was followed by increasing demand for new and improved agricultural products, which in turn stimulated increased specialization. Moreover, the demand for non-agricultural wares also increased rapidly. Combined with a process of social differentiation, this stimulated the growth of a home market, which was especially marked after 1820 (Schön 1979, 1985a, 1985b). Such social differentiation occurred widely, but was especially common outside the manorial areas, where regulation of the land market and inheritance patterns were both less strict. Particularly in such areas, the expansion of agriculture laid the foundation for an expansion of demand for consumption articles (textiles, furniture, food), capital goods (ploughs, harrows, threshing machines) and building materials (bricks, timber, tiles and so on).

So far, most research in this field has been concentrated on the expansion of textile production. Thus Schön has shown that demand for textiles was already increasing from the 1820s. During this decade it was still mainly restricted to high-quality varieties of cloth sold to peasants and other relatively well-off social strata. However, the industry exploded after 1850 when demand by low-income groups for cheaper wares rose rapidly (Schön 1979). However, other expanding activities must also be mentioned in this context. In particular, the building industry boomed after 1820. This tendency was reinforced by the enclosure movement which became a more active force from this decade onwards. It led to the break-up of villages, and forced peasants to re-build their farms on new sites. Although there is some debate concerning the extent to which the enclosure movement contributed to increased social differentiation in rural areas, it is still highly probable that it gave rise to an expansion in the home market in the manner we have discussed (Pettersson 1983; Olai 1983; Sivesand 1979).

Without doubt, the increase in agricultural production and productivity also stimulated the emergence and rapid expansion of proto-industries. Unfortunately, it is quite impossible to provide precise figures on the expansion of these industries, since proto-industrial workers were mainly registered as 'common peasants' or 'crofters' in tax lists and other censuses. Local studies can, of course, shed light upon the number of proto-industrial workers in smaller areas, but we are not able to measure the dimensions of proto-industry more generally (Ahlberger 1988; Jonsson 1994). We will therefore have to confine ourselves to presenting some qualitative data, and to mentioning briefly the main proto-industrial regions of the period.

The original model of proto-industrialization proposed by Mendels drew a clear division between town and country. Within towns there existed a system of regulation, including the guild system, which effectively hindered the emergence of small industry. Consequently, it was only in the countryside that proto-industry in its proper sense could develop. As has been discussed, especially with reference to Britain, this is an ideal-typical situation which seems not always to fit actual conditions (Clarkson 1985; see also Isacson and Magnusson 1987: 98f).

In many cases it is in fact difficult to draw a sharp distinction between town and country, since many town-like agglomerations emerged outside the jurisdiction of old towns (see, for example, Birmingham with its extensive toy industry, or Manchester with its textile industry). In Sweden, this sharp distinction between town and countryside can perhaps be maintained – but only until the first decades of the nineteenth century. In the following period, there occurred a de-regulation which included the gradual abandonment of the special jurisdictional and cameral status of the towns which had served to privilege them from interference; this meant that proto-industrial activities could now expand in old towns, or in their close vicinity. As a consequence, the great upsurge of proto-industrial production in Sweden only occurred when the towns were also drawn into the picture after the 1820s. Their opening up as markets for proto-industrial products most certainly stimulated a growing demand for such products.

The original model presented by Mendels also argued that only production for a distant market qualified as proto-industrial production. However, it is not easy to know what 'distant' means in this context. As a general trait, the early modern European economy was characterized by its complicated and inter-connected network of markets of different spatial ranges. Moreover, it would certainly be wrong to believe that selling over great distances was restricted to this period. From a much earlier period, a division of labour had prevailed between different regions in Europe. This gave rise to a trade which linked together economies which were characterized by distinct ecological and/or cultural preconditions. In addition, many producers in small villages combined local marketing with selling to rich putters-out who transported wares over long distances. Moreover, the expansion of long-distance and local markets presupposed each other's existence, and must be regarded as part of the same process. For both practical and analytical reasons, therefore, it is difficult to draw a clear demarcation line between 'real' proto-industries and something which perhaps could be called 'rural handicrafts' aimed at more local markets.

The proto-industrial expansion which took place in Sweden from the eighteenth century onwards certainly to some extent presupposed an earlier division of labour between different regions. Most pertinently, Scandinavia comprises a huge area, containing quite different socio-ecological types. However, the extent to which the different regions of Scandinavia were at an early period already involved in trading has been a subject of controversy in Swedish historiography. In earlier studies it was suggested that the clear social and economic distinction between western and eastern Sweden had provided a basis for a quite extensive division of labour, as well as the early development of exchange between an arable-orientated west and a corn-growing east. However, more recent research has questioned the extent to which different regions in Sweden relied upon each other in economic terms (Myrdal and Söderberg 1991). It is argued that, at least until the eighteenth century, specialization was not very highly developed. Instead, most regions were self-reliant in basic consumption goods and would only become involved in intra-regional trade insofar as surplus products were available. However, this interpretation, which supports Heckscher's view of pre-eighteenth-century Sweden as a predominantly 'natural economy', does not exclude the existence of certain forms of specialization and market exchange (Heckscher 1935–49: I; Hansen 1977; Myrdal and Söderberg 1991). It is conceivable that the bulk of such market exchange was predominantly local, and did not involve transportation over long distances. Thus a high degree of self-reliance does not have to exclude the possibility of some specialization within regions, nor does it exclude a relatively advanced degree of specialization in some speciality items and forms of trade.

However, long before the eighteenth century, certain proto-industrial activities which implied long-term trading already existed in Sweden. Most importantly, the production of iron, especially in the region of Bergslagen, was aimed at the export market. Moreover, the small-scale iron industry of this region, with its small furnaces and smithies, was in the hands of a specific kind of peasant who combined mining and iron production with agriculture, the so-called 'Bergsmän' (Florén and Rydén 1992). During the Middle Ages, marketing and selling in this industry was dominated by merchants from the cities around Lake Mälaren (Västerås, Köping, Stockholm), and sometimes these merchants would also operate as putters-out to the local producers. These merchants were in turn linked to – and most often financially dependent upon – the merchants of the Hanseatic League. Thus at an early stage the iron industry was already a 'model' proto-industry in all respects. However, from the seventeenth century on the role of the 'Bergsmän' gradually declined, and the iron industry became a large-scale industry which was in the hands of great capitalist magnates, often of Dutch origin. Other early proto-industries of the same kind were connected with the production and selling of tar, planks and limestone (from Gotland) – as well as, to some extent, the raising of oxen in the southern districts of Sweden, oriented toward export to Denmark and northern Germany. This certainly implied that in some regions a certain specialization had developed at an early period, which did not exclude a high degree of self-reliance as far as food was concerned.

Regional proto-industrialization from the eighteenth century onwards

At least to some extent, the later development of proto-industrialization was preconditioned by a regional specialization which had developed earlier. This helps to explain the localization of proto-industrial activities in particular regions from the eighteenth century onwards. Such proto-industries developed widely during the eighteenth and nineteenth centuries, but three regions stand out as particularly significant: southern Västergötland in the west of Sweden, the region stretching from Småland to northern Skåne in the south of the country, and Dalecarlia in the middle of Sweden, north-west of Stockholm (Isacson and Magnusson 1987: 18f; Isacson 1988). All three regions were characterized by rather poor agriculture and by farms which relied on a combination of cereal cultivation and cattle rearing.

In the first of these regions, south-western Sjuhäradsbygden, an area of the county of Västergötland characterized by a mixture of woodland and pasture, a flourishing textile industry emerged, together with wood and metal crafts. Even before the eighteenth century, this region was already highly regarded for its linen production. However, it was especially from the mid-eighteenth century onward that the rural linen industry of this area boomed. Gradually, and especially after 1820, linen wares were replaced by cotton goods as the main form of output. To a considerable extent, this industry was organized as a putting-out industry with powerful putters-out stationed in the cities of Borås and Gothenburg, who sold the fabrics outside the region. By the end of the 1820s, this domestic industry was the main occupation among the poorer strata in Sjuhäradsbygden, especially in Marks härad. Probably as a consequence, this region experienced a substantial rise in population, and the proportion of landless proletarians increased sharply (Isacson and Magnusson 1987; Palmqvist 1988; Ahlberger 1988).

In the second of these three proto-industrial regions, most of the county of Småland, including the southern segment which also extends into the wooded part of northern Skåne, can from the beginning of the nineteenth century best be described as an extremely widespread and diversified proto-industrial region. Especially in the area around the village of Gnosjö, there arose a diversified metal handicraft of metal wires, nails, pins and needles. In Markaryd, likewise, a number of metal-working and wood-working crafts flourished, for instance the making of weavers' tools. This product was sold, both within the region and outside it, according to a pattern whose complexity is illustrated by a study of eastern Skåne by Börje Hansen (1977). Hansen argues that we should not over-estimate the degree of direct exchange involved – for instance, the exchange of corn from the corn-growing areas for wood from the mixed farms in the woodland area: both regions were much more self-contained than might have been expected, and most of the exchange between the two areas took place, in any case, with the urban merchants as intermediaries. In the province of Kronoberg, too, a diversified cottage industry emerged during this period. This area produced everything from linen cloth to knives, locks and clocks. By and large, this whole region was highly regarded for its great diversity and skill in all sorts of crafts. Furthermore, it was characterized by rather poor agricultural conditions (Isacson and Magnusson 1987; Isacson 1988; Nelson 1963).

However, the most important proto-industrial area in Sweden was probably the third: Dalecarlia, in particular the part of this province which surrounds Lake Siljan. In villages such as Mora, a number of highly skilled metal crafts had developed gradually over the centuries. At the beginning of the nineteenth century, the manufacturing of files, knives, clocks and the so-called 'Mora-clocks' was widespread. Most of the goods were sold over a considerable distance, often by itinerant pedlars. In fact, at the beginning of the nineteenth century thousands of people around Siljan were engaged in metal working and wood working. Often each parish had its own distinct speciality. Våmhus, for example, north of Mora, was recognized for its women workers, who manufactured baskets and other products out of human hair. In Venjan, cooking utensils were manufactured, at Bonäs wood-turning wares, and in Malung, at some distance from Siljan, tanning was the main speciality (Isacson and Magnusson 1987: 68f).

Outside these three main regions, there were also many others which had flourishing proto-industries during this period of agrarian expansion. In Hälsingland and Ångermanland, along the northern coastline, linen cloth manufacturing was a dominant activity in the small parishes and villages (Jonsson 1994). The province of Halland, too, was recognized during the eighteenth century for its textile industry, mainly wool knitting. Kumla, in the middle part of Sweden, was well known for its widespread shoe making. In northern Västmanland, especially in Våla and Harbo, a furniture industry evolved during the course of the nineteenth century. These examples can, of course, be multiplied.

In many parts of Sweden, therefore, proto-industrial activities developed during this period. Their products were often sold over great distances, sometimes even for purposes of export. However, as already noted, it is difficult to distinguish between industries selling for a local market and those for more distant markets. Different types of industry all flourished because of rising incomes and the rapid expansion of a home market for both consumption goods and (mainly agricultural) capital goods. Industries selling tools and production utensils, especially to the flourishing agricultural sector, were to some extent also affected by this increase in demand. However, it is important to note that it was predominantly the home market which was important in this context. Although some of the goods produced by Swedish proto-industries were exported to nearby countries (Norway, Denmark, Russia and so on), this export activity had much less impact on the general development of such industry than did home markets.

Organizational forms of proto-industry

According to Mendels, the stylized organizational form for proto-industrialization was the putting-out system. This view was later modified by Kriedte, Medick and Schlumbohm, who argued that the 'Kaufsystem' or artisanal system was equally common. Although putting-out was by no means unknown in Sweden during the eighteenth and nineteenth centuries, the artisanal system seems to have dominated in most regions. Thus in Sweden there are only a few examples of a fully fledged putting-out system, in which powerful merchants provided producers with the raw material and then collected the finished wares. Instead, in a majority of cases, the producers seem to have been able to maintain fairly extensive control over both production and commercial activities. A clear example of such a proto-industry, one predominantly controlled by peasants, is provided by the textile regions in Hälsingland (Utterström 1957; Jonsson 1994; Schön 1982). Even in the parish and village of Delsbo, where at the beginning of the nineteenth century hundreds of workers already depended on linen manufacturing, putting-out failed to develop in its full form (Jonsson 1994). This was certainly also the case in the wood- and metal-working industries. For example, in the highly developed and widespread Mora metal industry, where the large and complicated Mora-clocks were manufactured by means of an advanced division of labour, the 'Kaufsystem' prevailed (Isacson and Magnusson 1987: 68f). As a consequence, in a majority of cases merchants from Stockholm and other cities travelled to rural regions to buy up proto-industrial products, or waited for peasant-sellers or pedlars to deliver them at their doorsteps. Very often, as well, locals would journey on foot to sell goods at fairs and market places all around the country (Rosander 1980). In some cases, however, closer links did emerge between producers and merchants, which resembled the putting-out form. In such cases, peasant producers would tend to sell wares on a long-term contractual basis to specific merchants. However, it seems that it was only rather infrequently that this was extended into a regular putting-out dominance by the merchant.

However, in one important region such a putting-out system certainly did develop: in the Sjuhäradsbygden of Västergötland. Here, an intricate net of relations was established which linked the cottage producer to a middleman located in a nearby small village, who provided the producer with his raw material. This middleman in turn worked on behalf of a merchant in Borås – who was also sometimes linked financially to a larger Gothenburg merchant house (Ahlberger 1988; Mannerfeldt and Danielsson 1924; Palmqvist 1988). However, this was a clear exception to the general rule of predominantly 'Kaufsystem' forms of proto-industrial organization. It is of course very complicated to explain this exceptional pattern or, for that matter, why the 'Kaufsystem' appears to have predominated in Sweden. In comparison with most of the other proto-industrial regions we have mentioned so far, Sjuhäradsbygden was early recognized for its many crofters and poor semi-proletarians. By contrast, the social organization of production in the proto-industrial linen districts in Hälsingland and Ångermanland, for example, was heavily dependent on a strong peasantry. As a consequence, in these areas the social power of the proto-industrial peasantry was strong enough for them to retain control both of the linen industry itself and of the channels of access to the market. Lack of social power – as well as of capital and other resources – was without doubt one of the most important reasons the crofters in Sjuhäradsbygden were not able to resist the introduction of a putting-out system.

Likewise, the social and household organization of proto-industrial production was far more complicated than the stylized version of proto-industrialization seems to admit. In Sweden, three different patterns seem to have predominated. First, in many areas proto-industrial production was integrated into an extended peasant household (of the same type as referred to by Brunner's term 'das ganze Haus' (Brunner 1956)). Here, the workers were part of the peasant's household, as daughters, sons and servants. This form was not uncommon in the linen districts of Hälsingland and Ångermanland, for example, as well as in the district around Lake Siljan in Dalecarlia (Jonsson 1994). One consequence was that the demographic results of proto-industrialization were certainly quite different than proposed in Mendels' standard model. Especially since in this case most producers stayed unmarried, it is not at all probable that the existence of proto-industry led to earlier marriages and thus to higher fertility. Only in a minority of cases did they form their own households as proto-industrial producers.

However, a second, mixed, organization was probably even more widespread. In Hälsingland, it was not uncommon for linen production to be integrated into the household of quite well-to-do peasants. Within such households, daughters, sons and servants would do much of the job. At the same time, women wage labourers would be hired in. So far, this arrangement clearly fits quite well with the previous model. However, additional crofters and small peasants with their own households but not enough land to support themselves would also be used to manufacture linen. Above all, the women in such households (which were much smaller than the households of the peasants) would be employed by the larger peasants, particularly for the spinning and swingle operations (Jonsson 1994, 1988).

This latter form – which is close to Mendels' original formula – also existed in a third, and distinct, variation. Thus, for example, in Sjuhäradsbygden the bulk of the workers – at least after 1820 – seem to have been crofter families with their own separate households (Schön 1982; Palmqvist 1988; Ahlberger 1988). In this case, the existence of proto-industrial opportunities may very well have given rise to lower marriage ages and higher fertility rates. However, not enough is known at the demographic micro-level to confirm this thesis. From crude figures on the level of the province, the conclusion can certainly be drawn that in provinces in which proto-industry was more common, such as Kronoberg and Värmland, the fertility rates of younger women were higher than in manorial areas (such as Södermanland) and especially than in areas of peasant farming (such as Skaraborg) (Fridlizius 1979: 372f). The same was also the case with marriage rates. To confirm the thesis, however, we would need more micro-level data, because the province is too large a unit to work with, and obviously often included economies of different ecological and socio-economic types. Nevertheless, it seems clear that the organizational mode which relied on the existence of independent crofter households taking part in proto-industrial production was not uncommon, and in many regions – especially Västergötland – may have predominated.

The political economy of proto-industrialization

During the eighteenth century, the Swedish political establishment propounded a strategy of state-administered industrialization and modernization of a 'mercantilistic' kind. Agricultural reforms were launched in order to increase population and help expand production and productivity. At the same time, the establishment of manufactures was very much supported. According to the leaders of the Swedish state, only a prosperous agriculture and a modern manufacturing sector could provide the means for a powerful and happy commonwealth. Moreover, in order to support the new state-supported manufactures, a policy of regulation was introduced. At the core, this policy implied that each occupation should be protected from interference from others. Hence, the peasants should not interfere in the proper activities of the town craftsmen, they should leave trading and marketing to proper merchants, and so on. Without doubt, this regulative order was especially directed against proto-industrial activities in the countryside. Thus it was made clear that the new manufactures – especially those in textiles – should be protected against competition from peasant handicrafts and proto-industries. According to this view, owing to the prevailing low opportunity cost of labour, 'cheating' peasants would always be able to sell more cheaply than the 'honest' manufacturers. Therefore, a proper regulative order was regarded as pivotal: it was argued that free enterprise and the loosening of the heavy restrictions upon peasant crafts and peasant marketing would only lead to chaos and the ruin of modern enterprise (Magnusson 1987b, 1992).

It is difficult to judge the extent to which this rather draconian regulative order was enforced, especially as it seems clear that both proto-industry and peasants' involvement in the market economy increased during the latter half of the eighteenth century. However, as many instances show, this order of regulation was not altogether a paper tiger. Thus by and large the prohibitions against peasants selling and buying outside the control of the city burghers seem to have been maintained by means of force at least until the 1820s. The heated conflict between the city of Borås and the linen-manufacturing peasantry in Sjuhäradsbygden at the end of the eighteenth century, for instance, provides a clear indication of the active role still played by the regulative control of trade and industry (Utterström 1957). By and large, it is probable that these regulations had a negative impact on the development and growth of proto-industry during this period.

As a consequence, this regulatory order was bitterly opposed by the peasants, both inside and outside the Diet. This struggle was combined with efforts to increase property rights in land and to improve agricultural conditions more widely. Especially during the reign of Gustavus III, this struggle was crowned with success (Kyle 1987). However, it was only after the end of the Napoleonic Wars that Sweden experienced a more distinct phase of de-regulation and liberalization. As a consequence, many of the restrictions on production and the establishment of free entreprise were gradually lifted. From the 1820s onwards, the so-called 'Bergverks-lagarna' (laws for the protection of the mining and iron industry) were abolished, which had up to then limited the production of iron and steel (on the grounds that it was important not to exhaust the supply of charcoal). In the same vein, the specific privileges governing the manufacturing sector were abolished, as was the system of state-supported manufactures orginally introduced in the 1720s. Such reforms made entry more easy for striving entrepreneurs. Of even more importance in this context was the abolition of the guilds in 1846, and the establishment of free enterprise in 1864. At the same time, the labour market was gradually 'liberalized' and other laws and regulations were repealed, in order to make industry and production for the market more easy (Eliasson 1988).

However, this did not mean that the state withdrew from all interference in the evolving industrial market economy which began to flourish, particularly from the 1850s onward. On the contrary, the abolition of the old structure of governance laid the ground for the establishment of a new set of institutions which served to promote and bolster modern economic growth and development. Thus the development of the Swedish economy from 1840 onwards was very much characterized by the introduction of new principles of state governance, which aimed explicitly at such modernization. Certainly, the 'departmental reform' of 1840 served such a cause. By means of this reform, an old and rather inefficient state apparatus, based upon the privileges and independence of the collegiums (independent administrative bodies responsible for different aspects of the economy such as commerce and mining) and, especially, the locally based 'länsförvaltningen' (county administrations), was replaced by a much more efficient and tightly knit state administration. Through the establishment of specially designed departments with their own exclusive functions, the state became a much more powerful machine for direct rule and governance. Previously, with the looser 'feudal' structure, the state's capacity to implement policies had been very limited indeed (Kyle 1989; Frohnert 1993). Nor did this process of 'de-regulation' imply that the costs of state administration were reduced. To the extent that figures of this kind can be calculated, it seems instead that the overall costs of state administration – in real prices – increased during most of the nineteenth century. And although the tax system was reformed in a series of stages during the century – for example, the old land-based taxes were abolished – there is no positive indication that the total tax burden decreased during the period. Rather, the opposite seems to be the case (Kyle 1987; Krantz 1987:186f).

All in all, these institutional developments were most certainly crucial for the rapid growth of a proto-industrial sector in Sweden after 1820.

Certainly, also, the struggle for 'liberal' reforms was in itself a sign of the rapid increase in proto-industrial production, which demanded such reforms for its sustainable growth. However, as the period of de-regulation was followed by the build-up of strong state structures, it is also possible that institutional factors contributed to the dual process of 'industrialization' and 'de-industrialization' which set in, particularly after 1870. The expanding state machinery craved and supported the emergence of modern industrial structures, and helped to bolster market institutions, patent regulations, restrictions against 'unsound' competition and so on, which especially stimulated the growth and survival of 'modern' factory-like production. In addition, the emergence of modern transportation, and especially the railroad system, which created the preconditions for the spread of mass-market organization and its technologies, seems to have had identical effects. Thus the changing institutional framework was certainly pivotal in the rapid process of industrialization which set in during the second half of the nineteenth century (Magnusson 1994). At the same time, as already noted, this change was stimulated by the very growth of proto-industrial forms of production which necessitated institutional changes.

Industrialization and de-industrialization

It has been convenient to argue that proto-industrialization contributed to later 'full' industrialization, particularly in three senses: proletarianization by means of population increase, expansion of markets and increased capital formation. In a certain sense, it is indeed plausible that an earlier 'stage' of proto-industrialization played an important role for later industrial development through contributing such endowments. However, its more exact consequences for later development are much harder to pinpoint. This is especially pertinent as it has been shown that de-industrialization was as common a consequence of proto-industry in many regions as was the emergence of centralized production in a factory-like environment. Moreover, the geographical context of proto-industrial achievements has not yet been very clearly formulated in the theories of proto-industrialization. Hence, in many localities the long-term effect of proto-industrialization seems to have been an increase in wage labour, capital, and markets which, through a process of competition and structural rationalization, stimulated the establishment of modern enterprises outside the region (Isacson 1988; Andersson and Haraldsson 1988). Moreover, it was not uncommon for merchants to start factories in the cities on the basis of their earlier putting-out activities. Often this meant that domestic proto-industries were out-competed.

Hence, the regional effects of proto-industry are very complicated, and can only be understood in relation to the industrialization process as a whole, and to the way in which this led to general concentration and geographical re-location of industries and branches of industry. However, against this background, what can be said of Sweden?

First, it is clear that Swedish proto-industry began to decline particularly after 1870. In some regions there was a clear transition from proto-industry to mechanized large-scale production, while in others de-industrialization occurred (Isacson and Magnusson 1987: 37f). The classic example of such a transition is provided by Sjuhäradsbygden in Västergötland. As we have seen, Sjuhäradsbygden had been the location of a widespread textile industry organized in the form of putting-out. With the establishment of Rydboholm's cotton mill in 1834, this district gradually emerged as a centre of modern textile industry. Rydboholm itself originated in the activities of a typical putting-out middleman, a peasant's wife called Kerstin of Stämmemad (Schön 1982; Mannerfeldt and Danielsson 1924; Isacson and Magnusson 1987: 41). In other regions with highly developed proto-industries, as well, factories were established on the basis of local skills. This was especially the case with wood working in the province of Småland, which laid the ground for a prosperous furniture industry from the late nineteenth century onward, and the wire making of Gnosjö in the same province, which was a precondition for the establishment here of many workshops and metal industries. Much the same can be said of Dalecarlia and especially the Mora region. Here a widely based metal craftsmanship led to the establishment, beginning around 1900, of a versatile industry of knife making, steel foundries and other forms of metal production. Numerous other examples can, of course, be mentioned: the tanning industry in Malung, the carpentry industry in Västmanland, scythe manufacturing and allied metal crafts in Dalecarlia and Gästrikland, shoe making in Örebro, weavers'-reed making in Markaryd and so on (Isacson and Magnusson 1987; Jonell-Ericsson 1975).

However, other regions with a strong heritage of de-centralized handicraft production instead experienced a decrease in their traditional activities. In this context, the most important example is the linen industry of Hälsingland and Ångermanland, which experienced a rapid decline after the 1870s. Other textile and garment industries also began to dwindle rapidly, perhaps even earlier. In 1876, the customs committee reported an actual decline of such 'female industries' in the provinces of Stockholm, Jönköping, Kronoberg, Gotland, Malmöhus, Blekinge, Gothenburg, Värmland and Västerbotten (Isacson and Magnusson 1987: 38). However, this decline was not restricted to the textile industry. In

Göinge, for example, the widespread forging industry underwent a rapid decline after 1910 and in Dalecarlia many regional specialities of wood working and metal manufacturing gradually disappeared.

Certainly, the causes behind such decline were multifarious and specific to each case. However, some more general causes can perhaps be emphasized.

First, we have already mentioned the effect of institutional change and transformation. Without any doubt, the changed regulative order was an important determining factor behind the industrialization process in general. It is probable that political and institutional change not only supported and propelled this process of change, but also actively helped to structure its actual form and content. As suggested by Sabel and Zeitlin, large-scale industry and the mass market were perhaps more than mere automatic consequences of the competitive process: they may have also been effects of institutional change and decision making (Sabel and Zeitlin 1985; Magnusson 1994). The same can probably be argued in general with regard to the geographical process of the localization of industry during the process of rapid industrialization.

Secondly, it is clear that a process of competition both within branches of industry and between different branches and sectors played a crucial role in this context. Thus it is clear from many instances how increasing demand for foodstuffs and wood led to local proto-industries being outcompeted by expanding agricultural sectors and forest industries. In Hälsingland, Ångermanland, Gästrikland and parts of Dalecarlia, this was certainly the main cause behind the decline of proto-industry. Hence, in the great linen districts of Hälsingland, for example, it is obvious how increased incentives in forestry led to the gradual abandonment of linen production (Schön 1982; Isacson and Magnusson 1987: 37f).

Thirdly, we must also of course deal with the location factors which are conventionally discussed by economic geographers. Hence, the existence of relative advantages such as vicinity to transport services, raw material supplies, and so on, could in a number of cases be of greater importance for the localization of large-scale industry than the earlier existence of proto-industry. This process was reinforced by the emergence of a more mobile labour market and the inauguration of less expensive transportation after the mid-nineteenth century. A clear example is the establishment of a large-scale saw-mill industry along the Norrland coast from 1850 onwards. To some extent, this replaced many of the small proto-industrial mills which had been widespread in Norrland, Gästrikland, Dalecarlia and Värmland (Haraldsson 1989).

For many decades after 1850, traditional workers from these areas would travel to do seasonal work in the new power-driven mills.

The role of proto-industry in Swedish industrial development?

As has already been remarked, it is difficult to draw any clear conclusion concerning the impact of proto-industrialization on the later industrial breakthrough in Sweden. This breakthrough was certainly caused by a combination of long-term factors such as the prevalence of proto-industry and of more short-term factors such as the export boom of the later nineteenth century. However, Sweden's long-term industrial tradition certainly played an important role for later industrial growth and specialization. A clear indication of this is surely that Sweden has remained strong in what were its distinctive specialities very early on: metal working and wood working. Such continuities can certainly not be regarded as pure chance. Nor can it be a mere coincidence that much industrial production in Sweden during the twentieth century has retained its localization in the countryside. Hence it can surely be argued that early proto-industrial production contributed to later industrial development in a number of senses. First, it helped to develop a network of markets linking up different provinces, as well as connecting towns with rural areas. Secondly, new and better transportation was stimulated by the expansion of proto-industrial production (for example, the building of canals and better roads). Thirdly, the growth of proto-industry helped to stimulate institutional reforms and the de-regulation of the old forms of regulation. Fourthly, capital generated in proto-industry was most probably channelled into the new industries which emerged after the middle of the nineteenth century (for example, the saw-mills).

To this extent, the Swedish path of development is certainly in line with what many other countries in western Europe also experienced. However, proto-industrialization in the Swedish context also manifested a number of peculiarities which I have discussed in this chapter. Together, these similarities and peculiarities formed the nucleus of the specific Swedish path of industrialization. And it was this combination which made Sweden what it is today – when the old industrial order is in flux, challenged by a third industrial revolution.

15 Proto-industrialization, economic development and social change in early modern Europe

Sheilagh C. Ogilvie and Markus Cerman

Proto-industries arose in almost every part of Europe in the two or three centuries before industrialization, and research on them encompasses almost every aspect of early modern European life. The chapters in this book discuss proto-industries from the Mediterranean to the North Sea and the Baltic, and from the Atlantic Ocean to the Oder and the Danube. They also reveal a multiplicity of perspectives on proto-industry. Some chapters, such as those on France, Sweden and Flanders, orient themselves around the hypotheses of Franklin Mendels; others, such as those on Bohemia, Austria, Switzerland, Germany and England, focus on the theories of Kriedte, Medick and Schlumbohm; while those on Ireland, Spain and Italy have simply chosen to discuss 'proto-industries' in these countries without systematic confrontation with one or another of the explanatory frameworks originally advanced along with the term 'proto-industrialization' in the 1970s.

Even under the rubric 'proto-industry', the various chapters encompass a number of different kinds of industrial production, reflecting the continuing debate about defining and circumscribing proto-industry (see Kriedte, Medick and Schlumbohm 1993: 217ff). Clarkson's chapter on Ireland criticizes the growing tendency to categorize all possible forms of pre-industrial manufacturing as proto-industries, and urges that a distinction be drawn between export-oriented proto-industries and locally oriented crafts. However, Magnusson's chapter on Sweden and Belfanti's chapter on northern Italy view rural location and freedom from guilds as more important than strict export orientation in defining a proto-industry. Thomson's chapter on Spain and Cerman's chapter on Austria, by contrast, also consider those industries which were urban, guild-dominated or centralized into manufactories – as long as they were export oriented. The various textile branches occupy centre-stage in the chapters on most countries, which reflects their overwhelming importance in early modern European industry, but the different technical demands of different branches of textiles, metal production and mining emerge from most contributions, and the mining and metal trades are discussed in detail in the chapters on Bohemia and Austria.

A wide variety of aspects of the original proto-industrialization theories are emphasized by the different chapters. Schlumbohm's conceptual chapter discusses the methodological and chronological dimensions of the theory, while Ogilvie's explores the neglected framework of social institutions. In the chapters on Italy, Ireland, France, Sweden and Spain, questions of economic development, and in particular the transition to factory industrialization, are at centre-stage. The chapter on Flanders concentrates on demographic change and standards of living. The chapters on England, Austria, Bohemia, Switzerland and Germany widen the focus not only to demography and agriculture, but also to questions of social history such as changes in gender roles, consumption behaviour, everyday life, social structure, the family economy, and family structures.

Research on European proto-industrialization thus covers an enormous geographical and thematic range, and its findings have become central to understanding many aspects of economy and society in early modern Europe. What general conclusions emerge from the array of case-studies surveyed in the present volume?

It is acknowledged by the original theorists that the demographic predictions of the original theory are not generally borne out by empirical findings (Kriedte, Medick and Schlumbohm 1993: 219ff). The country studies in the present volume confirm the variety, rather than the uniformity, of demographic responses to proto-industrialization. The predicted fall in age at marriage, rise in fertility, and rapid population growth are confirmed only for Catalonia and Bohemia, and for scattered regions of Austria, Switzerland, Germany and Italy. Fertility, nuptiality and population growth actually decreased in Flanders as proto-industrialization progressed. A very wide variety of demographic responses to proto-industries can be observed across England, Sweden, Austria, Italy, Switzerland and Germany.

Even where demographic behaviour changed, the cause could be agricultural expansion rather than proto-industry, as in parts of England, Ireland and Germany. Proto-industrial population growth was also capable of 'going into reverse', as Hudson points out for England. Mendels' 'ratchet mechanism' – whereby proto-industrial nuptiality and fertility increased in good years and did not decrease in bad years – has proved difficult to replicate. In the only duplication hitherto of Mendels' statistical model, Pfister, working on the Zürich highland, found that a shift in relative prices in favour of the proto-industrial sector increased birth and marriage rates, but only in certain time-periods, certain stages of production, and certain institutional contexts. Moreover, birth and marriage rates declined with falling relative prices just as strongly as they expanded with rising ones – Pfister ascribes Mendels' ratchet mechanism to faults in his statistical analysis (Pfister 1989a). French and German research, too, shows proto-industrial producers adjusting nuptiality and fertility to economic fluctuations. Swiss research suggests that rapid population growth in many proto-industrial regions was due to better nutrition and falling mortality, rather than rising nuptiality and fertility. Indeed, Pfister identifies three distinct models of proto-industrial demographic behaviour, all observed in early modern Switzerland; he argues that the relative marginal productivity of domestic labour and household capital are the main explanatory variables behind these differences (Pfister 1992b: 222 and *passim*). German findings suggest an even greater variety of demographic patterns, because demographic behaviour was affected by the ways in which social institutions constrained economic and social decisions in the specific region, as well as by the technological and organizational demands of the specific proto-industry. Similarly, the evidence from both England and Germany suggests that the position of women was not consistently affected by proto-industrial occupation, but rather depended on the organization of society and the economy in the particular proto-industrial region.

Originally it was argued that proto-industrialization led to impoverishment for its participants. However, the chapters in this book show that although some proto-industries saw falling living standards, others saw rising ones. Living standards appear to have been dependent upon the features of the particular proto-industry in question, and the fluctuations it went through, rather than the fact that it was a proto-industry. In the Po valley, proto-industry shielded peasants from falling incomes, and in Tuscany it protected them for a long time from the consequences of worsening shareholding contracts. Proto-industrialization unambiguously led to prosperity for rural producers in eighteenth-century Flanders, northern France and Catalonia. Most Swiss proto-industrial regions had lower mortality than average because of better and more varied nutrition. Where proto-industrial workers did see falling incomes, it was often because of a general downturn of the whole economy, as in nineteenth-century Flanders and northern France after 1789.

As Deyon concludes, 'the impoverishment of households has not been proved for all the very diverse models and all the successive phases of proto-industrialization'. Indeed, if we assume – as contemporary records suggest – that to marry and form a family was viewed as more desirable than lifelong celibacy by most people in early modern Europe, then wherever proto-industry was associated with earlier or more universal marriage, we may speculate that it increased human well being, even where it did not increase standards of material consumption.

Initially, it was argued that proto-industries were carried out by land-poor or landless groups, and that they furthered the process of rural 'proletarianization', the growth in the number of families dependent wholly on wages for survival. However, the chapters in this book show a much more variegated picture. In Italy, Germany, Austria, England and Sweden, research has shown that the families involved in domestic industry belonged to various social groups – small landowners, tenant farmers, cottagers, farm labourers and rural craftsmen – depending on the technical demands of the proto-industry, the nature of regional landholding and the institutional organization of both agriculture and industry. German, Swiss and Austrian research shows that the practice of some metal and textile proto-industries required expensive workshops and equipment, which could not be afforded by the poorest or landless groups in the rural population; instead, these proto-industries were practised by peasants. In some German regions, both peasants and cottagers practised proto-industry, with the peasants actually producing larger volumes of output.

Proletarianization in proto-industrial regions was often affected by agriculture more than by proto-industry. In the silk regions of Lombardy, for example, a progressive proletarianization of the rural classes took place because the landlords redefined the terms of share-cropping contracts. Resilient agrarian institutions maintained land-ownership by proto-industrial producers in a number of English, Austrian and German regions. In some Swiss, French and Flemish proto-industries, producers accumulated proto-industrial earnings in order to invest in buying land and setting up business as a farmer. On the whole, the pre-industrial social system proved flexible enough in the majority of investigated cases to absorb any changes in social structure which proto-industrialization might cause, rather than breaking down or preparing the way for a social upheaval.

Throughout Europe, the rise during the early modern period of a rural sub-stratum which could not live wholly from its own land is widely observed. According to the theories, proto-industrialization required a certain degree of such social polarization as a precondition, and there is evidence confirming this for a number of proto-industrial regions. However, very few case-studies provide a systematic examination of social structure before and after the appearance of proto-industry, and this is a fruitful and important area for future research. In a number of proto-industrial regions, social differentiation undeniably increased during the course of proto-industrialization, and by the end of the eighteenth century was higher than in many agrarian regions. This is not surprising, since availability of non-agricultural (or non-land-intensive) livelihoods made it possible – although not inevitable – for people to live with little or no land, and thus to swell the size of the rural sub-stratum. But labouring, small trading, peddling, rural crafts for local needs, and even certain forms of intensive agriculture such as vine growing, olive growing or market gardening which required very small plots of highly productive land, were also compatible with the rapid expansion of land-poor or landless rural groups. Thus proto-industry was only one sort of rural economic activity which enabled survival without much or any land, even if in many regions it was quantitatively the most important.

Moreover, although proto-industry created the potential for the rise and survival of large landless or land-poor rural groups, whether this potential was realized depended on social institutions. In many European proto-industrial regions, the unlimited growth in the number of households of the rural sub-stratum was restricted by the existing social system. Rather than obtaining their own cottages on the village commons, the proto-industrial producers became inmates in peasant households and remained part of the agrarian social system as well as of the agrarian economy, for instance as seasonal wage labourers for peasants (Berkner 1973; Kriedte, Medick and Schlumbohm 1993: 226–32; Schlumbohm 1994). Even in regions where there was a dramatic growth in the rural sub-stratum because of the availability of proto-industrial work, the social hierarchies within villages and the strong position of the landholding peasants were often maintained or even increased.

Proto-industrialization is supposed to have been associated with the commercialization of agriculture in neighbouring regions and subsistence by-employed farming in the proto-industrial region itself (Mendels 1972; Kriedte, Medick and Schlumbohm 1981). However, as Schlumbohm acknowledges in his chapter in this book, the bifurcation into regions of commercial agriculture and of proto-industry was 'merely a special case of a considerably more complex situation'. In Catalonia, proto-industry did not stimulate agricultural commercialization, but rather the survival of small-scale subsistence farming. In Switzerland, the system of complementary regions of commercial agriculture and proto-industry was more complex and segmented than the ideal-typical model, and Pfister identifies at least three sub-patterns. In Italy and in Germany, proto-industry arose alongside a wide variety of forms of farming, including feudal agriculture, cottager systems, peasant smallholdings and large commercial farms. In most parts of Europe, there were some proto-industries with little or no integration between agricultural activity and industrial work, while in others by-employment in agriculture, whether as labourer, cottager or small landowner, remained the norm. Food and raw material supplies came sometimes from neighbouring regions, sometimes from the proto-industrial region itself and sometimes from even further afield.

Nor was proto-industrialization always associated with the breakdown of feudalism, as was originally postulated (Kriedte, Medick and Schlumbohm 1981). Spanish historians argue that proto-industry sustained low-productivity agriculture, thereby serving 'as a prop to the survival of feudalism'. As Myška and Ogilvie point out, in Bohemia, Moravia and Silesia important proto-industries developed and lasted for centuries, despite the so-called 'second serfdom' and increasing involvement of the feudal nobility in non-agrarian economic activities. Myška shows the many ways in which feudal lords affected proto-industry directly, precisely through exploiting their monopoly rights over their peasants' labour. Feudalism was abolished only in the later eighteenth or early nineteenth century, and then because of state initiatives, not proto-industrialization. Feudalism was thus completely consistent with proto-industrialization, and was not broken down by it.

A central theme in almost all the country studies in this book is industrial organization: the form of production (craft, domestic industry, 'proto-factory'); the system of marketing (*Kaufsystem*, *Verlagssystem*, manufactory); and the division of labour (within or between households, by sex and age within the household, between full-time and by-employed producers). The dominance of the putting-out system in the original theories – even though consciously adopted as a correction to earlier studies – can hardly be justified, judging from the multiplicity of forms portrayed in the chapters of this book. The multiplicity of production forms arose partly from the variety of different branches of proto-industry, and partly from the variety of social and institutional contexts, which placed different technical and organizational constraints on producers. In some circumstances, different production forms could co-exist in one and the same industrial region. Similarly, the dominance of the 'family economy' in the original theories has been complicated by the emergence of various kinds of division of labour between households, sexes, age groups, and full-time industrial producers and those who worked part time in agriculture, labouring, peddling, trading in raw materials or other rural by-employments. Although the family was generally the unit of proto-industrial production, this was by no means always the case; and the organization of work within proto-industrial families varied widely.

The importance of other forms of production than the putting-out system, to some extent as supplements to it, emerges from most of the country studies in the book. For proto-industrial textile production in Bohemia and Austria, for silk processing in Italy and for cotton production in Catalonia, manufactories played an important role. That guilded industrial production is not necessarily incompatible with export-oriented rural domestic industry is shown by the textile industries in Castile, the linen and scythe-making industries in Austria, many textile and metal proto-industries in German territories and various forms of 'guild purchase' in Germany, Austria and Bohemia. Through merchants, guilded industrial producers could become just as integrated into the putting-out system as rural domestic workers were. Where this was the case, there no longer seems to be a clear demarcation between different groups of producers, and upon occasion – as is shown in the chapters on France, Spain and Germany – there could be co-operation between rural domestic industries and guild-organized finishing industries in towns. The widespread survival and new formation of guilds in rural proto-industries blurs the distinction between these and guilded export industries in the late medieval period. However, this does not necessarily mean that industrial production for local needs should be integrated into the concepts of proto-industrialization (Kriedte, Medick and Schlumbohm 1993: 226ff).

Even the *Kaufsystem* (artisanal system) and *Verlagssystem* (putting-out system) which are the main focus of the original theories turn out to have varied a great deal, and did not always show a progression from one to the other. In most proto-industrial regions of Sweden, for example, producers were able to retain control over the production process and the market by maintaining the artisanal system. The same is true for France, where case-studies have sought to clarify the transition mechanisms between artisanal and putting-out system. Similarly, in Catalonia, despite the involvement of merchant capital, merchants did not become more closely involved in the production process. For the wool industry in the West Riding of Yorkshire, Hudson explains the expansion of the putting-out system in the production of worsteds and the maintenance of an artisanal system operated by rural craftsmen in the production of woollens, in terms of differences in landownership and social structure. In the Black Forest of Württemberg, both artisanal system and putting-out system survived side by side among rural worsted weavers in the same communities over more than two centuries, sustained by the fine balance of institutional privileges between rural guilds and merchant company.

Finally, almost all contributions show that the division of labour within proto-industrial households depended on the sort of industry it was, the social groups which participated in production (whether they were peasants or sub-peasants), the structure of full-time industrial work and by-employments, and social and institutional factors (cf. Kriedte, Medick and Schlumbohm 1993). As Pfister points out on the basis of Swiss evidence, the family was not always the unit of proto-industrial production, but rather different family members carried out different forms of wage work as individuals; this had far-reaching effects on demographic behaviour and family structure.

The original theories assumed that proto-industrialization both required, and furthered, the replacement of 'traditional' social institutions with markets. However, the contribution by Ogilvie points out that urban privileges, guilds, merchant companies, village communities and seigneurial institutions remained important in many cases of European proto-industrialization, and this is amply borne out by the country studies in this volume.

Towns retained a variety of legal privileges to regulate proto-industries to a late date, except in England, Ireland and Flanders. In Italy, proto-industries could arise only in 'institutional enclaves' where urban privileges were neutralized. In other cases, urban privileges did not prevent the rise of proto-industries, but did shape their growth: in Castile and Catalonia throughout the eighteenth century, in Saxony, Westphalia, Württemberg and many other German regions until after 1800, and in Sweden until about 1820. Even in Switzerland, where urban powers declined during the seventeenth century, towns retained inspection rights and ensured customs privileges and monopolies for merchants; Zürich actually increased its controls over rural entrepreneurs after 1670, and these constraints contributed to delaying mechanization in the late eighteenth and early nineteenth centuries.

Partly because of the survival of urban privileges, but partly too because they obtained support from the growing early modern state, merchant groups enjoyed legal privileges in many proto-industries: the 'special corporative organizations' formed by merchants in many Swiss proto-industries; the 'franquicias' necessary to operate in the Catalan cotton proto-industry; the privileged manufactories characteristic of Austrian proto-industries; the urban inspection offices in the Westphalian linen proto-industries; the obligation to sell through urban merchant guilds in Saxon proto-industries; the monopoly and monopsony privileges of proto-industrial merchant companies in the Rhineland and Württemberg; and even the powers of the 'Blackwell Hall factors' in the southern English textile proto-industries.

Guilds, too, were widespread in European proto-industries until the end of the eighteenth century, except in England, Ireland and Flanders.

Guilds retained important economic influence over rural proto-industries in Switzerland until the early seventeenth century, in France and Westphalia until the late seventeenth century, in Bohemia and Saxony until the early eighteenth century, in Austria, Catalonia and parts of the Rhineland until the later eighteenth century, and in Sweden and Württemberg into the nineteenth century. In Castile and many parts of northern Italy, guilds excluded proto-industry altogether – even from the countryside. Long political struggles were required before the guilds could be weakened in proto-industries in Catalonia and many parts of Germany. In Austria, many parts of Germany and some parts of Bohemia, 'regional' guilds were formed which included rural as well as urban producers; exclusively rural proto-industrial guilds were formed in Germany and Italy. Many proto-industrial guilds were not simply survivals from the medieval period, but were specially formed in response to the challenges and pressures of proto-industrialization, including the desire on the part of producers to defend themselves against privileged merchants, and the desire on the part of the growing early modern state to tax and regulate the emerging proto-industrial sector.

Peasant communities and seigneurial institutions also helped to shape many proto-industries. In Austria and many parts of southern Germany, they regulated settlement and marriage until the later eighteenth century, preventing proto-industrial population explosion or proletarianization. In Bohemia, Moravia and Silesia, the strengthening of feudal institutions after *c.* 1650 influenced almost every aspect of proto-industrialization. Sharecropping institutions shaped several Italian proto-industries, and in Lombardy the powers of sharecropping landlords became greater, rather than weakening, as the silk proto-industry expanded. Even in England, 'both the location and longevity of proto-industry' was influenced by agrarian institutions. The 'ruralization' of export industries in early modern Europe did not necessarily mean their emancipation from institutional regulation and the growth of markets; it often simply meant exchanging one set of non-market regulatory institutions for another.

It is often argued that proto-industrialization led to changes in popular culture and mentalities, but there is wide debate about what these changes were. The original theories argued that although proto-industrial producers gradually adopted cultural practices no longer rooted in the agrarian society, at the same time they maintained some basic economic attitudes – subsistence orientation and willingness to engage in 'self-exploitation' – which are believed by some to be characteristic of 'peasant' and 'traditional' cultures. By contrast, the proto-industrial merchants and putters-out are supposed to have adopted a profit-oriented and capitalistic 'market' mentality. The interaction between 'self-exploitation' on the part of the producers and profit maximization on the part of the merchants was a central element in the growth process which the proto-industrial system was supposed to have unleashed in early modern Europe (Kriedte, Medick and Schlumbohm 1981: 50–4).

The contributions in this volume, however, show a wide variety of cultural practices and attitudes among both rural producers and merchants. Rural proto-industrial producers manifested both 'traditional' and 'market-oriented' attitudes. Thus, Hudson argues that the 'industrious revolution' in England involved new market-oriented mentalities among the proto-industrial producers. However, sometimes 'market-oriented' mentalities were clearly already in existence, as in parts of England where proto-industry was 'a vigorous response to additional opportunities for profit'. In other cases, proto-industrial workers retained a strong orientation toward the land: in the Po valley of Italy, in Flanders, in northern France and in parts of Germany, Austria and Switzerland. Finally, proto-industrial workers as far afield as England, Germany and Italy resisted new techniques and factory industrialization.

However, orientation to landholding or resistance to new techniques need not be seen as characteristic of 'traditional' rather than 'market' mentalities. Lombard peasants became involved in the silk proto-industry in order to diversify production and market risks, which is quite consistent with 'capitalist' economic rationality. Proto-industrial producers did not resist innovations because of inherent conservatism, but because these threatened their livelihoods: as the rural ribbon makers of Lusatia show, proto-industrial producers were ready enough to adopt new techniques which would benefit them. Similarly, the 'traditional mentalities' which are supposed to have lain behind Mendels' demographic 'ratchet mechanism', whereby proto-industrial workers increased their marriage rate in good years and did not decrease it in bad years, have failed to materialize for other regions; increasingly it appears that proto-industrial producers adjusted their demographic behaviour to livelihood expectations.

Nor was it always the case that the proto-industrial merchants were oriented toward commerce and capitalist profits (as, indeed, had already been partly acknowledged in Kriedte, Medick and Schlumbohm 1981: 107ff, 141ff). In parts of France, for instance, proto-industrial merchants were oriented toward landownership and noble status; in Bohemia, Moravia and Silesia, many proto-industrial 'entrepreneurs' were feudal nobles; and in many parts of Europe, the merchants themselves were organized into guild-like companies which resisted innovations and opposed entrepreneurial profit seeking. Even where proto-industry may have been associated with the growth of new economic and social attitudes, it did not always contribute to the diffusion of new mentalities to the society more generally, as is shown by the failure of 'the social values associated with the rise and development of modern capitalism' to diffuse from Catalonia to other parts of Spain.

A last question, common to all the contributions in this volume, concerns the transition from proto-industrialization to industrialization or de-industrialization. The studies in this volume show that this development was highly dependent on factors specific to the particular region. Moreover – and this is a finding not dealt with thoroughly in the debate hitherto – proto-industrial production forms often survived for a long time in co-existence with the factory system, both supplementing and resisting it.

As Jürgen Schlumbohm rightly points out, a major service performed by the theories of proto-industrialization was to have conceived the industrial revolution as a regional phenomenon, and to have explored the ways in which earlier proto-industrialization may have contributed to the regional sources of industrialization, whether directly through creating a regional industrial 'tradition' or 'path-dependency', or indirectly through its social and demographic consequences. However, as Deyon points out, subsequent research has now shown conclusively that proto-industrialization was only one of the possible paths toward the industrial revolution.

Even research on 'failed' transitions to industrialization in proto-industrial regions, however, has proved very illuminating, for it has generated a much more detailed analysis of the factors lying behind industrial continuity and discontinuity, and behind economic expansion and stagnation more widely. Deyon, Hudson and Ogilvie all trace industrial discontinuities – i.e. de-industrialization – back to social and institutional factors. These include both the institutional legacy of proto-industrialization, which could constitute a structural obstacle to industrialization, and direct resistance by proto-industrial producers to new techniques, new work practices or factory employment. For Hudson and Magnusson, geographical factors (such as transport connections or raw material supplies) which helped determine the location of proto-industry, constituted a further bundle of causes for industrialization or de-industrialization. According to Magnusson and Cerman, state liberalization of trade, industry and agriculture could also be decisive. But it must also be pointed out that discontinuities between proto-industrialization and later industrialization depended a great deal on the particular industry and its position relative to rival producers and competing sectors. Moreover, mechanization and concentration of production in an industry in one region could lead to the de-industrialization of other regions.

The role of international economic trends in this transition process is still not fully illuminated, although it is referred to in passing in most studies of continental Europe. The repeal of the Continental Blockade in 1815 and the influx of higher-quality English yarn threw early attempts at mechanized spinning in many parts of Europe into a severe crisis, or led to the final disappearance of proto-industrial domestic spinning, insofar as this had not already taken place. But even temporary discontinuities between proto-industrial and industrial textile production in Austria, Bohemia, France and many German territories can be traced back to this source (cf. Crouzet 1964: 572ff).

Several of the chapters in this volume point out the survival of proto-industrial production as a supplement or an alternative to factories, long into the nineteenth or even the twentieth century. The conditions for this survival were created by the very gradual rate of mechanization of particular branches of production. The sources of this gradualism in mechanization resided partly in technical difficulties in mechanization using particular raw materials, partly in the fact that proto-industry often still remained competitive in terms of costs, and partly in the only very gradual dissolution of various political, social and institutional obstacles to adopting new production practices. The fact that weaving was often mechanized decades or generations later than spinning – even though the technology was available in both processes – is well known. Less well known, by contrast, is the intentional maintenance of putting-out production alongside centralized factory production as a cushion for fluctuations in demand. Based on such observations, Pierre Deyon concludes that the industrial revolution did not displace the proto-industrial system in France, but rather 'encompassed, integrated, and further developed it'.

Theories of proto-industrialization have therefore not only brought about a re-evaluation of pre-factory industrial production in its own right, rather than as simply a precursor to the factory system (Mosser 1981: 382ff). They have also shed new light on the causes of the gradual and variegated nature of factory industrialization itself. The original theories of proto-industrialization stressed that the origins of capitalism and industrialization were to be found in the early modern period. Subsequent research on proto-industry, however, has also found that many features of early modern European societies and economies survived long into capitalism and industrialization. Indeed, this may be seen as the central conclusion of a change in historical perspectives which has been under way for some time. This new perspective emphasizes long-term continuities in the economic and social development of Europe between the medieval period and the nineteenth century, and in so doing opens up promising new avenues of approach to both proto-industrialization and industrialization.

References

Abt-Frössl, Victor 1988 *Agrarrevolution und Heimindustrie. Ein Vergleich zwischen Heimarbeiter- und Bauerndörfern des Baselbiets im 17. und 18. Jahrhundert* (Liestal).

Ågren, Maria 1992 *Jord och gäld. Social skiktning och rättslig konflikt i södra Dalarna ca 1650–1850* (Uppsala).

Ahlberger, Christer 1988 *Vävarfolket. Hemindustrin i Mark 1790–1850* (Göteborg).

Allen, Robert C. 1993 *Enclosure and the yeoman* (Oxford).

Almquist, E. L. 1979 'Pre-famine Ireland and the theory of European proto-industrialization: the evidence from the 1841 census', *Journal of Economic History* 39: 699–718.

Andersson, Roger and Haraldsson, Kjell 1988 'Geografiskt focus och proto-industriell locus', *Bebyggelsehistorisk Tidskrift* 16: 93–109.

Aracil, Rafael and García Bonafé, Mario 1978 'Industria domestíca e industrialización en España', *Hacienda Publica Española* 55: 113–29.

1983 'La protoindustrialització i la indústria rural espanyola al segle XVIII', *Recerques* 13: 83–102.

Armstrong, Alan W. 1972 'The use of information about occupation', in E. A. Wrigley (ed.), *Nineteenth-century society: essays in the use of quantitative methods for the study of social data* (Cambridge): 191–310.

Aubin, Gustav and Kunze, Arno 1940 *Leinenerzeugung und Leinenabsatz im östlichen Mitteldeutschland zur Zeit der Zunftkäufe. Ein Beitrag zur industriellen Kolonisation des deutschen Ostens* (Stuttgart).

Aubin, H. 1942 'Die Anfänge der grossen schlesischen Leinenweberei und -handlung', *Vierteljahrschrift für Sozial- und Wirtschaftsgeschichte* 35: 105–78.

1967 'Formen und Verbreitung des Verlagswesens in der Altnürnberger Wirtschaft', in *Beiträge zur Wirtschaftsgeschichte Nürnbergs*, vol. II (Nürnberg): 1635–41.

Aymard, Maurice 1991 'La fragilità di un'economia avanzata: l'Italia e le trasformazioni dell'economia', in Ruggiero Romano (ed.), *Storia dell'economia italiana*, vol. II, *L'età moderna: verso la crisi* (Torino): 5–137.

Baltzarek, Franz 1979 'Zu den regionalen Ansätzen der frühen Industrialisierung in Europa', in Herbert Knittler (ed.), *Wirtschafts- und sozialhistorische Beiträge. Festschrift für Alfred Hoffmann zum 75. Geburtstag* (Wien): 334–56.

Belfanti, Carlo Marco 1993 'Rural manufactures and rural proto-industries in the "Italy of the Cities" from the sixteenth through the eighteenth century', *Continuity and Change* 8: 253–80.

Bělina, Pavel 1983 'Státní podpora textilní výroby v českých zemích ve druhé polovině 17. a v 18. století', *Z dějin textilu* 5: 7–36.

Benedini, Bortolo 1880 *Le piccole industrie adatte a contadini nelle intermittenze de' lavori campestri* (Brescia).

Berg, Maxine 1985 *The age of manufactures. Industry, innovation and work in Britain 1700–1820* (London).

1987 'Women's work, mechanization and the early phases of industrialization in England', in Patrick Joyce (ed.), *The historical meanings of work* (Cambridge): 64–98.

1991 'Commerce and creativity in eighteenth century Birmingham', in Maxine Berg (ed.), *Markets and manufactures in early industrial Europe* (London): 173–205.

1993a 'Women's property and the industrial revolution', *Journal of Interdisciplinary History* 24: 233–50.

1993b 'Small producer capitalism in eighteenth-century England', *Business History* 35: 17–39.

1993c 'What difference did women's work make to the industrial revolution?', *History Workshop Journal* 35: 22–44.

1994 *The age of manufactures. Industry, innovation and work in Britain 1700–1820* 2nd edn (London).

Berg, Maxine and Hudson, Pat 1992 'Rehabilitating the industrial revolution', *Economic History Review* 45: 24–50.

Berger, Peter 1981 'Finanzwesen und Staatswerdung. Zur Genese absolutistischer Herrschaftstechnik in Österreich', in Herbert Matis (ed.), *Von der Glückseligkeit des Staates* (Wien): 105–36.

Berkner, Lutz K. 1973 'Family, social structure and rural industry: a comparative study of the Waldviertel and the Pays de Caux in the eighteenth century' (PhD dissertation, Harvard University).

Bernecker, Michael 1990 'Die Schweiz und die Weltwirtschaft: Etappen der Integration im 19. und 20. Jahrhundert', in Paul Bairoch and Martin Körner (eds.), *Die Schweiz in der Weltwirtschaft* (Zürich): 429–64.

Bielenberg, Andy 1991 *Cork's Industrial Revolution 1780–1880: development or decline?* (Cork).

Bietenhard, Benedikt 1988 *Langnau im 18. Jahrhundert. Die Biographie einer ländlichen Kirchgemeinde im bernischen Ancien Régime* (Thun).

Bilbao, Luis María and Fernández del Piñedo, Emiliano 1988 'Artesania e industria', in Miguel Artola (ed.), *Enciclopedia de Historia de España*, vol. I, *Economía y Sociedad* (Madrid): 96–190.

Bodmer, Walter 1960 *Die Entwicklung der schweizerischen Textilwirtschaft im Rahmen der übrigen Industrien und Wirtschaftszweige* (Zürich).

Bräuer, H. 1983 'Probleme der älteren Handwerksgeschichte. Einige aktuelle Forschungsaufgaben im Bezirk Karl-Marx-Stadt', *Regionalgeschichtliche Beiträge aus dem Bezirk Karl-Marx-Stadt* 5: 51–64.

1987 'Bemerkungen zur sozialökonomischen Entwicklung des Zunfthandwerks in Sachsen zwischen 1648 und 1763', in *III. Internationales*

Handwerksgeschichtliches Symposium Veszprém 18.–24.10.1986, 2 vols. (Veszprém): I.23–47.

Braun, Rudolf 1960 *Industrialisierung und Volksleben. Die Veränderungen der Lebensformen in einem ländlichen Industriegebiet vor 1800 (Zürcher Oberland)* (Erlenbach and Zürich).

1978 'Protoindustrialization and demographic changes in the Canton Zürich', in Charles Tilly (ed.), *Historical studies of changing fertility* (Princeton): 289–334.

1990 *Industrialisation and everyday life* (Cambridge and Paris).

Brunner, Otto 1956 'Das Ganze Haus und die Alteuropäische Ökonomik', in Otto Brunner, *Neue Wege der Sozialgeschichte* (Göttingen): 103–27 (2nd edn 1968).

Bücher, K. 1927 (4th edn) 'Art. Gewerbe', in *Handwörterbuch der Staatswissenschaften*, vol. IV (Jena): 966–89.

Bucher, Silvio 1974 *Bevölkerung und Wirtschaft des Amtes Entlebuch im 18. Jahrhundert* (Luzern).

Cafagna, Luciano 1989 *Dualismo e sviluppo nella storia d'Italia* (Venezia).

Cailly, Claude 1993a *Mutation d'un espace proto-industriel* (Le Mans).

1993b 'Contribution à la définition d'un mode de production proto-industriel', *Histoire et mesure* 8: 19–40.

Caizzi, Bruno 1968 *Industria, commercio e banca in Lombardia nel XVIII secolo* (Milano).

1972 *L'economia lombarda durante la restaurazione (1814–1859)* (Milano).

Camps, Enriqueta 1990 'Migraciones internas y formación del mercado de trabajo en la Cataluña industrial en el siglo XIX' (PhD dissertation, European University Institute, Florence).

Capecchi, Vittorio 1991 'Una storia della specializzazione flessibile e dei distretti industriali in Emilia-Romagna', in Frank Pyke, Giacomo Becattini and Werner Segenberger (eds.), *Distretti industriali e cooperazione fra imprese in Italia* (Firenze).

Cappello, Stefania and Prandi, Alfonso 1973 *Carpi: tradizione e sviluppo* (Bologna).

Carmona Badía, Joám 1990 *El atraso industrial de Galicia* (Barcelona).

Carpenter, Rebecca 1994 'Peasants and stockingers: socio-economic change in Guthlaxton Hundred, Leicestershire, 1700–1851' (PhD dissertation, University of Leicester).

Carrère, Claude 1967 *Barcelone, centre économique à l'époque des difficultés, 1380–1462*, 2 vols. (Paris).

1978 'Structures et évolution des entreprises pré-industrielles: le cas de Barcelone au bas Moyen-Age', *Studi in Memoria di Federigo Melis*, vol. III (Napoli): 37–57.

Caspard, Pierre 1979 'Die Fabrik auf dem Dorf', in Detlef Puls (ed.), *Wahrnehmungsformen und Protestverhalten. Studien zur Lage der Unterschichten im 18. und 19. Jahrhundert* (Frankfurt am Main): 105–42.

Cayez, Pierre 1978 *Métiers jacquard et hauts fourneaux. Aux origines de l'industrie lyonnaise* (Lyon).

Census 1841 *Report of the commissioners appointed to take the Census of Ireland for the year 1841* (Dublin [1843]).

1901 *Census of Ireland 1901*. Part 1, *Occupations etc.*: vol. 1, *Leinster*; vol. 2, *Munster*; vol. 3, *Ulster*; vol. 4, *Connaught*. Part 2, *General report* (Dublin).

Čermáková-Nesládková, Ludmila 1979 *Důsledky kapitalistické industrializace v populačním vývoji severní a severovýchodní Moravy* (Praha).

Cerman, Markus 1993 'Proto-industrialization in an urban environment: Vienna, 1750–1857', *Continuity and Change* 8: 281–320.

Chambers, J. D. 1957 'The vale of Trent 1660–1800', *Economic History Review Supplement* 30.

1962 'The rural domestic industries during the period of transition to the factory system, with special reference to the Midland counties of England', *Proceedings of the Second International Congress of Economic History (Aix-en-Provence)*, vol. II: 429–55.

Chassagne, Serge 1990 'Le rôle des marchands fabricants dans la transition entre proto-industrialisation et industrie cotonnière', *Annales de Bretagne* 97: 291–306.

1991 *Le coton et ses patrons* (Paris).

Chayanov, Aleksander V. 1966 *The theory of peasant economy*, ed. D. Thorner, B. Kerblay and R. E. F. Smith (Homewood, Ill.).

Cipolla, Carlo M. 1968 'The economic decline of Italy', in Brian Pullan (ed.), *Crisis and change in the Venetian economy in the sixteenth and seventeenth centuries* (London): 127–45.

Ciriacono, Salvatore 1983 'Protoindustria, lavoro a domicilio e sviluppo economico nelle campagne venete in epoca moderna', *Quaderni Storici* 18: 57–80.

Clark, Peter and Slack, Paul 1976 *English towns in transition 1500–1700* (Oxford).

Clarkson, Leslie A. 1985 *Proto-industrialization: the first phase of industrialization?* (London).

1989a 'The environment and dynamic of pre-factory industry in Northern Ireland', in Pat Hudson (ed.), *Regions and industries: a perspective on the industrial revolution in Britain* (Cambridge): 252–70.

1989b 'The Carrick-on-Suir woollen industry in the eighteenth century', *Irish Economic and Social History* 16: 23–41.

Clarkson, Leslie A. and Crawford, E. Margaret 1991 'Life after death: widows in Carrick-on-Suir at the end of the eighteenth century', in Margaret MacCurtain and Mary O'Dowd (eds.), *Women in early modern Ireland* (Dublin and Edinburgh): 236–54.

Clasen, Claus-Peter 1981 *Die Augsburger Weber. Leistungen und Krisen des Textilgewerbes um 1600* (Augsburg).

Coleman, Donald C. 1983 'Proto-industrialization: a concept too many', *Economic History Review* 36: 435–48.

Collins, Brenda 1982 'Proto-industrialization and pre-famine emigration', *Social History* 7: 127–40.

Coornaert, Emile 1930 *Un centre industriel d'autrefois. La draperie sayetterie d'Hondschoote* (Paris).

Corfield, Penelope J. and Keene, Derek (eds.) 1990 *Work in towns 850–1850* (Leicester).

Corner, Paul R. 1993 *Contadini e industrializzazione. Società rurale e impresa in Italia* (Roma and Bari).

Cova, Alberto 1987 'L'alternativa manifatturiera', in Sergio Zaninelli (ed.), *Da un sistema agricolo a un sistema industriale: il Comasco dal Settecento al Novecento. Il difficile equilbrio agricolo-manifatturiero (1750–1814)*, vol. I (Como): 132–265.

Crafts, N. F. R. 1985 *British economic growth during the industrial revolution* (Oxford).

Crafts, N. F. R. and Harley, C. Knick 1992 'Output growth and the British industrial revolution: a restatement of the Crafts–Harley view', *Economic History Review* 2nd ser. 45: 703–30.

Crawford, William H. 1988 'The evolution of the linen trade before industrialization', *Irish Economic and Social History* 15: 32–53.

Crouzet, François 1964 'Wars, blockade and economic change in Europe, 1792–1815', *Journal of Economic History* 24: 567–88.

Daly, Mary E. 1984 *Dublin the deposed capital: a social and economic history 1860–1914* (Cork).

Deane, Phyllis and Cole, W. A. 1962 *British economic growth, 1688–1950: trends and structure* (Cambridge).

de Kezel, Luc 1988 'Grondbezit in Vlaanderen, 1750–1850. Bijdrage tot de discussie over de sociaal-economische ontwikkeling op het Vlaamse platteland', *Tijdschrift Sociale Geschiedenis* 14: 61–102.

Deprez, Paul 1965 'The demographic development of eighteenth-century Flanders', in D. V. Glass and D. E. C. Eversley (eds.), *Population in history* (London): 608–30.

Dérival 1782–3 *Le Voyageur dans les Pays-bas Autrichiens ou lettres sur l'état actuel de ces pays*, 2 vols. (Amsterdam).

de Vries, Jan 1974 *The Dutch rural economy in the golden age, 1500–1700* (Berkeley).

1976 *The economy of Europe in an age of crisis, 1600–1750* (Cambridge).

1984 *European urbanization, 1500–1800* (London).

1993 'Between purchasing power and the world of goods: understanding the household economy in early modern Europe', in John Brewer and Roy Porter (eds.), *Consumption and the world of goods* (London): 85–132.

1994 'The industrial revolution and the industrious revolution', *Journal of Economic History* 54: 249–71.

Dewerpe, Alain 1985 *L'industrie aux champs. Essai sur la proto-industrialisation en Italie du Nord (1800–1880)* (Roma).

1986 'Genesi protoindustriale di una regione sviluppata: l'Italia settentrionale', in Andreina De Clementi (ed.), *La società inafferrabile. Protoindustria, città e classi sociali nell'Italia liberale* (Roma): 31–50.

1991 'Verso l'Italia industriale', in Ruggiero Romano (ed.), *Storia dell'economia italiana L'età contemporanea: un paese nuovo*, vol. III (Torino): 5–58.

Deyon, Pierre and Mendels, Franklin (eds.) 1982 *VIIIe Congrès International d'Histoire Economique, Budapest 16–22 août 1982. Section A2: La Protoindustrialisation: Théorie et Réalité* (Lille).

Dickson, David 1977 'Aspects of the rise and decline of the Irish cotton industry', in L. M. Cullen and T. C. Smout (eds.), *Comparative aspects of Scottish and Irish economic and social history 1600–1900* (Edinburgh): 100–15.

Dickson, P. G. M. 1987 *Finance and government under Maria Theresia, 1740–1780*, 2 vols. (Oxford).

Dloussky, Jocelyne 1990 *Vive la toile* (Mayenne).

Dohnal, Miloň 1966 *Původní akumulace a vznik manufaktur v severomoravské plátenické oblasti* (Praha).

Dubler, Anne-Marie and Siegrist, Jean-Jacques 1975 *Wohlen. Geschichte von Recht, Wirtschaft und Bevölkerung einer frühindustrialisierten Gemeinde im Aargau* (Aarau).

Ebeling, D. and Klein, P. 1988 'Das soziale und demographische System der Ravensberger Protoindustrialisierung', in E. Hinrichs and H. van Zon, (eds.), *Bevölkerungsgeschichte im Vergleich. Studien zu den Niederlanden und Nordwestdeutschland* (Aurich): 27–48.

Ehmer, Josef 1980 *Familienstruktur und Arbeitsorganisation im frühindustriellen Wien* (Wien).

1991 *Heiratsverhalten, Sozialstruktur, ökonomischer Wandel. England und Mitteleuropa in der Formationsperiode des Kapitalismus* (Göttingen).

Eley, Geoff 1984 'The social history of industrialization: "proto-industry" and the origins of capitalism', *Economy and Society* 13: 519–39.

Eliasson, Gunnar 1988 'Schumpeterian innovation, market structure, and the stability of industrial development', in H. Hanusch (ed.), *Evolutionary economics. Applications of Schumpeter's ideas* (Cambridge): 151–99.

Engels, W. and Legers, P. 1928 *Aus der Geschichte der Remscheider und Bergischen Werkzeug- und Eisenindustrie*, 2 vols. (Remscheid).

Engrand, Charles 1979 'Concurrences et complémentarités des villes et des campagnes, les manufactures picardes', *Revue du Nord* 61: 61–81.

Ericsson, Inger and Rogers, John 1978 *Rural labor and population change* (Uppsala).

Faipoult, F. 1800 *Mémoire statistique du département de l'Escaut* (ed. P. Deprez, Gent 1960).

Fenster, Aristide 1983 *Adel und Ökonomie im vorindustriellen Rußland. Die unternehmerische Betätigung der Gutsbesitzer in der großgewerblichen Wirtschaft im 17. und 18. Jahrhundert* (Wiesbaden).

Fiedler, S. 1972 *Grundriß der Militär- und Kriegsgeschichte*, vol. I, *1640–1789* (München).

Fine, Ben and Leopold, Ellen 1989 'Consumerism and the industrial revolution', *Social History* 15: 151–79.

Fink, Paul 1983 *Geschichte der Basler Bandindustrie 1550–1800* (Basel and Frankfurt am Main).

Fischer, Franz 1966 *Die blauen Sensen. Sozial- und Wirtschaftsgeschichte der Sensenschmiedezunft zu Kirchdorf-Micheldorf bis zur Mitte des 18. Jahrhunderts* (Graz and Köln).

Fitz, Arno 1981 'Die Frühindustrialisierung Vorarlbergs und ihre Auswirkungen auf die Familienstruktur' (PhD dissertation, University of Vienna).

1985 *Die Frühindustrialisierung Vorarlbergs und ihre Auswirkungen auf die Familienstruktur* (Dornbirn).

Flik, R. 1990 *Die Textilindustrie in Calw und in Heidenheim 1705–1870. Eine regional vergleichende Untersuchung zur Geschichte der Frühindustrialisierung und Industriepolitik in Württemberg* (Stuttgart).

Florén, Anders and Rydén, Göran 1992 'Arbete, hushåll och region. Tankar om industrialiseringsprocesser och den svenska järnhanteringen', *Uppsala Papers in Economic History* 29.

Florén, Anders, Isacson, Maths, Rydén, Göran and Ågren, Maria 1993 'Swedish iron before 1900', in Göran Rydén and Maria Ågren (eds.), *Ironmaking in Sweden and Russia. A survey of the social organisation of iron production before 1900* (Uppsala): 7–42.

Floud, Roderick and McCloskey, Donald (eds.) 1981 *The economic history of Britain since 1700* (Cambridge).

Flügel, A. 1993 *Kaufleute und Manufakturen in Bielefeld: Sozialer Wandel und wirtschaftliche Entwicklung im proto-industriellen Leinengewerbe von 1680 bis 1850* (Bielefeld).

Fortea Pérez, José Ignacio 1981 *Córdoba en el siglo XVI: las bases demográficas y económicas de una expansión urbana* (Córdoba).

Fremdling, R., Pierenkemper, T. and Tilly, R. H. 1979 'Regionale Differenzierung in Deutschland als Schwerpunkt wirtschaftshistorischer Forschung', in R. Fremdling and R. H. Tilly (eds.), *Industrialisierung und Raum: Studien zur regionalen Differenzierung in Deutschland des 19. Jahrhunderts* (Stuttgart): 9–26.

Freudenberger, Herman 1979 'Zur Linzer Wollzeugfabrik', in Herbert Knittler (ed.), *Wirtschafts- und sozialhistorische Beiträge. Festschrift für Alfred Hoffmann zum 75. Geburtstag* (Wien): 220–35.

1981 'Die proto-industrielle Entwicklungsphase in Österreich. Proto-Industrialisierung als sozialer Lernprozeß', in Herbert Matis (ed.), *Von der Glückseligkeit des Staates* (Berlin): 355–81.

Freudenberger, Herman and Mensch, Gustav 1975 *Von der Provinzstadt zur Industrieregion* (Göttingen).

Freudenberger, Herman and Redlich, Fritz 1964 'The industrial development of Europe: reality, symbols, images', *Kyklos* 17: 372–403.

Fridholm, Merike, Isacson, Maths and Magnusson, Lars 1976 *Industrialismens rötter* (Lund).

Fridlizius, Gunnar 1979 'Sweden', in W. R. Lee (ed.), *European demography and economic growth* (London): 340–406.

Fröbel, Folker, Heinrichs, Jürgen and Kreye, Otto 1980 *The new international division of labour: structural unemployment in industrialized countries and industrialization in developing countries* (Cambridge).

Frohnert, Per 1993 *Kronans skatter och bondens bröd. Den lokala förvaltningen och bönderna i Sverige 1719–1775* (Lund).

Frost, Pauline 1981 'Yeomen and metalsmiths: livestock in the dual economy of South Staffordshire 1560–1720', *Agricultural History Review* 29: 29–41.

Furger, F. 1927 *Zum Verlagssystem als Organisationsform des Frühkapitalismus im Textilgewerbe* (Stuttgart).

Gagliardo, John G. 1991 *Germany under the Old Regime, 1600–1790* (London).

García Sanz, Angel 1977 *Desarrollo y crisis del Antiguo Régimen en Castilla la Vieja. Economía y sociedad en tierras de Segovia, 1500–1814* (Madrid).

1987 'Mercaderes hacedores de paños en Segovia en la época de Carlos V: organización del proceso productivo y estructura del capital industrial', *Hacienda Publica Española* 108–9: 65–79.

1994 'Competitivos en lanas, pero no en paños: Lana para la exportación y lana para los telares nacionales en la España del Antiguo Régimen', *Revista de Historia Económica* 12: 397–434.

Gayot, Gérard 1981 'La longue insolence des tondeurs de draps dans la manufacture de Sedan au XVIIIe siècle', *Revue du Nord* 63: 105–34.

1995 *De la pluralité des mondes industriels, la manufacture royale de draps de Sedan, 1646–1870* (Paris).

Geary, Frank 1989 'The Belfast cotton industry revisited', *Irish Historical Studies* 26: 250–67.

Gill, C. 1925 *The rise of the Irish linen industry* (Oxford).

Giorgetti, Giorgio 1974 *Contadini e proprietari nell'Italia moderna* (Torino).

Göbel, G. W. 1988 *Bevölkerung und Ökonomie. Historisch-demographische Untersuchung des Kirchspiels Siegen in der Nassau-Oranischen Zeit* (St Katharinen).

González Enciso, Agustin 1975 'Inversión pública e industria textil en el siglo XVIII. La Real Fábrica de Guadalajara. Notas para su estudio', *Moneda y Credito* 133: 41–64.

1984a 'La protoindustrialización en España', *Revista de Historia Económica* 2, 1: 11–44.

1984b 'La protoindustrialización en Castilla la Vieja en el siglo XVIII', *Revista de Historia Económica* 2, 3: 51–82.

Good, David F. 1983 *The economic rise of the Habsburg Empire, 1750–1914* (Berkeley).

Gothein, E. 1892 *Wirtschaftsgeschichte des Schwarzwaldes und der angrenzenden Landschaften* (Strasbourg).

Gröllich, E. 1911 *Die Baumwollweberei der sächsischen Oberlausitz und ihre Entwicklung zum Grossbetrieb* (Leipzig).

Grüll, Georg 1974 'The Poneggen hosiery enterprise, 1763–1818: a study of Austrian mercantilism', *Textile History* 5: 38–79.

Guignet, Philippe 1977 *Mines, manufactures et ouvriers du Valenciennois au XVIIIème siècle* (New York).

1979 'Adaptations, mutations et survivances proto-industrielles dans le textile du Cambrésis et du Valenciennois du XVIIIe au debut du XXe siècle', *Revue du Nord* 61: 27–59.

Gullickson, Gay L. 1983 'Agriculture and cottage industry: redefining the causes of proto-industrialization', *Journal of Economic History* 43: 831–50.

1986 *Spinners and weavers of Auffay* (Cambridge).

Gutmann, Myron 1987 'Proto-industrialization and marriage ages in Eastern Belgium', *Annales de Démographie Historique*: 143–72.

Gyssels, Claire and Van Der Straeten, Lieve 1986 *Bevolking, arbeid en tewerkstelling in West-Vlaanderen, 1796–1815* (Gent).

Hajnal, John 1965 'European marriage patterns in perspective', in D. V. Glass and D. E. C. Eversley (eds.), *Population in history* (London): 101–43.

1983 'Two kinds of pre-industrial household formation system', in R. Wall, J. Robin and P. Laslett (eds.), *Family forms in historic Europe* (Cambridge): 65–104.

Halmdienst, Carmen 1993 *Die Entwicklung der Leinenindustrie in Oberösterreich (unter besonderer Berücksichtigung des Mühlviertels)* (Linz).

Hansen, Börje 1977 *Österlen* (Stockholm).

Haraldsson, Kjell 1989 *Tradition, regional specialisering och industriell utveckling – sågverksindustrin i Gävleborgs lán* (Uppsala).

Harder-Gersdorff, E. 1986 'Leinen-Regionen im Vorfeld und im Verlauf der Industrialisierung (1780–1914)', in H. Pohl (ed.), *Gewerbe- und Industrielandschaften vom Spätmittelalter bis ins 20. Jahrhundert* (Stuttgart): 203–53.

Harley, C. Knick 1982 'British industrialization before 1841: evidence of slower growth during the industrial revolution', *Journal of Economic History* 42: 267–89.

Harnisch, H. 1979 'Bevölkerungsgeschichtliche Probleme der Industriellen Revolution in Deutschland', in K. Lärmer (ed.), *Studien zur Geschichte der Produktivkräfte* (Berlin, GDR): 267–339.

Hasquin, Hervé 1978 *Les réflexions sur l'état présent du commerce fabriques et manufactures des Pais-Bas Autrichiens (1765) du négociant bruxellois N. Bacon (1710–1779)* (Brüssel).

Hassinger, Herbert 1964 'Der Stand der Manufakturen in den deutschen Erbländern der Habsburgermonarchie am Ende des 18. Jahrhunderts', in Friedrich Lütge (ed.), *Die wirtschaftliche Situation in Deutschland und Österreich an der Wende vom 18. zum 19. Jahrhundert* (Stuttgart): 110–76.

1986 'Die althabsburgischen Länder und Salzburg 1350–1650', *Handbuch der europäischen Wirtschafts- und Sozialgeschichte*, vol. III (Stuttgart): 927–67.

Head, Anne-Lise 1986 'Démographie, société et économie de montagne. Le pays glaronais de la fin du XVIe au milieu du XIXe siècle' (Thèse, University of Geneva).

Heaton, Herbert 1965 (1st edn 1920) *The Yorkshire woollen and worsted industries* (Oxford).

Heckscher, Eli F. 1935–49 *Sveriges ekonomiska historia sedan Gustav Vasa*, 4 vols. (Stockholm).

1954 *An economic history of Sweden* (Cambridge, Mass.).

Heitz, G. 1961 *Ländliche Leinenproduktion in Sachsen (1470–1555)* (Berlin).

Henderson, W. O. 1985 *Manufactories in Germany* (Frankfurt am Main, Bern and New York).

Hendrickx, François M. M. 1993 'From weavers to workers: demographic implications of an economic transformation in Twente (the Netherlands) in the nineteenth century', *Continuity and Change* 8: 321–55.

Herlitz, Lars 1974 *Jordegendom och ränta* (Göteborg).

Hey, David G. 1969 'A dual economy in south Yorkshire', *Agricultural History Review* 17: 108–19.

1972 *The rural metalworkers of the Sheffield region* (Leicester).

Hippel, W. von 1977 *Die Bauernbefreiung im Königreich Württemberg*, 2 vols. (Boppard am Rhein).

Hoffmann, Alfred 1952 *Wirtschaftsgeschichte des Landes Oberösterreich*, vol. I (Salzburg).

Hoffmann, W. G. 1931 *Stadien und Typen der Industrialisierung. Ein Beitrag zur quantitativen Analyse historischer Wirtschaftsprozesse* (Jena).

Hohenberg, Paul M. 1991 'Urban manufactures in the proto-industrial economy: culture versus commerce', in M. Berg (ed.), *Markets and manufacture in early industrial Europe* (London and New York): 159–72.

Hohenberg, Paul M. and Lees, Lynn Hollen 1985 *The making of urban Europe 1000–1950* (Cambridge, Mass., and London).

Hohorst, G. 1977 *Wirtschaftswachstum und Bevölkerungsentwicklung in Preussen 1816 bis 1914* (New York).

Hoppit, Julian 1990 'Counting the industrial revolution', *Economic History Review* 43: 173–93.

Horrell, Sara and Humphries, Jane 1992 'Old questions, new data and alternative perspectives: families' living standards in the industrial revolution', *Journal of Economic History* 52: 849–80.

Houston, Rab A. and Snell, Keith D. M. 1984 'Proto-industrialization? Cottage industry, social change and industrial revolution', *Historical Journal* 27: 473–92.

Hubler, Lucienne 1984 *La population de Vallorbe du XVIe au début du XIXe siècle. Démographie d'une paroisse industrielle jurassienne* (Lausanne).

Hudson, Pat 1981 'Proto-industrialization: the case of the West Riding wool textile industry in the eighteenth and nineteenth centuries', *History Workshop Journal* 12: 34–61.

1983 'From manor to mill: the West Riding in transition', in M. Berg, P. Hudson and M. Sonenscher (eds.), *Manufacture in town and country before the factory* (Cambridge): 124–46.

1986 *The genesis of industrial capital* (Cambridge).

1989 'The regional perspective', in Pat Hudson (ed.), *Regions and industries. A perspective on the industrial revolution in Britain* (Cambridge): 5–38.

1990 'Proto-industrialisation', *ReFresh* 10: 1–4.

1992 *The industrial revolution* (London).

Hudson, Pat and King, Steven 1994 'Rural industrializing townships and urban links in eighteenth-century Yorkshire', in Peter Clark and Penelope Corfield (eds.), *Industry and urbanization in eighteenth-century England* (Leicester): 41–79.

1995 (forthcoming) 'A sense of place: industrialising townships in eighteenth-century Yorkshire', in R. Leboutte (ed.), *Protoindustrialisation: Recherches récentes et nouvelles perspectives. Mélanges en souvenir de Franklin Mendels* (Genève).

forthcoming *Industrialization, material culture and everyday life.*

Iradiel Murugarren, Paulino 1974 *Evolución de la industria textil castellana en los siglos XIII–XVI. Factores de desarrollo, organización y costes de la producción manufacturera en Cuenca* (Salamanca).

1983 'Estructuras agrarias y modelos de organización industrial precapitalista en Castilla', *Studia Historica* 1: 87–112.

Isacson, Maths 1988 'Proto-industrins och fabriksindustrins regionala utbredning i Norden- en översikt', *Bebyggelsehistorisk Tidskrift* 16: 9–23.

Isacson, Maths and Magnusson, Lars 1987 *Proto-industrialization in Scandinavia* (Leamington Spa).

Jackson, R. V. 1992 'Rates of industrial growth during the industrial revolution', *Economic History Review* 45: 1–23.

Jäger, Reto, Lemmenmeier, Max, Rohr, August and Wiher, Peter 1986 *Baumwollgarn als Schicksalsfaden: Wirtschaftliche und gesellschaftliche*

Entwicklungen in einem ländlichen Industriegebiet (Zürcher Oberland) 1750–1920 (Zürich).
Jahn-Langen, Helene 1961 *Das böhmische Niederland. Bevölkerungs- und Sozialstruktur einer Industrielandschaft* (Bad Godesberg).
Janák, Jan 1983 'Brno jako středoevropské centrum výroby jemných suken', *Brno mezi městy střední Evropy* (Brno): 116–28.
Jaspers, Lieve and Stevens, Carine 1985 *Arbeid en tewerkstelling in Oost-Vlaanderen op het einde van het Ancien Régime* (Gent).
Jeannin, Pierre 1980 'La proto-industrialisation: développement ou impasse?' *Annales ESC* 35: 52–65.
John, Arthur H. 1961 'Aspects of English economic growth in the first half of the eighteenth century', *Economica* 28: 176–90.
Johnson, C. H. 1982 'De-industrialization: the case of the Languedoc woolens industry', in Pierre Deyon and Franklin Mendels (eds.), *VIIIe Congrès International d'Histoire Economique, Budapest 16–22 août 1982. Section A2: La Protoindustrialisation: Théorie et Réalité* (Lille).
Jonell-Ericsson, Britta 1975 *Skinnare i Malung* (Uppsala).
Jones, Eric L. 1968 'Agricultural origins of industry', *Past and Present* 40: 58–71.
Jonsson, I. 1988 'Kvinnor och män i Hälsinglands linhantering under 1800-talet', *Bebyggelsehistorisk Tidskrift* 16: 25–42.
1994 *Linhanteringen i Hälsingland* (Uppsala).
Jörberg, Lennart 1975 'The Nordic countries', in Carlo M. Cippolla (ed.), *The Fontana economic history of Europe*, vol. IV (London): 375–485.
Kao, C. H. C., Anschel, K. R. and Eicher, C. K. 1964 'Disguised unemployment in agriculture: a survey', in C. K. Eicher and L. Witt (eds.), *Agriculture in economic development* (New York): 129–43.
Kárníková, Ludmila 1965 *Vývoj obyvatelstva v českých zemích 1754–1914* (Praha).
Kaufhold, K.-H. 1976 *Das Metallgewerbe der Grafschaft Mark im 18. und frühen 19. Jahrhundert* (Dortmund).
1986 'Gewerbelandschaften in der frühen Neuzeit', in H. Pohl (ed.), *Gewerbe- und Industrielandschaften vom Spätmittelalter bis ins 20. Jahrhundert* (Stuttgart): 112–202.
Kellett, J. R. 1958 'The breakdown of guild and corporation control of the handicraft and retail trades in London', *Economic History Review* 11: 381–94.
Kelly, Patrick 1980 'The Irish Woollen Export Prohibition Act of 1699: Kearney revisited', *Irish Economic and Social History* 7: 22–44.
Kennedy, Liam 1985 'The rural economy', in Liam Kennedy and Phillip Ollerenshaw (eds.), *An economic history of Ulster* (Manchester): 1–61.
Kennedy, Liam and Clarkson, Leslie A. 1993 'Birth, death, and exile: Irish population history, 1700–1921', B. J. Graham and L. J. Proudfoot (eds.), *An historical geography of Ireland* (London): 158–77.
Kiesewetter, H. 1980 'Erklärungshypothesen zur regionalen Industrialisierung in Deutschland im 19. Jahrundert', *Vierteljahrschrift für Sozial- und Wirtschaftsgeschichte* 67: 305–33.
Kießling, Rolf 1989 *Die Stadt und ihr Land. Umlandpolitik, Bürgerbesitz und Wirtschaftsgefüge in Ostschwaben vom 14. bis ins 16. Jahrhundert* (Köln).
1991 'Entwicklungstendenzen im ostschwäbischen Textilrevier während der

Frühen Neuzeit', in J. Jahn and W. Hartung (eds.), *Gewerbe und Handel vor der Industrialisierung. Regionale und überregionale Verflechtungen im 17. und 18. Jahrhundert* (Sigmaringendorf): 27–48.

King, Steven 1993 'The nature and causes of demographic change in an industrialising township c. 1681–1820' (PhD dissertation, University of Liverpool).

Kisch, H. 1959 'The textile industries of Silesia and the Rhineland: A comparative study of industrialization', *Journal of Economic History* 19 (1959); reprinted with a postscriptum in Kriedte, Medick and Schlumbohm 1981: 178–200.

1964 'The growth deterrents of a medieval heritage: the Aachen-area woollen trades before 1790', *Journal of Economic History* 24: 518–37.

1968 'Prussian mercantilism and the rise of the Krefeld silk industry: variations upon an eighteenth-century theme', *Transactions of the American Philosophical Society* NS 58, Part 7: 1–50.

1972 'From monopoly to laissez-faire: the early growth of the Wupper valley textile trades', *Journal of European Economic History* 1: 298–407.

1981a 'The textile industries of Silesia and the Rhineland: a comparative study of industrialization [with a postscriptum]', in Peter Kriedte, Hans Medick and Jürgen Schlumbohm, *Industrialization before industrialization. Rural industry in the genesis of capitalism* (Cambridge): 178–200.

1981b *Hausindustrie und Textilgewerbe am Niederrhein vor der Industriellen Revolution. Von der ursprünglichen zur kapitalistischen Akkumulation* (Göttingen).

Klein, E. 1974 *Geschichte der öffentlichen Finanzen in Deutschland (1500–1800)* (Wiesbaden).

Klepl, Jan 1932 'Královská města česká počátkem 18. století', *Český časopis historický* 38: 260–84, 489–521; 39: 57–71.

Klíma, Arnošt: 1955 *Manufakturní období v Čechách* (Praha).

1959 'English merchant capital in Bohemia in the eighteenth century', *Economic History Review* 12: 34–48.

1974 'The role of rural domestic industry in Bohemia in the eighteenth century', *Economic History Review* 2nd ser., 27: 48–56.

1979 'Agrarian class structure and economic development in pre-industrial Bohemia', *Past and Present* 85: 58–83.

1985 'Probleme der Proto-Industrie in Böhmen zur Zeit Maria Theresias', in *Österreich im Europa der Aufklärung. Kontinuität und Zäsur in Europa zur Zeit Maria Theresias und Josephs II* (Wien): 173–95.

1991 *Economy, industry and society in Bohemia in the 17th–19th centuries* (Praha).

1993 'Die Länder der böhmischen Krone 1648–1850', in *Handbuch der europäischen Wirtschafts- und Sozialgeschichte*, vol. IV (Stuttgart): 688–719.

Knieriem, M. 1986 'Zur Migration spezieller Berufsgruppen in das östliche Wuppertal 1740–1800 am Beispiel der dezentralen Manufaktur der Gebrüder Engels in Barmen', in P. Assion (ed.), *Transformationen der Arbeiterkultur: Beiträge der 3. Arbeitstagung der Kommission 'Arbeiterkultur' in der Deutschen Gesellschaft für Volkskunde in Marburg, vom 3. bis 6. Juni 1985* (Marburg): 168–72.

Knittler, Herbert 1986 'Eisenbergbau und Eisenverhüttung in den österreichischen Ländern bis ins 18. Jahrhundert', in *Miniere e metallurgia, secc. XIII/XVIII. Dieciottesima Settimana di Studio, Istituto Internazionale di Storia Economica 'Francesco Datini'* (Prato).

1993 'Die Donaumonarchie 1648–1848', in *Handbuch der europäischen Wirtschafts- und Sozialgeschichte*, vol. IV. (Stuttgart): 880–915.

Knodel, John 1988 *Demographic behavior in the past: a study of 14 German village populations in the eighteenth and nineteenth centuries* (Cambridge).

Kocka, Jürgen 1990 *Weder Stand noch Klasse. Unterschichten um 1800* (Bonn).

Komlos, John 1980 'Thoughts on the transition from proto-industrialization to modern industry in Bohemia 1795–1830', *East Central Europe* 7: 198–206.

1983a 'Poverty and industrialization at the end of the "phase transition" in the Czech Crown Lands', *Journal of Economic History* 43: 129–35.

1983b *The Habsburg monarchy as a customs union* (Princeton).

1986 *Die Habsburgermonarchie als Zollunion. Die Wirtschaftsentwicklung Österreich-Ungarns im 19. Jahrhundert* (Vienna).

1990 'Bohemian and Moravian industry at the turn of the nineteenth century', in Erik Aerst and François Crouzet (eds.), *Economic effects of the French Revolutionary and Napoleon Wars. Session B-1. Proceedings Tenth International Economic History Congress* (Leuven): 104–13.

Komlosy, Andrea 1988 *An den Rand gedrängt. Wirtschafts- und Sozialgeschichte des oberen Waldviertels* (Wien).

1991 'Stube und Websaal. Waldviertler Textilindustrie im Spannungsfeld zwischen Verlagswesen, Heim- und Fabriksarbeit', in Andrea Komlosy (ed.), *Spinnen- Spulen - Weben* (Krems and Horn): 119–38.

Krantz, Olle 1987 *Historiska nationalräkenskaper för Sverige: Offentlig verksamhet* (Lund).

Krantz, Olle and Nilsson, Carl-Axel 1975 *Swedish national product 1861–1970* (Lund).

Kriedte, Peter 1982a 'Die Stadt im Prozeβ der europäischen Proto-Industrialisierung', *Die alte Stadt* 9: 19–51.

1982b 'Lebensverhältnisse, Klassenstrukturen und Proto-Industrialisierung in Krefeld während der französischen Zeit', in *Mentalitäten und Lebensverhältnisse. Rudolf Vierhaus zum 60. Geburtstag* (Göttingen): 295–314.

1983 'Proto-Industrialisierung und groβes Kapital. Das Seidengewerbe in Krefeld und seinem Umland bis zum Ende des Ancien Regime', *Archiv für Sozialgeschichte* 23: 219–66.

1986 'Demographic and economic rhythms: the rise of the silk industry in Krefeld', *Journal of European Economic History* 15: 259–89.

1991 *Eine Stadt am seidenen Faden. Haushalt, Hausindustrie und soziale Bewegung in Krefeld in der Mitte des 19. Jahrhunderts* (Göttingen).

Kriedte, Peter, Medick, Hans and Schlumbohm, Jürgen 1977 *Industrialisierung vor der Industrialisierung. Gewerbliche Warenproduktion auf dem Land in der Formationsperiode des Kapitalismus* (Göttingen).

1981 *Industrialization before industrialization. Rural industry in the genesis of capitalism* (Cambridge).

1983 'Proto-Industrialisierung auf dem Prüfstand der historischen Zunft. Antwort auf einige Kritiker', *Geschichte und Gesellschaft* 9: 87–105.

1986 'Proto-industrialization on test with the guild of historians: response to some critics', *Economy and society*, 15: 254–72.

1992 'Sozialgeschichte in der Erweiterung - Proto-Industrialisierung in der Verengung? Demographie, Sozialstruktur, moderne Hausindustrie: eine Zwischenbilanz der Proto-Industrialisierungs-Forschung', *Geschichte und Gesellschaft* 18: 70–87, 231–55.

1993 'Proto-industrialization revisited: demography, social structure, and modern domestic industry', *Continuity and Change* 8: 217–52.

Kropf, Rudolf 1982 'Die oberösterreichische Manufakturen und ihre Beziehungen zu Niederösterreich', in Helmuth Feigl and Andreas Kusternig (eds.), *Die Anfänge der Industrialisierung Niederösterreichs* (Wien): 288–314.

Kuczynski, J. 1981 *Geschichte des Alltags des deutschen Volkes*, vol. II (Berlin).

1984 'Zum Problem der Proto-Industrialisierung. Ein Briefwechsel mit Franklin F. Mendels', *Jahrbuch für Wirtschaftsgeschichte* 2: 151–60.

Kula, Witold 1963 'Przewrot przemysłowy. Historia i perspektywy. Klasifikacja udanych procesów industrializacyjnych', *Kwartalnik historyczny* 70: 3–22.

Kulczykowski, Mariusz 1989 'Zwischen Protoindustrie und Desindustrialisierung. Zu den ökonomischen Problemen der Textilindustrie in Polen und Ostmitteleuropa im 19. Jahrhundert', in Helena Madurowicz-Urbanska and Markus Mattmüller (eds.), *Studia polono-helvetica* (Basel): 67–78.

1991 'Le travail de manufacture dans les familles paysannes au 18e siècle', in Annalisa Guarducci (ed.), *Forme ed evoluzione del lavoro in Europa, 13 – 18 secc.* (Firenze): 267–88.

Kunze, A. 1960 'Der Weg zur kapitalistischen Produktionsweise in der Oberlausitzer Leineweberei im ausgehenden 17. und zu Beginn des 18. Jahrhunderts', in E. Winter (ed.), *E. W. von Tschirnhaus und die Frühaufklärung in Mittel- und Osteuropa* (Berlin): 207–13.

1961 'Vom Bauerndorf zum Weberdorf. Zur sozialen und wirtschaftlichen Struktur der Waldhufendörfer der südlichen Oberlausitz im 16., 17. und 18. Jahrhundert', in Martin Richter (ed.) *Oberlausitzer Forschungen* (Leipzig): 165–92.

Kyle, Jörgen 1987 *Striden om hemmanen* (Göteborg).

La Force, James Clayburn 1965 *The development of the Spanish textile industry* (Berkeley).

Landes, David 1973 *Der entfesselte Prometheus. Technologischer Wandel und industrielle Entwicklung in Westeuropa von 1750 bis zur Gegenwart* (Köln).

Lane, Frederic C. 1979 *Profits from power. Readings in protection and violence-controlling enterprises* (Albany).

Leboutte, René 1988 *Reconversions de la main-d'oeuvre et transition démographique. Les bassins industriels en aval de Liège 17e–19e siècles* (Paris).

Lee, C. H. 1979 *British regional employment statistics 1841–1971* (Cambridge).

Lee, R. 1979 'Regionale Differenzierung im Bevölkerungswachstum Deutschlands im frühen 19. Jahrhundert', in R. Fremdling and R. H. Tilly (eds.), *Industrialisierung und Raum. Studien zur regionalen Differenzierung im Deutschland des 19. Jahrunderts* (Stuttgart): 192–229.

Le Flem, Jean-Pierre 1976 'Vraies et fausses splendeurs de l'industrie textile ségovienne (vers 1460–vers 1650)', in *Produzione, commercio e consumo dei panni di lana. Atti della seconda settimana di studio* (Firenze): 525–36.

Lespagnol, André 1990 *Messiers de Saint Malo* (Saint Malo).
Levine, David 1976 'The demographic implications of rural industrialization: a family reconstitution study of Shepshed, Leicestershire, 1600–1851', *Social History* 1: 177–96.
1977 *Family formation in an age of nascent capitalism* (London).
1987 *Reproducing families: the political economy of English population history* (Cambridge).
Lewis, Gwynne 1993 *The advent of modern capitalism in France, 1770–1840: the contribution of Pierre-François Tubeuf* (Oxford).
Lewis, W. A. 1954 'Economic development with unlimited supplies of labour', *Manchester School of Economics and Social Studies* 22: 139–91.
Linde, Hans 1980 'Proto-Industrialisierung. Zur Justierung eines neuen Leitbegriffes der sozialgeschichtlichen Forschung', *Geschichte und Gesellschaft* 6: 103–24.
Little, I. D. M. 1982 *Economic development* (New York).
Macfarlane, Alan 1978 *The origins of English individualism: the family, property and social transition* (Oxford).
Machačová, Jana and Matějček, Jiří 1992 *Nástin vývoje textilní výroby v českých zemích v období 1781–1848, díl III, Sociální vývoj* (Opava).
McKendrick, Neil 1982 'The consumer revolution in eighteenth century England', in Neil McKendrick, John Brewer and Roy Porter (eds.), *The birth of a consumer society: the commercialisation of eighteenth century England* (London): 9–33.
Macůrek, Josef 1960 'K otázce přechodu od feudalismu ke kapitalismu v zemědělství ve střední Evropě – 16.–18. století', *Sborník prací filozofické fakulty Brněnské univerzity* 9, C-7: 321–32.
Mager, Wolfgang 1981 'Haushalt und Familie in protoindustrieller Gesellschaft: Spenge (Ravensberg) während der ersten Hälfte des 19. Jahrhunderts: Eine Fallstudie', in N. Bulst, J. Goy and J. Hoock (eds.), *Familie zwischen Tradition und Moderne: Studien zur Geschichte der Familie in Deutschland und Frankreich vom 16. bis zum 20. Jahrhundert* (Göttingen).
1982 'Protoindustrialisierung und agrarisch-heimgewerbliche Verflechtung in Ravensberg während der Frühen Neuzeit. Studien zu einer Gesellschaftsformation im Übergang', *Geschichte und Gesellschaft* 8: 435–74.
1983 'Die Rolle des Staates bei der gewerblichen Entwicklung Ravensbergs in vorindustrieller Zeit', in K. Düwell and W. Köllmann (eds.), *Rheinland-Westfalen im Industriezeitalter*, vol. 1, *Von der Entstehung der Provinzen bis zur Reichsgründung* (Wuppertal): 61–72.
1984 'Spenge vom frühen 18. Jahrhundert bis zur Mitte des 19. Jahrhunderts', in W. Mager (ed.), *Geschichte der Stadt Spenge* (Spenge): 93–194.
1988 'Protoindustrialisierung und Protoindustrie. Vom Nutzen und Nachteil zweier Konzepte', *Geschichte und Gesellschaft* 14: 275–303.
1993 'Proto-industrialization and proto-industry: the uses and drawbacks of two concepts', *Continuity and Change* 8: 181–216.
Magnusson, Lars 1987a 'The rise of agrarian productivity in Scandinavia 1750–1860: a review', in Patrick O'Brien (ed.), *International productivity comparisons and problems of measurements 1750–1939. Ninth International Economic History Congress, vol. B 6* (Bern): 86–95.

1987b 'Mercantilism and reform-mercantilism: the rise of economic discourse in Sweden during the eighteenth century', *History of Political Economy* 19: 415–33.

1991 'Markets in context: artisans, putting out and social drinking in Eskilstuna, Sweden 1800–50', in M. Berg (ed.), *Markets and manufacture in early industrial Europe* (London and New York): 292–320.

1992 'Economics and the public interest: the emergence of economics as an academic subject during the eighteenth century', *Scandinavian Journal of Economics* 94: 249–57.

1994 *The contest for control. Metal industries in Sheffield, Berg and Eskilstuna during industrialization* (Oxford).

Magnusson, L., and Isacson, M. 1982 'Proto-industrialization in Sweden: smithcraft in Eskilstuna and southern Dalecarlia', *Scandinavian Economic History Review* 30: 73–99.

Mainuš, František 1955 'Obchod přízí na severní Moravě a ve Slezsku po třicetileté válce', *Časopis Matice moravské* 74: 223–45.

1959 *Plátenictví na Moravě a ve Slezsku v XVII. a XVIII. století* (Ostrava).

1960 *Vlnařství a bavlnářství na Moravě a ve Slezsku v XVIII. století* (Praha).

Malanima, Paolo 1990 *Il lusso dei contadini. Consumi e industrie nelle campagne toscane del Sei e Settecento* (Bologna).

Mann, Julia de Lacy 1971 *The cloth industry of the West of England from 1640 to 1880* (Oxford).

Mannerfeldt, Otto and Danielsson, Hans 1924 *Sven Eriksons och Rydboholms fabrikers historia* (Borås).

Mantoux, Paul 1928 *The industrial revolution in the eighteenth century* (London).

Marquié, Claude 1993 *L'industrie textile carcassonnaise au XVIIIème siècle* (Carcassone).

Marshall, John D. 1989 'Stages of industrialization in Cumbria', in Pat Hudson (ed.), *Regions and industries* (Cambridge): 132–55.

Marx, K. 1857–8 *Grundrisse der Kritik der Politischen Ökonomie* (Berlin).

1973 *Grundrisse. Foundations of the critique of political economy*, transl. M. Nicolaus (Harmondsworth).

Matějček, Jiří 1987 'Rozmístění manufakturní a tovární textilní výroby v českých zemích v letech 1780–1848', *Z dějin textilu* 11: 47–94.

Matis, Herbert 1981a 'Staatswerdungsprozeβ und Ausbildung der Volkswirtschaft', in Herbert Matis (ed.), *Von der Glückseligkeit des Staates* (Berlin): 15–27.

1981b 'Die Rolle der Landwirtschaft im Merkantilsystem', in Herbert Matis (ed.), *Von der Glückseligkeit des Staates* (Berlin): 269–93.

1981c 'Betriebsorganisation, Arbeitsmarkt und Arbeitsverfassung', in Herbert Matis (ed.), *Von der Glückseligkeit des Staates* (Berlin): 411–49.

1991 'Protoindustrialisierung und "Industrielle Revolution" am Beispiel der Baumwollindustrie Niederösterreichs', in Andrea Komlosy (ed.), *Spinnen – Spulen – Weben* (Krems and Horn): 15–48.

Mattmüller, Markus 1983 'Die Landwirtschaft der schweizerischen Heimarbeiter im 18. Jahrhundert', *Zeitschrift für Agrargeschichte und Agrarsoziologie* 31: 41–56.

Medick, Hans 1976a 'The proto-industrial family economy: the structural function of household and family during the transition from peasant society to industrial capitalism', *Social History* 1: 291–315.

1976b 'Zur strukturellen Funktion von Haushalt und Familie im Übergang von der traditionallen Agrargesellschaft zum industriellen Kapitalismus: Die proto-industrielle Familienwirtschaft', in W. Conze (ed.), *Sozialgeschichte der Familie in der Neuzeit Europas* (Stuttgart): 254–82.

1983a '"Freihandel für die Zunft". Ein Kapitel aus der Geschichte der Preiskämpfe im württembergischen Leinengewerbe des 18. Jahrhunderts', in *Mentalitäten und Lebensverhältnisse. Rudolf Vierhaus zum 60. Geburtstag* (Göttingen): 277–94.

1983b 'Privilegiertes Handelskapital und "kleine Industrie". Produktion und Produktionsverhältnisse im Leinengewerbe des alt-württembergischen Oberamts Urach im 18. Jahrhundert', *Archiv für Sozialgeschichte* 23: 267–310.

1992/forthcoming 'Weben und Überleben in Laichingen 1650–1900. Untersuchungen zur Sozial-, Kultur- und Wirtschaftsgeschichte aus der Perspektive einer lokalen Gesellschaft im frühneuzeitlichen Württemberg' (Habilitation dissertation, Göttingen, 1992; Göttingen, forthcoming).

Meier, Theophil 1986 *Handwerk, Hauswerk, Heimarbeit. Nichtagrarische Tätigkeiten und Erwerbsformen in einem traditionellen Ackerbaugebiet des 18. Jahrhunderts* (Zürich).

Melton, Edgar 1987 'Proto-industrialization, serf agriculture and agrarian social structure: two estates in nineteenth-century Russia', *Past and Present* 115: 69–106.

Mendels, Franklin F. 1969/1981 *Industrialization and population pressure in eighteenth-century Flanders* (PhD dissertation, University of Wisconsin 1969; published version, New York, 1981).

1971 'Industrialization and population pressure in eighteenth-century Flanders (dissertation abstract)', *Journal of Economic History* 31: 269–71.

1972 'Proto-industrialization: the first phase of the industrialization process', *Journal of Economic History* 32: 241–61.

1975 'Agriculture and peasant industry in eighteenth century Flanders', in W. N. Parker and E. L. Jones (eds.), *European peasants and their markets* (Princeton): 179–204.

1980 'Seasons and regions in agriculture and industry during the process of industrialization', in Sidney Pollard (ed.), *Region und Industrialisierung. Studien zur Rolle der Region in der Wirtschaftsgeschichte der letzten zwei Jahrhunderte* (Göttingen): 177–95.

1981 'Les temps de l'industrie et les temps de l'agriculture. Logique d'une analyse régionale de la proto-industrialisation', *Revue du Nord* 63: 21–33.

1982 'Proto-industrialization: theory and reality. General report', *Eighth International Economic History Congress. 'A'-Themes* (Budapest): 69–107.

1984 'Des industries rurales à la proto-industrialisation: historique d'un changement de perspective', *Annales ESC* 39: 977–1008.

Merzario, Raul 1989 *Il capitalismo nelle montagne. Strategie familiari nella prima fase di industrializzazione del Comasco* (Bologna).

Miller, Edward 1965 'The fortunes of the English textile industry in the thirteenth century', *Economic History Review* 18: 64–82.

Milward, A. and Saul, S. B. 1973 *The economic development of continental Europe, 1780–1870* (London).

Mitterauer, Michael 1986 'Formen ländlicher Familienwirtschaft. Historische Ökotypen und familiale Arbeitsorganisation im österreichischen Raum', in Josef Ehmer and Michael Mitterauer (eds.), *Familienstruktur und Arbeitsorganisation in ländlichen Gesellschaften* (Wien): 185–323.

1992 'Peasant and non-peasant family forms in relation to the physical environment and the local economy', *Journal of Family History* 17: 139–59.

Moioli, Angelo 1981 *La gelsibachicoltura nelle campagne lombarde dal Seicento alla prima metà dell'Ottocento* (Trento).

Mokyr, J. 1976 'Growing-up and the industrial revolution in Europe', *Explorations in Economic History* 31: 371–96.

Montgomery, A. 1970 *Industrialismens genombrott i Sverige* (Stockholm).

Mooser, J. 1983 'Der Weg vom proto-industriellen zum fabrikindustriellen Gewerbe in Ravensberg, 1830–1914', in K. Düwell and W. Köllmann (eds.), *Rheinland-Westfalen im Industriezeitalter*, vol. I, *Von der Entstehung der Provinzen bis zur Reichsgründung* (Wuppertal): 73–95.

1984 *Ländliche Klassengesellschaft 1770–1848. Bauern und Unterschichten, Landwirtschaft und Gewerbe im östlichen Westfalen* (Göttingen).

Morineau, Michel 1969 'Histoire sans frontière: prix et révolution agricole', *Annales ESC* 24: 403–23.

1985 *Incroyables gazettes et fabuleux métaux* (Paris).

Moss, Michael and Hume, John R. 1986 *Shipbuilders to the world: 125 years of Harland and Wolff, Belfast 1861–1986* (Belfast).

Mosser, Alois 1981 'Proto-Industrialisierung. Zur Funktionalität eines Forschungsansatzes', in Herbert Matis (ed.), *Von der Glückseligkeit des Staates* (Berlin): 383–410.

Mottu-Weber, Liliane 1987 *Economie et refuge à Genève au siècle de la Réforme. La draperie et la soierie (1540–1630)* (Genève).

Muñoz, Josep-Maria 1984 'La contribució de la indústria rural a la industrialització: el cas de Sabadell i Terrassa al segle XVIII', *Primer Congrès d'Història Moderna de Catalunya*, vol. I (Barcelona): 399–410.

Muset, Asumpta 1989 'Protoindústria e indústria dispersa en la Cataluña del siglo XVIII. La pañeria de Esparraguera y Olesa de Montserrat', *Revista de Historia Económica* 7: 45–67.

Myrdal, Janken and Söderberg, Johan 1991 *Kontinuitetens dynamik. Agrar ekonomi i 1500-talets Sverige* (Stockholm).

Myška, Milan 1970 *Die mährisch-schlesische Eisenindustrie in der Industriellen Revolution* (Praha).

1979 'Pre-industrial iron-making in the Czech lands: the labour force and production relations circa 1350 – circa 1840', *Past and Present* 82: 44–72.

1983 'Das Unternehmertum im Eisenhüttenwesen in den Böhmischen Ländern während der Industriellen Revolution', *Zeitschrift für Unternehmensgeschichte* 28: 98–119.

1984 'K charakteristice výrobních vztahů a forem v předení lnu ve slezskomoravské "proto-industriální oblasti" v 16. až polovině 18. století', *Časopis Slezského muzea* 33, ser. B: 253–70.

1985 'Nákladnický systém a decentralizovaná manufaktura. Teoretická úvaha o podstatě těchto ekonomických kategorií na příkladu textilního průmyslu', *Z dějin textilu*, suppl. 4: 84–104.

1988a 'Der Adel der böhmischen Länder. Seine wirtschaftliche Basis und ihre Entwicklung', in Armgard Reden-Dohna and Ralph Melville (eds.), *Der Adel an der Schwelle des bürgerlichen Zeitalters 1780–1860* (Stuttgart): 170–89.

1988b 'Výrobní vztahy v tzv. domáckém průmyslu na Moravě a ve Slezsku na sklonku 19. století – ve světle výsledků ankety vídeňského ministerstva obchodu z 22. září 1897', *Z dějin textilu*, supplementum 5: 59–75.

1989 'Proto-industrializace. Realita, talentovaný omyl nebo mýtus?', in *II. setkání historiků textilního a oděvního průmyslu* (Ústí nad Orlicí): 47–68.

1991 *Opožděná industrializace. Lnářsky a bavlnářský průmysl na Frýdecku a Místecku do počátku tovární výroby* (Trutnov).

1992 *Proto-industriální železářství v českých zemích. Robota a jiné formy nucené práce v železářských manufakturách* (Ostrava).

Nadal, Jordi 1975 *El fracaso de la Revolución Industrial en España, 1814–1913* (Barcelona).

Nelson, Helge 1963 *Studier över svenskt arbetsliv, säsongsarbete och befolkningsrörelser under 1800 och 190-talen* (Lund).

Novotný, Karel 1983 'Rozmístění manufakturní výroby v Čechách kolem r. 1790', *Hospodářské dějiny* 11: 5–94.

O'Brien, George 1921 *Economic history of Ireland from the Union to the Famine* (London).

Ogilvie, Sheilagh C. 1985 'Corporatism and regulation in rural industry: woollen weaving in Württemberg, 1580–1740' (PhD dissertation, University of Cambridge).

1986 'Coming of age in a corporate society: capitalism, Pietism and family authority in rural Württemberg 1590–1740', *Continuity and Change* 1: 279–331.

1990 'Women and proto-industrialization in a corporate society: Württemberg woollen weaving 1590–1760', in Pat Hudson and W. R. Lee (eds.), *Women's work and the family economy in historical perspective* (Manchester): 76–103.

1992 'Germany and the seventeenth-century crisis', *Historical Journal* 35: 417–41.

1993a 'Proto-industrialization in Europe', *Continuity and Change* 8: 159–79.

1993b 'Women's work in a developing economy: a German industrial countryside, 1580–1797' (MA dissertation, University of Chicago).

1995 'Institutions and economic development in early modern Central Europe', *Transactions of the Royal Historical Society* Sixth Series, 5: 221–50.

forthcoming *State corporatism and proto-industry: the Württemberg Black Forest, 1580–1797* (Cambridge).

Ó Gráda, Cormac 1989 'Industry and communications, 1801–45', in W. E. Vaughan (ed.), *A new history of Ireland*, vol. V, *Ireland under the Union I: 1801–70* (Oxford): 137–57.

Olai, Brigitta 1983 *Storskiftet i Ekebyborna* (Uppsala).

Ollerenshaw, Phillip 1985 'Industry, 1820–1914', in Liam Kennedy and Phillip Ollerenshaw (eds.), *An economic history of Ulster* (Manchester): 62–108.

Othick, John 1985 'The economic history of Ulster: a perspective', in Liam

Kennedy and Phillip Ollerenshaw (eds.), *An economic history of Ulster* (Manchester): 224–40.

Otruba, Gustav 1981 'Die Wirtschaftspolitik Maria Theresias und Josephs II', in Herbert Matis (ed.), *Von der Glückseligkeit des Staates* (Berlin): 77–103.

Paas, Martha W. 1981 *Population change, labor supply and agriculture in Augsburg 1480–1618* (New York).

Palairet, M. R. 1982 'Woollen textile manufacturing in the Balkans 1850–1911: a study of protoindustrial failure', in Pierre Deyon and Franklin Mendels (eds.), *VIIIe Congrès International d'Histoire Economique, Budapest 16–22 août 1982. Section A2: La Protoindustrialisation: Théorie et Réalité* (Lille).

Palmqvist, Lena 1988 'Sjuhäradsbygdens bondefabrikörer', *Bebyggelsehistorisk Tidskrift* 16: 65–76.

Pedreira, J. M. 1990 'Social structure and the persistence of rural domestic industry in nineteenth century Portugal', *Journal of European Economic History* 19: 521–47.

Perlin, Frank 1983 'Proto-industrialization and pre-colonial south Asia', *Past and Present* 98: 30–95.

1985 'Scrutinizing which moment?', *Economy and Society* 14: 374–98.

Pescarolo, Alessandra and Ravenni, Gian Bruno 1991 *Il proletariato invisibile. La manifattura della paglia nella Toscana mezzadrile (1820–1950)* (Milano).

Petráň, Josef (ed.) 1990 *Počátky českého národního obrození 1770–1790* (Praha).

Pettersson, Ronny, 1983 *Laga skifte i Hallands län 1827–1876* (Stockholm).

Peyer, Hans Conrad 1975 'Wollgewerbe, Viehzucht, Solddienst und Bevölkerungsentwicklung in Stadt und Landschaft Freiburg im Übergang vom 14. bis 16. Jahrhundert', in Hermann Kellenbenz (ed.), *Agrarisches Nebengewerbe und Formen der Reagrarisierung im Spätmittelalter und 19./20. Jahrhundert* (Stuttgart): 79–95.

Pfister, Christian 1994 *Bevölkerungsgeschichte und historische Demographie 1500–1800* (Munich).

Pfister, Ulrich 1989a 'Proto-industrialization and demographic change: the Canton of Zurich revisited', *Journal of European Economic History* 18: 629–62.

1989b 'Work roles and family structure in proto-industrial Zurich', *Journal of Interdisciplinary History* 20 (1989): 83–105.

1992a *Die Zürcher Fabriques. Proto-industrielles Wachstum vom 16. zum 18. Jahrhundert* (Zürich).

1992b 'The proto-industrial household economy. Toward a formal analysis', *Journal of Family History* 17: 201–32.

1993 'Städtisches Textilgewerbe, Protoindustrialisierung und Frauenarbeit in der frühneuzeitlichen Schweiz', in Anne-Lise Head-König and Albert Tanner (eds.), *Frauen in der Stadt* (Zürich): 35–60.

forthcoming 'A general model of proto-industrial growth', in René Leboutte (ed.), *Protoindustrialisation: Recherches récentes et nouvelles perspectives. Mélanges en souvenir de Franklin Mendels* (Genève).

Pickl, Othmar 1986 'Die Steiermark als Gewerbe- und Industrielandschaft vom Spätmittelalter bis zur Gegenwart', in Hans Pohl (ed.), *Gewerbe- und Industrielandschaften vom Spätmittelalter bis zum 20. Jahrhundert* (Stuttgart): 16–38.

Pinchbeck, Ivy 1930 *Women workers and the industrial revolution 1750–1850* (London).
Piore, Michael J. and Sabel, Charles 1985 *Das Ende der Massenproduktion. Studie über die Requalifizierung der Arbeit und die Rückkehr der Ökonomie in die Gesellschaft* (Berlin).
Piuz, Anne-Marie and Mottu-Weber, Liliane 1990 *L'économie genevoise de la Réforme à la fin de l'Ancien Régime, XVIe–XVIIIe siècles* (Genève).
Pollard, Sidney (ed.) 1980 *Region und Industrialisierung. Studien zur Rolle der Region in der Wirtschaftsgeschichte der letzten zwei Jahrhunderte* (Göttingen).
Pollard, Sidney 1981 *Peaceful conquest. The industrialization of Europe 1760–1970* (Oxford).
1991 'Regional markets and national development', in Maxine Berg (ed.), *Markets and manufacture in early industrial Europe* (London): 29–56.
Poni, Carlo 1976 'All'origine del sistema di fabbrica: tecnologia e organizzazione produttiva dei mulini da seta nell'Italia settentrionale', *Rivista Storica Italiana* 88: 444–96.
1982a 'A proto-industrial city: Bologna sixteenth – eighteenth century', in Pierre Deyon and Franklin Mendels (eds.), *VIIIe Congrès International d'Histoire Economique, Budapest 16–22 août 1982. Section A2: La Protoindustrialisation: Théorie et Réalité* (Lille).
1982b 'Maβ gegen Maβ. Wie der Seidenfaden lang und dünn wurde', in Robert M. Berdahl *et al.* (eds.), *Klassen und Kultur. Sozialanthropologische Perspektiven in der Geschichtsschreibung* (Frankfurt am Main): 21–53.
1985 'Proto-industrialization, rural and urban', *Review* 9: 305–14.
1990 'Per la storia del distretto industriale serico di Bologna (secoli XVI–XIX)', *Quaderni Storici* 73: 93–167.
Poni, Carlo and Fronzoni, Silvio 1979 'L'economia di sussistenza della famiglia contadina', *Cultura popolare in Emilia Romagna. Mestieri della terra e delleacque* (Milano): 14–31.
Price, Jacob M. 1989 'What did merchants do? Reflections on British overseas trade 1660–1790', *Journal of Economic History* 49: 267–84.
Quataert, J. H. 1985 'Combining agrarian and industrial livelihoods: rural households in the Saxon Oberlausitz in the nineteenth century', *Journal of Family History*, 19: 145–62.
1986 'Teamwork in Saxon homeweaving families in the nineteenth century: a preliminary investigation into the issue of gender work roles', in Ruth-Ellen B. Joeres and Mary Jo Maynes (eds.), *German women in the eighteenth and nineteenth centuries: a social and literary history* (Bloomington): 3–23.
Ramella, F. 1984 *Terra e talai. Sistemi di parentela a manifattura nel Biellese dell'Ottocento* (Torino).
Randall, Adrian J. 1989 'Work, culture and resistance to machinery in the West of England woollen industry', in Pat Hudson (ed.), *Regions and industries: a perspective on the industrial revolution in Britain* (Cambridge): 175–98.
1991 *Before the Luddites: custom, community and machinery in the English woollen industry, 1776–1809* (Cambridge).
Ranzato, Gabriele 1987 *La aventura de una ciudad industrial: Sabadell entre el antiguo regimen y la modernidad* (Barcelona).

Redlich, Fritz 1964 'Europäische Aristokratie und wirtschaftliche Entwicklung', in *Der Unternehmer* (Göttingen): 268–99.

Reininghaus, W. 1990 *Gewerbe in der frühen Neuzeit* (München).

Reith, R. 1986 'Zünftisches Handwerk, technologische Innovation und protoindustrielle Konkurrenz. – Die Einführung der Bandmühle und der Niedergang des Augsburger Bortenmacherhandwerks vor der Industrialisierung', in R. A. Müller and M. Henker (eds.), *Aufbruch ins Industriezeitalter*, vol. II, *Aufsätze zur Wirtschafts- und Sozialgeschichte Bayerns 1750–1850* (München).

Riu, Manuel 1983 'The woollen industry in Catalonia in the later Middle Ages', *Cloth and clothing in medieval Europe: essays in memory of E. M. Carus Wilson* (London): 205–29.

Rollison, David 1992 *The local origins of modern society: Gloucestershire 1500–1800* (London).

Romano, Roberto 1990 *La modernizzazione periferica. L'Alto Milanese e la formazione di una società industriale (1750–1914)* (Milano).

Rosander, Göran 1980 *Gårdfarihandel i Norden* (Stockholm).

Röthlin, Niklaus 1986 *Die Basler Handelspolitik und deren Träger in der zweiten Hälfte des 17. und im 18. Jahrhundert* (Basel and Frankfurt am Main).

Rowlands, Marie B. 1975 *Masters and men in the west Midland metalware trades before the industrial revolution* (Manchester).

1989 'Continuity and change in an industrialising society: the case of the west Midlands industries', in Pat Hudson (ed.), *Regions and industries: a perspective on the industrial revolution in Britain* (Cambridge): 103–31.

Rudolph, R. L. 1980 'Family structure and proto-industrialization in Russia', *Journal of Economic History* 40: 111–18.

1985 'Agricultural structure and proto-industrialization in Russia: economic development with unfree labour', *Journal of Economic History* 45: 47–69.

Ruiz Martin, Felipe 1965 'La empresa capitalista en la industria textil castellana durante los siglos XVI y XVII', in *The Third International Conference of Economic History* (München): 267–76.

Sabean, D. W. 1990 *Property, production and family in Neckarhausen, 1700–1870* (Cambridge).

Sabel, C., and Zeitlin, J. 1985 'Historical alternatives to mass production: politics, markets and technology in nineteenth-century industrialization', *Past and Present* 108: 133–76.

Saito, Osamu 1981 'Labour supply behaviour of the poor in the English industrial revolution', *Journal of European Economic History* 10: 633–52.

Sánchez, Alejandro 1992 'La era de la manufactura algodonera en Barcelona, 1736–1839', *Estudios de Historia Social* 48–9: 65–114.

Sandgruber, Roman 1982 *Die Anfänge der Konsumgesellschaft* (Wien).

1991 'Weltspitze oder Nachzügler? Österreichs Textilindustrie und Österreichs Industrialisierung in der ersten Hälfte des 19. Jahrhunderts', in Andrea Komlosy (ed.), *Spinnen – Spulen – Weben* (Krems and Horn): 49–64.

1995 *Ökonomie und Politik. Österreichische Wirtschaftsgeschichte vom Mittelalter bis zur Gegenwart* (Vienna).

Schlözer, Ludwig August 1782 'Nachricht von der kaiserliche königliche

Wollen-Zeug-Fabrik in Linz', in August Ludwig Schlözer (ed.), *August Ludwig Schlözer's Briefwechsel X*, vol. LVIII (Göttingen): 212–14.

Schlumbohm, J. 1979 'Der saisonale Rhythmus der Leinenproduktion im Osnabrücker Lande während des späten 18. und der ersten Hälfte des 19. Jahrhunderts: Erscheinungsbild, Zusammenhänge und interregionaler Vergleich', *Archiv für Sozialgeschichte* 19: 263–98.

1982 'Agrarische Besitzklassen und gewerbliche Produktionsverhältnisse: Großbauern, Kleinbesitzer und Landlose als Leinenproduzenten im Umland von Osnabrück und Bielefeld während des frühen 19. Jahrhunderts', in *Mentalitäten und Lebensverhältnisse. Rudolf Vierhaus zum 60. Geburtstag* (Göttingen): 315–34.

1983 'Seasonal fluctuations and social division of labour: rural linen production in the Osnabrück and Bielefeld regions and the urban woollen industry in the Niederlausitz, ca. 1700–ca. 1850', in M. Berg, P. Hudson and M. Sonenscher (eds.), *Manufacture in town and country before the factory* (Cambridge): 92–123.

1991 'Lebensläufe, Familie, Höfe. Studien zu Bauern und Eigentumslosen in einem agrarisch-protoindustriellen Kirchspiel Nordwestdeutschlands: Belm 1650–1860' (Habilitation dissertation, Göttingen).

1992 'From peasant society to class society: some aspects of family and class in a northwest German proto-industrial parish, 17th–19th centuries', *Journal of Family History* 17: 183–99.

1994 *Lebensläufe, Familien, Höfe. Die Bauern und Heuerleute des Osnabrückischen Kirchspiels Belm in proto-industrieller Zeit, 1650–1860* (Göttingen).

Schmoller, G. 1900/4 *Grundriß der allgemeinen Volkswirtschaftslehre*, 2 vols. (Leipzig).

Schön, Lennart 1979 *Från hantverk till fabriksindustri* (Lund).

1982 'Proto-industrialization and factories. Textiles in Sweden in the mid-nineteenth century', *Scandinavian Economic History Review* 30: 57–71.

1985a 'Marknad och industrialisering under 1800–talet', *Historisk Tidskrift* 4: 453–69.

1985b 'Jordbrukets omvandling och konsumtionens förändringar 1800–1870', *Meddelande från Ekonomisk-historiska institutionen vid Lunds universitet* 41.

Schöne, B. 1979 'Lausitzer Bandweberei vom Zunfthandwerk zur Manufaktur und zur frühen Fabrik', in *Internationales Handwerksgeschichtliches Symposium Veszprém 20–24.11.1978* (Veszprém): 176–81.

1981 'Kultur und Lebensweise Lausitzer und erzgebirgischer Textilproduzenten sowie von Keramikproduzenten im Manufakturkapitalismus und in der Periode der Industriellen Revolution', in H. Zwahr (ed.), *Die Konstituierung der deutschen Arbeiterklasse von den dreißiger bis zu den siebziger Jahren des 19. Jahrhunderts* (Berlin): 446–67.

1982 'Posamentierer – Strumpfwirker – Spitzenklöpplerinnen. Zu Kultur und Lebensweise von Textilproduzenten im Erzgebirge und im Vogtland während der Periode des Übergangs vom Feudalismus zum Kapitalismus (1750–1850)', in R. Weibhold (ed.), *Volksleben zwischen Zunft und Fabrik. Studien zu Kultur und Lebensweise werktätiger Klassen und Schichten während des Übergangs vom Feudalismus zum Kapitalismus* (Berlin, GDR): 107–64.

Schremmer, Eckart 1970 *Die Wirtschaft Bayerns. Vom hohen Mittelalter bis zum Beginn der Industrialisierung. Bergbau. Gewerbe. Handel* (München).

1976 'The textile industry in South Germany, 1750–1850. Some causes for the technological backwardness during the industrial revolution', *Textile History* 7: 60–89.

1980 'Industrialisierung vor der Industrialisierung: Anmerkungen zu einem Konzept der Proto-Industrialisierung', *Geschichte und Gesellschaft* 6: 420–48.

1981 'Proto-industrialisation: a step towards industrialisation?', *Journal of European Economic History* 10: 653–70.

Schultz, H. 1979 '"Proto-Industrialisierung" in der Manufakturperiode', *Jahrbuch für Wirtschaftsgeschichte* Part 4: 187–96.

1983 '"Protoindustrialisierung" und Übergangsepoche vom Feudalismus zum Kapitalismus', *Zeitschrift für Geschichtswissenschaft* 31: 1079–91.

Schwarz, Leonard D. 1992 *London in the age of industrialization: entrepreneurs, labour force and living conditions, 1700–1850* (Cambridge).

Sée, Henri: 1925 *La France économique et sociale au XVIIIème siècle* (Paris).

Seibold, Gerhard 1977 *Die Viatis und Peller. Beiträge zur Geschichte ihrer Handelsgesellschaft* (Köln and Wien).

Sella, Domenico 1976 'European industries 1500–1700', in Carlo M. Cipolla (ed.), *The Fontana economic history of Europe*, vol. II, *The sixteenth and seventeenth centuries* (London): 354–426.

1979 *Crisis and continuity. The economy of the Spanish Lombardy in the seventeenth century* (Cambridge, Mass., and London).

Sharpe, Pamela 1991 'Literally spinsters: a new interpretation of local economy and demography in Colyton in the seventeenth and eighteenth centuries', *Economic History Review* 44: 46–65.

1995a (forthcoming) 'De-industrialization and re-industrialization: women's employment and the changing character of Colchester, 1700–1850', *Urban History Yearbook* 22.

1995b (forthcoming) 'The women's harvest: straw plaiting and the representation of labouring women's employment, c. 1793–1885', *Rural History* 6.

Shaw, J. 1788 *Essai sur les Pays-Bas Autrichiens* (London).

Short, Brian 1989 'The deindustrialization process: a case study of the Weald', in Pat Hudson (ed.), *Regions and industries: a perspective on the industrial revolution in Britain* (Cambridge): 156–74.

Sivesand, Kent 1979 *Skifte och befolkning. Skiftenas inverkning på byar och befolkning i Mälarregionen* (Uppsala).

Slicher van Bath, B. H. 1982 'The economic situation in the Dutch Republic during the seventeenth century', in M. Aymard (ed.), *Dutch capitalism and world capitalism* (Cambridge): 23–35.

Snell, Keith D. M. 1985 *Annals of the labouring poor: social change and agrarian England, 1660–1900* (Cambridge).

Sombart, Werner 1891 'Die Hausindustrie in Deutschland', *Archiv für soziale Gesetzgebung und Statistik* 4: 103–56.

1900 (2nd edn) 'Hausindustrie', in *Handwörterbuch der Staatswissenschaften* (Jena), vol. IV: 1138–69.

1916; 1928 (2nd edn) *Der moderne Kapitalismus* (München and Leipzig).

Sommer, Karel and Gímeš Emil 1970 *Z dějin oděvního průmyslu na Prostějovsku* (Prostějov).

Sorgesa Miéville, Béatrice 1992 *De la société traditionnelle à l'ère industrielle. Les comportements familiaux face au changement économique. Mutations démographiques d'un village horloger du Jura neuchâtelois, Fleurier, 1727–1914* (Neuchâtel).

Špiesz, Anton 1961 *Manufakturné obdobie na Slovensku 1725–1825* (Bratislava).

Spree, R. 1977 *Die Wachstumszyklen der deutschen Wirtschaft von 1840 bis 1880* (Berlin).

Spufford, Margaret 1984 *The great reclothing of rural England: petty chapmen and their wares in the seventeenth century* (London).

Stauffacher, Hans Rudolf 1989 *Herrschaft und Landsgemeinde. Die Machtelite in Evangelisch-Glarus vor und nach der Helvetischen Revolution* (Glarus).

Stromer, Wolfgang v. 1978 *Die Gründung der Baumwollindustrie in Mitteleuropa. Wirtschaftspolitik im Spätmittelalter* (Stuttgart).

1986 'Gewerbereviere und Protoindustrien in Spätmittelalter und Frühneuzeit', in Hans Pohl (ed.), *Gewerbe- und Industrielandschaften vom Spätmittelalter bis ins 20. Jahrhundert* (Stuttgart): 39–111.

Šůla, Jaroslav 1985 'Pěstování a zpracovávání lnu a konopí v Orlických horách a v Podorlicku', *Z dějin textilu* 9: 37–82.

Svoboda, Jiří 1957 'Ke studiu sociálního rozvrstvení venkovského lidu v Čechách v druhé polovině 18. století', *Československý časopis historický* 5: 447–73.

Swain, John T. 1986 *Industry before the industrial revolution* (Manchester).

Takei, Akihiro 1994 'The first Irish linen mills, 1800–1824', *Irish Economic and Social History* 21: 28–38.

Tanguy, Jean 1966 'La production et le commerce des toiles "Bretagne" du XVIe au XVIIIe siècle. Premiers résultats', in *91ème Congrès des Sociétés Savantes (Rennes 1966), Section d'histoire moderne*, vol. I (Paris): 105–41.

Tanner, Albert 1982 *Spulen – Weben – Sticken. Die Industrialisierung in Appenzell Ausserrhoden* (Zürich).

1986 'Arbeit, Haushalt und Familie in Appenzell-Ausserrhoden. Veränderungen in einem ländlichen Industriegebiet im 18. und 19. Jahrhundert', in J. Ehmer and M. Mitterauer (eds.), *Familienstruktur und Arbeitsorganisation in ländlichen Gesellschaften* (Vienna): 449–94.

Tarlé, Victor 1910 *L'industrie dans les campagnes en France à la fin de l'Ancien Régime* (Paris).

Terrier, Didier 1994 *Les deux âges de la protoindustrialisation* (Paris).

Tesseyre Sallmann, Line 1993 'Une croissance industrielle. Le textile du Bas Languedoc aux XVII et XVIIIèmes siècles' (Thèse, Sorbonne, Paris).

forthcoming *Un développement industriel. Le textile du Bas Languedoc aux XVIIième et XVIIIième siècles* (Genève).

Thirsk, Joan 1961 'Industries in the countryside', in F. J. Fisher (ed.), *Essays in the economic and social history of Tudor and Stuart England* (Cambridge): 70–88.

1978 *Economic policy and projects: the development of a consumer society in early modern England* (Oxford).

Thirsk, Joan (ed.) 1984 *The agrarian history of England and Wales*, vol. V (Cambridge).

Thomson, James K. J. 1982 *Clermont-de-Lodève 1633–1789: fluctuations in the prosperity of a Languedocian cloth-making town* (Cambridge).

1983 'Variations in industrial structure in pre-industrial Languedoc', in Maxine Berg, Pat Hudson and Michael Sonenscher (eds.), *Manufacture in town and country before the factory* (Cambridge): 61–91.

1990 *La indústria d'indianes a la Barcelona del segle XVIII* (Barcelona).

1991 'State intervention in the Catalan calico-printing industry in the eighteenth century', in Maxine Berg (ed.), *Markets and manufactures in early industrial Europe* (London): 57–89.

1992 *A distinctive industrialization: cotton in Barcelona, 1728–1832* (Cambridge).

Thümmler, H. 1977 'Zur regionalen Bevölkerungsentwicklung in Deutschland 1816 bis 1871', *Jahrbuch für Wirtschaftsgeschichte*, Part I: 55–72.

Thun, A. 1897 *Die Industrie am Niederrhein und ihre Arbeiter*, 2 parts (Leipzig).

Tilly, Charles, and Tilly, Richard 1971 'Agenda for European economic history in the 1970s', *Journal of Economic History* 31: 184–98.

Tilly, R. H. 1979 'Zur Frühindustrialisierung', *Geschichte und Gesellschaft* 5: 173–4.

Tipton, F. B. 1976 *Regional variations in the economic development of Germany during the ninteenth century* (Middletown, Conn.).

Topolski, Jerzy 1963 *Narodziny kapitalizmu w Europie XIV–XVII wieku* (Warszawa).

Torras, Jaume 1984 'Especialización agrícola e industria rural en Cataluña en el siglo XVIII', *Revista de Historia Económica* 2, 3: 113–27.

1987 'Fabricants sense fàbrica. Estudi d'una empresa llanera d'Igualada (1726–1765)', *Recerques* 19: 145–60.

1989 'Early manufacturing and proto-industry in Spain', *Workshop 'Manufacture and trade in the Mediterranean in the eighteenth and nineteenth Centuries'* (unpublished MS, University of Warwick).

1991 'The old and the new. Marketing networks and textile growth in eighteenth-century Spain', in Maxine Berg (ed.), *Markets and manufacture in early industrial Europe* (Cambridge): 93–113.

Troeltsch, W. 1897 *Die Calwer Zeughandlungskompagnie und ihre Arbeiter: Studien zur Gewerbe- und Sozialgeschichte Altwürttembergs* (Jena).

Urdank, Albion 1990 *Religion and society in a Cotswold vale: Nailsworth, Gloucestershire, 1780–1865* (Berkeley).

Urfus, Valentin 1955 'O právní úpravě manufakturní výroby u nás v 18. století', *Právně historické studie* 1: 122–55.

Utterström, Gustaf 1954 'Some population problems in pre-industrial Sweden', *Scandinavian Economic History Review* 2: 103–65.

1957 *Jordbrukets arbetare*, 2 vols. (Stockholm).

Válka, Josef 1972 'K typologii "druhého nevolnictví"', *Historické štúdie* 17: 179–89.

1982 'Le grand domaine feodale en Bohême et en Moravie du 16e au 18e siècle. Un type d'économie parasitaire', in Péter Gunst and Tamás Hoffmann (eds.), *Grands domaines et petites exploitations en Europe au moyen-âge et dans les temps modernes* (Budapest): 289–315.

Vandenbroeke, Christiaan 1975 *Agriculture et alimentation dans les Pays-Bas Autrichiens* (Gent and Leuven).

1979 'Sociale en konjunkturele facetten van de linnennijverheid in

Vlaanderen, late 14de-midden 19de eeuw', *Handelingen Maatschappij Geschiedenis en Oudheidkunde Gent* 33: 117–74.

1981 'Mutations économiques et sociales en Flandre au cours de la phase proto-industrielle, 1650–1850', *Revue du Nord* 63: 73–94.

1984 'Le cas flamand: évolution sociale et comportements démographiques aux XVIIe–XIXe siècles', *Annales ESC* 39: 915–38.

1987 'The regional economy of Flanders and industrial modernization in the eighteenth century: a discussion', *Journal of European Economic History* 16: 149–70.

Vandervelde, Emile 1902 *Essais sur la question agraire en Belgique* (Paris).

Van Isterdael, Herman 1980 'Evolutie van de grond- en pachtprijzen te Okegem, 17de–18de eeuw', *Land van Aalst* 32: 195–225.

Vardi, Liana 1993 *The lord and the loom: peasants and profit in northern France, 1680–1800* (Durham and London).

Vicens Vives, Jaume 1972 *Manual de historia económica de España* (Barcelona).

Vilar, Pierre 1962 *La Catalogne dans l'Espagne moderne. Recherches sur les fondements économiques des structures nationales*, 3 vols. (Paris).

Vondruška, Vlastimil 1984 'Problematika homogennosti zemědělských výrobních oblastí v Čechách v 1. polovině 19. století', *Hospodářské dějiny* 12: 379–406.

Wadsworth, J. P. and Mann, Julia de Lacy 1931 *The cotton trade and industrial Lancashire 1600–1780* (Manchester).

Wagner, G. 1986 'Protoindustrialisierung in Berg und Mark? Ein interregionaler Vergleich am Beispiel des neuzeitlichen Eisengewerbes', *Zeitschrift des Bergischen Geschichtsvereines* 92: 163–71.

1993 *Bauer und Schmied. Die Hagener Sensenarbeiter und die Eisenindustrien des Süderlandes 1760–1820* (Bielefeld).

Wall, Richard 1978 'The age at leaving home', *Journal of Family History* 3: 181–202.

Wallerstein, Immanuel 1974 *The modern world-system: capitalist agriculture and the origins of the European world-economy in the sixteenth century* (New York, etc.).

Walton, J. K. 1989 'Proto-industrialization and the first industrial revolution: the case of Lancashire', in P. Hudson (ed.), *Regions and industries: a perspective on the industrial revolution in Britain* (Cambridge): 41–68.

1990 *Lancashire: a social history 1558–1939* (Manchester).

Weatherill, Lorna 1988 *Consumer behaviour and material culture in Britain 1660–1760* (London).

Weitensfelder, Hubert 1991 *Interessen und Konflikte in der Frühindustrialisierung: Dornbirn als Beispiel* (Frankfurt am Main).

Whyte, Ian D. 1989 'Proto-industrialization in Scotland', in Pat Hudson (ed.), *Regions and industries: a perspective on the industrial revolution in Britain* (Cambridge): 228–51.

Williamson, Jeffrey G. 1984 'Why was British growth so slow during the industrial revolution?', *Journal of Economic History* 44: 687–712.

Wilson, Richard G. 1973 'The supremacy of the Yorkshire cloth industry in the eighteenth century', in N. B. Harte and K. G. Ponting (eds.), *Textile history and economic history: essays in honour of Miss Julia de Lacy Mann* (Manchester): 225–46.

Winberg, Christer 1975 *Folkökning och proletarisering* (Göteborg).

Wohlin, Nils 1909 *Den jordbruksidkande befolkningen i Sverige 1751–1900 Statistisk-demografisk studie på grundval af de svenska yrkesräkningarna* (Stockholm).

Wolff, K. H. 1979 'Guildmaster into millhand: the industrialization of linen and cotton in Germany to 1850', *Textile History* 10: 7–74.

Wood, Andrew 1993 'Industrial development, social change and popular politics in the mining area of north west Derbyshire c. 1600–1700' (PhD dissertation, University of Cambridge).

Wrightson, K. 1982 *English society 1580–1680* (New York and London).

Wrigley, E. A. 1983 'The growth of population in eighteenth-century England. A conundrum resolved', *Past and Present* 98: 121–50.

1985a 'Urban growth and agricultural change: England and the continent in the early modern period', *Journal of Interdisciplinary History* 15: 683–728.

1985b 'The fall of marital fertility in nineteenth-century France: exemplar or exception?', *European Journal of Population* 1: 141–77.

Wrigley, E. A. and Schofield, Roger 1981 *The population history of England, 1541–1871: a reconstruction* (London).

1983 'English population from family reconstitution: summary results, 1600–1799', *Population Studies* 37: 157–84.

Zeitlhofer, Hermann 1995 'Textile Verbindungen. Lebensformen und Heiratsverhalten der Waldviertler Heimweber im 18. und 19. Jahrhundert', in Andrea Komlosy and František Svátek (eds.), *Kulturen an der Grenze* (Wien): 131–9.

Zell, Michael 1994 *Industry in the countryside: Wealden society in the sixteenth century* (Cambridge).

Zorn, Wolfgang 1988 'Ein neues Bild der Struktur der ostschwäbischen Gewerbelandschaft im 16. Jahrhundert', *Vierteljahrschrift für Sozial- und Wirtschaftsgeschichte* 75: 153–87.

Index